BANK OF ENG
INFORMATION

Accn Cod: BA

Copy No.

Class No. 343.032 GLE

GW01513686

## THE INFORMATION CENTRE
**Bank of England**
**Threadneedle Street**
**London EC2R 8AH**

This book should be returned not later than the last date stamped below.

3 0 SEP 2019

# THE LEGAL CONCEPT OF MONEY

# The Legal Concept of Money

SIMON GLEESON

Great Clarendon Street, Oxford, OX2 6DP,
United Kingdom

Oxford University Press is a department of the University of Oxford.
It furthers the University's objective of excellence in research, scholarship,
and education by publishing worldwide. Oxford is a registered trade mark of
Oxford University Press in the UK and in certain other countries

© Simon Gleeson 2018

The moral rights of the author have been asserted

First Edition published in 2018

Impression: 1

All rights reserved. No part of this publication may be reproduced, stored in
a retrieval system, or transmitted, in any form or by any means, without the
prior permission in writing of Oxford University Press, or as expressly permitted
by law, by licence or under terms agreed with the appropriate reprographics
rights organization. Enquiries concerning reproduction outside the scope of the
above should be sent to the Rights Department, Oxford University Press, at the
address above

You must not circulate this work in any other form
and you must impose this same condition on any acquirer

Crown copyright material is reproduced under Class Licence
Number C01P0000148 with the permission of OPSI
and the Queen's Printer for Scotland

Published in the United States of America by Oxford University Press
198 Madison Avenue, New York, NY 10016, United States of America

British Library Cataloguing in Publication Data
Data available

Library of Congress Control Number: 2018961270

ISBN 978–0–19–882639–2

Printed and bound by
CPI Group (UK) Ltd, Croydon, CR0 4YY

Links to third party websites are provided by Oxford in good faith and
for information only. Oxford disclaims any responsibility for the materials
contained in any third party website referenced in this work.

In memorium
My father and mother
Joe and Teresa Gleeson

# *Preface*

One of the greatest gifts that the world can give any analyst is a genuinely new factual context to which to apply an existing set of ideas. This is the gift that financial lawyers have been given by the creation of virtual currency.

In this respect, it does not matter how prevalent virtual currency becomes. Even if the current generation of virtual currencies were to disappear without trace, the questions raised by their existence would remain open. The key fact is that instruments have been created by private entities which are explicitly intended to be used (and to some extent are used) as money. In this respect, virtual currency is not new—indeed, it is exactly cognate with the large variety of other instruments that have been created over the years to substitute for sovereign currency. How the law should treat such instruments is a question which, once having been raised, deserves an answer. More importantly, by addressing the question, we learn something about money as it exists today.

This book was largely written during my time as a Visiting Fellow of All Souls College Oxford. I would like to record my enormous thanks, both for the opportunity to live and work in such an outstanding institution, and for the great kindness and tolerance shown to me by the Warden and Fellows, and particularly by my fellow Visiting Fellows, throughout my time there. I would also like to record a significant debt of gratitude to Professor Charles Goodhart, who encouraged me to pursue what at times seemed an unachievable goal. As always, my immeasurable gratitude goes to my wife and children for tolerating my absence and uplifting me with their presence. Finally, it would be churlish not to mention those who faithfully assisted by sleeping on the couches and rugs of the study—Zeus, Bailey, Wellington, and Pinto.

Simon Gleeson<br>
Clifford Chance<br>
Canary Wharf

*July 2018*

# Table of Contents

| | |
|---|---:|
| *Table of Cases* | xvii |
| *Table of Legislation* | xxiii |
| Introduction | 1 |
| 1. What is Money? | 7 |
| 2. Money, Government, and Sovereignty | 27 |
| 3. Money and Credit | 47 |
| 4. Money and Value | 65 |
| 5. The Rise of Private Payment Instruments | 85 |
| 6. Banking, Payments and Money | 93 |
| 7. The Legal Character of Money | 115 |
| 8. Private and Public Virtual Currency | 149 |
| 9. Virtual Currency and the Law | 163 |
| 10. Financial Regulation in the New World | 195 |
| *Index* | 217 |

# *Detailed Table of Contents*

| | |
|---|---|
| Table of Cases | xvii |
| Table of Legislation | xxiii |

| | |
|---|---|
| Introduction | 1 |
| **1. What is Money?** | **7** |
|   1.1 The Sociology of Money | 1.05 |
|     1.1.1 Money as an institution | 1.08 |
|     1.1.2 The origins of the money institution | 1.09 |
|     1.1.3 The formation of new institutions | 1.12 |
|   1.2 Does Money 'Exist'? | 1.16 |
|     1.2.1 Does traditional money exist? | 1.17 |
|     1.2.2 Intangibles as things | 1.19 |
|     1.2.3 Money and payment instruments | 1.20 |
|     1.2.4 Tangible money as a 'thing' | 1.23 |
|     1.2.5 Social perception of bank money | 1.27 |
|     1.2.6 Bank money as imaginary property | 1.30 |
|   1.3 Is Money a Commodity? | 1.34 |
|     1.3.1 Do we need 'real' sovereign money? | 1.36 |
|   1.4 What Gives Money its Value? | 1.40 |
|     1.4.1 Why is money valuable? | 1.42 |
|     1.4.2 Can law make a thing valuable as money? | 1.49 |
|     1.4.3 How should the courts decide what is money? | 1.50 |
|     1.4.4 Is characterisation as money once-and-for-all? | 1.53 |
| **2. Money, Government, and Sovereignty** | **27** |
|   2.1 Money and the Sovereign Authority | 2.02 |
|     2.1.1 The origins of money | 2.07 |
|   2.2 The Function of Money | 2.15 |
|     2.2.1 Alternatives to state money | 2.17 |
|   2.3 The State in the Economy | 2.20 |
|     2.3.1 Coins | 2.23 |
|     2.3.2 Precious Metal Coins—weight or tale? | 2.29 |
|     2.3.3 Banknotes | 2.32 |
|     2.3.4 Sovereign values versus real values | 2.33 |
|   2.4 Multiple Currencies within a Country | 2.38 |
|     2.4.1 Valuing coins | 2.39 |
|     2.4.2 Why multiple currencies? | 2.40 |
|     2.4.3 Debasement and inflation | 2.41 |
|   2.5 What Makes a Monetary Sovereign? | 2.45 |
|   2.6 Conclusion | 2.46 |

## 3. Money and Credit — 47

### 3.1 The Origins of Credit — 3.02
- 3.1.1 Coexistence of money and credit — 3.08
- 3.1.2 The study of credit — 3.10
- 3.1.3 Business and credit — 3.14

### 3.2 Credit and Money Distinguished — 3.16
- 3.2.1 Clearing houses as a substitute for money — 3.20
- 3.2.2 Girobank(s) as substitutes for money — 3.23
- 3.2.3 Mercantile agency as a substitute for money — 3.25
- 3.2.4 Open versus closed systems — 3.26
- 3.2.5 The reified promise to pay — 3.28
- 3.2.6 The reified instruction to pay — 3.29

### 3.3 The Discharge of Credit Obligations — 3.30
- 3.3.1 The pig/egg paradigm — 3.32
- 3.3.2 Usefulness of payment to the debtor — 3.37
- 3.3.3 Usefulness of payment to the creditor — 3.41
- 3.3.4 Money as the vehicle for credit risk transfer — 3.47
- 3.3.5 Credit risk transfer as the foundation for lending banking — 3.48
- 3.3.6 Risk transfer and risk pooling — 3.49
- 3.3.7 Virtual currency as a risk transfer mechanism — 3.50

## 4. Money and Value — 65

### 4.1 Thing Value versus Money Value — 4.02
- 4.1.1 Intertemporal reallocation of value — 4.04
- 4.1.2 Commercial bank money as a store of value — 4.09

### 4.2 Other Theories of Money Value — 4.11

### 4.3 Metallism — 4.13
- 4.3.1 Gresham's law — 4.16
- 4.3.2 Explaining metallic coin — 4.19
- 4.3.3 Metallic coin and international trade — 4.24
- 4.3.4 Why maintain the metal content of coins? — 4.26
- 4.3.5 Metal content as a constraint on money creation — 4.28

### 4.4 Money as a Claim on Government — 4.30
- 4.4.1 Central banknotes and government bonds — 4.31
- 4.4.2 Is money a credit claim? — 4.34
- 4.4.3 Private banknotes — 4.36
- 4.4.4 Private banknotes backed by assets — 4.37
- 4.4.5 Central banknotes — 4.38
- 4.4.6 Central bank money — 4.41

### 4.5 Money as a Risk-free Asset — 4.42
- 4.5.1 Information insensitivity of money — 4.47
- 4.5.2 The unit of value as risk-free — 4.53
- 4.5.3 The riskiness of near-money — 4.55
- 4.5.4 The riskiness of virtual currency — 4.56

## Detailed Table of Contents

| | | |
|---|---|---|
| **5.** | **The Rise of Private Payment Instruments** | **85** |
| 5.1 | Private Payment and Book Credit | 5.02 |
| | 5.1.1 The shortcomings of book credit | 5.03 |
| | 5.1.2 Private payment instruments | 5.04 |
| | 5.1.3 Private payment instruments in the form of physical tokens | 5.05 |
| | 5.1.4 Private payment instruments in the form of bills and notes | 5.07 |
| | 5.1.5 Foreign currencies as private payment instruments | 5.10 |
| 5.2 | Private Banknotes and Bank Cheques | 5.11 |
| | 5.2.1 Banknotes as private payment instruments | 5.13 |
| | 5.2.2 Limitation of the power to create private banknotes | 5.15 |
| | 5.2.3 Banknotes and cheques compared | 5.18 |
| 5.3 | Virtual Currency Issued by Banks | 5.20 |
| **6.** | **Banking, Payments, and Money** | **93** |
| 6.1 | Payment in a Modern Economy | 6.02 |
| | 6.1.1 Commodity and Credit money | 6.08 |
| | 6.1.2 The role of central bank money | 6.10 |
| | 6.1.3 Exogenous and endogenous credit money | 6.13 |
| | 6.1.4 The form of Private Bank Money | 6.14 |
| | 6.1.5 Virtual currency within the monetary system | 6.17 |
| 6.2 | Why Bank Money? | 6.20 |
| 6.3 | Are Private Money and Deposit-taking Interdependent? | 6.27 |
| | 6.3.1 Payment, deposit-taking, and credit creation | 6.29 |
| | 6.3.2 Instruments of Payment | 6.34 |
| | 6.3.3 Ownership of deposited money | 6.37 |
| 6.4 | Transfer and Negotiability of Private Payment Instruments | 6.45 |
| | 6.4.1 What does transfer of a payment instrument actually transfer? | 6.49 |
| | 6.4.2 Private payment in virtual currency | 6.51 |
| 6.5 | Commercial Bank Credit Money as Private Money | 6.54 |
| | 6.5.1 The state and bank credit money | 6.58 |
| | 6.5.2 Payment in commercial bank credit money | 6.60 |
| | 6.5.3 Virtual currency as commercial bank money | 6.61 |
| **7.** | **The Legal Character of Money** | **115** |
| 7.1 | Legal Definitions of 'Money' | 7.02 |
| | 7.1.1 Characterisation as 'money' | 7.03 |
| | 7.1.2 The argument that only sovereign currency is 'money' | 7.06 |
| | 7.1.3 How free are the courts to recognise private intention as determinative of money status? | 7.12 |
| | 7.1.4 Are different characterisations in different circumstances permissible? | 7.15 |
| | 7.1.5 Case-by-case versus once-and-for-all characterisation | 7.17 |
| | 7.1.6 Impracticality of once-and-for-all determination | 7.21 |
| | 7.1.7 Hard and soft boundaries in legal classifications | 7.23 |

|     |       |                                                                       |      |
| --- | ----- | --------------------------------------------------------------------- | ---- |
|     | 7.2   | The Attributes of Money                                               | 7.26 |
|     | 7.3   | Currency                                                              | 7.29 |
|     |       | 7.3.1 Currency and negotiability                                      | 7.36 |
|     |       | 7.3.2 Virtual currency as currency                                    | 7.40 |
|     | 7.4   | Abstraction                                                           | 7.46 |
|     | 7.5   | Untraceability through Mixtures                                       | 7.49 |
|     | 7.6   | Tender                                                                | 7.53 |
|     |       | 7.6.1 Legal tender                                                    | 7.54 |
|     |       | 7.6.2 Determination of the value of the thing tendered                | 7.56 |
|     |       | 7.6.3 The *Case de Mixt Moneys*                                       | 7.58 |
|     |       | 7.6.4 Divergence of common and civil law                              | 7.61 |
|     |       | 7.6.5 Practical significance of legal tender legislation              | 7.62 |
|     |       | 7.6.6 Tender and the discharge of debts                               | 7.65 |
|     |       | 7.6.7 Discharge of debts—Can the debtor unilaterally discharge a debt? | 7.67 |
|     |       | 7.6.8 Discharge of debts—Can the creditor unilaterally discharge a debt? | 7.68 |
|     |       | 7.6.9 Contractual provisions regarding payment                        | 7.69 |
|     |       | 7.6.10 Tender through the provision of a payment mechanism            | 7.72 |
|     |       | 7.6.11 The relevance of tender                                        | 7.74 |
|     |       | 7.6.12 Tender of money and tender of goods                            | 7.76 |
|     |       | 7.6.13 Tender of virtual currency                                     | 7.78 |
|     | 7.7   | Payment                                                               | 7.84 |
|     |       | 7.7.1 What is a 'sale'?                                               | 7.86 |
|     |       | 7.7.2 The two elements of payment                                     | 7.88 |
|     |       | 7.7.3 Methods of payment                                              | 7.91 |
|     |       | 7.7.4 Payment in virtual currency                                     | 7.93 |
| 8.  | **Private and Public Virtual Currency**                                     || 149  |
|     | 8.1   | Private Virtual Currency                                              | 8.02 |
|     |       | 8.1.1 A taxonomy of private virtual currencies                        | 8.04 |
|     | 8.2   | Central Bank Digital Currency (CBDC)                                  | 8.05 |
|     |       | 8.2.1 CBDC compared with other payment instruments                    | 8.10 |
|     |       | 8.2.2 Designs for CBDC                                                | 8.12 |
|     |       | 8.2.3 CBDC as a replacement for commercial bank money                 | 8.17 |
|     |       | 8.2.4 CBDC as a control mechanism for commercial bank money           | 8.21 |
|     |       | 8.2.5 A centralised banking model                                     | 8.26 |
|     |       | 8.2.6 Economic consequences of the adoption of a centralised money model | 8.33 |
|     |       | 8.2.7 Interaction of central bank digital currency and private virtual currency | 8.38 |
| 9.  | **Virtual Currency and the Law**                                           || 163  |
|     | 9.1   | Virtual Currency as Property                                          | 9.04 |
|     |       | 9.1.1 Property in an entry in a distributed ledger                    | 9.08 |
|     |       | 9.1.2 Ownership or mere right to transfer?                            | 9.12 |
|     |       | 9.1.3 Transfer of ownership of virtual currency                       | 9.17 |
|     |       | 9.1.4 Virtual currency and nominalism                                 | 9.21 |

| | |
|---|---|
| 9.2 Virtual Currency and Set-off | 9.30 |
|     9.2.1 The rules of set-off | 9.35 |
|     9.2.2 What can be set-off—common law? | 9.39 |
|     9.2.3 What can be set-off—equity? | 9.44 |
|     9.2.4 Set-off and virtual currency | 9.45 |
| 9.3 Virtual Currency, Transferability, and Negotiability | 9.46 |
| 9.4 Taking Security Over Virtual Currency Units | 9.49 |
|     9.4.1 Virtual currency unit balances maintained with a bank | 9.53 |
| 9.5 Repo of Virtual Currency | 9.57 |
| 9.6 Recovery of Misappropriated Virtual Currency | 9.62 |
|     9.6.1 Proprietary and possessory remedies | 9.63 |
|     9.6.2 Personal restitution | 9.67 |
| 9.7 Situs of Virtual Currency | 9.70 |
| 9.8 Loan of Virtual Currency Units | 9.84 |
| 9.9 Claims for Payment in Virtual Currency | 9.87 |
|     9.9.1 Foreign money and virtual currency | 9.88 |
|     9.9.2 Consequences of treatment of money as a commodity | 9.90 |
|     9.9.3 Recognition of non-UK currency as money | 9.92 |
|     9.9.4 Deciding the relevant currency of a contract | 9.97 |
|     9.9.5 Virtual currency and obligations | 9.109 |
| **10. Financial Regulation in the New World** | **195** |
| 10.1 Financial Regulatory Structures and Virtual Currency | 10.02 |
| 10.2 The Regulation of Investments | 10.10 |
|     10.2.1 Virtual currency and securities regulation | 10.13 |
|     10.2.2 Debt securities | 10.14 |
|     10.2.3 Public offering | 10.17 |
|     10.2.4 Receipts and units with underlyings | 10.19 |
|     10.2.5 Collective Investment Scheme regulation | 10.21 |
| 10.3 The Regulation of Deposits and Payment Systems | 10.29 |
|     10.3.1 E-money | 10.33 |
|     10.3.2 Payment services | 10.40 |
|     10.3.3 Lending and credit | 10.50 |
| 10.4 The Regulation of Virtual Currency | 10.51 |
|     10.4.1 Investment business | 10.51 |
|     10.4.2 Deposit-taking | 10.60 |
|     10.4.3 E-money | 10.62 |
|     10.4.4 Payment services | 10.63 |
| 10.5 The US Experience | 10.64 |
|     10.5.1 The CFTC—futures and derivatives regulation | 10.65 |
|     10.5.2 The SEC—securities regulation | 10.67 |
| *Index* | 217 |

# Table of Cases

## UNITED KINGDOM

A Ltd v B Bank [1997] 6 Bank LR 85 CA (Civ Div) ................................. 9.107
Adelaide Electric Supply Company Ltd v Prudential Assurance Company Ltd
   [1934] AC 122.................................................................. 2.33
Aectra Refining and Marketing Inc. v Exmar NV [1994] 1 WLR 1634 .................... 9.43
Aldridge v Johnson (1857) 7 E & B 885 .............................................. 7.86
Alloway v Phillips [1980] 1 WLR 888, CA ............................................ 9.72
Arkin v Borchard Lines Ltd [2005] EWCA Civ 665 ..................................... 7.47
Armstrong DLW GmbH v Winnington Networks Ltd [2012] EWHC 10 (Ch),
   [2013] Ch 156 ................................................................. 9.09
Asset Land v FCA See FSA v Asset Land Investment Inc
Attorney General v Bouwens (1838) 4 M & W 171...................................... 9.76
Attorney General v Higgins (1857) 2 H & N 3-39 .................................... 9.78
Attorney General of Hong Kong v Nai-Keung [1987] 1 WLR 1339, PC .................... 9.09
Axel Johnson Petroleum AB v MG Mineral Group AG [1992] 1 WLR 270 ........ 9.35, 9.42, 9.43

Baden v Société Générale pour Favoriser le Developpement du Commerce et de l'Industrie
   de France SA [1993] 1 WLR 509 ................................................. 6.43
Bagshaw v Playn (1595) Cro. Eliz. 536 .............................................. 9.88
Bank of Credit and Commerce (Overseas) Ltd v Akindele [2001] Ch 437 ................ 6.43
Barclays Bank International Ltd v Levin Bros (Bradford) Ltd [1977] QB 270 QBD (Comm) ... 9.95
Barnes Will Trust [1972] 1 WLR 587 Ch D ............................................ 7.02
Bechuanaland Exploration Co. v London Trading Bank Ltd [1898] 2 QB 658, QBD ........ 7.36
Bentley (Dick) Productions Ltd v Harold Smith (Motors) Ltd [1956] 1 WLR 623 ........ 7.16
Beswick v Beswick [1968] 1 AC 58 ................................................... 9.66
Blumberg v Life Interests and Reversionary Securities Corp [1897] 1 Ch 171, aff [1898]
   1 Ch 27 ....................................................................... 7.75
Bolt & Nut Co (Tipton) Ltd v Rowlands, Nicholls & Co [1964] 2 QB 10................. 6.36
Bonython v Commonwealth of Australia [1950] AC 201 ................................. 2.35
Bordin v St. Mary's NHS Trust [2000] Lloyds Rep Med 287 ........................... 9.103
Boys, Re (1870) LR 10 Eq. 467...................................................... 6.33
British American and Continental Bank, Re Lisser and Rosenkranz claim, Re [1923]
   1 Ch 276 ................................................................7.68, 9.105
British Eagle International Air Lines Ltd v Cie Nationale Air France [1975] 1 WLR 758 ....... 3.21
Broderick v Centaur Tipping Services (2006) 103(34) LSG 32 ........................ 10.25
Burdett v Willett (1708) 2 Vern 638 ................................................ 7.51
Buttes Oil & Gas Co v Hammer (No 3) [1982] AC 888 .................................. 9.23

Camdex International Ltd v Bank of Zambia (No 3) [1997] EWCA Civ 798; [1997]
   6 Bank LR 44 CA (Civ Div) .......................................... 7.79, 7.80, 9.105
Canmer International Inc v UK Mutual S.S. Assurance Association (Bermuda) Ltd
   (The Rays) [2005] EWHC 1694 (Comm), [2005] 2 Lloyds Rep 479................... 7.67
Carreras Rothmans v Freeman Matthews Treasure [1985] Ch 207....................... 9.50
Case de Mixt Moneys; Gilbert v Brett (1604) Davis 18; 2 State Trials 114 ...... 7.09, 7.57, 7.58, 7.71
Cebora SNC v SIP (Industrial Products) Ltd [1976] 1 Lloyds Rep 271 ................ 6.35
Charge Card Services Ltd, Re [1989] Ch 497 ........................................ 6.33
Chesterman's Trusts, Re [1923] 2 Ch 466 ....................................9.23, 9.26

Chikuma, The [1981] 1 WLR 314 ................................................6.32, 7.92
Clarke v Shee (1774) 1 Cowp 197..................................................7.34, 9.67
Co-operative Insurance Society Ltd v Argyll Stores (Holdings) Ltd [1998] AC 1 ............. 9.66
Coinstar v The Commissioners for Her Majesty's Revenue and Customs [2016]
    UKFTT 0610 (TC) ................................................................ 7.97
Colonial Bank v Whinney (1885) 30 Ch D 261 ........................................ 9.09
Commissioners of Inland Revenue v Maple & Co Ltd [1908] AC 22..................... 9.78
Courage Ltd v Crehan [1999] 2 EGLR 145........................................... 9.42
Crampton v Walker (1860) 3 El & El 321............................................ 9.42
Crouch v Credit Foncier of England Ltd (1873) LR 8 QB 374 ......................... 7.36

Daintrey, Re [1900] 1 QB 546 ....................................................... 9.40
Davies v Customs & Excise Commissioners [1975] 1 WLR 204 ......................... 7.96
Despina R, The [1979] 1 Lloyds Rep 1 ......................................... 9.96, 9.102
Di Ferdinando v Simon Smits & Co. Ltd [1920] 3 KB 409............................. 9.89
Dixon v Clarke (1848) 5 CB 365 (CP) ......................................... 7.53, 7.76
Dumas, Ex parte (1754) 1 Atk 232 .................................................. 7.51

Edelstein v Schuler & Co. [1902] 2 KB 144, Com Ct .................................. 7.36
English, Scottish and Australian Bank v IRC [1932] AC 238............................ 9.71
Esso Petroleum v Milton [1997] 1 WLR 938......................................... 9.44
Ewing, In the Goods of (1881) 6 PD 19 .............................................. 9.79

Feist v Société Intercommunale Belge de L'electricite [1934] AC 161..................... 6.59
Fletcher v Dyche (1787) 2 TR 32, 100 ER 18 ......................................... 9.43
Flightline v Edwards [2003] 1 WLR 1200, CA ....................................... 9.52
Flory v Denny (1852) 21 LJ Ex 223, 7 Exch 581...................................... 9.19
Foley v Hill (1848) 2 HLC 28....................................................... 6.54
Folias, The [1979] AC 685, HL............................................ 9.95, 9.96, 9.99
Fons HF (In liquidation) v Corporal Ltd [2014] EWCA 304............................ 10.14
Forman v Wright (1851) 11 CB 418................................................. 6.35
Foskett v McKeown [2001] AC 102 ............................................. 9.62, 9.63
Fouldes v Willoughby (1841) 8 M & W 540 .......................................... 9.64
FSA v Asset Land Investment Inc [2016] UKSC 17................................10.23, 10.54
FSA v Fradley [2005] 1 BCLC, [2006] BCLC 216 (CA) ............................... 10.24

Garey v Pyke (1839) 10 Ad & El 512 ................................................ 7.86
Geldof Metaalconstructie NV v Simon Carves Ltd [2010] EWCA Civ 667 ............. 9.32, 9.44
Gilbert v Brett *See* Case de Mixt Moneys
Gilchrist, Ex Parte; Re Armstrong (1886) 17 QBD 521............................ 9.12, 9.13
Golden Ocean Group Ltd v Salgaocar Mining Industries Pvt Ltd [2012] EWCA Civ 265;
    [2012] 1 Lloyds Rep 542 ........................................................ 9.47
Golden Victory, The [2007] UKHL 12............................................... 7.01
Goldshede v Cottrell (1836) 2 M. & W. 20........................................... 6.33
Goodwin v Robarts (1874–5) LR 10 Ex 337; affd (1876) 1 App Cas 476 HL........ 0.09, 7.36, 7.40
Gordon v Strange (1847) 1 Exch 477 ................................................ 7.71
Government of India v Taylor [1955] AC 491......................................... 9.22
Government of Newfoundland v Newfoundland Railway Co (PC) (1888) 13 App Cas 199..... 9.44
Green v Farmer (1768) 4 Burr 2214, 98 ER 154 ...................................... 9.41

Hadley v Baxendale [1854] 9 Exch 341.......................................... 7.01, 9.108
Halcyon the Great, The [1975] 1 WLR 515 .......................................... 7.79
Hallett's Estate, Re (1880) 13 Ch D 696.......................................... 7.51, 7.52
Handyside's Case (1750) East PC 652................................................ 9.05

Harrison v Luke (1845) 14 M. & W. 139 .............................................7.95, 9.61
Haynes' Case (1614) 12 Co Rep .................................................................9.05
Helbert Wagg & Co, Re [1956] Ch 323 ......................................................9.74
Helden v Strathmore Limited [2011] EWCA Civ 542.............................. 10.12
Henriksens Rederi A/S v THZ Rolimpex (The Brede) [1974] 1 QB 233 ...................9.42
Hibbert v Pigou (1783) 3 Doug. K.B. 224 ..................................................0.09
Higgs v Holiday (1599) Cro Eliz 746 ..........................................................7.31
Hill v Lewis (1709) 1 Salk 132 ...........................................................6.32, 6.34
Hodgson, In re [1936] Ch 203 ....................................................................7.02

Indian Oil Corp Ltd v Greenstone Shipping Co SA (Panama) (The Ypatianna) [1988]
 1 QB 345...............................................................................................7.52
Investor Compensation Scheme Ltd v West Bromwich Building Society [1998] 1 W.L.R. 896 ....9.11
Isherwood v Whitmore (1843) 11 M & W 347..........................................7.76

Jabbour v Custodian of Israeli Absentee property [1954] 1 WLR 139 .......9.73
Jackson v Anderson (1811) 4 Taunt 24 .......................................................9.64
James Lamond v Hyland Ltd (No. 2) [1950] 1 KB 585 ..............................6.35
Jeffs v Wood (1723) 2 P Wms 128...............................................................9.36
Joachimson v Swiss Bank Corp [1921] 3 KB 110 (CA) ..............................6.54
John Laing Construction v Dastur [1987] 1 WLR 686 ..............................7.77
Johnson v Agnew [1980] AC 367 ................................................................7.01
Jugoslavenska Oceanska Plovidba v Castle Investment Co Inc [1974] QB 292................9.92

Kalaher v Midland Bank [1950] AC 24, HL ...............................................9.22
Kaupthing Singer and Friedlander Ltd (In Administration), Re [2009] EWHC 740 (Ch);
 [2009] 2 Lloyd's Rep 154 ..............................................................9.34, 9.40
King v Milsom (1809) 2 Camp 7 ................................................................7.34
Kuwait Airways Corporation v Iraqi Airways Co (Nos 4 and 5) [2002] UKHL 19,
 [2002] 2 AC 883 ....................................................................................9.64
Kwok Chi Leung Karl v Commissioner of Estate Duty [1988] 1 WLR 1035 (PC) ........9.73, 9.74
Kynaston v Moore (1627) Cro Car 89..........................................................7.43

Lagos v Grunwaldt [1910] 1 KB 41.............................................................9.43
Laidly v Lord Advocate (1890) 15 App Cas 468 .........................................9.79
Le Neuville v Nourse (1813) 3 Camp 351....................................................7.87
Lee v Abdy (1886) 17 QBD 309 ..................................................................9.71
Lehman Brothers International (Europe) (In Administration), Re [2015] Ch 1, affd
 [2016] Ch 50 ........................................................................................9.108
Lesotho Highlands Development Authority v Impreglio SpA [2005] UKHL 43 .............9.92
Levy v Abercorris Slate Co. (1888) 37 Ch D 260........................................10.14
Libyan Arab Foreign Bank v Bankers Trust Co [1989] QB 728 ..................6.54
Libyan Arab Foreign Bank v Manufacturers Hanover Trust Co [1989] 1 Lloyds LR 608 (QB) ...7.91
Lipkin Gorman v Karpnale Ltd [1991] 2 AC 548 ...........................7.34, 9.63, 9.68
London and County Banking Co v London and River Plate Bank Ltd (1888) 21 QBD 535......7.37
London Joint Stock Bank Ltd v Macmillan [1918] AC 777........................6.54
London Joint Stock Bank Ltd v Simmons [1892] AC 201..................6.41, 6.42
Lunn v Thornton (1845) 1 CB 379..............................................................9.19

MacMillan Inc v Bishopsgate Investment Trust Plc (No. 3) [1995] 1 WLR 978; affd
 [1996] 1 WLR 387 (CA) ..............................................................9.62, 9.78
Manners v Pearson [1898] 1 Ch 581............................................................9.89
Mardorf Peach & Co v Attica Sea Carriers Corp of Liberia [1976] QB 835, CA; reversed
 [1977] AC 850, HL .........................................................................6.32, 7.74

Marrache v Ashton [1943] AC 311 . . . . . . . . . . . . . . . . . . . . . . . . . . . . . . . . . . . . . . . . . . 7.69, 7.79
May v Chapman (1847) 16 M. & W. 355 . . . . . . . . . . . . . . . . . . . . . . . . . . . . . . . . . . . . . . . . 6.42
Mehta v J. Pereira Fernandes SA [2006] EWHC 813 (Ch); [2006] 2 Lloyds Rep 244 . . . . . . . . . . 9.47
Mercuria Energy Trading v Citibank [2015] EWHC 1481 . . . . . . . . . . . . . . . . . . . . . . . . . . 9.57
Metliss v National Bank of Greece [1959] AC 509 . . . . . . . . . . . . . . . . . . . . . . . . . . . . . . . . 9.27
Milan Nigeria Ltd v Angelika B Maritime [2011] EWHC 892 . . . . . . . . . . . . . . . . . . . . . . 9.102
Miliangos v George Frank (Textiles) Ltd [1976] AC 443, HL . . . 9.93, 9.94, 9.95, 9.96, 9.104, 9.106
Miller v Race (1758) 1 Burr 452 . . . . . . . . . . . . . . . . . . . . . . . . . . 5.16, 6.42, 7.31, 7.32, 7.37, 7.51
Momm v Barclays Bank [1976] 3 All ER 588 (QB) . . . . . . . . . . . . . . . . . . . . . . . . . . . . . . . . 7.91
Monrovia Tramp Shipping Co v President of India [1978] 2 Lloyds Rep 193, affd
   [1979] 1 WLR 59 . . . . . . . . . . . . . . . . . . . . . . . . . . . . . . . . . . . . . . . . . . . . . . . . . . . . . . . 9.104
Morley v Inglis (1837) 4 Bing (NC) 58 . . . . . . . . . . . . . . . . . . . . . . . . . . . . . . . . . . . . . . . . . 9.42
Morrison v London County and Westminster Bank Ltd [1914] 3 KB 356 . . . . . . . . . . . . . . . . . 9.65
Mosconi, The [2002] 2 Lloyds Rep 313 . . . . . . . . . . . . . . . . . . . . . . . . . . . . . . . . . . . . . . . . 9.102
Moses v Macferlan (1760) 2 Burr 1005 . . . . . . . . . . . . . . . . . . . . . . . . . . . . . . . . . . . . . . . . . 7.95
Moss v Hancock [1899] 2 QB 111 . . . . . . . . . . . . . . . . . . . . . . . . . . . . . . . . . . . . 7.07, 7.17, 7.54
Multiservice Bookbinding Ltd v Marden [1979] Ch 84 . . . . . . . . . . . . . . . . . . . . . . . . . . . . . 6.59

National Provincial and Union Bank of England v Charnley [1924] 1 KB 431 . . . . . . . . . . . . . . 9.50
National Provincial Bank v Ainsworth [1965] AC 1175, HL . . . . . . . . . . . . . . . . . . . . . . . . . . 9.04
New York Breweries Co. v Attorney General [1899] AC 62 . . . . . . . . . . . . . . . . . . . . . . . . . . . 9.78
New York Life Insurance v Public Trustee [1924] 2 Ch 101, CA . . . . . . . . . . . . . . . . . . . . . . . 9.72

OGB v Allan [2007] UKHL 21 . . . . . . . . . . . . . . . . . . . . . . . . . . . . . . . . . . . . . . . . . . . . . . . 9.65
Orwell v Mortoft (1505) CP 40/972, M 123 . . . . . . . . . . . . . . . . . . . . . . . . . . . . . . . . . . . . . . 7.30
Ottoman Bank v Chakarian (No. 1) [1930] AC 277 . . . . . . . . . . . . . . . . . . . . . . . . . . . . . . . . 9.90
Owen v Tate [1976] QB 402 . . . . . . . . . . . . . . . . . . . . . . . . . . . . . . . . . . . . . . . . . . . . . . . . . 7.67
Owners of Turbo Electric Bulk Carrier Teh Hu v Nippon Salvage Co Ltd (the Teh Hu)
   [1970] P. 106 CA (Civ Div) . . . . . . . . . . . . . . . . . . . . . . . . . . . . . . . . . . . . . . . . . . 9.89, 9.91
Ozalid Group (Export) Ltd v African Continental Bank Ltd [1979] 2 Lloyds Rep
   231 QBD (Comm) . . . . . . . . . . . . . . . . . . . . . . . . . . . . . . . . . . . . . . . . . . . . . . . . . . . . . 9.106

Palmer v Bramley [1895] 2 QB 405 . . . . . . . . . . . . . . . . . . . . . . . . . . . . . . . . . . . . . . . . . . . 6.33
Perrin v Morgan [1943] AC 399 HL . . . . . . . . . . . . . . . . . . . . . . . . . . . . . . . . . . . . . . 7.02, 7.25
Phillips v Homfray (1883) 24 Ch D 439 . . . . . . . . . . . . . . . . . . . . . . . . . . . . . . . . . . . . . . . . 9.69
Pollway Ltd v Abdullah [1974] 1 WLR 493 . . . . . . . . . . . . . . . . . . . . . . . . . . . . . . . . . . . . . . 7.72
President of India v Lips Maritime Corp (the Lips) [1988] AC 395, HL . . . . . . . . . . . . . . . . . 9.108

R v Grimes (1752) Fost 79n . . . . . . . . . . . . . . . . . . . . . . . . . . . . . . . . . . . . . . . . . . . . . . . . . 9.59
R v Leigh (1764) 1 Leach. 52 . . . . . . . . . . . . . . . . . . . . . . . . . . . . . . . . . . . . . . . . . . . . . . . . 9.59
R v Preddy [1996] AC 815 . . . . . . . . . . . . . . . . . . . . . . . . . . . . . . . . . . . . . . . . . 1.31, 1.32, 1.35
Rastell v Draper (1605) 80 ER 55 . . . . . . . . . . . . . . . . . . . . . . . . . . . . . . . . . . . . . . . . . . . . . 9.89
Rawson v Samuel (1841) Cr and Ph 161 . . . . . . . . . . . . . . . . . . . . . . . . . . . . . . . . . . . . . . . . 9.44
Read v Hutchinson (1813) 3 Camp 352 . . . . . . . . . . . . . . . . . . . . . . . . . . . . . . . . . . . . 7.95, 9.61
Robshaw Brothers v Mayer [1975] Ch 125 . . . . . . . . . . . . . . . . . . . . . . . . . . . . . . . . . . . . . . 7.86
Rogers v Markel Corp [2004] EWHC 2046 . . . . . . . . . . . . . . . . . . . . . . . . . . . . . . . . . . . . 9.106
Rolls v Miller (1884) 27 Ch D 71 . . . . . . . . . . . . . . . . . . . . . . . . . . . . . . . . . . . . . . . . . . . . . 10.12
Romer and Haslam, Re [1863] 2 QB 286 . . . . . . . . . . . . . . . . . . . . . . . . . . . . . . . . . . . . . . . 6.33
RSM Bentley Jennison (A Firm) v Ayton [2015] EWCA Civ 1120, CA . . . . . . . . . . . . . . . . . . . 7.78
RSPCA v Sharp [2011] 1 WLR 980 . . . . . . . . . . . . . . . . . . . . . . . . . . . . . . . . . . . . . . . . . . . 7.02

Schorch Meier v GmbH v Hennin [1975] QB 416 . . . . . . . . . . . . . . . . . . . . . . . . . . . . 9.93, 9.94
Shearer v Spring Capital [2013] EWHC 3148 . . . . . . . . . . . . . . . . . . . . . . . . . . . . . . . . . . . . 7.66

Simpson v Connolly [1953] 2 All ER 474 .......................................... 7.86
Sinclair v Brougham [1941] AC 398 ................................................. 7.33
Solomons v Bank of England (1810) 13 East 136 ................................... 7.34
Startup v Macdonald (1843) 6 M & G 563 .......................................... 7.76
Stein v Blake [1995] 2 All ER 961 ............................................ 9.38, 9.42
Stooke v Taylor (1880) 5 QBD 569 .................................................. 9.42
Street v Mountford [1985] UKHL 4 ................................................. 1.54
Swiss Bank Corp v Lloyds Bank [1982] AC 584 ....................................... 9.52

Tasarruf Mevduati Sigorta Fonu v Merill Lynch Bank and Trust Company (Cayman)
  [2011] UKPC 17 .............................................. 9.12, 9.14–9.16
Tenax Steamship Co v Reinante Transoceania Navegacion SA, The Brimnes [1975]
  QB 929 (CA) ................................................................. 7.75
Texaco Melbourne, The [1994] 1 Lloyds Rep 473 ................................... 9.101
Thoni GmbH & Co KG v R.T.P. Equipment Ltd [1979] 2 Lloyds Rep 282 ................. 6.35
Treseder-Griffin v Co-Operative Insurance Society [1956] 2 QB 127 .................. 6.59
Triffitt's Settlement, Re [1958] Ch 852 ............................................ 9.14
TSB Bank of Scotland v Welwyn Hatfield District Council [1993] 2 Bank LR 267 ....... 7.67
TXU Europe Group Plc [2003] EWHC 3105 (Ch) ..................................... 9.52

United Railways of Havana and Regla Warehouses Ltd, Re [1961] AC 1007, HL ... 9.89, 9.91

Vogrie Farms v Revenue and Customs Commissioners [2015] UKFTT 531 (TC) ......... 6.32
Volturno, The [1921] 2 AC 544 ..................................................... 9.90

Ward v Evans (1702) 2 Ld. Raym. 928 ................................... 5.13, 6.32, 6.34
Ward v Ridgwin (1625) Latch 84 .................................................... 9.88
Weldon v SRE Linked Life Assurance [2000] 2 All ER 914 (Comm) ..................... 7.73
Whitecomb v Jacob (1710) 1 Salk 160 ............................................... 7.51
Wilton Park Ltd v The Commissioners for Her Majesty's Revenue and Customs [2015]
  UKUT 0343 (TCC) ............................................................ 7.97
Woodhouse AC Israel Cocoa Limited v Nigerian Produce Marketing Ltd [1971] 2 QB 23 (CA) .... 7.70
Wookey v Pole (1820) 4 B & Ald 1 ............................................ 7.31, 7.43
Wyer v The Dorchester and Milton Bank (1833) 11 Cush (65 Mass) 51 .................. 7.34

EUROPEAN UNION

First National Bank of Chicago v Customs and Excise Commissioners (C-172/96)
  [1999] QB 570 ECJ ........................................................... 7.01
Skatteverket v Hedqvist (C-264/14) EU:C:2015:718; [2016] S.T.C. 372 ................ 10.18
T-Mobile Austria GmbH v Verein für Konsumenteninformation (C-616/11)
  EU:C:2014:242 .............................................................. 10.49

INTERNATIONAL CASES

**Australia**

Doodeward v Spence (1908) 6 CLR 406 .............................................. 9.05
Foley v Hill (1848) 2 HLC 28 ....................................................... 9.53
Grant v the Queen (1981) 147 CLR 503 .............................................. 7.33
Luxtrend Pty Ltd, Re [1997] 2 Qd R 86 ............................................. 9.41
O'Dea v Merchants Trade-Expansion Group (1938) 37 AR (NSW) 410 ................... 7.86
One.Tel Pty Ltd, In the matter of [2014] NSWSC 457 ................................ 9.41

Penfolds Wine Pty Ltd v Elliot (1946) 74 CLR 204 .................................... 9.64
R v Curtis ex p. A-G (1988) 1 Qd R 546 ............................................ 7.33
Usine de Melle's Patent, Re (1954) 91 CLR 42 ...................................... 9.80

**Canada**
Braun v The Custodian [1944] 4 DLR 209 (Sup Ct Can) ......................... 9.72, 9.78
Brown, Gow, Wilson v Beleggings-Societeit NV (1961) 29 DLR (2d) 673, 691 (Ont) .... 9.72, 9.78
Secretary of State for Canada v Aline Property Custodian [1931] 1 DLR 890 ............... 9.78

**Ireland**
Flynn v Mackin [1974] IR 101 .................................................... 7.86
Jennings, Re, Caldbeck v Stafford [1930] IR 196 .................................... 7.25

**New Zealand**
Davey v Paine Brothers (Motors) Ltd [1954] NZLR 1122 ............................. 7.86
Hamilton Ice Arena Ltd v Perry Developments Ltd [2002] 1 NZLR 309 ................. 9.41
Tony Lee Motors Ltd v M S McDonald & Son (1974) Ltd [1981] 2 NZLR 281 ............. 9.41

**United States**
Barclays PLC, In re, CFTC Docket No. 15-25 (May 20, 2015) ....................... 10.65
Coinflip, Inc., d/b/a Derivabit, and Francisco Riordan, In the matter of, CFTC Docket
    No. 15-29 (Sep 17, 2015) .................................................. 10.65
Commodity Futures Trading Commission v Patrick K. Mcdonnell, and Cabbagetech,
    Corp. D/B/A Coin Drop Markets, No. 18-CV-361, 2018 WL 1175156, at *12
    (E.D.N.Y. Mar. 6, 2018) ................................................... 10.65
Edwards v Kearzey, 96 US 595, 24 L.Ed 793 (1877) ................................ 7.54
Factors etc. Inc v Pro Arts, 579 F. 2d 215 .......................................... 9.06
First Victoria National Bank v United States, 620 F. 2d 1096 ......................... 9.05
Haelan Laboratories v Topps Chewing Gum, 202 F 2d 866 .......................... 9.06
Knox v Lee, 79 US 457 (1871) .................................................... 2.23
Koreag, Controle et Revision SA, In re, 961 F. 2d 341 ............................... 9.61
Munchee, In the matter of, Securities Act of 1933 Release No. 10445/December 11, 2017 .... 10.69
SEC v Edwards, 540 US 389 (2004) .............................................. 10.69
SEC v WJ Howey Co, 328 US 293 (1946) ................................... 10.21, 10.69
United Housing Fund, Inc v Forman, 421 US 837 (1975) ........................... 10.69
Vick v Howard, 136 Va. 101, 109,116 SE. 465 (1923) ............................... 7.54

# Table of Legislation

## STATUTES

Arbitration Act 1996
  s 48(4) .......................... 9.92
Bank Act 1844 ...................... 5.17
Bank of England Act 1708 ............ 5.15
Bank of England Act 1833 ............ 5.16
Banking Act 1742..................... 5.15
Banking Act 2009
  Pt 6 ............................ 4.37
Bankrupt Laws (England) Act 1822
  s 3 ............................. 9.12
Bills of Exchange Act 1882 ........ 4.38, 7.36,
                                       9.47, 9.48
  Pt IV ........................... 9.46
  Pt 4A ........................... 9.48
  s 2 ............................. 9.46
  s 29(1)(b)....................... 6.42
  s 31 ............................ 7.36
  s 47(2) ......................... 7.48
  s 73 ............................ 5.12
  s 83 ............................ 9.46
Bubble Act 1720..................... 5.15
Civil Procedure Acts Repeal Act 1879
  s 2 ............................. 9.40
Coinage Act 1971................. 7.71, 7.72
  s 2(1) .......................... 7.04
Consumer Rights Act 2015
  s 5 ............................. 7.86
Country Bankers Act 1826 ............ 5.15
Criminal Law Act 1967 ............... 7.47
Currency Act 1751.................... 2.23
Currency Act 1764.................... 2.23
Currency and Bank Notes Act 1954 ... 7.71, 7.72
  s 1(1) .......................... 7.04
  s 1(2) .......................... 4.38
  s 3 ............................. 4.38
Electronic Communications Act 2000
  s 7 ............................. 9.47
Exchange of Gold and Silver Act 1351 .... 2.29
Factors Act 1889..................... 7.15
  s 2(1) .......................... 7.15
Financial Services and Markets
    Act 2000 ..................... 10.65
  s 21 ...................... 10.10, 10.27
  s 22(1) ......................... 10.12
  s 22(2) ......................... 10.10
  s 85 ............................ 10.17
  s 102A(3) ....................... 10.17
  s 235 ........................... 10.22
  s 238 ........................... 10.27
  Sch 2 ........................... 10.10
Insolvency Act 1986
  s 130(5) ........................ 9.12
Insolvent Debtors Relief Act 1729 ....... 9.37
Interpretation Act 1978
  s 5 ...................... 9.46, 10.15
  Sch 1 ........................... 10.15
Lord Liverpool's Act 1816............. 2.29
Money Act 1551...................... 2.29
Patents Act 1977
  s 30(1) ......................... 9.09
Sale of Goods Act 1979.......... 7.26, 7.85,
                                       7.87, 9.18
  s 2 ......................... 7.86, 7.88
  s 17 ............................ 7.26
  s 17(2) ......................... 9.18
Senior Courts Act 1981
  s 49(2) ......................... 9.40
Statute of Acton Burnell *See* Statute of
    Merchants 1283
Statute of Frauds 1677
  s 4 ............................. 9.47
Statute of Merchants 1283 ............ 7.14
Statute of Merchants 1285 ............ 7.14
Statute of Set-off 1735 .............. 9.37
  s 4 ............................. 9.39
Statute of the Staple 1353............ 7.14
Supply of Goods and Services Act 1982.... 7.87
  s 1(3) .......................... 7.87
Torts (Interference with Goods)
    Act 1977
  s 14(1) ......................... 9.64
Value Added Tax Act 1994
  Sch 9, Group 5, Item 1 ............. 7.97

## STATUTORY INSTRUMENTS

Civil Jurisdiction and Judgements Order
    2001, SI 2001/3929 .............. 9.75
Civil Jurisdiction and Judgements
    (Amendment) Regulations 2014,
    SI 2014/2947 ................... 9.75
Civil Procedure Rules 1998,
    SI 1998/3132............... 7.77, 7.83
  r 16.6 ................. 9.34, 9.40, 9.45
  r 37.2 .......................... 7.77

Electronic Money Regulations 2011,
SI 2011/99
 reg 63 . . . . . . . . . . . . . . . . . . . . . . . . 10.39
Financial Collateral Arrangements
(No. 2) Regulations 2003,
SI 2003/3226 . . . . . . . . . . . . . . . . . . 9.54
Financial Markets and Insolvency
(Settlement Finality) Regulations
1999, SI 1999/2979 . . . . . . . . . . . . . 9.81
 reg 23 . . . . . . . . . . . . . . . . . . . . . . . . . 9.81
Financial Services and Markets Act 2000
(Carrying on Regulated Activities
by way of Business) Order 2001,
SI 2001/1177
 Art 2 . . . . . . . . . . . . . . . . . . . . . . . . . 10.31
Financial Services and Markets Act 2000
(Collective Investment Schemes)
Order 2001, SI 2001/1062
 Sch 1, para 3 . . . . . . . . . . . . . . . . . . 10.26
Financial Services and Markets Act
2000 (Promotion of Collective
Investment Schemes (Exemptions))
Order 2001, SI 2001/1060 . . . . . . . 10.27
Financial Services and Markets Act 2000
(Regulated Activities) Order 2001,
SI 2001/544 . . . . . . . . . . . . 10.10, 10.11,
        10.14, 10.30, 10.56
 Art 3 . . . . . . . . . . . . . . . . . . . . . . . . . 10.56
 Art 5 . . . . . . . . . . . . . . . . . . . . . . 10.30, 10.61
 Art 5(1) . . . . . . . . . . . . . . . . . . . . . . 10.31
 Art 5(2) . . . . . . . . . . . . . . . . . . . . . . 10.36
 Art 9AB . . . . . . . . . . . . . . . . . . . 10.36, 10.48
 Art 9B . . . . . . . . . . . . . . . . . . . . . . . 10.39
 Art 15(1)(a) . . . . . . . . . . . . . . . . . . . 10.12
 Art 17 . . . . . . . . . . . . . . . . . . . . . . . 10.14
 Art 60C(3) . . . . . . . . . . . . . . . . . . . 10.50
 Art 65 . . . . . . . . . . . . . . . . . . . . . . . 10.57
 Art 77 . . . . . . . . . . . . . . . . . . . . . . . 10.14
 Art 77(2) . . . . . . . . . . . . . . . . . . . . . 10.14
 Art 77(2)(c) . . . . . . . . . . . . . . . . . . . 10.16
 Art 79 . . . . . . . . . . . . . . . . . . . . . . . 10.20
 Art 80 . . . . . . . . . . . . . . . . . . . . . . . 10.20
 Art 83 . . . . . . . . . . . . . . . . . . . . . . . 10.19
 Art 84 . . . . . . . . . . . . . . . . . . . . . . . 10.19
 Art 84(1) . . . . . . . . . . . . . . . . . . . . . 10.66
 Art 84(1A) . . . . . . . . . . . . . . . . . . . 10.66
 Art 84(1B) . . . . . . . . . . . . . . . . . . . 10.66
 Art 84(5) . . . . . . . . . . . . . . . . . . . . . 10.66
 Art 85 . . . . . . . . . . . . . . . . . . . . . . . 10.20
 Art 85(2)(a) . . . . . . . . . . . . . . . . . . . 10.20
 Art 89 . . . . . . . . . . . . . . . . . . . . . . . 10.20
Payment Services Regulations 2017,
SI 2017/752 . . . . . . . . . . . . . 10.40, 10.63
 reg 2 . . . . . . . . . . . . . . . . . . . . . 10.33, 10.46

 reg 2(1) . . . . . . . . . . . . . . . . . . . . . . 10.37
 reg 33 . . . . . . . . . . . . . . . . . . . . . . . 10.46
 reg 58 . . . . . . . . . . . . . . . . . . . . . . . 10.43
 reg 138 . . . . . . . . . . . . . . . . . . . . . . 10.40
 reg 141 . . . . . . . . . . . . . . . . . . . . . . 10.43

## EUROPEAN LEGISLATION

### Treaties and Conventions

Convention on jurisdiction and
the enforcement of judgments
in civil and commercial matters
(Lugano, 1988) . . . . . . . . . . . . . . . . 9.75
 Art 2 . . . . . . . . . . . . . . . . . . . . . . . . . 9.75
European Convention on Foreign
Money Liabilities 1967, Council
of Europe Treaty No.60 . . . . . . . . . . 9.91

### Regulations

Regulation (EC) No 593/2008
of the European Parliament
and of the Council of 17 June
2008 on the law applicable to
contractual obligations (Rome I)
 Art 12(2) . . . . . . . . . . . . . . . . . . . . . 9.83
Regulation (EC) No 207/2009 of
26 February 2009 on the
Community trade mark . . . . . . . . . . 9.80
 Art 16 . . . . . . . . . . . . . . . . . . . . . . . . 9.80
Regulation (EU) No. 1215/2012 of the
European Parliament and of the
Council on Jurisdiction and the
recognition and enforcement of
judgements in civil and commercial
matters (Brussels I recast) . . . . . . . . . 9.75
 Art 4 . . . . . . . . . . . . . . . . . . . . . . . . . 9.75
Regulation (EU) No 596/2014 of
the European Parliament and
of the Council of 16 April 2014
on market abuse (market abuse
regulation) . . . . . . . . . . . . . . . . . . . . 10.66

### Directives

Directive 98/26/EC of the European
Parliament and of the Council
of 19 May 1998 on settlement
finality in payment and securities
settlement systems . . . . . . . . . . . . . . 9.81
Directive 2002/47/EC of the European
Parliament and of the Council of
6 June 2002 on financial collateral
arrangements . . . . . . . . . . . . . . . . . . 9.54
 recital 18 . . . . . . . . . . . . . . . . . . . . . 9.54

Directive 2009/110/EC of the European
  Parliament and of the Council of
  16 September 2009 on the taking up,
  pursuit and prudential supervision
  of the business of electronic money
  institutions................... 10.33
  recital 7 ...................... 10.33
  recital 13 ..................... 10.36
Directive 2014/65/EU of the European
  Parliament and of the Council of 15
  May 2014 on Markets in Financial
  Instruments and Amending
  Directive 2002/92/EC and
  Directive 2011/61/EU...... 10.17, 10.66
  Art 4(21) ..................... 10.59
  Art 4(22) ..................... 10.59
  Art 4(23) ..................... 10.59
  Art 4(44) ..................... 10.17
Directive (EU) 2015/2366 of the European
  Parliament and of the Council of 25
  November 2015 on payment services in
  the internal market............ 10.40

# INTERNATIONAL LEGISLATION

**United States**

Commodity Exchange Act 1936
  s 1(a)(9) ...................... 10.65
  s 2 ........................... 10.65
  s 2(c)(2)(C)(i)(II)(bb)(AA) ......... 10.65
  s 21(a) ....................... 10.67
Currency Act 1873.................. 7.54
Securities Act 1933................. 10.69
  s 2(a)(1) ...................... 10.69
Securities Exchange Act 1934
  s 3(a)(1) ...................... 10.70
  s 3(a)(10) ..................... 10.69
Uniform Commercial Code .......... 7.87
  s 1-201(24)..................... 7.06
  s 2-304(1)...................... 7.87
Uniform Sales Act 1906
  s 9(2) ......................... 7.87

# Introduction

The reason that fitting virtual currency into modern monetary law is so difficult is  0.01
that the high water mark of monetary legal theory more or less coincided with the
high water mark of the gold standard. Thus, the old masters were broadly in no
doubt as to what money was. Any of them, if asked, could have picked up a gold
coin of some denomination or other and demonstrated that this, ultimately, was
what they meant when they spoke of money. It bore the stamp of a sovereign issuing
authority, was of a weight and fineness broadly consistent with its monetary value;
it was clearly a store of value and a medium of exchange, and its denomination constituted the unit of account in the economy concerned. They realised that it was not
the only form of currency, but they would have been in no doubt that it was the basis
of the idea of money.

This coincidence led to the belief that there was a clear distinction between  0.02
'money' and 'not-money', and the only challenge with respect to any particular form
of circulating medium was to decide which side of the line it fell. This was not always
entirely straightforward—there was some debate in the early twentieth century as to
whether cheques might properly be regarded as a species of money—but the existence of the bright line was not in doubt.

The idea of the bright line was compounded by the economic theory of the "quan-  0.03
tity theory of money"[1] (QMT). This is based on the simple but deeply misleading
idea that there is a specific quantity of money in circulation in the economy.

The origins of the QMT lie in what Schumpeter called the "Ricardian vice" of  0.04
the economics profession[2] – that is, the tendency to view the world through a prism
of oversimplified approximations. In this case, the approximation was the idea that
because in any given period there are a measurable number of transactions, each at
a measurable price,[3] it must be possible to calculate the total amount of money in
use at any given time. This approach appears rational in the abstract, but is based
on a fundamental misunderstanding of the nature of both money and commerce.
In reality, a sale transaction is an exchange of goods for a credit claim. Money is one

---

[1] Fischer *The Purchasing Power of Money* (New York; The MacMillan Co, 1911) is the *ur*-text, but there is an enormous literature on the topic.
[2] Schumpeter, *History of Economic Analysis* (Routledge, 1987) *passim*.
[3] Clearly some monetary units can change hands more than once in any period, so the total of all transactions is divided by the velocity of circulation to arrive at the aggregate amount of money in circulation.

of the mechanisms by which the resulting credit claim may be discharged, but it is trivially true that not all credit claims are discharged by money payment – indeed the vast majority of them are satisfied by the creation of other credit claims on other economic actors. However, for our purposes the problem with the QMT approach was that it induced those thinking about the economy to assume without examination the existence of a lump of stuff called 'money' whose quantity could be established by sufficient statistical analysis. Once this idea had become established, it created scope for all sorts of concerns about where this stuff came from, who could create it, and on what terms it should be created, and the lineaments of these concerns are visible today in some of the thinking on the dangers posed by virtual currency to central bank's control of the economy.

0.05  The reason that this idea is a problem is that it leads to an approach to money based on the idea of identifying 'what it is'—does any particular thing form part of the "lump of stuff". In reality, however, money is characterized by what it does, not what it is—that which is universally accepted in payment is money, regardless of the views of the relevant authorities.

0.06  The 'lump of stuff' idea, even if it performs some useful function in the field of economics, is useless when it comes to examining the real world. The more any definition of money is examined, the less clear the precise location of the border between money and not-money seems to be. In particular, the conventional idea that money can be defined as a unit of account, a mechanism of exchange, and a store of value is an excellent description of a gold coin, but disintegrates on first contact with monetary reality. There are historical precedents for monetary items which are units of account but neither stores of value nor media of exchange (e.g. the ghost units which are frequently encountered in monetary history, which have a theoretical but not a real existence[4]), items which are media of exchange but not stores of value (currency in hyperinflating economies), and stores of value but neither units of account not media of exchange (such as the stone money of Yap[5]). Equally there are examples of things which can be both money and not—money at the same time (e.g. cigarettes in prison camps,[6] slave girls in second-century Ireland[7]). Society can make anything money, and money is fundamentally different from other forms of property in that its essence is its social function. The usefulness of any thing treated as 'money' derives precisely and exactly from the extent to which the recipient expects other members of society to accept it in payment. Whereas most social behaviour can be regarded as arrangements between people in respect of things, money is an arrangement between people as to their future behaviour. More importantly, these arrangements are 'social' in the sense that they are absolutely not private contracts. If A accepts X in payment from B, in the expectation that he will be able to give it to C in payment in due course, he almost certainly has not made an explicit

---

[4] For example, the shilling and the pound were units of account in England in the reign of King Offa, but were not minted as coins until the reign of Henry VII.
[5] Furness, *The Island of Stone Money* (JB Lippincott 1910).
[6] Radford, *The Economic Organization of a P.O.W. Camp* (Economica November, 1945).
[7] Yes, really. Nolan, *A Monetary History of Ireland* (PS King 1926) Vol. I at 117–18.

agreement with C in advance to accept X in payment—not least because at the time when he accepts X in payment, he probably has no clearly formed intentions to give it to C as opposed to D, E, F, or whomsoever else he wishes. The basis of the 'moneyness' of X is that all of the members of the group have a firm expectation that all of the other members will accept it as money. Thus, in any society, the question of whether a particular thing is 'money' or not can only be answered by examining social behaviour and social norms.

It cannot be too strongly emphasised that this question of 'moneyness' is entirely separate from the issue of legal tender. The laws of legal tender take effect when a person owes a debt, and determine what instruments the creditor is obliged to accept in payment of that debt. These laws have no relevance in the situation where a seller, debating whether or not to sell goods in exchange for a particular instrument, is considering how useful that instrument will be in buying things from others. If the seller does not wish to accept the instrument in payment he can secure that outcome simply by refusing to enter into the transaction in the first place or by demanding some other thing as payment, and the laws of legal tender are powerless to affect his decision. It is not the law, or the legal status of the thing proffered in payment, which determines his decision. It is sometimes said that money is a legal institution.[8] It is not. It is a social institution. Law is a phenomenon of society, not a determinant of it.

If we reject law as a source of social practice, why therefore, if money is a social phenomenon, is the law of money of any interest at all? A simplified answer to this question is that when sociology and economics had their celebrated parting of the ways in the Methodenstreit controversy at the end of the nineteenth century,[9] one of the issues which subsequently divided the controversialists was Menger's theory of money (an economic phenomenon) as a socially constructed device. Both sides of the debate would have asserted that money was a legal phenomenon, but both would have argued (for different reasons) that the law surrounding the topic was nothing more than a manifestation of the ineluctable logic of their positions. This is why, if we want to examine social attitudes to particular things at particular times, the law is a good place to look. Court decisions are generally little more than expressions of consensus social attitudes to particular issues, and because of their nature are likely to be more precisely recorded than other manifestations of social attitudes. In many respects, laws and court decisions may be regarded as similar to the palaeontological record—patchy and incomplete, but providing high levels of information of specific cases. Thus, by examining the legal treatment of particular things at particular times we can understand where the balance of forces between social and economic pressures lie, and by doing so see more clearly the social reality.

The argument of this book can be put very simply. There is no rule of law whose effect is that virtual currency is money. Equally, there is no rule of law whose effect

---

[8] See e.g. Desan, 'Money as a Legal Institution' in Fox and Ernst, *Money in the Western Legal Tradition* (OUP 2016).
[9] The (almost certainly correct) argument that this development was critical for the development of the twentieth-century study of money is developed by Geoffrey Ingham in *The Nature of Money: New Directions in Political Economy* (Polity Press 2004).

is that virtual currency is not money. There is a legal doctrine of money, whose effect is that if a thing is characterised as money, certain consequences follow as to the conduct of claims in respect of it. However, that doctrine determines only the consequences of being money, not the question of what is money. Thus, the question which we have to address is how we answer the question of whether the law should apply these doctrines to virtual currency or not, and the way that we address this question must involve abandoning *a priori* legal analysis. There is a striking comparison here with the development of negotiable instruments law under Lord Mansfield in the eighteenth century. There was no body of established English law which could have been used to create the doctrine of negotiability. However, Mansfield was quite clear that in deciding questions arising between merchants, 'a great deal must be referred to the usage of merchants'.[10] Thus, when questions arose as to whether particular and how particular instruments might be transferred in the market, the courts in effect looked to market usage to answer these questions—thus, in *Goodwin v Robarts*, when the question arose as to whether a scrip certificate was negotiable, the court held that 'the usage of the money market has solved the question whether the certificate should be considered security'.[11]

0.10   The development of new monetary instruments in the United Kingdom, and their treatment within the legal system, should be managed no less sensitively in the twenty-first century than it was in the eighteenth century. Thus, it is necessary—uncomfortable though it may be—to abandon an approach based on existing rules and to look to social practice in developing private law. This means that the court must ask 'how do people generally treat these instruments?'. Where there is a discontinuity between legal structure and commercial usage (as there is today as regards commercial bank money) the law must adapt its analysis to accommodate practice. It seems clear that the question of what the law should regard as money can only be answered by looking at what society itself regards as money.

0.11   In order to answer the question of how society determines money-ness, it is necessary to look in a number of different directions. First, we need to accept that money is a social institution with an exceptionally long history, and that how we think about money today is heavily influenced by how we thought of money in the past. We therefore need to consider how money developed. Next, we need to consider where money comes from—to what extent is the answer to the question 'what is money?' answerable by reference to who makes it—in particular, whether there is a rule to the effect that only units created by a sovereign issuer can be money. Next, we need to consider how the modern economy works, and in particular how payments are actually made. This means we need to look at the banking system of today, and ask how payment made using private bank money compares with payment made using other types of currency—in particular virtual currency. Next, we need to venture into the realms of hypothesis. We need to look at what the actual legal consequences are of treating virtual currency units as money or not. This involves

---

[10] *Hibbert v Pigou* (1783) cited in Oldham, *English Common Law in the Age of Mansfield* (University of North Carolina Press 2014) at 134.
[11] Per Cockburn CJ (1874–5) L.R. 10 Ex. 337 at 353.

hypothesising a series of potential disputes concerning virtual currency, and asking how they would be decided differently on the alternative hypotheses that it is or that it is not money. Finally, we need to think about how the ordinary rules of the road of the financial system—in particular the doctrines of financial regulation—should apply to virtual currencies.

The scheme of this book is therefore roughly as follows. In Chapter 1, I seek to establish some of the basic attributes of money and consider how money comes to have those attributes. In Chapter 2, I examine the extent to which money acquires its value because of its association with the state as its creator. In Chapter 3, I consider the job which money does in society and, in particular, the relationship between money and credit. In Chapter 4, I consider in more detail the question of how it is that money comes to be considered to be valuable. In Chapter 5, I look at the history and development of private payment instruments through history and consider whether and how much they provide precedents for virtual currency. In Chapter 6, I consider how payment is actually accomplished in the modern economy and, in particular, how deposits with commercial banks form the basis of the modern payment system. In Chapter 7, I look at the attributes which the law accords to money per se and identify the unique characteristics which money has but other types of property do not. In Chapter 8, I consider virtual currency as it currently exists and provide a taxonomy of both private and public virtual currencies. In Chapter 9, I review the various legal issues which transactions in virtual currency units give rise to. Finally, in Chapter 10, I consider how virtual currency interacts with the existing financial regulatory system.

0.12

# 1

# What is Money?

| | |
|---|---|
| 1.1 The Sociology of Money | 1.05 |
|    1.1.1 Money as an institution | 1.08 |
|    1.1.2 The origins of the money institution | 1.09 |
|    1.1.3 The formation of new institutions | 1.12 |
| 1.2 Does Money 'Exist'? | 1.16 |
|    1.2.1 Does traditional money exist? | 1.17 |
|    1.2.2 Intangibles as things | 1.19 |
|    1.2.3 Money and payment instruments | 1.20 |
|    1.2.4 Tangible money as a 'thing' | 1.23 |
|    1.2.5 Social perception of bank money | 1.27 |
|    1.2.6 Bank money as imaginary property | 1.30 |
| 1.3 Is Money a Commodity? | 1.34 |
|    1.3.1 Do we need 'real' sovereign money? | 1.36 |
| 1.4 What Gives Money its Value? | 1.40 |
|    1.4.1 Why is money valuable? | 1.42 |
|    1.4.2 Can law make a thing valuable as money? | 1.49 |
|    1.4.3 How should the courts decide what is money? | 1.50 |
|    1.4.4 Is characterisation as money once-and-for-all? | 1.53 |

Money is conventionally regarded as having three characteristics—a unit of account, a medium of exchange, and a store of value—and this can reasonably be described as the social scientist's traditional rule of recognition for 'money-ness'.[1] This trifecta is a good description of a gold coin, but unhelpful as regards other forms of money. However, these three attributes are all, to some extent, indicia of money-ness, and each individually is helpful in constructing a rule of recognition to enable us to recognise money when we see it.

1.01

Our starting point, however, is that it is absolutely not the case that only things having all three of these characteristics are money. The status of unit of account is a purely theoretical construct—a coin or note may be created to represent the unit of account, but it is the unit of account which defines the coin and not vice versa.

1.02

---

[1] See 'Fiat Money' in *The New Palgrave: A Dictionary of Economics* (Palgrave Macmillan 1987).

Equally, money may be useless as a store of value (as it is in hyperinflating economies) whilst retaining its characteristics as both a unit of account and a medium of exchange. Finally, money need not exist to be money—the shilling and the pound existed as units of account in England since the days of King Offa, but were not given physical existence by the mint until the reign of King Henry VII—and it seems clear that a unit which does not exist cannot easily function as a medium of exchange. Central bankers have recently tried to add a fourth criterion to this list—that the unit should be created by a central bank—but since it follows from this argument that the United States did not have a currency at all between 1836[2] and 1913,[3] this too must be abandoned. Consequently, although during the era of the gold standard it might have been possible to say that a gold coin satisfying these conditions was the only 'real' money in existence, this belief disappeared from monetary theory and practice a sufficiently long time ago that we should spend no more time on it.

1.03 There is considerable debate amongst theorists as to the interaction of these three characteristics. Keynes, for example, explains that the true definition of money is as a unit of account—he observes:

> Something which is merely used as a convenient medium of exchange on the spot may approach to being money, inasmuch as it may represent a means of holding General Purchasing Power. But if this is all, we have scarcely emerged from the stage of Barter. Money-Proper in the full sense of the term can only exist in relation to a money of account.[4]

Conversely, Menger takes the view that money has only one fundamental function; that being its function as a medium of exchange, and that its function as a standard of value is a mere phenomenon of its status as a medium of exchange.[5] In this regard, it is Menger who appears to be closest to the truth, in that something which cannot be used as a medium of exchange (i.e. which is not capable of being used to extinguish obligations) cannot by definition function as money, whereas there is no principle that the thing which is used to extinguish obligations must have the same value as the unit in which the obligation is denominated (it is perfectly practicable, if not always convenient, to pay sterling debts in dollars and vice versa).

1.04 The short-term conclusion from this is that the idea of money as a unit of account is simply wrong—as we shall see, currency developed to embody units of value, not the other way around—and the concept of a store of value is unhelpful, since anything valuable is capable of being a store of value for the period for which it endures. Thus, it is only the idea of the medium of exchange which is the real determinant of money-ness. This takes us to the conclusion that the only way to see whether a particular thing is a medium of exchange is to see whether it is actually used for that purpose in the marketplace. This in turn means that it is observation rather than analysis which will answer our question as to what constitutes money.

---

[2] When the Second Bank of United States ceased to operate because of President Jackson's veto of the renewal of its charter.
[3] When the current Federal Reserve was established.
[4] *Treatise on Money* in the *Collected Writings of John Maynard Keynes* (CUP, published for the Royal Economic Society 2013) at 1.
[5] Menger, *On the Origin of Money*, The Economic Journal, Vol. 2, No. 6. (June, 1892).

## 1.1 The Sociology of Money

If money is that which society treats as money, determining what is money requires an assessment of social behaviour. However, when we speak of social behaviour in this context, we are really speaking of social norms—the question is not 'do some people accept this as money?', but 'do people generally accept this as money?'. This latter question immediately raises the preliminary issue of 'which people?'. There is nothing which can be said to be universally accepted as money by everyone in the world—in reality, the world contains many monies, each circulating within a particular social sub-group. Thus, we need to begin by defining a social group before we can ask whether a particular thing circulates as money within that group. This is important because the question to be asked is as to whether a money thing is accepted generally as money. In order to answer this question, it is irrelevant how many people accept it—what matters is how many do not accept it. Since we can assume that no one outside the relevant social group will accept its money as such, casting the net too widely will secure the outcome that the thing is not money. Conversely, casting the net too narrowly runs the risk of defining the social group as that group of persons who do accept the thing as money, and this definition also pre-decides the question to be asked. Thus, knowing precisely what is meant by 'society' in this context is an essential element of the analysis to be undertaken.

1.05

The idea that money is a social creation is unremarkable. Aristotle in the *Nicomachean Ethics*[6] sets out the basic principle that:

1.06

Money has become by convention a sort of representative of demand; and this is why it has the name 'money' ('nomisma')—because it exists not by nature but by law (nomos) and it is in our power to change it and make it useless,

Hume compares money and language in this regard in the *Treatise of Human Nature*:[7]

[L]anguages [are] gradually establish'd by human conventions without any explicit promise. In like manner do gold and silver become the common measures of exchange, and are esteem'd sufficient payment for what is of a hundred times their value.

The analogy between money and language is peculiarly accurate. Commerce and language are both forms of social interaction which require a common medium, and once a particular medium has become established, adopting it has clear and immediate benefits for the adopter. This creates a substantial incentive for new users to adopt it. This in turn broadens the scope of its establishment and increases the incentive for new adopters still further.

David Lewis[8] offers a theory of linguistic conventions, and that theory, regardless of its applicability in the field of language, seems to work well in the field of money. Lewis' basic contention is that conventions are the result of predictions by people as to the future behaviour of others. This is illustrated by game theory mechanics

1.07

---

[6] At V.5.II33a (Penguin Classics 2004).   [7] 1738–40 (OUP 2000) at 490.
[8] *Convention: A Philosophical Study* (Blackwell 2002).

derived from pure coordination games, and demonstrates that in an environment where individual actors are aware of the behaviour of other actors and can draw conclusions from that behaviour as to future behaviour, the result will be coordination hardening into convention.

### 1.1.1 Money as an institution

1.08 If this is correct, then money is clearly a Northian institution—a 'humanly devised constraint that structures political, economic and social interactions'.[9] The origins of Northian institutions can best be established in a game theoretic context—they are in effect attempts to reduce transaction costs where transactions spread beyond tightly knit groups by enabling economic actors to predict the likely behaviours of other actors with whom they may engage in games in the future. North postulates a world in which institutions become increasingly necessary as the need for transactions expands beyond small groups where transactions are repeated and each participant possesses complete information about the other participant's past performance.[10] This precisely replicates conclusions which sociologists and others have reached about the development of money—that it is a concomitant of increasing geographical spread of trade, fragmentation of distribution chains, and division of labour. As exchange expands beyond tightly knit communities, the development of institutions reduces transaction and production costs by reducing uncertainties and increasing the probability of certain specified outcomes.[11]

### 1.1.2 The origins of the money institution

1.09 The origin of a Northian institution is in effect a feedback loop between the societal behaviours of people and the mentality which the existence of those behaviours creates. Thus, like all institutions, it has a social origin. The best explanation of the mechanic by which this is produced is from H. Peyton Young:

> ... complex economic and social structure can emerge from the simple, un-co-ordinated actions of many individuals. When an interaction occurs over and over again and involves a changing cast of characters, a feedback loop is established whereby past experiences of some agents shape the current expectations of other agents. This process yields predictable patterns of equilibrium and disequilibrium behaviour that can be construed as social and economic 'institutions'.[12]

Young goes on to point out that although major players matter in the development of social institutions, small variations in individual behaviour, which are more subtle and difficult to pinpoint, are likely to be more important for the development of some kinds of institutions. This seems to catch more or less perfectly the position as

---

[9] North, *Institutions*, The Journal of Economic Perspectives, Vol. 5, No. 1 (Winter, 1991) 97–112 at 97.
[10] Ibid.
[11] North, *Understanding the Process of Economic Change* (Princeton University Press 2005).
[12] Peyton Young, *Individual Strategy and Social Structure* (Princeton University Press 2001).

regards royal or imperial proclamations regarding the future use of money, and their relative importance as against the myriad small determinations by individuals about what they will, and what they will not, accept as payment. As Young concludes, 'we suspect that influential actors often get the credit for things that were about to happen anyway'.[13]

In this regard, North[14] points out that although such institutions may develop through a process capable of being understood through evolutionary game theory built on learning and imitation, he also points to the observation of Merlin Donald that 'Culture can literally reconfigure the use patterns of the brain; and it is probably a safe inference from our current knowledge of cerebral plasticity that those patterns of use determine much about how the exceptionally plastic human central nervous system is organised in terms of cognitive structure'.[15] It may well be that our notion of the idea of money—and it is doubtful that there are more than a handful of people on the face of the planet who do not have an idea of money—is a result of our inhabiting a society in which it is one of the most universal institutions. 1.10

Institutions are incidents of societies. They differ from social group to social group, and change over time as the society of which they are a phenomenon changes. Thus, there can be no arbitrary definition of money which is good for all societies at all times—no thing is always money. The fact that different societies have different monies is too well-known to be worthy of comment, but the fact that the same society may have different monies at different times is of more importance for the purpose of the discussion in this book. No person can single-handedly change a social institution, and it is very questionable whether legislation unaccompanied by broad social acceptance can change such institutions either—for example, if the UK Parliament were to pass a law tomorrow designating bitcoin as legal currency of the United Kingdom, it is very unlikely that this would have any real impact on the commercial behaviour of individuals. However, the question which we are dealing with here is as to what the position should be if one or more cybercurrencies were to gain broad acceptance within at least some sections of society over time, such that as between those persons the expectation of future behaviour as regards dealing in cybercurrencies were to become institutionalised. 1.11

### 1.1.3 The formation of new institutions

It seems clear that we cannot deal with the formation of new institutions simply by reasserting old rules. If social change has resulted in institutional change, the correct way to deal with this cannot be simply the repetition of rules which constituted the old rule in the old state of society.[16] However, monetary status is a social and not a private arrangement—the law may reflect social preferences, but should not 1.12

---

[13] Ibid. at 145.
[14] North, *Understanding the Process of Economic Change* (Princeton University Press 2005) at 69.
[15] Donald, *Origins of the Modern Mind: Three Stages in the Evolution of Culture and Cognition* (Harvard University Press 1991) at 14.
[16] And if North is correct that change in human society is non-ergodic, this is axiomatic.

mandate individual preferences. Consequently, it must not and should not simply accept individual agreements as creating institutional arrangements. There are public policy issues as well as private arrangements to be considered in institution-building, and both must be taken into account.

1.13  So how do we go about deciding when institutional change has reached the point that a particular thing has become money? As with any issue involving legal classification, it is unhelpful to approach it in the abstract. Any attempt to apply legal classifications to any individual situation should always begin with the question 'why do you care?'—or more precisely, 'what are the consequences of this or that classification?'. This question is not extraneous to the classification, but an integral part of it. In this particular case, the question of whether or not a particular unit or instrument should be classified as 'money' determines the application of a number of legal rules to it relating to transfer, ownership, and recoverability of the units concerned, along with a number of regulatory rules prohibiting certain dealings with the unit or instrument without appropriate authorisation. Thus, for example, if we classify a particular unit as money, we apparently determine whether handing it over constitutes payment, whether looking after it for another constitutes deposit-taking, how it can be recovered if it is misappropriated, and what happens if it is mixed with other property of the same kind?

1.14  However, this takes us to a further question. Currently, we operate with unitary concepts of money and not-money, and the applicability of all of these rules is determined by a single classification. Thus, our current mental model is that there is a single institution called 'money', and the debate about new payment mechanisms is as to whether they should be treated as belonging within that institution. This translates into an idea that the idea of 'money' is unitary and indivisible. However, is there any reason why this should be the case? Could we determine that a particular unit should be classified as money for the purposes of recognising it as payment, but as not-money to the extent that holding it for another should not constitute the regulated activity of deposit-taking? It is clearly easier and intellectually tidier to answer this question with a resounding 'no', and argue that money status is unitary and indivisible, and if it is sought to obtain the benefits of money status for an instrument, then the disadvantages of that status must be applied in full to it. However, no matter how appealing this approach may be in terms of intellectual coherence, there is no rule of law which mandates it. The idea of a unit which is treated as money for some purposes but not others is no different from ideas such as goodwill and confidential information, which are equally treated as property for some purposes but not others.[17]

1.15  Translated into institutional terms, the question that is being asked here is whether new forms of payment should be dealt with by bringing them within existing institutions, or whether we might need to develop new institutions to accommodate them? It is submitted that the latter may well be the case, and that the correct approach to this issue may well not be to apply the existing definition of 'money' on

---

[17] See Bridge and Gullifer et al., *The Law of Personal Property* (2nd edn, Sweet & Maxwell 2018) Ch. 9.

a once-and-for-all basis. This is not least because this is absolutely not the way that users will approach it. If a person accepts virtual currency from another in exchange for goods, he is very likely to perceive the transaction as a sale rather than a barter, and in that regard will regard the virtual currency as money. However, if he holds the resulting virtual currency for the benefit of a third party, he is very unlikely to regard himself as deposit-taking, as opposed to simply custodying an asset. In each case, the particular expectations and arrangements between the parties need to be considered, and an appropriate outcome determined. It is very unlikely that a single answer of the form 'this is money' or 'this is not money' will address all of these issues satisfactorily.

## 1.2 Does Money 'Exist'?

One of the most common objections to the idea that virtual currencies might be money is the argument that they 'don't really exist'. This is self-evidently true as regards cryptocurrencies, which are literally nothing but a string of code in a distributed ledger. However, the implication of the objection is that 'real' money does, somehow, exist in a way in which virtual money does not. The only way that this can be usefully approached is to ask whether and to what extent the money which we use today can be said to 'exist'. 1.16

### 1.2.1 Does traditional money exist?

Physical currency, of course, does exist in physical form. However, it is generally accepted that if the Bank of England were to decide to automate its operations in such a fashion as to eliminate physical cash completely,[18] such that sterling existed only in the form of its electronic ledgers, the pound would still 'exist' in exactly the same way in which it is considered to exist now. This seems entirely reasonable—the 'pound' is the platonic ideal which is substantiated in the pound coin, and the disappearance of all the pound coins in the world would not affect the existence of the ideal. 1.17

However, this leaves us with the idea that money is an existing intangible. For lawyers, this raises the question of whether it is a 'claim' or a 'thing'. 1.18

### 1.2.2 Intangibles as things

The point here is that law distinguishes two broad classes of legal relationships; one deriving from relationships between persons, the other deriving from ownership of things. Intangibility is not an obstacle to ownership—intangibles can be owned in exactly the same way that any other item of property can be owned. Intellectual property in all its forms provides an obvious example of intangibles which can be 1.19

---

[18] See Rogoff, *The Curse of Cash* (Princeton University Press 2016) for an impassioned argument for precisely this policy measure, along with an account of how it could be achieved.

owned, and the law of real property is replete with rights which are clearly property, which can be transferred by law and defended in the courts by the transfer, but which constitute nothing more than a right to do a thing, or to require some other person to do a thing.[19] Some confusion occasionally arises from the fact that the way in which property rights are protected by the law is through the enforcement or rejection of claims, and this has occasionally led to the oversimplification that there is no real difference between property rights and relationship claims.[20] However, there is in fact a reasonably clear distinction between the two—a claim is a claim on a particular person (or persons); a property right is a claim on all people. It is perfectly possible to own a claim—if you owe me £5, there is a legal mechanism called assignment by which I can transfer my claim on you to a third party, and the laws which apply to that transfer are broadly the same as the laws which apply to any other transfer of property. However, it is equally possible to own an intangible which is not a claim against any particular person—again, intellectual property being the most commonly encountered example.

### 1.2.3 Money and payment instruments

1.20 When this model is applied to money today, it seems clear that, rightly or wrongly, there is a more or less universal assumption both by society and by the courts that money is a thing which is owned, which is capable of being transferred, and which is protected from interference by the ordinary doctrines of property law. A little introspection will demonstrate that this is a good proxy for the way that people generally think of and contract in respect of money—when a person speaks of paying a debt, they will generally conceptualise the payment as a transfer of property from them to the payee, despite the fact that if the payment passes through the banking system at no point will any physical thing ever be transferred. Thus, money is best regarded as an item of intangible property.

1.21 This can most easily be seen if we imagine a person paying for a purchase with a cheque. Most people would say that the cheque itself was not the payment, but merely a payment mechanism which enables the seller to obtain payment.[21] Consequently, it is wrong to say that the seller has sold in exchange for the cheque—the seller has sold in exchange for the promise of the payment of money, along with the delivery of a mechanism by which performance of that promise may be obtained. Conversely, if the buyer makes payment by handing over notes and coins, we would say that the

---

[19] Known as incorporeal hereditaments. These rights are as old as property law—2 Bl Comm 20. A good example of an incorporeal hereditament is an advowson: the right to present a particular clergyman to a particular parish. Such a right is a 'pure' right, in that it has no physical aspect at all. It is nonetheless an item of property and can be sold, leased or mortgaged.

[20] This position is generally attributed to Hohfeld (*Some Fundamental Legal Conceptions as Applied in Judicial Reasoning*, Yale Law Journal, Vol. 23, No. 16 (1913) at 32), and is notable primarily in that it is entirely rejected by ordinary people in real life, to whom the idea that their ownership of their car can be expressed as 6 billion individual rights, one against each of the other people in the world, appears incomprehensible. A good account of the position as it is perceived in real life can be found in Merrill and Smith, *The Property/Contract Interface*, Columbia Law Review, Vol. 101, No. 4 (May 2001) at 773–852.

[21] *Chitty on Contracts* (32nd edn, Sweet & Maxwell 2015) at para 21-075.

delivery of the notes and coins is itself payment. This seems to illustrate that there is a simple distinction between money, which is a 'thing', and payment instruments, which are claims to money.

1.22 This tidy classification seems at first glance to be straightforward. Sadly, however, it relies on a nineteenth-century mental model of money and payment which bears no relation to the way in which payments are actually effected today. We can best illustrate this by imagining that we have stopped a man who has just bought a cup of coffee on the way to work and ask how he paid for it. He will reply—probably rather testily—'with money'. He almost certainly did not. If he paid by tapping a contactless card on a payment terminal, what he actually did was to send an instruction to a card company which caused the card company to instruct its bank to transfer an amount to the bank which maintains the account of the coffee shop. The card company will then present an electronic request to the coffee-buyers' bank, which will in turn reduce the amount which regards itself as owing to the coffee-buyer, and make a corresponding payment out of its own resources to the card company. One (oversimplified and legally incorrect) way of looking at this is that what has happened is that he has paid with a claim on his bank by transferring it to the coffee shop, but even this would strike our hypothetical coffee-buyer as wrong. When he thinks of his balance at his bank, he does not think of it as a credit claim against the bank, he thinks of it as 'money' which he 'owns'. If asked what 'money' actually is, the result might be some vague reference to either the state or the Bank of England, or more likely the production of notes and coins from his wallet along with the exasperated response 'this is'. The key point here is that when economic participants in a modern economy think about money and payment, they think of it using a mental model of handing over notes and coins, and no matter how far removed their actual transaction execution mechanism may be from the simple act of handing over notes and coins, that is how they will conceptualise it. However, there will be no doubt in the minds of either the coffee-buyer or the coffee-seller that what has happened is a transfer of a thing, not a mere exchange of credit claims.

### 1.2.4 Tangible money as a 'thing'

1.23 Thus money—even intangible book-entry commercial bank money—seems to be universally regarded as property. The question therefore is simply as to what sort of property is it.

1.24 We begin with physical money, which we initially characterised as clearly a thing and not a claim. Is this actually clear? It seems unquestionable that coins are not a credit claim on the person minting them, but the debate as to whether bank-issued notes (whether issued by private banks or central banks) are things or credit claims is less straightforward.

1.25 The first point to make about this debate is that it is probably a distinction without a difference. Assume I have £100 on deposit with a Scottish Bank,[22] and I have

---

[22] Scottish banks have the privilege of issuing their own banknotes.

agreed with my neighbour to pay him £100. If I go into a branch of the bank and ask for £100 in £10 notes, what I will receive is ten notes issued by the bank itself. Conversely, if I go into the same bank and ask for a banker's draft (a draft drawn by the bank on itself) for £100, what I will receive is a single note drawn by the bank on itself, which broadly performs the same function as a banknote. Both of these pieces of paper have the common attribute of being 'claims' on the issuing bank. The difference between the two is that if I give the notes to my neighbour, he will regard them as things whose delivery satisfies my payment obligation. However, if I give him the bankers draft, he will regard it as a payment mechanism, and will only regard my obligation as discharged once he has provided the draft to his bank, his bank has collected it from my bank, and advised him that this account has been credited. Thus, two instruments which are legally identical are treated as falling on different sides of our thing/claim line. What this tells us is that the test for determining whether a particular item is a thing or a claim is not a purely legal test. Put simply, in the context of payment at least 'thing-ness' is an attribute derived from social practice and use, not from legal analysis.

1.26 This point becomes more important when we come to consider the position of Bank of England banknotes. A Bank of England banknote is ostensibly a credit claim on the Bank of England—indeed it bears on its face a promise by the Bank of England to pay to the bearer a sum of money—but in practice Bank of England banknotes are universally treated as 'things' whose delivery constitutes settlement of monetary obligations. Thus, we should have little difficulty in concluding that, regardless of their legal form and characterisation, Bank of England banknotes, like private banknotes, are things and not claims.

### 1.2.5 Social perception of bank money

1.27 Most people do not in fact discharge the majority of their obligations with physical banknotes, but with credit claims on private banks. If I have a credit balance with a commercial bank, what I have is clearly a claim on that bank. However, the way that most people think about their claim on their bank is that they have a claim to things held by that bank. Thus, the idea of a £100 balance at a bank translates in the common mind into the idea that the bank is somehow 'holding' £100 for the customer—thus when a £50 payment is made out of the account, the customer generally thinks of the transaction as involving £50 which was previously held by the bank for him being transferred to the seller's bank, where it will be held for the seller. Most customers probably know that this is not in fact the case, but the operation of the payment system is based on a common pretence that it is. It is probably wrong to describe this common pretence as a legal fiction, since the law does not always operate as if this were in fact the case. However, the basic model that when considering a bank account, the common appreciation is of a claim on a bank for a thing.

1.28 However, although it may well be true that people think of their bank accounts as containing banknotes, they do not. Private bank accounts pretend to hold considerably more government-created money than the government has in fact created, and as noted below the amount of government-created money in existence does not appear to be connected to the amount of private money in existence. Commercial bank money is a claim on a commercial bank for an abstract unit of account. In this regard, a claim on a private bank for pounds is no different from a claim on a private bank for bitcoins.

The point at issue here is that for individuals who are active in a modern economy, the pounds in their bank accounts are 'things', despite the fact that they have no existence at all. This, interestingly, is the point at which law and practice reconnect—a great deal of legal development around the recovery of misappropriated money is based on property law doctrines of recovery which only make any sense at all in this context if the starting point is the popular perception that money in a bank account is a thing which is capable of being owned, and which therefore simply disregard the true legal position. Thus, we can conclude that private bank money is thought of as a 'thing' which is 'owned'.   1.29

This brings us to the (important) legal distinction between the intangible and the imaginary. A claim on a bank for the balance of an account is an intangible thing, which the depositor clearly owns at law. The pounds which the depositor thinks of as being held for him by the bank are entirely imaginary—they are a mental device which enables him to comprehend the position as between him and the bank, but they have no existence at all. Does this matter?

### 1.2.6 Bank money as imaginary property

For practical purposes money is a claim for an imaginary thing on a commercial bank—imaginary in the sense that nobody believes that the bank actually holds an amount of money equal to its liabilities, but every holder of those liabilities behaves as if that were the case.   1.30

The fact that there is a gulf between the common approach to money in a bank account as a thing which is owned and transferred and the legal position of money as a credit claim on the bank where it is held causes less difficulty in the courts than might be expected. However, this is largely because the courts themselves are generally less than rigorous in applying technical legal analysis to this issue. When they do, the results can be highly disruptive. In *R v Preddy*,[23] the House of Lords was required to consider whether a transfer of (imaginary) money from one bank account to another constituted a transfer of ownership of a thing (the case concerned a charge of obtaining money by deception, and the question was as to whether the accused, by having money paid into their bank accounts, had 'obtained money'). The conclusion reached was that (a) there was no transfer of any underlying property, because no such property actually existed, and (b) there was no transfer of a claim—the effect of the transaction was that one man's account balance at one bank was reduced, and another man's account balance at another bank was increased, but there was no transfer of ownership of the claim from one person to another. There are two   1.31

---

[23] *R v Preddy* [1996] AC 815.

points of interest for us about *Preddy*. First is the fact that it caused real consternation amongst criminal lawyers—the idea that money in a bank account is real, and is actually transferred when a payment is made, was so widely held amongst lawyers and judges that the fact that this was not in fact how the banking system worked seems to have come as a great shock, and required rapid change in law.[24] Second is that the only way in which the court could have reached the conclusion it did was by positively asserting that the claim on the bank for the imaginary money concerned was the only claim that existed. If the underlying money had itself been a claim of any form, then the transfer of that claim would have been necessary to give effect to the transaction.

1.32 In summary, what *Preddy* affirms is that currency in normal commercial banking use constitutes a claim on an intermediary for an imaginary thing. If this is compared with a claim for (say) a bitcoin held in an account maintained by a bitcoin service provider, it should immediately be clear that there is a real distinction between the two, in that the underlying bitcoin does in fact 'exist', and is in fact 'transferred' on the ledger. Conversely, money held in a bank account is never transferred, but is created and destroyed by book entry.

1.33 The conclusion is that the pound which is represented by my deposit with a commercial bank has slightly less 'real' existence than the virtual currency unit which I may own by virtue of an entry in a distributed ledger. Both are simply tokens representing accrued value, usually received in respect of value given, and held for the sole purpose of being transferred on, usually in respect of value received. Consequently, viewed from the perspective of the man in the street, the virtual currency unit can be (and is) thought of as 'the same sort of thing' as the money in his bank account or in his pocket. This view is eminently justifiable.

## 1.3 Is Money a Commodity?

1.34 It is sometimes objected that the argument that money is a thing means that it must be a commodity. There are all sorts of arguments as to why money should not properly be regarded as a commodity, which can collectively be summed up under the heading that the measure of all things cannot be itself a thing. However, this is to confuse the monetary unit with the thing that it represents. There may well be a piece of metal in Paris which is labelled as the standard metre, but it is not itself a metre. Equally, there may well be a coin issued by the Bank of England to the value of a pound, but it is not a pound. A metre is a concept, a pound is equally a concept. A metal bar is a thing; a pound coin is also a thing.

1.35 In order to understand this it is necessary to understand an important distinction. Economic transactions are denominated in monetary units, but do not necessarily involve money. A basic economic transaction involves delivery of goods and services for credit, and the subsequent extinction of that credit by the delivery of money.

---

[24] See Brindle and Cox, *Law of Bank Payments* (Sweet & Maxwell 2010) at para 3-093 for more on this.

*What is Money?*  19

In some transactions the extinction may be almost instantaneous, in others it may be very prolonged, but in almost no case is the transaction a barter of one thing for another. The credit which is granted is measured in a unit called the pound, and those who grant credit agree that each pound of obligation can be discharged by the delivery, in one form or another, of something with a unit value of one pound. However, there is no requirement that the pound so delivered be real—if I pay for goods with a cheque for £10 drawn on my commercial bank, what *R v Preddy* tells us is that what happens is that my bank stops pretending it holds £10 for me and the seller's bank starts pretending that it holds £10 for him. These 'pretend' pounds are nothing to do with the 'real' pounds created by the Bank of England. Leaving aside physical notes and coins, the 'real' pounds created by the Bank of England exist in the form of credit balances maintained (almost exclusively by private banks) directly with the Bank of England. The only utility that these 'real' pounds have is the settlement of transactions between private banks—they almost never touch the real economy.[25]

### 1.3.1 Do we need 'real' sovereign money?

This does seem to take us to an extraordinary idea. If the pounds which are used for payment in the real economy are entirely imaginary, and the vast majority of the pounds created by the Bank of England are entirely notional,[26] to what extent can the pound be said to exist at all. As physical currency takes up an ever-smaller role in actual commerce,[27] and we replace tangible things with intangible things, could we simply abolish the central bank and state-provided money, and rely exclusively on commercial banks to provide money to the economy?  1.36

The short answer is that we could, but it would be a bumpy ride. Although it is highly arguable that the money market is a self-adjusting mechanism, and that the commercial banking system will eventually provide the correct amount of money required by the economy, there have been sufficient recent incidents where this does not appear to have been the case to demonstrate that mere faith in the efficiency of the market may be as poor a policy in this area as it proved in others. Recent experience has demonstrated that there are occasions on which the commercial banking system provides very significantly less money than the economy appears to require, to the extent that the injection of money into the economy from outside it (usually through the creation of new money by the central bank) is essential.  1.37

One reason for this is that the amount of credit in an economy fluctuates over time. This fluctuation appears to be neither predictable nor stable. However, at  1.38

---

[25] One way of looking at this is that Bank of England 'real' money is commodity money, whereas bank 'pretend' money is credit money.

[26] In its February 2018 accounts, the Bank of England's money provision to the commercial banking system through deposits stood at £502m, whereas the volume of cash placed by it into circulation was £73m.

[27] Cash payments constituted 61% of all payments in the United Kingdom in 2007 but only 34% in 2017, and are expected to fall to 16% by 2027—see *UK Payments Market 2018* published by UK Finance.

moments of significant credit expansion the price of assets with fixed supply (such as land) will inflate disproportionately, and at moments of rapid credit contraction the otherwise stable economy is capable of substantial value destruction unless external stabilisation is provided. In the first case, there is little that can be done—the development of a credit bubble is unlikely to be impacted by the reduction of the supply of money to the system. However, in the second case, the system as a whole finds itself in need of increased monetary resources in order to extinguish excess credit exposures, and those resources can only be supplied exogenously. One way of looking at this is to say that the amount of debt in the system and the credit capacity of the system are independent variables—as long as the credit appetite of the system is sufficient to absorb the amount of debt created, all is well, but if the credit appetite of the system suffers a crisis of confidence and falls below the level of debt in the system,[28] a damaging destruction of value will be experienced if new credit is not granted to the system by an outside source.

1.39 All this is a long-winded way of saying that the supply of money does matter to an economy, and in particular that that the endogenous money within the system may from time to time require supplementing through the creation and injection of exogenous money. It is at this point that a currency, although not itself a commodity, resembles a commodity in one very important respect—that is, that its value is capable of being affected by an imbalance between supply and demand. If the supply of pounds increases in a situation where nothing else changes, the value of the pound will decrease (i.e. prices expressed in pounds will rise) and everything would get more expensive, in exactly the same way that if the authorities were to decree a reduction in the standard metre, everything would get longer. Interestingly, however, the reverse is not the case. There is plentiful evidence that an economy can expand significantly whilst its supply of real money is static or declining. This is because the supply of credit can be infinitely expanded. However, where the extension of credit replaces the payment of debts, the result is a complex web of extended credit chains which is not economically efficient, and multiple different mechanisms (referred to collectively as private money, or more properly private payment instruments) have been invented at different times to address this problem. However, a shortage of money does not appear of itself to drive deflation. Looked at in simplistic terms, we can say that increasing credit is a good substitute for shortage of money, but a surplus of money must be accommodated by a repricing of credit.

It is notable that the conclusion to which this takes us is not that sovereign money is essential, but that the capacity of the sovereign to create money at certain times may be essential. It is therefore arguable that an economy could function without sovereign money, provided that the sovereign retained the capacity to create money. Lest it be assumed that this is a modern phenomenon, it should be noted that the injection of money into the economy by the sovereign

---

[28] See Calomiris and Gorton, *The Origins of Banking Panics: Models, Facts and Bank Regulation in Financial Markets and Financial Crises*, Ed. Hubbard (University of Chicago Press 1991).

was the technique used by the Emperor Augustus to address the financial crisis of AD 33.[29]

## 1.4 What Gives Money its Value?

The historical filter created by the worldwide adoption of the gold standard led many into the error of believing that a coin was intended to be merely a stamped ingot—the fact of coining being merely a certification that the metal value of the coin was equal to its face value. Coins of this kind could be said to have an absolute value determined by the physical weight of the gold, silver, or electrum which the coin included. The prevalence of this belief is somewhat mysterious, in that in the absence of an interventionist central bank or similar authority (not generally encountered in the ancient or medieval worlds), any such coin would immediately have had two divergent values; one in respect of the unit of currency which it represented, the other in respect of the value of the precious metal which composed it. Unless we assume that the value of the relevant precious metal did not vary *at all* against the unit of currency concerned, we have to assume that the users of such coins must have been indifferent to either the real value of the coin, or to its face (currency unit) value. Since it would be very odd indeed to assume that users of a coin were indifferent to its face value and focused primarily on its commodity value, we have to assume the opposite. However, as soon as we assume this we are assuming that users are indifferent to the physical metal content of the coin, and this in turn forces us to the conclusion that the coin does not derive its value from its physical metal content. 1.40

A coin can only be treated in one of two ways; either as a physical piece of metal whose value is determined by the value of that metal (that is, a commodity), or as a payment mechanism whose value is determined by its face value (that is, as money). It is only likely to be treated as a commodity if its intrinsic value is significantly in excess of its face value, and coins of this kind effectively cease to perform the function of currency and tend to disappear rapidly from circulation. Thus, it is a good general rule that the only coins which actually circulate are those whose face values are broadly equal to or higher than their metal content. Even in the era where money consisted of physical coins with a significant intrinsic value, it is wrong to say that that money derived its value to any material extent from its physical composition. This is *a fortiori* true in the world in which every one of the readers of this book was born into and has grown up in, where money does not have a significant commodity value. However, by eliminating the idea that money has an intrinsic value, we simply intensify the fundamental question of what it is that gives money its value. 1.41

---

[29] Tacitus, Annals, VI, 16-17. A good account is to be found in *The Financial Crisis of A.D. 33: A Keynesian Depression?* Thornton and Thornton The Journal of Economic History Vol. 50, No. 3 (Sep, 1990), pp. 655–62.

### 1.4.1 Why is money valuable?

1.42  The fundamental purpose of money is to discharge credit obligations—a good working definition of money might be 'that whose delivery extinguishes payment obligations', and a payment obligation is simply a credit claim. Thus, in order to get to the value of money it is necessary to think about credit. However, this is not as helpful as it might at first appear. Assume that B has paid C in advance[30] to do something for him—whether to supply something or to do something at some point in the future. B is now exposed to the credit risk of C.

1.43  In broad terms, the idea of credit risk is straightforward—if someone has an obligation to me which is due to be performed at some point in the future, even if the obligation is undisputed and undisputable, there is a risk that it might not be performed. This may happen either because the person obliged cannot perform—he does not have the resources—or because he chooses not to and challenges me to bring enforcement action against him. Credit risk is an inherent part of any non-barter economy, and arises every time any obligation is created—the failure of a supplier to deliver goods may be regarded as credit risk in exactly the same way as the failure of a creditor to pay money. Credit risk is, at its simplest, the risk that tomorrow may not be as we expect it to be today.

1.44  Now assume that A has created money. If C wishes to be discharged from his obligation to B, he can extinguish it by the payment of money. However, if money is a claim on its creator, then all that happens when C pays his debt to B is that B is exchanging a claim on one person (C) for a claim on another (A). What is it that makes one claim—the claim on A as the issuer of the currency—different from the other—the claim on B?

1.45  The answer is definitional - the claim on A is 'money', whereas the claim on C is not. The difference between the two lies not in the fact that they are claims, but that one of them is a type of thing which is treated by persons generally as 'money', whereas the other is not. Reverting to our definition of money as that whose delivery extinguishes a debt or obligation, the point about the claims on A is that they have that character. It should be emphasised that this is not a unique property of money—it is perfectly possible to provide by private contract that the delivery of any thing has the effect of absolutely extinguishing an obligation in this way. However, money has this characteristic by default, whereas non-money assets have it only have it only if that character is specifically conferred on them by a particular agreement in respect of a particular transaction.[31]

---

[30] If we do not assume this, then we get into complex issues of set-off and mitigation which are irrelevant to the current discussion.

[31] An example of this is the position where a car buyer trades in his existing car as part of the purchase price of a new model. Once the exchange value of the old car has been agreed, the delivery of the car will absolutely discharge that amount of the purchase price as if money had been handed over. However, what is happening here is not that the car has become money, but that the parties to the sale contract of the new car have agreed, in the context of their particular agreement, to treat the car as if it were money. This is a critically important distinction in considering sales for a price determined in virtual currency units.

1.46 From the point of view of the seller (B), acceptance of money issued by A in payment constitutes the absolute discharge of C. Why does the seller agree to this? The short answer is that he agrees to it because what he receives is potentially useful to him in that it will be accepted by others in exchange for goods. If he does not accept payment in this way, then he will have to wait for C to deliver value to him in some way. Thus, the options which face B are that he can either accept payment in money from C, thereby terminating C's obligation to him, but allowing him to buy what he needs elsewhere, or require C to perform his contract in the future. The risk that C will fail to perform this obligation is referred to as credit risk.[32]

1.47 By accepting payment today the creditor extinguishes his exposure to misfortune tomorrow arising out of the default of his creditor. However, he assumes risk in respect of the monetary unit which he has accepted in payment. Money is that which can immediately be used to purchase.

However, since no one can know for certain what will happen in the future, we must rephrase this as money is that which it is most confidently expected will be accepted as a purchase price. In this context, it is wrong to think of a binary distinction between money and not-money. It is perfectly possible to imagine a market in which only some traders will accept certain types of money in payment. Thus, in a US market in the late-nineteenth century, the 'Bank Note Reporter' would have circulated setting out the relative values of banknotes issued by different banks,[33] and it may well be that some traders will accept the banknotes of banks A, B, and C in payment, but not the notes of banks X, Y, and Z, whilst other traders will accept all such notes. This does not mean that the notes issued by banks X, Y, and Z are not 'money'—indeed what this helpful thought experiment reveals is that the idea of trying to define a bright line between that which is money and that which is not is simply nonsense. Money is that which people generally accept in payment of debts—the more people accept a thing, the more money-like it is, the fewer people accept a thing, the less money-like it is.

1.48 In an environment of this kind, a commercial actor would have to consider which instruments it would consider as 'payment', and which it would not. This really is an example of a case where the creditor will be exposed to credit risk whatever he does—if he accepts bank issued notes from his creditor in discharge of the creditor's debt, he relieves himself of the risk of credit failure of his customer at the cost of accepting the risk of failure of the bank issuer of the notes. Thus, from the creditor's perspective the term 'money' means simply 'that which my creditor will accept in payment of my debt'. This is, ultimately, the core definition of money. However, viewing the same issue from the perspective of the creditor, the answer to the question 'what shall I accept as payment?' is simply 'that which I confidently expect to be

---

[32] Note that credit risk is not simply the risk of the failure of a payment obligation. Credit risk is the term that applies to the risk of failure to perform any obligation where the obligor has already been paid, in part or in full, in respect of his obligation.
[33] A copy of *Thompson's Bank Note Reporter* from February 1846 is available online at https://archive.org/details/thompsonsbanknot0246thom from Washington University Libraries, and illustrates the thousands of different banknotes issued by different issuers whose values were reported.

able to use immediately to procure whatever I might otherwise have received'. Thus, a creditor needs to perceive a thing as capable of performing a money function before he will accept it as payment, and from a debtor's point of view 'money' is simply 'that which my creditor will accept in absolute discharge of my obligation'. In a commercial economy, this is the true answer to the question 'what gives money value?'. A monetary unit derives its economic value precisely and exactly from the fact that it is confidently expected to be accepted in complete discharge of obligations.

### 1.4.2 Can law make a thing valuable as money?

1.49 It is worth noting at this point that there is a curious idea sometimes encountered amongst non-lawyers that what makes a thing money is law, and the relevant law is the law of legal tender. This is wrong. The law of legal tender determines how a person who is owed money under a pre-existing debt can elect to be paid. Once I have agreed to sell something to a person, my claim on him for payment arises under the law, and the law provides that I must accept legal tender in discharge of his obligation to me. The law of legal tender has nothing at all to say to the question of whether I must contract with him in the first place. Loosely, if a seller won't agree to accept it in payment, it isn't money, whether it is legal tender or not.[34] This phenomenon can be seen where sovereign currencies fall out of use in their domestic markets. The Zimbabwean Dollar, Argentine Peso, and German Reichsmark remained legal tender throughout the periods when they ceased to be regarded as money in their own countries; and in all of those cases the fact that the instruments concerned were legal tender had little, then less, and finally no impact on the question of whether individuals and businesses were prepared to accept them as a purchase price.

### 1.4.3 How should the courts decide what is money?

1.50 If money is not created by law, how is it created? Clearly, by social acceptance—the more people there are who will accept a thing in payment, the more money-like that thing is. In a world in which all debts could be settled by the delivery of cigarettes, cigarettes would be money. This, however, creates a problem for the law. Current legal theory sets a clear dividing line between money and not-money—the legal characteristics of money are different from the legal characteristics of not-money, the mode of action is different, and the consequences of breach of a contract to pay money are different from the consequences of a contract to deliver not-money. This line has never been as bright as it is sometimes presented, but it nonetheless exists, and the appearance in circulation of things which have some but not all of the characteristics of money creates a significant problem for businesses, for commercial lawyers, and ultimately for the courts.

---

[34] This point is likely to be painfully familiar to anyone who has ever tried to pay for anything in the south of England with a Scottish banknote.

The gravamen of this book is that it is useless to try and approach this problem by 1.51 seeking to create a bright-line test based on legal principles between what is money and what is not money, and to apply that test to new forms of payment as they appear. We must accept—and the courts must accept—that in between the class of things which are clearly money and the class of things which are clearly not-money, there will appear a class of things which are treated-as-money. This last class of things is likely to have been used in transactions, and to appear in litigation in circumstances where the parties to the litigation have used them precisely in that way—as sort-of-money. Forensic examination of the intentions of the parties as to precisely whether they thought of these instruments as money or not is unlikely to produce any useful result, since the parties will simply not have thought of the transaction in those terms.

The upshot of this is that the courts should avoid the construction of abstract 1.52 rules in the hope that the world will accommodate them, but should accommodate themselves to the way of the world. A comparison may be drawn here with what has sometimes been described as the reception of commercial law into English law under Lord Mansfield. The idea that there was a concrete, existing commercial law which was absorbed into common law has been long exploded—the reality is that the law adopted the practices of commerce as they were developed on the basis that the primary function of commercial law is to give effect to, and not to contradict, the arrangement which the parties have made between themselves. One way of looking at this is as a recognition of private law—that once it is accepted that the parties to an agreement may agree to make the terms of that agreement binding as between themselves, the role of the court should be to implement that agreement to the extent that it is not contrary to public law.

## 1.4.4 Is characterisation as money once-and-for-all?

However, the issue in this case is precisely as to how public law applies in this con- 1.53 text. In particular, if public law prescribes that there is one law for obligations to deliver money (debt) and another for obligations to deliver things (damages), should the parties be able to elect by private agreement which category the specific obligation created by the specific contract belongs to? And, if they take the view that the obligation belongs to one category for one purpose, should they be able to argue that it belongs to a different category for a different purpose?

The answer to this question involves a little investigation into the idea of legisla- 1.54 tive policy. It is trite law that where the legislator has provided that arrangements of a particular kind should be treated in a particular way, it should not be possible for the parties to a contract to avoid that treatment simply by classifying their arrangement differently. Thus, to take a simple example, once the legislator has determined the characteristics of a lease and of a licence to occupy, and prescribed different consequences for the two, a mere agreement between the parties that an arrangement is a licence and not a lease should be simply disregarded by a court. In this case the proper approach is that set out by Lord Templeman in *Street v Mountford*[35]—that as

---

[35] [1985] UKHL 4.

a matter of law 'The manufacture of a five pronged implement for manual digging results in a fork even if the manufacturer, unfamiliar with the English language, insists that he intended to make and has made a spade'. However, there is all the difference in the world between the application of deliberately formulated legislative policy and the application of principles developed for other times and other systems to present day problems. An attempt to characterise bitcoins by application of principles developed in the era of the gold standard is not only unwise, but unjustifiable, and the challenge for the current generation of lawyers is to develop a law of quasi-money. This is not a different, or a harder, challenge than that faced by our predecessors in the nineteenth century seeking to develop a law of negotiable instruments, or our predecessors in the twentieth century seeking to develop a law of unjust enrichment. However, it does require an acceptance that the primary function of commercial law is to facilitate rather than to frustrate commercial transactions, and that for this purpose a man should not be permitted to escape the commercial consequences of his commercial actions through the invocation of historical legal principles formulated in different circumstances to address different problems.

# 2

# Money, Government, and Sovereignty

| | |
|---|---|
| 2.1 Money and the Sovereign Authority | 2.02 |
| 2.1.1 The origins of money | 2.07 |
| 2.2 The Function of Money | 2.15 |
| 2.2.1 Alternatives to state money | 2.17 |
| 2.3 The State in the Economy | 2.20 |
| 2.3.1 Coins | 2.23 |
| 2.3.2 Precious Metal Coins—weight or tale? | 2.29 |
| 2.3.3 Banknotes | 2.32 |
| 2.3.4 Sovereign values versus real values | 2.33 |
| 2.4 Multiple Currencies Within a Country | 2.38 |
| 2.4.1 Valuing coins | 2.39 |
| 2.4.2 Why multiple currencies? | 2.40 |
| 2.4.3 Debasement and inflation | 2.41 |
| 2.5 What Makes a Monetary Sovereign? | 2.45 |
| 2.6 Conclusion | 2.46 |

'One of the most robust regularities of monetary economics [is] the one to one correspondence between countries and currencies.'[1] We have grown up in a world where money is in practice created by countries, and in general the unit of payment in the territory of a country is the currency unit designated by the sovereign of that territory. However, the world is changing. The development of privately created virtual currencies poses a series of challenges to the idea that all currency is created by the exercise of sovereign power. In particular, it poses a question which would have been almost incomprehensible only a few years ago—can a payment instrument which is entirely unconnected with a sovereign properly be described as money?

---

[1] Eichengreen, *A More Perfect Union? The Logic of Economic Integration*, Essays in International Finance, No. 198. Princeton International Finance Section, Princeton, NJ.

## 2.1 Money and the Sovereign Authority

2.02 There is a vast array of literature across the different branches of the social sciences discussing the linkage between money and sovereign authority. The best account is Charles Goodhart's paper on *The Two Concepts of Money*.[2] Goodhart begins from the observation that there are two predominant theories of origin and use of money; these being the theories of the cartalists,[3] who argue that the use of currency is based on the power of the issuing authority, which effectively orders its subjects to use its tokens as money, and those theories which argue that the origin of currency lies in the market. This latter group can be sub-divided into those who argue that the basis of the value of money is the intrinsic value of the coins used (metallists) and those who argue that money originated as a private-sector, market-oriented, response to overcome the transaction costs inherent in barter (Mengerians[4]). Since metallism is somewhat out of fashion these days, Goodhart considered the applicability of the cartalist and Mengerian theories in the light of the development of the Euro area— his point being that if the Mengerian theory were correct then the development of a single Euro area containing separate governments would be unexceptionable, whereas if the cartalist theory were correct then the idea would seem to do violence to the basic nature of currency as a sovereign creation. He argues that if market-based ideas of money as simply a solution to an economic efficiency problem were correct, we should be seeing the widespread adoption of a smaller and smaller number of monies across multiple territories, since optimal currency area theory would suggest that it is extremely unlikely that optimal currency areas are congruent with national boundaries. However, not only do we not see this development in practice, but in fact exactly the opposite appears to be the case—indeed it has been robustly but accurately stated that 'The standard theory of optimum currency areas is falsified by the empirical evidence'.[5] He therefore concludes that although the Mengerian theory lends itself to mathematical formalisation, it is the cartalist theory which provides by far the best explanation of the world as it is. Thus, he concludes that there is an inherent linkage between money and sovereignty which is sufficiently powerful to override the market drivers which would otherwise lead to a Mengerian solution.

2.03 This argument is clearly correct to the extent that it emphasises that there is an interlinkage between money and sovereignty which derives from something other than economics. However, it has sometimes been pushed to absurd lengths, and in particular to the conclusion that nothing which is not issued by a sovereign can ever be treated as money.

---

[2] Goodhart, *The Two Concepts of Money: Implications for the Analysis of Optimal Currency Areas*, European Journal of Political Economy, Vol. 14 (1998) 407–32.
[3] So-called because they believe that money derives its status from a sovereign designation, or 'charter'. The father of cartalism was Knapp in *The State Theory of Money* (1924).
[4] So-called in reference to Karl Menger's 1892 paper *On the Origin of Money*, The Economic Journal, Vol. 2, 238–266, trans. C. A. Foley.
[5] Cesarano, *Currency Areas and Equilibrium*, Open Economics Review, Vol. 8 (1997) 51–9 at 57.

The more prosaic answer, of course, is that there is something in both positions. 2.04
Mengerians are correct that money originated through interactions, and was developed, not decreed. The cartalists are equally correct that money developed through the interaction of individuals and the state. The error, which seems to be an error of assumption rather than analysis, is on the cartalist side, and involves the idea that the state creates money by decreeing it into being, as opposed to validating it by transacting in it. When cartalists think of the state, they think of it as a legislative institution, and envisage that money is rendered such by legal decree. This is clearly wrong, as market theorists repeatedly point out. However, a state that wishes to create money has more weapons than mere legislation at its disposal. In particular, it can make the units which it creates 'money' simply by accepting them in payment.[6]

It follows from this that the state could therefore make any other instrument money 2.05 by the same route. The question of whether a thing has the status of money-ness is answered not by the question of who produced the instrument concerned, but of who accepts it in payment, and anything which is accepted in payment by the state is de facto money. However, it is important to note that this is not a statement about the state *per se*—it can be validly reformulated as that anything which is accepted in payment by the largest economic participant in any market will be de facto money in that market. Since in almost all economies 'the largest economic participant in the market' and 'the state' are synonymous concepts, anything which is generally and customarily accepted in payment by the sovereign can be potentially regarded as money. This does, however, take us to the more pressing issue of whether it is only the sovereign which has this right. In particular, is there a level of general social acceptance in payment which can make a thing 'money', regardless of the position of the sovereign?

To some extent, the answer to this question is that it must be so—the primary— 2.06 and unanswerable—challenge of the Mengerians to the pure cartalists is that the briefest examination of the historical record shows that money was not in fact created out of nothing by royal decrees, but developed slowly and over time through social interactions. However, this idea of money as a market phenomenon 'nationalised' by sovereigns is also somewhat overstated. In order to establish the true state of affairs it is necessary to consider—briefly—the origins of money.

## 2.1.1 The origins of money

There is a commonly held (but erroneous) view that once a society passes a particular 2.07 level of economic sophistication (expressed in the development of non-trivial division of labour) it is in effect forced to adopt money because the inconvenience of multilateral barter becomes too great.[7] This does not seem to be ethnographically accurate—Paul Einzig, in his masterly survey of commerce in early-stage societies *Primitive Money*,[8] points out:

---

[6] This was entirely clear to Knapp—see The State Theory of Money Trans. Lucas and Boner, Macmillan 1924) at 95.
[7] See, e.g., Jevons, *Money and the Mechanism of Exchange* (Appleton & Co 1896).
[8] Eyre & Spottiswoode 1949.

There is ample ethnological evidence to show that most primitive communities had a number of favourite media of barter in use at any given moment. Many of these communities could get on very well without the adoption of a common medium of exchange, as their trade was limited, and barter with the aid of media of barter suited their purpose tolerably well. Nonetheless, they gradually came to adopt a medium of exchange—not because they came to realise that this was the 'right thing to do', nor because the old system of barter was becoming intolerable, but simply because in practice they found it more convenient.[9]

2.08   Einzig also points out that not all transactions are commercial, and that it is very likely that in many primitive societies non-commercial transactions—religious offerings, bride-prices and dowries, fines, tribute, blood-money—were already established social practices at times when commerce was beginning to emerge.

All these and other non-commercial requirements must have led in innumerable instances to a widespread and systematic demand for objects eminently qualified to fulfil the functions of a medium of exchange, long before the need for the employment of a medium of exchange was sufficiently strong to overcome conservatism and other factors responsible for the survival of pure barter... It seems probable that when the growing diversity of goods and services and the growing division of labour made the use of a medium of exchange increasingly necessary, the object chosen as an intermediary was very often not a favourite medium of barter but the ready-made medium of payment which was already widely used in the community for non-commercial payment.[10]

2.09   This argument is also powerfully made by Grierson,[11] who emphasises that early tribal customs of blood-money (Anglo-Saxon Wergild) required a degree of quantification, and such quantification is encountered in very early sources (e.g. the use of oxen as a unit of account in the *Iliad* and *Odyssey*) which seem to pre-date money concepts.

2.10   Einzig also points out that the establishment of a standard of value is very likely to have pre-dated commercial exchange:

Given human nature being what it is, there must always have been a natural desire to compare the size of the wealth of one chief against that of another chief. Unless they keep their wealth in precisely the same form there could be no comparison without the use of some form of common denominator in terms of which the various forms of wealth could be expressed for the sake of comparison... In this way a medium of exchange may have originated through the function of the standard of value.[12]

The major point here is that the relationship between the individual and the state which necessitates the creation of a unit of value is considerably older than the idea of commercial transaction. This should come as no surprise—taxes are older than commerce.

---

[9] Ibid. at 355.   [10] Ibid.
[11] Grierson, *The Origins of Money*, Creighton lecture (delivered Cambridge 1970, published Athlone Press, University of London 1977).
[12] Einzig, *Primitive Money* (2nd edn, Pergamon Press 1966) at 367.

*Money, Government, and Sovereignty*     31

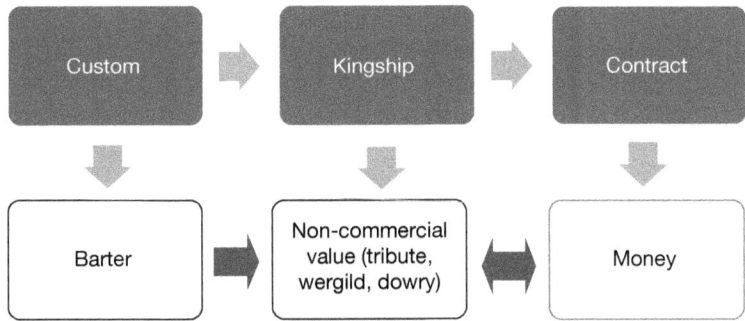

**Figure 2.1** Simplified model of the development of payment

Thus, a simplified model of the development of payment media might be as shown in Figure 2.1.[13] The arrow in the bottom right-hand corner emphasises that the processes are self-reinforcing—it seems likely that when an object was to be utilised to perform a non-commercial function such as tribute, over time that object would come to be the favourite medium for commercial barter.[14] However, an object which was in use for commercial barter would be attractive to a king, court or taxing authority simply by virtue of its commercial acceptability—thus in a society where taxes were collected in cowrie shells but silver coins were used in payment for commercial transactions, we should expect (and usually encounter) a rapid transition by the taxing authority towards the collection of taxes in silver coins. Finally, it should be noted that there would be a strong centripetal relationship between these two factors—those receiving tribute, blood-price, or whatever would seek to receive it in the most useful possible form. Put simply, it is unlikely that any asset came to be valued because it was used as money—it is much more likely that it came to be used as money because it was already valued.    2.11

In this regard, the creation of the English value measurement system is of interest. In the first half of the seventh century the primary unit of account in England seems to have been the penny.[15] However, the primary coin in circulation in England was generally the sceat[16] (plural sceattas). Sceat coins appear to have been created by a variety of providers, both royal and private—the major producer was the royal mint, but significant quantities were also created by a number of private mints, including notably the ecclesiastical mints of York and Canterbury. There appears to have been relatively little standardisation—few sceattas carried the image of the King, and as    2.12

---

[13] Based on Maine, *Ancient Law: Its Connection with the Early History of Society and its Relation to Modern Ideas* (13th edn, John Murray 1906) and Einzig, *Primitive Money* (2nd edn, Pergamon Press 1966).
[14] Max Weber, in his *General Economic History* (London 1923), placed great emphasis on the importance of political payments in the origin of money.
[15] The term 'penig', the old English word for penny, compares almost exactly with the Friesian and Dutch equivalents, and with the Danish word for money in general (Penge)—see Davies, *A History of Money* (4th edn, University of Wales Press 2016) at 130.
[16] Derived from Old English *sceatt*, meaning 'wealth'.

time went on they diverged significantly in design. It also appears that as demand grew they were significantly debased, with wide variations in the level of debasement being found between mints. Also, in Northumberland at least, smaller coins representing a fraction of a sceat (stycas) were minted and circulated entirely privately. Thus, we are presented with an economy which has a single unit of account, but a variety of circulating payment media, some sovereign, some not. It seems highly unlikely that there was any difference of treatment of sceattas according to whether they proceeded from the royal mint or from other mints.

2.13 King Offa (757–96) was responsible for the development of the English penny coin (first minted around 765),[17] which became a European phenomenon. However, the important thing was that although Offa was introducing a coin, he was not introducing a unit of account—the coin which he created was created in order to match a unit of account which was already in use. Thus, the sequence of events which is often assumed to exist, in which a sovereign commences by creating a currency, and the grateful populous responds by using those coins as units of value, appears to be almost the reverse of the actual truth—that a unit of account (the penny) is created by social acceptance, and the state responds by creating coinage which reflects that unit of account.

2.14 If money is a social creation, we can legitimately ask why it was created—what is the social problem that money is created to solve?

## 2.2 The Function of Money

2.15 It is necessarily the case that the idea of debt must pre-date the idea of money, since the concept of money only makes sense in the light of the idea of a payment obligation which it may discharge; that is, a debt. Such debts are not necessarily commercial debts—it is almost certain that money was initially created first to quantify and then to discharge debts which have the nature of societal rather than economic obligations—what we would describe as tax liabilities.[18] Money therefore pre-dates commerce, as anthropologists have abundantly demonstrated. However, the existence of money, and its application to commercial arrangements, enabled the development of commerce by solving one of its most pressing problems.

2.16 That problem is credit. In any social arrangement where A wants something from B now, but will only be able to deliver something to B at a point in the future, there are two problems which need to be solved, not one. The first problem is the creation

---

[17] Technically Heberth and Ecgbert of Kent got there first, and it was only really on Offa's takeover of Kent that the English penny took off. See Davies, *A History of Money* (4th edn, University of Wales Press 2016) at 129.

[18] It is important to understand that 'tax' in this context includes every exaction which a person in a social position is entitled to claim from others. Thus, medieval serfs would have said that they did not pay tax, but they paid rents and heriots, and medieval nobles did not pay tax, but they paid entry fines in respect of their accession to their lands and titles which took may years to pay off. Franklin's observation that 'In this world nothing can be said to be certain, except death and taxes'(letter to Jean-Baptiste Leroy, 1789, in *The Works of Benjamin Franklin* (1817)) appears to be universally valid.

of an exact record of the existence of the debt, such that B is confident that he will in due course be able to recover value from A. This 'scorekeeping' function has been explained by Kocherlakota in the pithy phrase 'money is memory',[19] and this is of course correct in the sense that money is a scorekeeping device intended to equalise transfers of value over time. However, money is more than memory. A single central record of all transactions would perform this function equally well, and, as envisaged by Wicksell, it would be perfectly possible to create an economic system where 'money does not actually circulate at all, neither in the form of coin ... nor in the form of notes, but where all domestic payments are effected by means of the *Giro* system and bookkeeping transfers ... [T]his purely imaginary case ... provides a precise antithesis to the equally imaginary case of a pure cash system, in which credit plays no part whatever.'[20]

### 2.2.1 Alternatives to state money

Money, in the sense of notes and coins issued by the state, is only one of a number of solutions to this problem. To begin with a small example, two merchants who regularly deal with each other by exchanging goods may never 'pay' their debts, but may simply set off their mutual obligations. Even in this case there is an identifiable 'moment of payment'—each will regard himself as indebted to the other until the moment when they agree to reduce their mutual exposures. This can be projected onto more complex situations with larger numbers of participants, but at all times there will be an accumulation phase followed by a point at which mutual exposures are cancelled. It is perfectly possible that there could be a centralised omniscient clearing system which recorded accurately every transaction between two persons within the system—which would, as Wicksell said, eliminate the necessity for the use of money completely—but even within that system there would still be periodic 'payments' in which claims were extinguished by being set off against other claims. The important point here is that when we come to ask 'what is money', the answer is that it is a mechanism for the discharge of debts due.

2.17

This, of course, is what goes on today within the commercial banking system. In a modern developed economy, the commercial banking system effectively provides exactly such a record-keeping mechanic. In effect, each private bank acts as a complete clearing system as regards transactions between two persons who are both its clients, and two private banks can, by settlement between themselves, collectively act as a clearing system between two persons who are their clients. Thus, if we think of the private banking system as providing such a record-keeping function, we can dispense with the traditional notion of 'money' altogether.

2.18

---

[19] Journal of Economic Theory, Vol. 81, No. 2 (August 1998) at 232–51.
[20] *Interest and Prices* (Geldzins und Güterpreise 1936 (1898)) at 68ff. The insuperable practical problem with this idea at the time of its initial formation was that every person in the economy, both economically active and inactive, would have to have an account with the Girobank. Technology may, however, make this a practical proposition in the future.

2.19    From this perspective, the function of the various virtual currency systems is reasonably clear. If our functional definition of money becomes 'that which, when delivered, constitutes payment', then a balance maintained with a private bank is no different in this regard from a balance maintained on a distributed ledger. The only difference between the two is that the balance on the bank account is denominated in terms of units which are in turn designated by the government of a country as units in which it is prepared to transact, whereas the balance of a virtual currency is designated in units of its own devising.

## 2.3 The State in the Economy

2.20    That takes us to one of the most important relationships in the idea of money, and one which is somewhat hidden in European (although not US) consideration. The key to this is the fact that the state is not only an economic actor, but in most societies is the primary economic actor. Not only are there very few societies in which the public fisc is not the largest single participant[21] in terms of turnover, but the public fisc is, in every society, the primary participant in non-commercial transactions. This of course becomes particularly true in times of war, when the role of the state becomes the mobilisation of a large proportion of the assets of society towards a common aim, and the state becomes a major participant in commercial transactions. However, it is true at all times that whatever the state collects in taxation is only useful if it can be used to acquire that which the state needs, be it service (military or otherwise), victuals for servitors, or prestige goods for enhancing the status of the king. Again, it should be noted that this role of the state in society potentially precedes the development of commercial transactions—as Scyld and Beow in *Beowulf* would have understood, in order to be a ring-giver, you need to have acquired rings to give. The purpose of taxation is expenditure, and tax paid in in things that are neither immediately useful nor usable to purchase is worse than useless.

2.21    This is all well set out in the judgment of Bradley J in *Knox v Lee*, where he said:[22]

> A constitutional government, notwithstanding the right of eminent domain, cannot take physical and forcible possession of all that it may need to defend the country and is reluctant to exercise such a power where it can be avoided. It must purchase, and by purchase command materials and supplies, products of manufacture, labour, service of every kind. The government cannot, by physical power, compel the workshops to turn out millions of dollars worth of manufactures in leather, and cloth, and wood, and iron, which are the very first conditions of military equipment. It must stimulate and set in motion the industry of the country. In other words, it must purchase. But it cannot purchase with specie. That is soon exhausted, hidden or exported. It must purchase by credit.

---

[21] One of the better-observed regularities of public affairs is that anyone with deeper pockets than the government tends to become the government.
[22] 79 US 457 (1871) at 558–9.

The judge made clear that this power was entirely separate from the power conferred on the federal government to regulate the coinage.

Thus, when we think of the state, we must think of it as the first purchaser in the kingdom. In a perfect world (for kings), this would entail a grateful populace accepting whatever promissory notes the crown chose to give them in exchange for their goods. In reality, 'put not thy trust in princes'[23] has been a guiding principle for the economically active for the majority of the history of the human race, and if kings are to obtain goods on credit, they must give some substance to their promises of repayment beyond the mere fact of their kingship. There are in practice two ways of doing this. One is to give the token that you give as an earnest of repayment some real value—this is the basis of precious metal currency. The other is to announce that you will accept the token in payment of taxes. In reality, monarchs tended to do both.

### 2.3.1 Coins

A coin is a token issued by a taxing authority on the basis of a promise that it will be accepted in discharge of tax obligations. It is for all practical purposes an IOU issued by the taxing authority.

For a tax authority issuing such tokens, the immediate policy question is as to whether they should or should not be transferrable. Prima facie it is strongly in the interests of the taxing authority to treat such tokens as non-transferable, since this will reduce the number of them being presented in any given year (some of those who hold IOUs may have lower or no tax obligations, if only by reason of being dead). Thus, there is no necessary reason why the tokens should be transferable. This seems to have been the case in the United States in the run-up to the war of independence, since under the Currency Act of 1751 the English Parliament prohibited the New England colonies from permitting their bills of credit to stand as legal tender for the payment of all bills public and private (the prohibition was extended to all of the US colonies by the Currency Act 1764, and is often cited as one of the primary causes of the American revolution[24]).

However, this argument is overborne by the contrary argument, which is simply that such tokens are much less likely to be presented at all if they have another use—that is, if they can be used as currency. Thus, once a society has decided that it needs currency, it is very strongly in the interests of the fisc to supply that requirement with its own obligations. For the majority of our recorded history, this was done through the creation and circulation of metal coins.

Now it is important to dispel any notion that there is a magic to gold, silver, electrum, or cowrie shells which makes them valuable in the absence of exchange. Metal is not prized because it is valuable, it is valuable because it is prized. The reason for

---

[23] Psalm 146 v3 King James version.
[24] See, e.g., per Bradley J in *Knox v Lee* 79 US 457 (1871) at 559.

gold jewellery is public display of wealth—if gold was not perceived as valuable, there would be little or no gold jewellery. The fact that things are in short supply and cannot be easily obtained makes them candidates for the role of money, but does not make them money. Indeed, the most widely used ancient proto-money, the cowrie shell, has no merits at all apart from its rarity.[25]

2.26 We are accustomed to thinking of coins as things having a real metallic value, and for much of recorded history this has been the case. Some coins were deliberately created to have a metal value which was to some extent equal to the value of the underlying obligation. However, this is a baffling policy. If the state can create its own currency, what it should clearly do is to create money which costs it nothing to create—wooden notched tallies are an excellent example. Why, it may be asked, should a state care what the metal content of its coin was?

2.27 A desire to include a certain amount of precious metal in a coin may have been motivated by desires to inhibit forgery, enhance the prestige of the currency, and secure its circulation outside the country (a measure which would also enrich the fisc—a coin which has left the country is very much less likely to be presented in payment of tax, putting the fisc in the position of a creditor who has issued an IOU which will never be redeemed[26]). However, eliminating the fiduciary element of coinage by coining the metal value of the unit seems to be not so much retrograde as pointless.

2.28 Part of the explanation for this type of coinage seems to be the simple fact that it is necessary to establish coinage as a concept before moving to the next stage of fiduciary value. After all, the primary purpose of Pepin and Offa's coinage appears to have had more to do with establishing a medium of exchange than with creating a fiscal vehicle. This approach explains the idea of 'free coinage'—profits from minting cannot have been great, and encouraging the circulation of full value coins will have established the idea of monetisation and therefore helped monetary development.[27] This is likely to be the incentive which drove the minting of full value gold coins in the United Kingdom until the nineteenth century. The fact that the unit of account exists in tangible form appears to facilitate intangible transactions.

---

[25] The cowrie shell was the original currency of China—indeed, the classical Chinese character for money started life as a picture of a cowrie shell. The only reason that the Chinese can have had for using cowrie shells as money was that they originated a long way away from China and the supply of them could only be expanded with great difficulty (see Goetzmann, *Money Changes Everything* (Princeton University Press 2016) at 147–51 for a short account of cowrie shells as Chinese currency). These appear to be the same characteristics that drove the adoption of rare metals as the basis of the payment mechanisms of China and Europe.

[26] This of course was exactly the strategy that the United States embarked on when it created the 'trade dollar' in 1873. The subsequent fate of this coin is instructive—despite having a higher metal content than the normal US dollar, it seems to have traded at a discount to it because of concerns about its legal status.

[27] It is freely accepted that it cannot be the case that rulers in non- or semi-monetised economies must have perceived the benefits of, and worked towards, a fully monetised economy. However, it does seem likely that rulers confronted with taxpayers seeking to pay their taxes in chickens, cows, or other kind, must have been keenly aware of the advantages of monetisation.

## 2.3.2 Precious Metal Coins—weight or tale?

For reasons that we will discuss in due course, sovereigns generally chose to give their tokens an intrinsic value, and so was born the metal coin. It is entirely clear that regardless of the actual metal content of the tokens, they were intended to operate as tokens rather than as commodities—that is, they were to be valued by tale (number) rather than by weight,[28] and there is no doubt that from a very early stage the value ascribed to any given coin was ascribed by the exercise of royal power. In England as early as 1352 the statute 25 Edw. III Ch. 12 prohibited the exchange of gold and silver coins at anything other than their face value, and by 5&6 Edw. VI Ch. 19 if any person gave or received a premium for coin over its nominal value, the money was liable to be forfeited and they were liable to imprisonment. This statute was eventually replaced by Lord Liverpool's Act of 1816,[29] which prohibited the exchange of gold coins for paper money at anything other than the face value of the coins. This does seem to make it reasonably clear that although coins were made of precious metal, they were never intended to circulate at anything other than their face value.

2.29

The issue this raises is therefore what happens when such a coin is debased? In principle, the answer is that the nominal value remains whilst the actual value decreases—thus Matthew Boulton was famously able in 1772 to buy more than 1,000 gold coins of the realm with a £1,000 banknote[30]—an interesting demonstration of the fact that once the value of a currency has been established by the creation of commodity value, that value can continue even when the actual commodity value of the coins declines. A bigger and better example is the creation of the continental deposit banks[31] during the currency crisis brought on by the Thirty Years War (1618–48). As described by Schnabel and Schin:

2.30

The thirty years war ... was associated with one of the most severe economic crises ever recorded, with rampant hyperinflation and the breakdown of trade and economic activity. The crisis became known as the *Kipper- und -Wipperzeit* (the clipping and culling times), after the practice of clipping coins and sorting good coins from bad.[32]

---

[28] This position is not universally accepted (see Rolnick et al., *The Debasement Puzzle: An Essay on Medieval Monetary History*, Journal of Economic History Vol. 56 (1996) at 789–808). However, it is the more common and much more probable view—see Volckart, *The Big Problem of the Petty Coins, and How it Could be Solved in the Late Middle Ages* (LSE 2008) Working Paper No. 107/08.
[29] 56 Geo III, Ch 68.
[30] Davies, *A History of Money* (4th edn, University of Wales Press 2016) at 304. This did not contravene the statute 5&6 Edw. VI, since that statute only prevented the payment of a premium for coin, not its sale at a discount. What it actually demonstrates is the existence of an 'agio' in the United Kingdom between coins and bank deposit money—see Smith, *The Wealth of Nations*, Book IV Chapter 3 for an extended discussion of the origin and operation of bank agios which were common among the merchant's clearing banks of Europe. See also Schnabel and Shin, *Money and Trust: Lessons from the 1620s for the Digital Age* (BIS February 2018) Working Paper No. 698.
[31] The Bank of Amsterdam in 1609, the Bank of Hamburg, and the Banco Publico de Nuremberg.
[32] Schnabel and Shin, *Money and Trust: Lessons from the 1620s for the Digital Age* (BIS February 2018) Working Paper No. 698.

However, this serves only to reinforce the basic point that coins circulated by tale—coin clipping or sweating would be a completely redundant exercise if coins circulated by weight.[33]

2.31 This seems to support a pure state (cartalist) theory of money—a metallist argument that transactions in coins with a fixed metal value reflects a transaction in the underlying metal is insupportable unless coins circulated by weight, and all the evidence we have suggests that this was never the case. Thus, the starting point is the cartalist one that a coin was worth what the mint ordinance specified, and it was prohibited to exchange it for any other value. It should also be noted that determining what counts as 'a coin' in this context is not entirely straightforward. The problem with coin clipping was that there was a point at which a sufficiently heavily clipped coin ceased to be acceptable in payment at all, and a fine judgement was required to determine where this line was drawn. The problem was similar to that described by Keynes in volume 1 of the *Treatise on Money*:

> A district commissioner in Uganda today, where goats are the customary native standard, tells me that it is part of his official duties to decide, in cases of dispute, whether a given goat is or is not too old or too scraggy to constitute a standard goat for the purposes of discharging a debt.[34]

This brings us back to the difference between the idea of a unit of currency and the reality of any particular coin. In the same way that Keynes' district commissioner was seeking to determine whether the goat concerned deviated so far from the ideal goat that it no longer embodied its Platonic form, the same determination would be made by money-changers throughout the world when asking whether a clipped, sweated or defaced coin had been so degraded that it was no longer a 'coin' for this purpose. However, the mere existence of the enquiry demonstrates the truth of the concept. In order to enquire whether a particular item is a valid coin, it is necessary to have a clear vision of what an ideal coin is. Note that it is not necessary to believe that any such coin actually exists – what matters is not belief in the substantiated ideal, but belief in the ideal.

### 2.3.3 Banknotes

2.32 A similar problem arises at a later stage in history when banknotes become the predominant medium of exchange in the nineteenth century. The value of a banknote is a function of the bank issuing it, and in the United States and the United Kingdom notes were issued by very large numbers of different banks with very different credit standings. It appears that in England in 1802 these notes passed widely into currency, and were generally accepted at their face value. Thornton[35] lamented the fact that although commercial men might be properly equipped to evaluate the different values of notes issued by different banks, these notes circulated widely and were treated by their holders as carrying their face value 'for the time during which they intend to hold it is very short, and their responsibility will cease almost as soon as

---

[33] Volckart, London School of Economics Working Paper No. 107/08 (2008).
[34] (First published 1930, Martino Publishing 2011), Vol. 1 at 11.
[35] *An Enquiry into the Nature and Effects of the Paper Credit of Great Britain* (1802, Routledge 2017) at 172–3.

they shall have parted with it'. This tendency to treat anything resembling a unit of currency at its face value is both entirely understandable and a useful demonstration that once a particular unit has acquired that status in general usage, the mere fact that its intrinsic value deteriorates may have no effect on its value in circulation.

### 2.3.4 Sovereign values versus real values

Having established that cartalism rules as regards the valuation of currency, we must now start to unpick that conclusion. The essence of cartalism is the idea that the state determines the value of a particular payment instrument issued by it, but there is no shortage of instances of units circulating at valued very different from those formally ascribed to them by the state. There is even precedent for the position where the same units of currency have different values in different territories. This sounds bizarre, but is a documented historical phenomenon. For example, Irish currency before the 1601 debasement circulated at a different value in Ireland and England—thus an Irish shilling was worth 9 shillings in England,[36] and considerable effort was devoted to persuading contracting parties to specify whether, when they said shillings, they meant English or Irish Shillings. Although this may seem like a quirk of history, the same problem has resurfaced at regular intervals—see, for example, *Adelaide Electric Supply Company Ltd v Prudential Assurance Company Ltd*.[37] Note that the obvious conclusion—of assuming that the two territories each had a separate monetary system—was the approach taken by Lord Simonds in *Bonython v Commonwealth of Australia*,[38] but was rejected by Lord Tomlin and the majority in the *Adelaide* case. The basis of Lord Tomlin's approach was a simple application of the state theory of money—that only a sovereign could make or alter money, there was no evidence that the sovereign had intervened in order to alter the status of the relevant monetary units; therefore they had the status which they had at their creation, regardless of the actual divergence of value.[39] Thus, it is English law that the same unit of account may have two different values ascribed to it by the same sovereign in two different places.

2.33

The real challenge for cartalism, however, arises where the state attempts to ascribe a value to something which does have an intrinsic value—usually a metal coin—where that intrinsic value is different from the commercial value of the metals which comprise the coin. There are three possible states of an currency made of a valuable material—it can have an intrinsic value which is more than, equal to, or less than its face value.[40] Also, economic change (and in particular inflation) can change that relationship.[41] Thus, although there are very few examples of the minting of

2.34

---

[36] See Fox, *The Case of Mixt Moneys*, Cambridge Law Journal (2011) 144 at 163.
[37] [1934] AC 122.    [38] [1950] AC 201.
[39] See Mann on the Legal Aspect of Money (7th edn OUP 2012) paras 2.55–2.65.
[40] Even coins which do not have a formal face value (such as the English Guinea) have an implicit face value, in that the relevant state will accept them for a specified value of tax due.
[41] It is a common trope amongst governments (and sometimes historians) considering the interrelationships of metallic currencies and inflation that the inflation is a consequence of the devaluation of the currency. In reality (and despite Locke's support of this position in his *Further Considerations Concerning*

coins whose token value is lower than their metal component,[42] there have been many historical instances where the metal value of a coin was less than the token value on minting, but where decline in the real value of the token through inflation, or appreciation of the value of the metal, caused the physical coin to be worth more than the token value.

2.35　Coins in this situation tend to be hoarded rather than spent,[43] and the mints will be disinclined to make more of them. Consequently, inflation and the hoarding of coin tend to be encountered together in the historical record. This problem is, of course, magnified considerably if a currency has both silver and gold coins in issue, since changes in the relative prices of silver and gold will almost inevitably mean that one series of coins is overvalued relative to the other.[44] Given this problem, it may be asked why precious metal was used at all, since in general the optimal position for the fisc would have been to create tokens which were inherently worthless (and therefore cheapest to create).

2.36　This theory would take us to the idea that the fisc need only supply tokens, and there are clearly cases where this was the case—wooden tallies in England, for example, were fiscal tokens whose intrinsic value was zero.[45] Even in the later Roman Empire, where metallic coinage was the norm, we know that coinage was intended to have a token value—Diocletian's recoinage at the end of the third century AD was intended to have a value 60 per cent above its metal content.[46] However, by the time we get to the recoinage of Europe (which broadly begins with Pepin in Paris and Offa in England)[47] the denier (or penny) is a coin whose silver content exactly matches its value.[48] Why would this happen, and—more importantly—is this evidence that the sovereign does not have the power to decree the value of coins?

2.37　The answer seems to have been that whereas valueless tokens such as wooden tallies optimise the position as between sovereign and direct subjects, in order for a country's currency to be accepted internationally, it was necessary for it to have some inherent value to give it credibility.[49] Having one's currency used internationally was a great benefit, both for the state itself, which was likely to have been the largest

---

*Raising the Value of Money* (1695, 2nd edn 1696), it seems overwhelmingly likely that the causation is the other way around.

[42] Although the UK Royal Mint does this today—the UK Gold Sovereign, with a legal tender value of £1, is valued at £238 at the time of writing.

[43] One manifestation of Gresham's law, see section 4.3.1 above.

[44] For example, Newton's revaluation of UK gold against silver currency in 1717—see Fay, *Newton and the Gold Standard*, Cambridge Historical Journal, Vol. 5, No. 1 (1935) at 109–17.

[45] Fitz Nigel, *Dialogue of the Exchequer* (1180) online at The Avalon Project, Yale Law School, at http://avalon.law.yale.edu/medieval/excheq.asp.

[46] Cascio, *State and Coinage in the Late Republic and Early Empire*, Journal of Roman Studies, Vol. 71 (1981) 76–86 at 79.

[47] This represented the eighth-century rebasing of the European economy on a silver standard. Prior to this the coin most commonly used in international trade seems to have been the Byzantine gold coin (Bezant). The earliest silver pennies seem to have been issued in the late seventh century. Spufford, *Money and Its Use in Mediaeval Europe* (Cambridge University Press 1989).

[48] It is noteworthy that although the basic structure of the monetary system—12 pennies (denarii, deniers) to a shilling (solidi, sols, sous), and 20 shillings to a pound (libra, lira, livre) was established at this time, only the penny was actually minted—the larger units existed only as money of account.

[49] See below s.4.3.2.

participant in international transactions, and for the merchants of that state, who obtained preferential access to a scarce resource. It is therefore likely that the reason for the creation of King Offa's silver coins was simply to facilitate international trade. It therefore seems to have been worth the while of states to try and enhance the international credibility of their currency by increasing precious metal content. Thus, the logic of states creating full-bodied coins (i.e. coins whose metal value was broadly equal to their nominal value) was not that they could not otherwise secure the circulation of those coins at their stated value within their borders, but that they could not otherwise secure the circulation of those coins outside their borders. The trade-off was a simple one—reducing the metal value of domestically circulating currency created seignorage revenues but disadvantaged export and import trade, whereas enhancing the metal value reduced seignorage but promoted trade. In an era where customs levies were the mainstay of royal revenues, it is not hard to see how this balance might have tipped heavily towards facilitation of trade and away from seignorage.

## 2.4 Multiple Currencies within a Country

The next challenge to a cartalist view of money is the fact that what circulated throughout most of our history was not money, but monies. This was true both as regards foreign coins, a large number of which circulated in every country, often with traditionally prescribed values, but also as regards different coins issued by the home sovereign. Sovereigns were effectively obliged to produce multiple monies with different metal compositions, and these could and did fluctuate in value against each other. This is almost incomprehensible to modern currency users. We are so used to the idea that a certain number of pennies or cents make up a certain number of pounds or dollars, that any other state of affairs seems almost unimaginable. However, it should be clear that in an environment where two sorts of coin circulate, one of silver and one of gold, then simple variation in the values of the two metals will result in significant changes in the ratios between them. Thus, for example, Cipolla observes that the Florentine gold florin, struck for the first time in 1252, and intended to have a value of 240 Florentine pennies, was by 1500 worth 1,500 Florentine pennies.[50] The same development can be seen in the English guinea, which, priced at 21s 6d in 1690, passed for 29s 6d in 1695.[51] This phenomenon was even more problematic in a world where multiple different currencies circulated as a matter of course. The 'Lex Paulus',[52] whose effect at civil law was that a person who had tendered particular coins could claim payment in exactly those coins, seems absurd to us today—why should a person who as advanced ten £5 notes be able

2.38

---

[50] 'Ghost Moneys' in *Money Prices and Civilisation in the Mediterranean World* (Gordian Press 1967) at 43.
[51] Mayhew, *Sterling; The History of a Currency* (Penguin 1999) at 94.
[52] The colloquial name for the citation from Paulus at D. 46.3.99 that '... a creditor cannot be required to accept money in any other form lest he suffer some disadvantage [damnum] thereby'.

to reject a tender of five £10 notes? However, in a world where relative values even within the same currency continuously fluctuated, it seems an entirely reasonable rule. It must, however, have significantly harmed the easy circulation of money. More importantly, it draws attention to an important limit on the power of the state to determine the value of money—even the state cannot buck the market, and a law which requires £1 of value to be exchanged for 19s of value will be invariably and routinely broken. Thus, we see that the power of the state over its currency is by no means absolute.

### 2.4.1 Valuing coins

2.39    It is also the case that the willingness to accept coins at their face value may have been driven less by respect for the sovereign and the rule of law, and more by the fact that the owner of a coin generally could not, without the expenditure of a great deal of effort, determine the precise metallic composition of that coin.[53] This of course assumes that the mint concerned had the intelligence, when debasing coins, to adulterate the debased coins in such a way that there was no change in weight, size or physical appearance between pre- and post-adulteration coins—a task to which most of them appear to have been fully equal. The problems which arise with a debased currency are as much information problems as they are valuation problems—in particular, receiving payment in coins creates a variation of Ackerloff's 'lemons' problem.[54] However, the 'lemons' problem is only a real problem if the purchaser of the lemon is certain—or very highly likely—to find out at some stage after the purchase that what he has bought is in fact a lemon. Thus, the fact that a coin has a low (or lower) precious metal component than other coins of the same fiat value is only relevant if the value of the coin is affected to some extent by its metal composition. If information about the coin's metal content is irrelevant, the problem does not arise. More importantly, it follows from this that the problem equally does not arise where information about a coin's composition is unavailable to both sides of the transaction, and is unlikely to be determinable by an ordinary third party. Where information is unavailable to either side of a transaction, and is unlikely to be discovered in a relevant time, the information can rationally be disregarded. Thus, debasement is only relevant if it can be detected without excessive effort.

---

[53] See Gandall and Sussman, *Asymmetric Information and Commodity Money: Tickling the Tolerance in Medieval France*, Journal of Money, Credit and Banking, Vol. 29, No. 4 (1997) at 440–7, which explains just how difficult it was, using available technology, accurately to determine the metal composition of any coin..

[54] The 'lemons' problem is an application of Gresham's law to physical goods. Assume a car market contains 'peaches'—good cars—and 'lemons'—cars with some defects. Assume further that buyers cannot tell whether any particular car is a lemon. Buyers who buy peaches will keep them; buyers who buy lemons will seek to sell them on through dealers. As buyers realise that the proportion of lemons on the market is rising, the price they are prepared to pay for any car will fall. The lower the price falls, the greater the disincentive for owners of peaches to sell, and the higher the proportion of lemons on the market. However, as the proportion of lemons increases, buyers' willingness to buy will diminish, and eventually the market will cease to operate at all. Akerloff, *The Market for 'Lemons': Quality Uncertainty and the Market Mechanism* Quarterly Journal of Economics, Vol. 84, No. 3 (1970) at 488–500.

## 2.4.2 Why multiple currencies?

It may be worth explaining how it came to be that states issued within their territory  2.40
what were in effect competing currencies which fluctuated in value against each
other. This is known as the 'big problem of small change'.[55] If gold is the medium
of exchange for international transactions, coins must be high-value enough to be
usable for those transactions without requiring impractically large physical volumes
of metal. Such coins are likely to be impractically highly denominated for the purpose of everyday use. The obvious solution to this is to create two (or more) types of
coin, made of different metals and having different values. This generally results in
gold or silver coins for big transactions and copper coins for small ones. The effect
of this strategy is that the economy rests on two (or more) metal standards, and is
therefore generally known as bimetallism.[56] Bimetallism can be made to work in a
closed economy where an absolute value ratio can be maintained between the two
metals (assuming, broadly, that the monetary value of each can only be established
by reference to the value of the other). However, in an open economy where there
are external factors driving the price of the two metals, the ratio between them
will inevitably diverge. This creates well-known problems, generally involving the
disappearance of one or other of the units as it becomes relatively more valuable.
There are also more practical problems related to the fact that even a small amount
of precious metal is high value in terms of the price of a loaf of bread or a pint
of beer. For example, the English farthing introduced by Edward 1 in 1279—the
smallest coin minted in England—weighed 0.34 g, or one-tenth of the weight of a
modern 5p coin, but still constituted one-quarter of the daily wage of the average
paid workman.[57] Thus, it is likely that most daily life involved either the extension
of credit or the use of tokens, thereby adding a further settlement mechanism into
an already complex mix.

## 2.4.3 Debasement and inflation

One of the illusions which has still not been entirely discarded is the idea that debasement of coinage causes inflation. The rationale for this connection is clear—if  2.41
an authority debases its coins, what is happening is that the same amount of available metal is being converted into a larger amount of coin—in other words, the
money supply is being increased with no corresponding increase in the quantity of

---

[55] Initially identified by Cipolla in *Money, Prices and Civilization in the Mediterranean World, Fifth to Seventeenth Century* (1956) published for the University of Cincinnati by Princeton University Press and addressed in a book of this title by Sargent and Velde, *The Big Problem of Small Change* (Princeton University Press 2002).

[56] The whole process is clearly described and analysed in Redish, *Bimetallism: An Economic and Historical Analysis* (Cambridge University Press 2006).

[57] Some European issuers (notably Venice) dealt with this problem by issuing lower-value coins with a correspondingly lower proportion of precious metal (known as billon). However, the English appear to have taken the view that this was cheating. As a result, there were regular petitions from the commons to the crown lamenting the lack of small change—see Sargent and Velde, *The Big Problem of Small Change* (Princeton University Press 2002).

other assets. Orthodox economics tells us that this will result in prices increasing to absorb the amount of new money created (the doctrine of monetary neutrality).[58] However, this disregards one important aspect of currency debasement; that where a government increases the supply of money without changing any other variable, the money thus created is put into circulation by the government. This has the same effect as an increase in government borrowing—government's gross purchases are increased beyond the level at which they would stand otherwise.

2.42 A sovereign who needs money is unlikely to confine himself to only one way of raising it. Sovereigns in this position are likely to draw heavily on the credit both of their citizens and of external lenders. A common technique was also the 'crying up' of the currency, by which new coins identical to existing coins were given a higher value,[59] as well as borrowing and debasement. All of this, by increasing their buying power, will increase prices in their territories. The key point is that coins because of inflationary policies, not the other way around, and it is availability of credit, not availability of currency, which drives price inflation. Where credit is created by government borrowing, government may seek to monetise debt, and in the absence of an increase in available precious metal, this necessitates debasement.

2.43 However, it is important to understand that there is no necessary link between a change in the metallic composition of coins and price levels. If a government with a full-bodied metal currency took action to reduce the metal content of that currency to 50 per cent of its fiat value, but did not increase the total fiat value of the coins in issue, price levels in its economy should be unaffected. Adulteration and inflation are frequently encountered together, but they are not directly causally linked.

2.44 Another way of looking at this is that a metal standard in a relatively closed economy prevents the sovereign from borrowing in this way, since for any given amount of physical metal there is only a certain amount of coin that can be created. This in turn means that the government is incentivised to maintain the level of metal in its currency at a level no higher than that used in other trading countries as a percentage of fiat value, since if its currency has a higher metal content then international trade will result in a net loss of metal to the country and therefore a reduction in the effective borrowing limit.[60]

## 2.5 What Makes a Monetary Sovereign?

2.45 The argument above leads to the conclusion that any entity with the power to raise taxes has the potential to create its own currency. This is clearly true. However, there are a large number of entities which have taxation powers but which do not in

---

[58] See 'Friedrich August von Hayek' in *The New Palgrave: A Dictionary of Economics* (Macmillan 1987).

[59] Coins generally did not have a face value relative to other coins, so it was practical to decree that as from tomorrow a penny is worth twopence. Simple debasement, whereby a smaller, lighter coin is produced and decreed to be worth the old value is the same technique in reverse. See Davies, *A History of Money* (University of Wales Pres 4th Ed 2016 at 2014–15).

[60] See Schnabel and Shin, *Money and Trust: Lessons from the 1620s for the Digital Age* (BIS February 2018) Working Paper No. 698.

practice issue their own currency. This group includes regional governments (such as the Scottish and Welsh Assemblies in the United Kingdom). However, there are a number of at least nominally sovereign entities which have also eschewed money issuance—the member states of the Eurozone and the states of the United States are both examples. However, both of these circumstances provide us from time to time with demonstrations of the fact that any entity with tax-raising powers can in effect create money at will. The most recent example is the state of California, which in 2009 issued IOUs to its creditors. These instruments had a term of six months and bore a coupon of 3.75 per cent, and were generally regarded as bonds rather than money proper.[61] However, the fact that they were state obligations appears to have been sufficient to cause them to circulate as money and, more importantly, for banks to accept them as deposits into cash accounts for a period. Equally, in discussions about the possible position of Greece and Italy as members of the Eurozone, it has frequently been suggested that these countries could escape the burden of EU restrictions on borrowing by creating their own domestic money which could circulate alongside the Euro and would derive its money-ness from the fact that the government concerned would agree to accept it in payment of tax.[62] The interesting thing about these proposals from our perspective is the characterisation issue that they create. Considering the Greek example, if the instruments were held to be bonds, then their issue would presumably breach the limits on sovereign borrowing to which those governments are subject, and if they were held to be money, they would contravene the requirement that Euro member states must have the euro as their sole currency. Consequently, such proposals postulate a new state-issued instrument which is neither money nor debt. This possibility is not considered further in this book, which proceeds on the (old-fashioned) basis that a thing either is money or it is not. However, if it turns out to be possible to create a sovereign-issued instrument which has these characteristics, then a second edition will be required.

## 2.6 Conclusion

The history of money seems to demonstrate that it is a mixed product of law and social conduct. There is no doubt that physical money is generally (although not quite invariably) created by the act of a sovereign. However, more often than not the actual action of the sovereign was the creation of new mechanisms of exchange to facilitate the settlement of claims denominated in pre-existing socially determined units of account. Such coins derived their value from the denomination ascribed to them by law, not their metal intrinsic value (except in extreme cases). The basis for this valuation, and the underpinning of the social acceptance of the statutory valuation

2.46

---

[61] Especially by the SEC—see https://www.sec.gov/investor/pubs/californiaiou-alert.htm.
[62] Sometimes referred to as 'Fiscal Money' proposals—see Varoufakis, *The Promise of Fiscal Money* at https://www.project-syndicate.org/commentary/fiscal-money-end-central-bank-independence-by-yanis-varoufakis-2017-08?barrier=accesspaylog and https://monetafiscale.it/english-version/.

of these coins, was their acceptance by the sovereign in discharge of public (non-commercial) obligations owed by citizens to it, with the metal content serving as a backstop. However, sovereign money has probably never formed the whole of the circulating payment media of any economy, and at times of stress private media have flourished to fill gaps resulting from a shortfall in the supply of sovereign money.

# 3

# Money and Credit

| | |
|---|---|
| **3.1 The Origins of Credit** | **3.02** |
|    3.1.1 Coexistence of money and credit | 3.08 |
|    3.1.2 The study of credit | 3.10 |
|    3.1.3 Business and credit | 3.14 |
| **3.2 Credit and Money Distinguished** | **3.16** |
|    3.2.1 Clearing houses as a substitute for money | 3.20 |
|    3.2.2 Girobank(s) as substitutes for money | 3.23 |
|    3.2.3 Mercantile agency as a substitute for money | 3.25 |
|    3.2.4 Open versus closed systems | 3.26 |
|    3.2.5 The reified promise to pay | 3.28 |
|    3.2.6 The reified instruction to pay | 3.29 |
| **3.3 The Discharge of Credit Obligations** | **3.30** |
|    3.3.1 The pig/egg paradigm | 3.32 |
|    3.3.2 Usefulness of payment to the debtor | 3.37 |
|    3.3.3 Usefulness of payment to the creditor | 3.41 |
|    3.3.4 Money as the vehicle for credit risk transfer | 3.47 |
|    3.3.5 Credit risk transfer as the foundation for lending banking | 3.48 |
|    3.3.6 Risk transfer and risk pooling | 3.49 |
|    3.3.7 Virtual currency as a risk transfer mechanism | 3.50 |

One of the more basic facts about money in pre-modern societies is that in none of them was there sufficient metal to provide enough coin to meet the presumed demand for it as deduced from estimates of commercial activity and of gross domestic product (GDP) in those economies. There has been a dispiriting tendency to assume that in these economies this demonstrates that the level of commercial activity was lower than the level of GDP might lead us to expect. However, this is to put the cart a long way before the horse. If the level of coinage in existence does not match the level of economic activity projected, the ordinary conclusion from that phenomenon should be that the missing proportion of commercial activity was conducted using means of payment other than coin, not that it was absent altogether. In later societies this function was supplied by a variety of instruments ranging from negotiable bonds through to bank cheques, but it seems likely that in almost any society, where there are discrepancies between the levels of coin in circulation and the estimated GDP, the difference is likely to represent simple credit claims.

## 3.1 The Origins of Credit

3.02 There have occasionally been attempts to argue that credit money is a late creation, and that there are societies (or states of society) in which all money is commodity money. This is clearly wrong. We know that exchange based on credit obligations was a feature of Babylonic economic activity in the twenty-fifth century BC[1] and it is transparently clear from the historic record that payment systems existed thousands of years before the invention of coin in the west in the seventh century BC. The reason for this is simply that it is inevitable—it is impossible to imagine any society in which all reciprocal dealings are always immediately settled with physical transfer of the relevant goods (and what about service obligations?). Thus, there seems to be good evidence that credit is as old as markets, and considerably older than coin, with which it has coexisted for the whole period of the latter's existence.

3.03 This point was made by Mitchell Innes in 1913–14. In a pair of powerful articles,[2] he demolished the argument that commercial activity was synonymous with the use of coin, and argued that the true monetary sphere was constituted by the aggregate credit appetite of the participants. One way of expressing this would be precisely to say that endogenous monetary (credit) capacity was a function of the credit risk appetite of participants in the system, and that exogenous money supply was largely irrelevant to monetary (credit) capacity. Mitchell Innes advances evidence ranging from China and Babylon to the great cloth fairs of Champagne, but we can begin considerably nearer to home. Craig Muldrew,[3] working on the records of medieval Kings Lynn, demonstrates that if the local economy had operated on a purely coinage basis, the velocity of circulation of the coin must have been nearly thirty times—whereas the conventional economic expectation in most normal economies is around four times. Thus, either our estimates for the total amount of coinage are wildly out, or the vast majority of transactions were settled using something other than coins. Muldrew concludes that 'every household in the country from those of paupers to the royal household, was to some degree enmeshed within the increasingly complicated webs of credit and obligation'.[4]

3.04 The length and breadth of these credit chains can be seen in the boom in litigation over unfilled obligations. In the central courts of Kings Bench and Common Pleas, the number of cases heard increased from around 5,000 in 1563 to nearly 29,000 in 1640. Most of these suits were actions of debt, and concerned instances where the conditions of bonds had been broken.[5] This was, however, only the tip of the iceberg

---

[1] See Van De Mieroop, *The Invention of Interest: Sumerian Loans* in Goetzman and Rouwenhorst (eds), *The Origins of Value* (OUP 2005).

[2] Mitchell Innes, *What is Money*, The Banking Law Journal (May 1913) 377-408 and *The Credit Theory of Money*, The Banking law Journal, Vol. 31 (1914) 151-168. For an assessment, see *Credit and State Theories of Money: The Contributions of A. Mitchell Innes* Ed. Wray (Edward Elgar 2004).

[3] Muldrew, *The Economy of Obligation: The Culture of Credit and Social Relations in Early Modern England* (Macmillan 1998).

[4] Ibid. at 95.

[5] Ibid. at 203 and 240, and see Brooks, *Pettyfoggers and Vipers of the Commonwealth: The Lower Branch of the Legal Profession in Early Modern England* (Cambridge University Press 1986) at 56–71.

as regards the total numbers of suits being conducted in all of the various courts which existed across England—in Kings Lynn alone, an average of 2,000 cases a year were brought before the borough court in the early seventeenth century.[6]

It is not difficult to see the explanation for this explosion of credit—between 1544 and 1590 the amount of money in circulation increased by 63 per cent.[7] In this period food prices trebled, industrial prices doubled, and the number of commercial transactions at least doubled.[8] The upshot of all this was that the demand for money had increased by somewhere around 500 per cent.[9] However, the supply of money had simply not kept pace with this demand, and the shortage was exacerbated by the operation of Gresham's law—scarce coin was hoarded, and Pepys observed that the total amount of coin circulating in England in 1665 was probably only around £7m because so much of what existed was hoarded.[10] Thus, on Muldrew's estimates, for the town of Kings Lynn (where the total value of all transactions undertaken was probably around £390,000) there may have been less than £11,000 of physical cash in the entire town, much of which would have been unavailable for circulation because it was being hoarded for use in large-scale transactions. In such an environment, the rapid development of credit was unavoidable.

3.05

The point about complicated webs is important. The issue is not that you owe money to, and are owed money by, a lot of people. That is not a web. The issue is that Fred owes you money, but John owes him money, and if John can't pay Fred, then Fred can't pay you. Even if you know all this, then in order to know whether Fred is likely to be able to pay you, you need to know who John's creditors are, and how likely they are to be able to pay him. In the absence of cash, obligations are not settled and the web becomes more complex—and harder to understand—with every transaction. The outcome is that every economically active citizen is potentially credit-dependent on every other citizen.

3.06

As a diversion, it is plausibly suggested that this may be the reason why the repayment of debts is so often seen in so many societies as having a social or moral aspect to it. In societies where money is scarce there is no alternative to assuming credit exposure to others, and members of society know that they may well be exposed to other members through mechanisms which are entirely invisible to them. In such a society we would expect to find—as we do in practice—strong cultural pressures to the effect that it is a moral and social as well as a legal requirement for any man not only to repay his debts, but also to conduct himself in such a fashion that he does not become unable to repay his debts. Such cultures can be expected to—and do—make a significant distinction between those affected by misfortune, whose debts should be forgiven, and those whose default is a result of improvidence, who thereby endanger not only themselves but the whole community. Thus, in a community which

3.07

---

[6] Muldrew, ibid. at 204.
[7] Challis, *The Tudor Coinage* (Manchester University Press 1978) at 245–7.
[8] Brenner, *The Inflation of Prices in England, 1551–1650*, Economic History Review, 2nd ser, XV #2 (1962) at 270.
[9] Muldrew, *The Economy of Obligation: The Culture of Credit and Social Relations in Early Modern England* (Macmillan 1998) at 100.
[10] Pepys Diary, IV, at 147–8, VI, at 23.

is strongly connected by credit relationships, any sign of improvidence (whether ostentation, gambling, speculation or any other form of high-risk behaviour) by any member is likely to be strongly disapproved by other members, since cascading default potentially threatens all.[11]

### 3.1.1 Coexistence of money and credit

3.08  It is well-known that economic theory does not require the existence of money—the most advanced form of modern economic models—Walrasian[12] or Arrow-Debreu[13] models—are described as frictionless precisely because they preclude any role for money.[14] This is because they assume that money is a veil, whose only function is to conceal the fact that all economic exchanges are ultimately exchanges of commodities for other commodities.[15] Alternative approaches have considered the idea that the lack of money is an absolute constraint to economic activity, but have approached that problem by assuming that although there may be a counterparty for every (economically efficient) transaction, the issue is that they cannot find each other. This 'search-friction' approach[16] is based on the same assumptions as the classical models. The position is accurately summed up by Ugolino:

> Despite their differences, both lines of research have focussed on why some goods acquire the property of 'moneyness'. This means that, de facto, their actual goal has been to justify the existence of commodity money—although, de jure, their results have been claimed to justify also the existence of fiat money by showing that the intrinsic value of the money-good is irrelevant to the assumption of the 'moneyness' property.[17]

3.09  It is to be hoped that anyone who has stayed the course this far will understand that demonstrating that the value of fiat money is not connected to its physical value does not constitute a major advance in the theory of money. The real challenge is best articulated by Nosal and Rochteau:

> one of the key challenges in monetary theory is to provide an explanation for the coexistence of money and credit. One reason why coexistence is a challenge is that the frictions that are needed to make money essential typically make credit infeasible, and environments where credit is feasible are ones where money is typically not essential.

---

[11] This may well be the true source of the 'spirit of capitalism' and 'protestant work ethic' identified by Max Weber.

[12] Walras, *Elements of Pure Economics, or the Theory of Social Wealth* (Allen & Unwin 1954).

[13] Debreu, *Theory of Value: An Axiomatic Analysis of Economic Equilibrium* (Willey 1959).

[14] It is possible to introduce into such models a 'cash-in-advance constraint' (also known as the Clower constraint). This assumes that each consumer or firm must have sufficient cash available before they can buy goods; and that therefore the total amount of goods that can be bought at any given time cannot exceed the amount of available money.

[15] See Starr, *Why is there Money? Walrasian General Equilibrium Foundations of Monetary Theory* (Edward Elgar 2012).

[16] The key paper here is Kiyotaki and Wright, *A Contribution to the Pure Theory of Money*, Journal of Economic Theory, Vol. LIII (1991) at 215–35, and for recent developments see Nosal and Rochteau, *Money, Payments, and Liquidity* (MIT Press 2011).

[17] Ugolino, *The Evolution of Central Banking: Theory and History*, Palgrave Studies in Economic History (Palgrave 2017) at 168–9.

Given that the authors lived (as do we all) in a society in which both money and credit flourish in harmony, it is clear why this should have been such an uncomfortable position to have reached.

### 3.1.2 The study of credit

The trouble with credit in this regard is that it is difficult to measure. The amount of credit that I have given is a material, quantifiable fact; the amount of credit that I am prepared to give must be forever unknown. It is necessarily clear that in the normal state of any economy the total amount of credit actually outstanding is less than the total credit capacity of that economy. Just to make things harder, the credits and debits of all individual participants within an economy sum to zero when that economy is considered as a whole, and are therefore to some extent invisible. Finally, it is of course possible to measure the actual amount of credit extended by any particular group of business, and as a result it is possible to measure how much credit is extended by the banking system to the rest of the economy. However, banks are by no means the only suppliers of credit—it has long been a cliché amongst corporate treasures that the primary supplier of credit to business is other business, and it is certainly true that suppliers who could not obtain bank credit are frequently kept going by trade credit. Measuring the credit appetite of the real economy is a difficult task, and forecasting changes in that appetite a more difficult one (although since we have just gone through a financial crisis caused by a sudden shrinkage in global financial credit appetite, one whose study might repay a little more effort). 3.10

It is because the study of credit appetite appears impossible today and the study of actual credit levels impossible for most of recorded history that we are to some extent forced to fall back on the study of physical currency. In this area we suffer very badly from what has been called the palaeontologists curse—that no matter how much we may wish to know about the thinks which have not survived, we are restricted to studying only those things which have survived. Physical coins leave physical traces which can be examined, notional accounts, credits, debits, and promises of payment generally do not. Thus, although we know that concepts of money have existed in notional form for a very long time, there is always a tendency to think of money as a physical thing, with notional uses of it as unusual. In reality, the position is almost certainly the other way around. The point is most clearly put by Schumpeter:[18] 3.11

[F]rom the fourteenth and fifteenth centuries on (and even in the Graeco-Roman world) the gold or silver or copper was the familiar thing. The credit structure—which moreover was incessantly developing—was the thing to be explored and to be analysed ... Logically, it is by no means clear that the most useful method is to start from the coin ... in order to proceed to the credit transactions of reality. It may be more useful to start from these in the first place, to look upon capitalist finance as a clearing system that cancels claims and debts and carries forward the differences—so that 'money' payments come in only as a special case without any

---

[18] *History of Economic Analysis* (1954, Routledge 1987) at 717.

particularly fundamental importance. In other words: practically and analytically, a credit theory of money is possibly preferable to a monetary theory of credit.

3.12 The study of credit has always fallen on the outskirts of economics. This is partly because it is proverbially hard to measure, and partly because unlike money balances, which can only be created by banks, credit exposures can be created by every participant in the economy. However, it is also the case that many people have difficulty in conceiving of a debt as a 'thing'. This idea, unremarkable amongst lawyers, seems to be counterintuitive for many, and it is interesting that the first British economist to propound the idea that credit rather than money was the proper subject of economic analysis, Henry Dunning McLeod, was a lawyer by training.[19] The reason that this matters at a practical level is that in order to understand the operation of virtual currency units, the question to which we most urgently require an answer is as to how they differ both from money and from ordinary credit and whether, in Schumpeter's phrase, they require a credit theory or a money theory.

3.13 Thus, before we consider concepts of money and payment, we must begin by thinking about credit.

### 3.1.3 Business and credit

3.14 It can probably be taken for granted that international trade has always operated on the basis of some sort of credit. However, the more interesting issue arises when we focus on local business. In that regard, in particular where business is done within a relatively small town or tribe, the position is—unusually—clearer. F. A. Walker's description of the origin of US banking is instructive in this regard. He wrote:

> Under the modern system of credit, an enormous amount of indebtedness exists in every civilised community, not occasionally, or as the result of commercial misfortune, but in the usual course of business. To a degree, the mutual cancellation of debts is effected without the intervention of any separate agency. The farmer credits his hands with their wages, and charges them for his advances, from time to time, and at the end of the year or season a balance is struck... Farmers who are neighbours do the same thing in respect of their mutual accommodations... The country storekeeper, on his part, sets off the value of produce received from the farmer against the entries of goods sold...
>
> Now if we suppose all these debts to be owing in the same town or city, and to fall due on the same day, we see what a great saving of time and labour, of annoyance and disappointment... would be saved if all the persons engaged in trade in such town or city could be made debtors to one person or corporation, in respect of all their obligations falling due, and creditors in respect to all debts owing them, and thus a cheap and easy extinguishment of indebtedness take place, through the intervention of a third party, who, by putting himself now in the debtor's and now in the creditor's place—that is, by becoming debtor and creditor alternately, at the request and on the warrant of the trading individuals concerned, should effect that mutuality of obligations which is the condition of the cancellation. It is in the bank

---

[19] McLeod's *Theory of Credit* (1889) is now almost forgotten (although see Skaggs, *H. D. Macleod and the Origins of the Theory of Finance in Economic Development* in *History of Political Economy* (Duke University Press, Vol. 35, No. 3, Fall 2003) 361–84 for a reappraisal of his impact.

that the claim of the creditor and the obligation of the debtor thus meet, and are simultaneously discharged.[20]

If it is true that for the vast majority of the period that coins and tokens were the only form of money handled by the majority of the population, then we should not assume that there were no commercial transactions, but rather that the absence of money led to the continuing existence of such multiple credit obligations. 3.15

## 3.2 Credit and Money Distinguished

However, this takes us to the discussion as to why credit obligations should be so sharply distinguished from money. It must be true that, as Hicks says: 3.16

> Credit money is just part of a whole credit structure that extends outside money; it is closely interwoven with a whole system of debts and credits, or claims and obligations, some of which are money and, some of which are not, and some of which are on the edge of being money.[21]

The point here is that it is not necessary for a claim to be reified into a coin or document in order to function as 'money'. A mutual exchange of promises which is not embodied in any sort of token is a perfectly valid and workable system of payment, and highlights one of the fundamental paradoxes of the concept of money, that although it is universal it does not appear to be necessary. An economy could in theory function perfectly happily on the basis of an exchange of obligations extinguished by performance without any reification of those obligations.[22] 3.17

In Walker's frontier town, a farmer who owed money to another would have no difficulty in saying to the storekeeper/merchant charged with selling the town's crops that upon receipt of the proceeds of sale, part of the amount due to him should in fact be credited to his neighbour.[23] Such obligations would be recorded in the books of the merchant, but only needed to be given some more permanent legal form where either the amounts involved were very large or the parties were strangers to each other.[24] Thomas Jefferson is reported as having remarked in 1813 that 'a farmer with a revenue of ten thousand dollars a year may obtain all his supplies from his merchant and liquidate them at the end of the year by the sale of his produce to him without the intervention of a single dollar of cash'.[25] The same pattern can be 3.18

---

[20] Walker, *Money in its Relation to Trade and Industry* (New York 1889) at 250.
[21] Hicks, *Critical Essays in Monetary Theory* (OUP 1979) at 157–8.
[22] Hawtrey, *Currency and Credit* (Longmans, Green 1919) Ch. 1.
[23] And indeed, this seems to have been how commercial payments were made for much of English history—see Postan, *Credit in Mediaeval Trade*, The Economic History Review, Vol. a1, No. 2 (January 1928) 234–61, and also Salzman, *English Trade in the Middle Ages* (Clarendon Press 1931) at 25–42. When transferable bills appeared in seventeenth-century English trade they were a very small amendment to a very old mechanism—see Rodgers, *Early History of the Law of Bills and Notes* (Cambridge University Press 1995) at 109ff.
[24] Atherton, *The Southern Country Store 1800–1900* (Louisiana State University Press 1949) at 14; Atherton, *The Frontier Merchant in Mid-America* (University of Missouri Press 1971) at 18–19, 125.
[25] Quoted in Hammond, *Banks and Politics in America from the Revolution to the Civil War* (Princeton University Press 1957) at 71.

seen in fourteenth-century France,[26] and it seems very highly likely that this sort of centralised non-cash account-based system would have been encountered in any society which had trading arrangements but suffered from a shortage of cash.

3.19 Of course the book entries in the accounts of merchants of this kind are no more than payments, and to that extent the merchants are no more than paymasters (in Geva's terms[27]) or banks (in the colloquial use today). However, this system only works where there is a single, central agent intermediating transactions between multiple persons. Such a central agent is generally referred to as a clearing house.

### 3.2.1 Clearing houses as a substitute for money

3.20 Interestingly, structures of this kind are more common than might be imagined. Clearing houses are as old as commerce, and it seems that one of the important features of a medieval fair of any size was a payment settlement procedure (*rescontrire*) in which obligations between merchants were to the greatest extent possible set off against each other so as to minimise the requirement for cash settlement.[28] Such arrangements are also common amongst banks—after the elimination of the US central bank in 1835, US banks responded by creating a clearing house to manage payment settlement risk.[29]

3.21 However, clearing houses do not abolish credit risk, and, depending on the periodicity of the clearing, they may increase it. Thus, in the early medieval fairs, where clearing occurred four times a year,[30] merchants may have been constrained from seeking early settlement of individual debts from doubtful debtors by the requirements of the clearing system.[31] The only way that clearing systems can genuinely eliminate credit risk is by assuming a central counterparty (CCP) function. This means that the clearing house ceases to be simply an arrangement for identifying and executing netting obligations and becomes a single central entity dealing with and acting as counterparty to all transactions.[32] However, because a CCP effectively assumes the credit risk of every member which it takes on, CCPs in general tend to

---

[26] Lopez and Raymond, *Mediaeval Trade in the Mediterranean World* (Columbia University Press 1955) at 98–100.

[27] See Geva, *Bank Collections and Payment Transactions: A Comparative Legal Analysis* (OUP 2001).

[28] See Borner and Hatfield, *The Design of Debt Clearing Markets: Clearinghouse Mechanisms in Pre-Industrial Europe*, Journal of Political Economy Vol. 125, No. 6 (December 2017) at 1991–2037.

[29] Gibbons, *The Banks of New-York, their Dealers, the Clearing House and the Panic of 1857* (Appleton 1858) at 292–6.

[30] See Verlinden, *Markets and Fairs* in Postan, Rich, and Miller (eds), *The Cambridge Economic History of Europe from the Decline of the Roman Empire* (Cambridge University Press 1963) at 119–54.

[31] Under the rules of Besancon, the most common model for medieval fair customs, merchants were required to specify in advance if they wanted payment other than through the clearing system, and were thereafter prohibited from demanding early payment of a debt submitted to clearing. This was also the case with other fair rules—see Borner and Hatfield, *The Design of Debt Clearing Markets: Clearinghouse Mechanisms in Pre-Industrial Europe*, Journal of Political Economy, Vol. 125, No. 6 (December 2017) at 1991–2037. For an examination of the unfortunate economic effects of the collapse of a clearing system see *British Eagle International Air Lines Ltd v Cie Nationale Air France* [1975] 1 WLR 758.

[32] This is the function which clearing houses such as the London Clearing House (LCH) perform for certain markets today.

be distinctly selective about who they will allow to become a member. A CCP which threw open its doors to all comers would rapidly find itself insolvent.

If a clearing house is to be a true substitute for money, however, it will have to provide not only a way of netting transactions, but also a way of settling the transactions which are left.

### 3.2.2 Girobank(s) as substitutes for money

A clearing gouse which seeks to settle all of the transactions which occur within it must be a girobank.[33] A girobank differs from a cheque (or private-payment-instrument-issuing) bank in that in order to make a payment through a girobank both parties have to have accounts with that girobank. A system-wide girobank would have to operate accounts for every participant in an economic system, both permanent and transient. This is why the bank must be a girobank, since if it is a cheque-based deposit bank then the cheques thus created can effectively circulate as money outside the system provided that the recipient of the cheque can persuade a third party who is within the system to collect the payment embodied in the cheque on his behalf—and then we are back to circulating money.

If we could create a single central intermediary within an economy which was both a giro bank for that economy, and a CCP clearing house for credit risk arising from payment default,[34] with every economically active participant in the economy as a member, it is clearly the case that we could eliminate money from that economy.[35]

### 3.2.3 Mercantile agency as a substitute for money

However, we are getting ahead of ourselves. Our hypothetical mid-western merchant is neither a CCP nor a pure payment service provider—indeed what he resembles more than anything else is the Roman *coactores argentarii*, who combined in one business the activities of finance provision and commercial agency. The book entry service which he provides is unquestionably a payment service, but the provision of payment services is not his business—indeed, it is a mere ancillary activity to his main activity as a commercial agent. This point is a specific instance of a fact which recurs throughout the history of money—that where actions are undertaken for an owner by a mercantile agent, that mercantile agent will be in possession of money which he can then be directed to pay to a third person, thereby rendering the credit

---

[33] The difference between a giro bank and a cheque bank is that in a giro bank payment is made by the account holder instructing the bank to make a transfer to another named account, whereas in a cheque bank the payer writes the instruction to the bank to transfer on a cheque and hands it to the payee. The reason that this matters is that a cheque can serve as a circulating medium outside the banking system, whereas a giro only facilitates payment between persons within the banking system.
[34] The purpose of a CCP is to mutualise risk across a system, such that where a claim between two persons is submitted to the CCP, then the two parties are no longer exposed to each other but each is exposed to the CCP, such that the failure of the creditor does not affect the amount owed to the debtor, and the amount of the loss caused by the debtor's default is spread over all of the users of the clearing house.
[35] This is the point made by Kotcherlatoka, *Money is Memory*, Staff Report 218, Federal Reserve Bank of Minneapolis (1996).

balance concerned to some degree transferable.[36] Herein lies the problem for the users of his service. For as long as any one client is prepared to put all of his business through one agent, he will receive in effect the services of a central clearing house. However, that will remain the case only to the extent that he is prepared to confine his commercial relationships only to other clients of the same merchant. However, as clients grow and diversify, they will no longer be satisfied to confine their business to other clients of the same merchant, and will wish to deal through different agents in different transactions. As soon as the agents need to settle obligations amongst themselves, we are back to a world in which money is required—unless the merchants themselves are part of a larger system.

### 3.2.4 Open versus closed systems

3.26  The common denominator of all of these arrangements is that they are closed systems—that is, that they only permit settlement between persons who are members of the system. The point about circulating media of exchange is that they are open systems. A coin or a banknote can be handed over by any person to any person, and there does not need to be any pre-existing arrangement between them for the transfer to be an effective payment. Cash payment massively expands the universe of people with whom business can be done.

3.27  This point that payment within a closed system is useful but insufficient is an important one. In principle, as a farmer expands the universe of people with whom he wishes to deal, he can invite those people into the system. However, this takes us back to the issue of credit appetite. Storekeepers may be happy to take moderate credit risks on well-known parties, but are unlikely to be prepared to take credit risks on moderately known parties. Thus, in the absence of credit appetite, the only way that the farmer can expand his business is by securing payment.

### 3.2.5 The reified promise to pay

3.28  This takes us to the 'reified promise to pay'. These take two forms. One is the transferrable promise (more commonly referred to as an IOU). No purpose is served by reifying a bilateral obligation which both parties accept already exists unless the reification results in transferability, so we assume that the creation of an IOU enables the promise to pay to be transferred to a third party. However, the third party will still have to come back to the person who made the IOU in order to be paid. The point about a reified promise to pay is that it can be transferred without restriction—there is no need for the holder to have any pre-existing relationship with any other party, provided that he knows where the payee can be found. A reified transferrable promise to pay is a good description of a bank note.

---

[36] This quasi-payer function of the mercantile agent is visible from the Roman *coactores argentarii* to the Dutch merchant bankers of the seventeenth century. The development of the mercantile agent into the acceptance of bills and ultimately to freestanding credit provision is described in Rogers, *The Early History of Bills and Notes* (Cambridge University Press 1995).

### 3.2.6 The reified instruction to pay

A 'reified instruction to pay' is an instruction to a person (in our example, the storekeeper) to pay money to the holder of the instrument. Reified instructions to pay come in two forms: those which are bilateral—that is, where the document is simply an instruction to the recipient to make a payment; and those which are trilateral, that is, where the recipient has endorsed the instrument, thereby accepting liability on it. This instrument is a direct promise to pay made by a paymaster, and is the closest cognate to money that can be created. Like a reified promise to pay, it has the overwhelming advantage that it can be transferred to any person at any time, and is likely to retain its value in the hands of that person. A reified accepted instruction to pay is a good description of a bill of exchange or cheque.

## 3.3 The Discharge of Credit Obligations

It is necessary at this point to delve a little more deeply into the question of the function which money actually performs. Although we have established that its function is the discharge of debts, it is necessary to consider why the discharge of debts, considered in the abstract, is a useful function to have performed.

This point can best be elucidated by beginning with Jevons' 'double coincidence of wants'. If I want what you have, and you want what I have, then we do not need currency—we can simply exchange things in a barter. However, for a true barter to happen, it is necessary not only that A and B should each want what the other has, but that they should both want what the other has at a time when the other has it to hand and available for immediate delivery. This is in many respects the most unlikely part of the double coincidence, and—it should be noted—is particularly unlikely in primitive agricultural communities. Consequently, any commercial exchange is likely to involve a time gap between the performance of one part of the deal and the performance of the other, and any such time gap, as we have seen, creates credit risk. In order to think about this, it is easiest to begin with a stylised example.

### 3.3.1 The pig/egg paradigm

Assume that, in a primitive economy, I am a chicken farmer and you are a pig farmer. If I give you an egg every day for a year on the basis that you will give me a pig twice a year, one of us will be a creditor of the other for an extended period of time. This can happen either way around—you can start by giving me a pig on the basis that I will agree to deliver eggs for the next six months (in which case you assume a large credit exposure to me on the day you deliver your pig), or I can start by giving you eggs on the basis that you will deliver a pig to me in six months' time (in which case I will have a large credit exposure to you on the day before that delivery). Neither of us can do very much about the periodicity of our supplies. Thus, the question of whether we can deal at all depends on (a) credit risk appetite, and (b) if the proposed

3.33 It is important in this example to understand the basis of credit-risk aversion. Issues of this kind are frequently mischaracterised as primarily involving 'trust'. However, this is a very small part of the problem. One possibility for the egg supplier is that, having given the pig supplier eggs for six months, the pig supplier will simply deny the debt when the pigs are slaughtered. However, even if both were autarkic backwoodsmen existing entirely outside a social framework this is an improbable outcome—if for no other reason than that the pig supplier would probably like his egg supply to continue. Within almost any social framework, a barefaced denial of a publicly known obligation is an extreme strategy likely to result in the withdrawal of the cooperation which that network provides, and therefore likely to have consequences which are more severe than the benefit derived from the repudiation.

3.34 Trust is not the issue. What is the issue is the possibility that, through a variety of external events, the pig supplier will simply not be able to perform his side of the bargain. This could range from the affliction of the pig-supplier with any one of a number of illnesses rendering him unable to curate his pigs, to the affliction of his pigs with any one of a number of illnesses rendering them unsaleable, to fire, flood, famine, armed incursion, confiscation, appropriation, or nationalisation. Every creditor becomes, to some extent, an equity investor in the person to whom he has credit exposure, and the risk which lies at the base of any credit risk is not the risk that the creditor will not perform his obligation, but that he cannot.

3.35 Lest this all appear too hypothetical, it may be noted that this is exactly Muldrew's web of credit problem (see para 3.03 above). In his detailed study of the economy of Kings Lynn in the sixteenth century, he noted that (as a result of a shortage of money) there developed long chains of credit relationships. These long chains created social problems, since a default anywhere along the chain might cascade default down it. This in turn meant that the credit risk being assumed in any one transaction included an element based on the likelihood of those who owed money to the creditor repaying their debts, and those who owed money to those debtors repaying theirs. The immediate point there is that the risk of the pig supplier can at least be analysed in terms of the risk to his pigs—if we have to add another layer of risk—for example, if we know that the pig supplier is critically dependent on the pig-swill supplier, who is critically dependent on the local tavern, and so on—it becomes easy to see how credit-risk aversion develops.

3.36 The best way of mitigating credit exposure is payment, and consequently the best tool for mitigating the credit risk involved in the relationship is money. This illustrates the major interaction of money and credit—that money is a tool for managing and reallocating credit risk. However, there is more to it than that. Before considering the how of credit risk mitigation, we should first consider the why—in particular, why might a debtor wish to discharge an obligation by paying money, and why might a creditor be prepared to have an obligation discharged through the receipt of money.

### 3.3.2 Usefulness of payment to the debtor

If I supply you with goods, on the basis that you will at some later stage supply me with other goods, as soon as you have accepted my goods you have committed yourself to supply those other goods. Going back to our pig/egg example, as soon as the pig farmer has accepted the first egg he has effectively undertaken to continue as pig farmer for at least the next six months. If he is suddenly seized by the idea of going on a pilgrimage, taking holy orders, or simply moving to another village, he will find that the network of obligations in which he is enmeshed is quite sufficient to prevent him doing any of those thing—or, to be precise, sufficient to ensure that his neighbours will prevent him from doing so. In order to acquire the individual freedom to make any significant change in his life, he must first be able to settle his open accounts, such that no one is significantly disadvantaged by his decision. This will be true even if the only change that he wants to make is to move from rearing pigs to rearing goats. It should be noted that the effluxion of time will not help here—given that the development cycle of the pig is determined by some of the better-known laws of nature, there is nothing he can do to discharge his obligation to deliver the pig early, or to vary it. Neither can he absolve his obligation by redelivering the eggs which he has received, since he has eaten them. It is likely that there will be no time at which all of his social obligations are set at zero such that he can free himself from his obligations by performing them without having acquired any new ones. For the debtor, only payment of debts can purchase freedom of action. This is well put by Mitchell Innes: 'the really important characteristic of a credit is not the right which it gives to "payment" of a debt, but the right that it confers on the holder to liberate himself from debt by its means'.[37] This of course is the classical picture of the transition from serfdom to equality in medieval societies—the commutation of service obligations to rent obligations is itself a substantial grant of freedom to those subject to the obligations.[38]

3.37

This point is also, of course, the basis of much of the Marxist analysis to the effect that money dissolves social relationships. The Marxist position is that if in a primitive society a lord is owed a duty of service, but in return owes a duty to provide for his man for an extended period, the lord is very significantly benefited if he can eliminate his long-term, structured obligation to his man by a cash payment. It is also true that the effect of the payment is to transfer responsibility for the care and provisioning of the man from the lord to the man. However, what this does is to loosen an obligation of co-dependence (which some would call slavery), and what it permits is for both sides of the agreement to structure the arrangement between them in such a fashion that it increases both of their freedoms of action.

3.38

It seems to follow from this that the level of individual freedom in any state may be a function of the utility of money in that state as a mechanism for dissolving social obligations, and it appears that there is something in this. In particular the Peruvian

3.39

---

[37] Mitchell Innes, *What is Money*, The Banking Law Journal (May 1913).
[38] See, for example, North and Thomas, *The Rise and Fall of the Manorial System: A Theoretical Model*, The Journal of Economic History, Vol. 31, No. 4 (December 1971) 777–803.

Incas, arguably the most sophisticated civilisation not to have developed money, seem to provide an instance of this—modern analysis would characterise Inca society as a slave-state, with individual obligations descending to an obligation to wear the specific clothing provided and prescribed by the state.[39]

3.40    It is also notable that where individuals are subject to a high degree of individual restriction in an economy which does have a monetary function, those individuals will in general devote a disproportionate amount of their time and effort to liberating themselves from those constraints—generally considerably more than would be commercially justified. Buying yourself out of slavery is clearly more than a merely commercial transaction.[40] But the point that a person who assumes an obligation can—potentially, and with appropriate social safeguards—free himself of that obligation by doing a thing is an important one, and consequently the wise debtor ensures that whatever obligations he assumes, they should always be capable of being discharged by the payment of money.

### 3.3.3 Usefulness of payment to the creditor

3.41    All commercial creditors have a finite credit appetite, both for each individual debtor and for all debtors together. Most commercial businesses operate somewhere near the limits of their credit appetite, and thus in order for them to take on a new obligation, an existing obligation must usually be discharged. Such an obligation may be discharged by performance, but here again the date of performance may be immovable. Set-off may help to some degree—if I owe you something and you owe me something, then the credit risk arising out of the transaction may be only the net balance between the two. However, every creditor has a point beyond which he will not go in assuming the risk of performance of others. Once a creditor has reached this point, only payment will induce him to enter into further transactions with a particular counterparty.

3.42    Viewed from this perspective, it is clear that the function of money in the pig and egg example is as a credit risk allocation technique. Assume that we restructure the transaction so that the egg supplier is the creditor (that is, it is he who incepts the transaction, and on the day before the delivery of the pig he is fully exposed to the credit of the pig supplier). The egg supplier is not prepared to accept this much credit risk. Consequently, each day the pig supplier pays the egg supplier a penny for the egg, and twice a year the egg supplier pays the pig supplier 15s 2d[41] for a pig. Now at

---

[39] Although, to be fair, we have almost no idea how the Inca economy actually operated. One possibility is that the uniqueness of the Inca economy was that the economic actors were local lords and the currency in use between them was actually people—see La Lone, *The Inca as a Nonmarket Economy: Supply on Command Versus Supply and Demand* in Ericson and Earle (eds), *Contexts for Prehistoric Exchange* (Academic Press 1982) for an overview of this puzzle.

[40] See, e.g., the narrative of John Berry Meachum, born a slave in Virginia in 1789 (National Humanities Center 2008) at nationalhumanitiescenter.org/pds/. Many slaves who had 'self-purchased' seem to have made it their next priority to purchase members of their immediate family, at the same non-economic prices. See, generally, Schweninger, *Black Property Owners in the South, 1790–1915* (University of Illinois Press 1997).

[41] For younger readers, 182 pennies at 12 pennies to one shilling and 20 shillings to one pound.

any point during the transaction the egg supplier's credit exposure to the pig supplier is no more than one penny. Now it should be clear that if the pennies involved here were simply a private currency in use between the two participants, then the position would be absolutely unchanged—if the only thing that the egg supplier can do with the pennies is to buy a pig from that particular pig supplier, then he is in no different position than he was beforehand. However, if the pennies will be accepted elsewhere in payment, then he is in a considerably better position, since he is no longer confined to dealing with the one particular supplier, and if swine fever hits that supplier he can simply buy his pig from someone else—or, if all of the pig farmers have been affected by swine fever, he can buy a sheep instead. At this point we have in effect made the transition to 'cash' payment.

3.43 This raises the question as to where the 'pennies' come from. For the time being we will simply assume that they are provided by someone other than the two parties to the transaction. At first glance the risk profile of the parties has been improved. However, in fact all we have actually done is to reallocate risk between the parties. If we assume that the pig supplier acquired the pennies by promising to pay for them in the future, then all that has happened is that the credit exposure to the pig supplier which was previously borne by the egg supplier is now borne by the penny supplier. In particular, it should be clear that the risk of the failure of the supplier has been transferred, not eliminated. The question in respect of any particular risk is simply one of who bears it. Thus, when we come to think of the incidence of credit risk, the question we are really asking is who bears which risk, and how can the incidence of that risk be most efficiently allocated.[42]

3.44 At this point it may well be surmised that this achieves nothing—if risk exists, and cannot be eliminated, what good purpose can be served by transferring it? The answer is very simple—that by pooling many risks, the riskiness of the outcome is reduced—fire insurance is a good model here. In the same way that a company which assumes many small individual risks can construct a risk position which mitigates the risks of individual insureds, a company which assumes many individual credit risks can construct a risk position which mitigates the risk of many individuals exposed to individual credit risk.

3.45 In our pig/egg example, imagine that the parties have agreed that the egg supplier will begin by supplying eggs every day, and the pig supplier will deliver a pig after six months. Our egg supplier will say to the pig supplier: 'I am not prepared to grant you such a large amount of credit. You wish to sell your pig, and you want eggs. However, I am not prepared to give you credit equal to more than 5 per cent of your total wealth, which, since your total wealth is £5, means that my credit ceiling as regards you is 5s, or 60 pennies. Very well; you can pay me (i.e. reduce my credit claim on you) every time the amount you owe me goes above 5s. That way you ensure your supply of eggs, and enable me to buy your pig from you assuming nothing goes wrong.' The pig supplier will respond: 'But if I have to pay you, I need to get

---

[42] See Kiyotaki and Moore, *Evil is the Root of all Money*, American Economic Review, Vol. 92, No. 2 (May 2002), for an elegant statistical presentation of this problem.

the money to pay you from somewhere, and until I sell my pigs I have no cash of my own. Thus, in order to pay you I will have to borrow from another.' To this the egg purchaser will respond: 'I understand that, and I understand that it will cost you money to borrow the money you need to pay me. However, what I am doing if I grant you credit is lending you money, and if I am to lend you money, I will charge you for the risk I am taking in lending it to you, in the same way that any other lender would—let's say in the form of 10 per cent discount on the eventual price of the pig. Thus, the only question for you is whether it is cheaper for you to borrow the money from a moneylender or from me.'

3.46 What follows from this little imaginary dialogue is that the binding constraint on both sides is their risk appetite for the credit risk of the other. In a money-free system, no transaction can take place where the resulting transaction would involve one person assuming a credit exposure to the other which exceeded their risk tolerance.[43] At its best, this would result in an economy in which the maximum possible transaction volume was significantly lower than the total credit risk appetite of the participants in that economy.

### 3.3.4 Money as the vehicle for credit risk transfer

3.47 In our pig/egg example, if the pig supplier does deal with his egg problem by borrowing money from a moneylender, the total amount of credit exposure in the economy has not changed—all that has happened is that the credit risk of the pig farmer is being borne by the moneylender rather than the egg supplier. It should be emphasised at this point that what the moneylender is doing is taking a risk for a price. Moneylenders are traders in credit risk, and their fundamental business proposition is exactly that of a bookmaker or an insurance company—that is, the amount they receive for taking on a portfolio of risks will exceed the losses resulting from the crystallisation of some of those risks. Thus, economically the pig supplier has paid a third party to do two things—to accept the ultimate risk of his own economic failure, and to enable him to continue to eat eggs for breakfast. This is because the risk has been transferred from the egg supplier to the moneylender. Why is this an improvement? Because the egg supplier is absolutely constrained by his risk appetite for one highly idiosyncratic risk, which probably exceeds both his total risk appetite and his risk appetite for that particular exposure. The moneylender, by contrast, has a diversified portfolio of risks and is—like all financiers—a credit trader. His business is taking credit risk for reward. This means both that he is likely to be a more efficient supplier of credit risk capacity to the economy than individual traders, and that his business has the capacity to move credit risk around the economy such that the aggregate appetite for credit risk in the system is matched as efficiently as possible with the demand for credit in the system.

---

[43] If this idea is plugged into the cash-in-advance constraint, what you end up with is a cash-plus-private-credit-appetite-constraint. Sadly, since credit appetite is arguably unmodellable this is no practical use to economists.

### 3.3.5 Credit risk transfer as the foundation for lending banking

This point—that transferability of credit exposures facilitates specialist credit trading—is an important one. One of the features of credit as an asset class is that it benefits substantially from diversification—for example, credit card debts are famously less likely to be repaid on time than any other form of debt, but securitisation vehicles issuing bonds backed by credit card receivables can obtain very high credit ratings for those bonds because the high levels of diversification lead to relatively predictable default levels and therefore to a highly stable asset type. If participants in an economy can transfer their debts to a specialist debt trader, and the specialist debt trader can construct a properly diversified portfolio, then the cost of credit provision by that credit trader will be substantially lower than the perceived cost to the participants of the risk that they face. Thus, the magic of portfolio theory can operate to create economic structures which demonstrably benefit all parties.

3.48

### 3.3.6 Risk transfer and risk pooling

It seems reasonably clear that the mutualisation and pooling of risks, although technically a zero-sum game at the level of the economy as a whole, can significantly increase the level of exposure which any particular trader can maintain. The origin of clearing in the commodities markets was fundamentally that traders in goods wished to carry exposure to the volatility of forward prices in those goods, but did not wish to carry credit exposure to individual counterparties, and the reduction of their exposure to the latter enabled them to take on more exposure to the former. This is why North argues that the development of marine insurance in the fifteenth century was a major driver of the increase in seaborne trade by converting uncertainty into risk.[44] Interestingly, this is not a simple argument about risk transference. The Romans had a form of contract (*fenus nauticum*) equivalent to a modern bottomry loan[45] under which the borrower borrowed on the security of a ship or its cargo, but did not have to repay if the ship was lost. This was equivalent to marine insurance for the borrower, but had no risk-reducing element, since it merely transferred risk from one person to another. It is only where risks are pooled and allocated between a large number of co-insurers that there is any real possibility of converting uncertainty into manageable risk.[46] The same is true for banks engaged in the credit business.

3.49

### 3.3.7 Virtual currency as a risk transfer mechanic

The question which arises from the foregoing is simply one of whether a virtual currency token could perform the credit risk management and allocation function

3.50

---

[44] North, *Understanding the Process of Economic Change* (Princeton University Press 2005) at 17.
[45] Although bottomry transactions are undertaken today, it is unfair to describe them as modern—they appear in the Code of Hammurabi.
[46] Our Roman forebears were well aware of this. We know that Cato the elder tried to organise what appears to be the first marine underwriting syndicate that we know of by arranging a consortium of lenders to take on fifty loans of this kind collectively—Plutarch, Vitae, Cato Maior 21, 5–7.

described above in the same way that that function is performed by other kinds of money. The answer is straightforward—there is no reason why it could not, *provided that it was regarded as money.* As we shall see in later chapters, the function of transferring credit risk can only be performed by an instrument which extinguishes that risk – giving security from a debt is a different thing from extinguishing it. Transfer of an obligation can only be effected by an extinction of the obligation to the transferor obligor. However, if virtual currency is accepted by a creditor in extinction of the obligation due to him, then the risk concerned has been effectively transferred.

# 4

# Money and Value

| | |
|---|---|
| 4.1 Thing Value versus Money Value | 4.02 |
|     4.1.1 Intertemporal reallocation of value | 4.04 |
|     4.1.2 Commercial bank money as a store of value | 4.09 |
| 4.2 Other Theories of Money Value | 4.11 |
| 4.3 Metallism | 4.13 |
|     4.3.1 Gresham's law | 4.16 |
|     4.3.2 Explaining metallic coin | 4.19 |
|     4.3.3 Metallic coin and international trade | 4.24 |
|     4.3.4 Why maintain the metal content of coins? | 4.26 |
|     4.3.5 Metal content as a constraint on money creation | 4.28 |
| 4.4 Money as a Claim on Government | 4.30 |
|     4.4.1 Central banknotes and government bonds | 4.31 |
|     4.4.2 Is money a credit claim? | 4.34 |
|     4.4.3 Private banknotes | 4.36 |
|     4.4.4 Private banknotes backed by assets | 4.37 |
|     4.4.5 Central banknotes | 4.38 |
|     4.4.6 Central bank money | 4.41 |
| 4.5 Money as a Risk-free Asset | 4.42 |
|     4.5.1 Information insensitivity of money | 4.47 |
|     4.5.2 The unit of value as risk-free | 4.53 |
|     4.5.3 The riskiness of near-money | 4.55 |
|     4.5.4 The riskiness of virtual currency | 4.56 |

As noted in chapter 1, the characteristics which are sometimes said to define money—a unit of account, a medium of exchange, and a store of value—are all phenomena of the fundamental attribute of money—that it is something *which is perceived as having value*. It should be reasonably clear that something which was not perceived as having value would by definition have none of these characteristics. However, assessing the value of money per se is a difficult exercise—it is in some respects akin to asking how long is a yard. Nonetheless, if we are to address our core question of whether and to what extent virtual currency can be said to be money, we need to understand what it is that gives fiat money value so that we can answer the question of whether virtual currency can be said to be valuable in the same way.

## 4.1 Thing Value versus Money Value

4.02 An interesting approach to this topic is to ask what the criterion of a 'store of value' is doing amongst the three traditional indicia. Of all of the three, it is the one which is least unique—indeed almost any commodity can function as a store of value. However, this may be to underappreciate one of the most important aspects of money. Other things—gold bars, real estate, diamonds—are regarded as valuable because they appear to have an intrinsic value. The owner looks at them and thinks 'there is a market for gold in which the price is $x per ounce, I have a bar of gold weighing 400 ounces, therefore the value stored in the bar is $400x'. However, money is not like this—there is no external market for money in which it is valued relative to something else. Its value is purely socially determined.

4.03 However, if we think of a debt, it is immediately clear that a debt *is* capable of being a store of value—if I owe you £100 on terms that I will pay you whenever you ask for payment, for as long as I remain solvent what you own is about as good a store of value as it is possible to get, since it has no carrying or safeguarding costs, is capable of being immediately converted into currency for a known value, and does not deteriorate over time. But all of these characteristics are equally true of both physical money and credit money. This takes us to the conclusion that if a debt is a store of value to the extent that it can immediately be converted into money at a point in the future, money is equally a store of value to the extent that it will already be money at that same point in the future. What makes money a store of value is the belief that it will have value at the time in the future when it is sought to release its value—or, put another way, if other things are potentially stores of value to the extent that they can be converted into money in the future, money is a store of value to the extent that it can be converted into other things in the future.

### 4.1.1 Intertemporal reallocation of value

4.04 It is this characteristic of money—to give an entitlement today to obtain something tomorrow—which is most important to economists. As Keynes observes: 'The importance of money essentially flows from its being a link between the present and the future.'[1] Further, it is the point where money ceases to serve as a useful store of value (e.g. in periods of high inflation) that its social usefulness ceases.

4.05 Jevons realised that this function might be the oldest of the three functions of money, pointing out that the use of gold in the Homeric period preceded by some time the development of any other aspect of monetary character,[2] and Menger admitted that hoarding must have preceded money.[3] Also, there are multiple

---

[1] *The General Theory of Employment, Interest and Money* (1936, Cambridge University Press 2013) at 293.
[2] Jevons, *Money and the Mechanism of Exchange* (Appleton & Co. 1896) at 16.
[3] Ibid. at 55.

instances in historic and prehistoric evidence of prestige articles being accumulated as stores of value by chiefs and others before those articles acquire any monetary function.[4]

Interestingly, in order to perform this function, the primary characteristic which any token requires is a degree of permanence—and we do observe that across societies the items used as money tend to have that characteristic. However, it is also notable that one of the advantages of bank money over physical money is the complete absence of deterioration risk—assuming, of course, the continuation of the bank. It may well be that virtual currencies—at least in their cybercurrency form—may provide a higher level of comfort in this regard even than traditional bank balances. A distributed ledger is in theory immortal.  4.06

It should, however, be remembered that money can lose this characteristic without ceasing to function as money. In high inflation economies, it is not uncommon for sellers of goods who cannot immediately acquire what they need to take the money received from the sale and immediately use it to purchase some reasonably liquid commodity (frequently cigarettes) which will be relied upon to hold value until the desired commodity becomes available for sale. At that point, the cigarettes will be sold and the resulting currency applied in the purchase of the commodity, the assumption being that the relative values of the commodity and the cigarettes will have remained relatively constant regardless of the movements of the relevant currency.  4.07

It is therefore clear that the store of value criterion remains both useful and relevant. However, where it becomes interesting is at the point where we drag it out of its comfortable residence amongst the gold coins of the 1930s and bring it into the present day.  4.08

### 4.1.2 Commercial bank money as a store of value

It is absolutely clear that the commercial bank money today performs the function of a store of value perfectly well—people hold substantial parts of their personal savings in bank deposit accounts, and for the vast majority of citizens the bank is by definition the place where they keep money in the period between the time when they receive it and the time when they require it. However, unlike the gold coins of the gold standard era, modern money has no commodity value at all. This is particularly true if we consider the fully imaginary money which constitutes the conceptual underpinning of the individual bank account (or even for that matter central bank money in the form of deposits maintained with the central bank), but it is equally true of the circulating notes and coins of today, whose intrinsic value is no greater than that of medieval wooden tallies.  4.09

Since modern circulating money has no intrinsic value, the value which it has must therefore be extrinsic. This raises the question of what we mean by value.  4.10

---

[4] Einzig gives the example of African chiefs, who accumulated ivory even before it became a medium of exchange following the appearance of European traders in Africa.

Even if we disregard Marxist labour theory of value (which is clearly inapplicable to modern money, let alone virtual currencies), it is clear that the question of whether money can be said to 'have a value' can only be answered in Austrian terms—that is, that its value is determined not by any inherent property of the good, nor by the amount of labour necessary to produce the good, but is determined instead by the importance an acting individual places on a good for the achievement of his desired ends.[5] Put simply, modern money is worth solely what you think others will give you for it.

## 4.2 Other Theories of Money Value

4.11 It must be acknowledged at this point that this argument is not universally accepted. In particular, there are two alternative schools of thought which would reject it out of hand. One of these it the metallist school, which in general believes that money derives its value from its intrinsic worth. The other is the 'governmentalist' school, which maintains that money is a 'claim' on government, and therefore has an intrinsic value independent of its acceptability as a payment mechanism. The 'metallist' position can be best summarised as that the origins of money lie in its physical value; that it is because money at some point in the past had a real value that it continues to be treated as if it still had a value through social convention. This argument is sometimes unkindly summarised as the belief that people are so stupid that they do not realise that the gold standard has gone. Those holding this belief frequently also believe that it is only a matter of time before the current experiment with non-metal-backed currency ends in failure, and society reverts to gold as the proper basis for a monetary system.[6] The other—governmentalist—position is based on the idea the idea that modern money is 'backed' by a promise to pay, either from a central bank or from the issuing sovereign, and that this promise makes sovereign money qualitatively different from currency units which have no such backing. It should be emphasised that there is a distinction here between value created by a government's readiness to accept its currency in payment for obligations—which is uncontroversial—and value created by the exercise of governmental power to order that its currency be accepted by others. It is the latter which is the essence of the governmentalist position as discussed here. Modern governmentalists tend to argue that the performance of the central bank function is part of the function of a currency, such that nothing which is not operated by a central bank can properly be described as money.[7]

4.12   We shall consider both of these positions in turn.

---

[5] Menger, *Principles of Economics* (Institute for Humane Studies 1976) at 120.
[6] Although to be fair there are a number of other candidates for this role—the Petro, a cryptocurrency launched by the government of Venezuela in February 2018, purports to be backed by oil.
[7] Sáinz de Vicuña, *An Institutional Theory of Money* in Mario Giovanoli and Diego Devos (eds), *International Money and Financial Law: The Global Crisis* (OUP 2010).

## 4.3 Metallism

The validity of metallism today depends on its validity yesterday—that is, in order for it to be a useful concept, it is necessary to show that throughout the period of human history when money had a significant metal content, that metal content was directly relevant to the value of that money.   4.13

As the owner of a precious metal coin, what difference does the metal value of that coin make to me? Clearly, if it has an intrinsic value of more than its face value it will remain in circulation as a coin for no longer than it takes for its holder to discover that fact. Consequently, we can disregard the class of coins whose intrinsic value is higher than their face value. The question is therefore in principle how much I, as the holder of the coin, care whether its intrinsic value is 60 per cent of its face value, 40 per cent of its face value, or nothing at all. The answer is that I should be utterly indifferent to this fact—as indeed I am likely to be.   4.14

Where this becomes more complex is if we imagine an economy with two types of coins in circulation, one with a metal value of 60 per cent of its face value and one with a value of 40 per cent of its face value. Conventional wisdom says that in this circumstance Gresham's law[8] will operate—that is, that *ceteris paribus* people will prefer the coin with the higher monetary value, that these coins will therefore disappear into hoards, and the economy will be left with only the lower value coins. If this could be shown to have occurred, it would be a good indicator that some significance was attached to the metal content of the coin.   4.15

### 4.3.1 Gresham's law

The problem is that it did not. A basic application of Gresham's law based on metal content of coin is not even remotely consonant with actual historical experience. In this regard, the monetary history of the United States provides a magnificent set of experimental results.[9] What we discover is that there is relatively little differentiation between coins where the metal content of both coins is at a discount to face value. If I have one dollar with an intrinsic metal value of 70 per cent of its face value and another with an intrinsic metal value of 50 per cent of its face value, I am only very weakly incentivised to hoard one rather than the other—my primary utility for both of them will be in transactions. We also see the reverse happening—where a coin is created whose metal value is in excess of its face value, one possibility is simply that it circulates at a value above its face value. This was the experience as regards the   4.16

---

[8] The law was named in 1860 by Henry Dunning Macleod (The Elements of Banking, Longmans 1858), after Sir Thomas Gresham (1519–79). However, it was a discovery, not an invention: it was stated by Nicolaus Copernicus in the fourteenth century; by Oresme (*c*.1350) in his treatise *On the Origin, Nature, Law, and Alterations of Money;* by jurist and historian Al-Maqrizi (1364–1442) in the Mamluk Empire; and alluded to by Aristophanes in his play *The Frogs*, which dates from around the end of the fifth century BC.
[9] See Rolnick and Weber, *Gresham's Law or Gresham's Fallacy?*, Journal of Political Economy, Vol. 94, No. 1 (February 1986) at 185–99.

English golden guinea in the seventeenth century—minted with a nominal value of 20s (and accepted in tax for only that 20s value), it immediately circulated at a value of 21s, going as high as 30s before settling at 21s. However, it was not 'driven out', but continued to circulate.[10]

4.17 The true statement of Gresham's law in this regard is that bad money drives out good only where there is a positive cost to the holder in using good money—that is, if the holder were to seek to spend the good money, he would suffer a detriment compared with some other use to which he could put it. This is most likely to happen where: (a) a coin has significant inherent value over and above its nominal value; (b) there is some way of realising that value (e.g. by melting it down) which is not itself costly; and (c) people generally are not prepared to accept the coin at its commodity value. Interestingly, this is most likely to happen as regards a coin-based economy with small-denomination coins, since the smaller the denomination of the coin the more likely it is that the commodity value of the metal composing it will exceed the notional value of the coin.[11] However, the fact that 240 pennies, melted down, would yield 245-pence worth of copper is unlikely to render the melting down an attractive proposition, and it is only where the money premium becomes significant that Gresham's law will operate in its traditional sense.

4.18 What follows from all of this is that even where coins have a valuable metallic component, that valuable component does not appear to be particularly determinative of the way in which they are actually used.

### 4.3.2 Explaining metallic coin

4.19 This conclusion, however, is strongly resisted by metallists on what appear to be rigorously logical grounds. If it is true that users of a currency are indifferent to its metal content, then sovereigns who create metal currency are simply picking their own pockets. In order to sustain the argument that metal content is almost completely irrelevant to coin in circulation, it is necessary to produce a convincing explanation of why it came to have a metal content in the first place, and why this apparently futile policy continued for as long as it did.

4.20 The answer to this is to be found in the fact that money has traditionally operated in two distinct spheres. One is within the national economy. The other is as a medium for international trade. In a completely closed economy, it is highly arguable that money can very rapidly be converted into valueless specie, and indeed this is exactly how Goetzman argues that paper currency was so rapidly introduced in China.[12] However, autarky was never an option in Europe, where at all times and in all places trade has been with people outside a country as well as people inside it.

4.21 It is important to note that the term 'country' for this purpose should be read to mean 'currency area'—for these purposes country A is simply the area in which currency A is produced, and where it is accepted in payment. There may be many

---

[10] See ibid. at 191.
[11] See Sargent and Velde, *The Big Problem of Small Change* (Princeton University Press 2002).
[12] Goetzmann, *Money Changes Everything* (Princeton University Press 2016).

currency areas in a country—for example, as Schnabel and Shin set out,[13] trade in the Holy Roman Empire in the seventeenth century was largely 'international', in that it took place in an environment in which large numbers of regional rulers had and exercised the right to mint their own coins. Thus, the Empire was composed of a large number of currency areas, and any trade between those areas was 'international' for this purpose. This has the interesting consequence that where a territory which was fragmented into different currency areas is consolidated into a single currency area under a single authority, trade that was previously 'international' for this purpose becomes domestic. Thus, the transition in France in the thirteenth and fourteenth centuries from local lords' mints to royal mints made France into a single currency area. Interestingly, it also significantly increased the power of the crown to debase the currency and derive revenue from such debasement.[14]

4.22 Using a national coin in international trade poses a whole new set of problems. For one thing, my trading counterparties in other countries are unlikely to have tax obligations to my sovereign, the issuer of my coins. Consequently, the utility of my coins to them is much reduced—indeed their only immediate usefulness to them is if they need to buy things from people in my territory. However, given that we are by definition talking about merchants engaged in cross-border trade, the fact that a thing has a determined value in a particular territory is itself a potential source of profit, so the debate between buyer and seller is likely to turn on exchange rates rather than acceptability, provided the economic future of the sovereign issuing the relevant coins remains reasonably assured.

4.23 It is these last few words which catch the justification for metal currency. For most of recorded history the survival of the particular issuing authority of any particular currency was anything but assured. Consequently, a merchant in country A, dealing with counterparties in countries B and C, would deal for choice with those who paid in currency which had some other merit, such that if it was repudiated or devalued by its issuer, it might have some secondary use. The easiest way of achieving this outcome is to give money a precious metal content.

### 4.3.3 Metallic coin and international trade

4.24 Consequently, metal currency is predominantly a phenomenon of international trade. Goetzman demonstrates that the sequence of events appears to have been that trading based on silver ingots was replaced by trading based on coin with a silver value.[15] It is entirely possible that early international trade went through a period where 'coins' really were simply small pieces of precious metal with a stamp which

---

[13] Schnabel and Shin, *Money and Trust: Lessons from the 1620s for the Digital Age* (BIS February 2018) Working Paper No. 698.
[14] Sussman, *Debasements, Royal Revenues and Inflation in France During the Hundred Years War, 1415–1422*, Journal of Economic History (March 1993) 53(1) 44-70.
[15] Goetzman, *Money Changes Everything: How Finance Made Civilisation Possible* (Princeton University Press 2016) at 63. Athens is the prime exemplar of this last point—it used silver to import goods (ibid. at 88).

indicated their weight.[16] However, by the time we get to classical Athens it seems clear that even in international trade money was circulating exclusively by tale.[17]

4.25 It is interesting to pause here and think what the world looked like to the classical Athenians. Athens itself has relatively few exports, but what it did have was the enormous silver mine at Lavrion, whose output it used to purchase wheat and other necessities. The fact that even as early as the fifth century BC silver was an established medium of exchange in international trade meant that they had something to sell, and it was a matter of the most obvious logic to mint this silver into the tetradrachm 'owl' coin. Once these were created in sufficiently large quantities, they appear to have circulated widely outside Athens, and to have become in many respects the basic payment mechanism for trade over a wide area. We have no idea what the value of a tetradrachm was in relation to its metal weight, but it would be very surprising if the coins had not circulated at some premium to their metal content, and that premium in turn would have been pure profit to the Athenian treasury in respect of those coins which did not return to Athens.

### 4.3.4 Why maintain the metal content of coins?

4.26 Why might the Athenians not have sought to increase their minting profits by reducing the precious metal component of the currency? The answer is precisely because Athens was creating a currency for use in international trade, and not one for purely domestic use. Imagine a sovereign issuing currency with a precious metal value of 60 per cent of its unit value. Every unit of that currency which circulates outside the territory is effectively a pure profit of 40 per cent of the currency value to the sovereign, since it will by definition not be presented in payment of tax. Imagine, however, that the sovereign of the next-door country creates a currency whose precious metal value is 70 per cent of its unit value. *Ceteris paribus*, third country merchants will tend to deal with merchants in that other country, since their payment will be the same in nominal value, but their security will be greater. The government of the next-door country will of course suffer in terms of the loss of seignorage, but may well gain in terms of their total tax take. This creates a 'race to the top' amongst governments, who eventually produce a coin with a sufficiently high value to be acceptable amongst those who are not their taxpayers. In a perfect world, of course, government would simply produce two types of coin—a full-bodied coin for international trade and a nearly worthless coin for use in internal payments. Sadly, however, this is not possible—international trade and national trade are two sides of the same coin; no one having ever imported goods except with the intention of selling or using them domestically. Thus, governments have found themselves forced to create coins

---

[16] This appears to have been the position of early Lydian coins of the seventh century BC. However, although these were made to precise weights, the nature of electrum meant that the weights did not necessarily tell the holder what he needed to know about the intrinsic metal content, and therefore the commodity value, of the coin. Consequently, even here it is hard to see that metal content was the determining factor of value.

[17] Schaps, *The Invention of Coinage and the Monetization of Ancient Greece* (University of Michigan Press 2004).

whose value is equal to an international standard simply through a desire to enhance trade. A trading nation requires a strong international currency.

The function of facilitating payment in international trade transitioned over time from silver to gold. In general, gold is too highly valued to be of much use in day-to-day transactions, and the only real use for gold coins is in high-value and international trade.[18] As Keynes pointed out, even in the era of the gold standard there was no country for which gold formed the whole, or even a significant part, of its internal circulating currency. 'Gold is an international, but not a local currency. The currency problem of each country is to ensure that they shall run no risk of being unable to put their hands on international currency when they need it, and to waste as small a proportion of their resources on holdings of actual gold as is compatible with this'.[19]

### 4.3.5 Metal content as a constraint on money creation

We have said a great deal about the reasons why the precious metal content of coins does not determine their value. However, for large tranches of history, the maintenance of high levels of precious metals within the national coinage has been regarded as a benefit in its own right and a duty of kings.[20] Why was this believed? The answer to this can be most clearly seen in the work of Nicolaus Copernicus.[21] This is largely because he had had personal experience of it as an administrator in the province of Ermland in the early sixteenth century. The province was on the periphery of the wars between the Teutonic Knights and the Kings of Poland, in which all sides sought to increase their financial resources by increasing their output of coins and therefore debasing their currencies. The result was economic and social distress.[22] Copernicus's treatise is therefore an early but perfect statement of the social and economic case against monetary inflation. However, because he correctly perceived that the cause of the inflation was the increase in the volume of coins circulating, and that this had been caused by the debasement of the currency, his proposed remedy was the reinstatement of the currency at a minimum metal content standard for coins. This is the case for a gold standard, and it is a respectable case. In discussing the return of the UK to the gold standard after the Napoleonic wars, Schumpeter summed up the position perfectly:

At present we are taught to look upon such policy as wholly erroneous—as a sort of fetishism that is impervious to rational argument. We are also taught to discount all rational and all

---

[18] Thus, for example, Copernicus's main complaint about the debasement of the Prussian coinage in the early sixteenth century is that this will stop *foreign* trade. See Copernicus, *Monetae Cudendae Ratio: On the Evils of Inflation and the Establishment of a Sound Currency*, trans. Taylor, Journal of the History of Ideas, Vol. 16 (1526) at 540–7.
[19] Keynes, *Indian Currency and Finance* (1913, Cambridge University Press 2013) at 21.
[20] Elisabeth's recoinage, Spain.
[21] Copernicus, *Monetae Cudendae Ratio: On the Evils of Inflation and the Establishment of a Sound Currency*, trans. Taylor, Journal of the History of Ideas, Vol. 16 (1526).
[22] Interestingly Copernicus's final report, delivered to King Sigismund I of Poland in 1526, formed the basis of the monetary union of Poland and Prussia in 1528.

purely economic arguments which may actually be adduced in favour of it. But ... there is one point about the gold standard which would redeem it from the charge of foolhardiness, even in the absence of any purely economic advantage ... An 'automatic' gold currency is part and parcel of a laissez-faire and free trade economy ... It links every nation's money rates and price levels with the money rates and price levels of all the other nations that are 'on gold'. It is extremely sensitive to government expenditure and even to attitudes or policies that do not involve expenditure directly, for example, to foreign policy, to certain policies of taxation and, in general, to precisely all those policies that violate the principles of economic liberalism. *This* is the reason why gold is so unpopular now, and why it was so popular in the bourgeois era. It imposes restrictions upon governments or bureaucracies which are much more powerful than parliamentary criticism. It is both the badge and the guarantee of bourgeois freedom.

This passage explains more or less perfectly why support for the gold standard has been so deep, so firm, and has endured for so many centuries. It is arguably one of the formative economic factors of the modern age. But it has nothing to do with the value of money per se.

4.29    The key point of all of this is that even where coins have had high metal content, and even where they are 'full-bodied', the metal content is not the thing which gave the coin its value. There have been instances where coin is simply stamped bullion, with the stamp being no more than a certification of the gold content of the coin. However, the vast majority of precious metal coins seem to have worked the other way around—for example, Keynes described the silver currency circulating in India as simply a token which happened to be stamped on silver rather than paper.[23]

## 4.4  Money as a Claim on Government

4.30    The idea that money derives its value from sovereign backing is one which is commonly held but possibly not widely understood. The paradox of English banknotes, which bear on their face the legend that the Bank of England promises to pay the bearer on demand the face value of the note, has caused generations of children to speculate as to in what medium the bank might discharge that obligation. The explanation that the owner of a £10 note has the right to take it to the Bank of England and have it exchanged for another £10 note does not always provide complete enlightenment in such cases. This does usefully demonstrate that the idea that currency is 'backed' by the undertakings of its issuer is not a substantial contributor to its value.

### 4.4.1  Central banknotes and government bonds

4.31    Another way to approach this question is to ask what the difference is between a government-issued note and a government bond. These two instruments appear to have

---

[23] Keynes, *Indian Currency and Finance* (1913, Cambridge University Press 2013) at 26.

different legal characteristics but the same economic essence. More importantly, no one would dispute that the value of a government bond is established precisely by reference to the credit claim which it embodies on the government which issues it. Is the same true of its money?

In principle, the answer is clear. When a government bond matures, the holder of the bond surrenders it to the government in exchange for payment—in other words, he surrenders one written promise of payment by a person in exchange for another promise of payment of the same amount by the same person. Structurally, a government bond and a banknote are nearly identical. In principle, the difference between a central bank issued note and a government bond are: (a) the government bond (sometimes) pays interest; (b) the government bond has a maturity date, prior to which it can only be converted into currency through sale to a third party; and (c) the note is, but the bond is not, designated by law as legal tender. However, all of these characteristics are contestable. Short-term government paper generally does not carry a yield, almost all government paper can be immediately exchanged for currency with the relevant central bank (albeit at a cost), in the financial markets it is common to satisfy an obligation by the transfer of high-quality government paper in settlement of obligations, and we are satisfied that legal tender status is irrelevant to monetary status. Thus, there is no necessary difference between the two in law—and yet, in the marketplace, there is. 4.32

Given this difference of treatment, it seems to be a necessary conclusion that the mere fact that an instrument is a credit claim on a government is not of itself sufficient to make that instrument money. Even if a supporter of the governmentalist position wishes to argue that only claims on government can constitute money, he cannot reasonably argue that the fact that an instrument embodies a claim on government is of itself sufficient to make that thing money. Something more is clearly needed. However, before we get to that point it is necessary to as to what extent it is reasonable to regard sovereign money as a credit claim at all? 4.33

### 4.4.2 Is money a credit claim?

Consider a spectrum of money instruments ranging from coins at one end to central bank notes at the other. It seems quite clear that the coin does not represent a credit claim on anyone—it is a mere token, created for the purpose of circulation, and whose value is derived from its social acceptability and its potential utility for discharging tax obligations. What is the position of the banknotes? 4.34

Banknotes occur in three forms—private banknotes, private banknotes backed by holdings of public debt, and public banknotes.[24] These are used to different extents in different ways, but the primary function of all of them is to substitute for the 4.35

---

[24] There are some examples of governments issuing notes directly—US treasury greenbacks in the nineteenth century and the original UK £1 and 10 shilling notes issued during the First World War are examples—but in general governments choose to issue notes through central banks, so we shall assume for this purpose that when we speak of legal tender we mean central-bank-issued notes.

'token' function of coinage. They are transaction media, not investment media—in other words their value to their holder is what they can be used for tomorrow, not what they may eventually be valued at when redeemed.[25]

### 4.4.3 Private banknotes

4.36   If we start with private banknotes, these are clearly credit claims on the banks which create them. There are broadly three things which a depositor of cash with a bank can do with the deposit. First, he can withdraw it in cash. Second, he can draw on the bank with a cheque, negotiable instrument, or similar instrument. Third, he can obtain a banknote—basically an IOU issued by the bank—which he hopes will be accepted in payment on delivery. In the first two of these cases, it is reasonably clear that what is being created is a credit claim on the bank. In the third case, the transaction is a purchase of tokens rather than the creation of a credit claim.

### 4.4.4 Private banknotes backed by assets

4.37   An intermediate case arises when a private bank creates private notes which are explicitly backed by government assets. This is a very common form of banknote creation. It was most commonly encountered in the United States during the free banking era. During this period, although there was no licence required to open a bank or engage in banknote issuance, the law in almost all states remained that anyone who engaged in the business of banknote creation was required to hold a balance of bonds (mostly bonds issued by the state of incorporation of the bank) equal to the value of notes issued.[26] This architecture is also still in existence in the United Kingdom, where the Scottish[27] and Northern Irish[28] banks are permitted to issue their own banknotes provided that they hold an equivalent value of UK government central bank money.[29] Notes of this kind are genuine hybrids—in effect, the bank is repackaging government claims, and although the bank clearly does have a claim on the government concerned in respect of the assets that it holds, it is by no means clear that this fact is of any relevance as regards the holders of the notes which it has issued.

---

[25] For this purpose, by 'redeemed' I mean surrendered back to their original issuer in settlement of claims by that issuer.

[26] This explains, amongst other things, why default concentration in that era was closely correlated with the creditworthiness of the relevant state—states whose bonds depreciated tended to bankrupt their banks. The same phenomenon was clearly visible in the Eurozone crisis of 2012, suggesting that there really is nothing new under this particular sun.

[27] Royal Bank of Scotland, Bank of Scotland, and Clydesdale.

[28] Bank of Ireland, AIB Group (trades as First Trust Bank in Northern Ireland), Northern Bank (trades as Danske Bank), and Ulster Bank.

[29] See Part 6 of the Banking Act 2009 and rules and orders made thereunder for the regime relating to Scottish banknotes. Interestingly, Scottish banknotes are not legal tender either in England or in Scotland.

### 4.4.5 Central banknotes

This takes us to the even harder case of the typical central bank. A central banknote 4.38
issuer is in this regard in the same position as the private banknote issuer. Legally, the
position is very straightforward—in order to qualify as currency, a note must be issued by the Bank of England and expressed to be payable to the bearer on demand,[30]
and it will therefore constitute a promissory note under the Bills of Exchange Act
1882,[31] and there is little doubt that in theory a promissory note creates a credit obligation. However, this takes us to the paradox which lies at the heart of a Bank of
England note. It unquestionably does bear a promise to pay the bearer on demand,
but what is it that it promises to pay? If a customer went into the Bank of England,
handed a £10 note over the counter and demanded payment, the bank would discharge its obligation by handing him the same £10 note back again. It seems relatively clear that if this is a credit obligation, it is a credit obligation of a unique kind.
The better view is therefore that it is probably wrong to describe such instruments as
credit instruments in any meaningful sense of the word.

What, then—if anything—is the difference between a note issued by the Bank 4.39
of England and a note issued by a private bank (or, for that matter, an IOU issued
by a private citizen)? Once more, in order to answer this question, we have to leave
the realms of legal theory and enter the realm of human behaviour. In this lower
realm, the question has a very simple answer—there is none. The reason a bank
customer gives money to a bank in exchange for a banknote is precisely because he
wishes to obtain an instrument which he expects to use for the purposes of payment of debts by physical delivery. A purchaser of banknotes does not see himself
as purchasing credit claims against the bank, and a bank selling banknotes does not
perceive itself as granting credit to the purchaser (although it is creating a future
liability for itself). Here again, we have a distinction which is purposive rather than
conceptual, to the extent that it is the intention of the parties which gives character
to the transaction.

If we apply this test to notes issued by a central bank, it gives us a very clear answer 4.40
to our question. Central banknotes are created to function as tokens, and are universally treated as such. It is simply wrong to think of them as credit claims on anyone.
In this regard, they differ fundamentally from government bonds, which are almost
never used as tokens.[32] What the central bank does, and what private note issuers
generally do, is to sell tokens and invest the proceeds in the purchase of credit claims
on the relevant sovereign authority. The fact that the notes are in effect a repackaging
of those claims is irrelevant to the question of whether or not the notes themselves
constitute credit claims.

---

[30] Currency and Bank Notes Act 1954, ss. 1(2) and 3.
[31] Gleeson (ed.), *Chalmers & Guest on Bills of Exchange and Cheques* (18th edn, Sweet & Maxwell 2016) at 15-025.
[32] 'Almost' because there are some specialist areas of wholesale financing where it is conventional to deliver government bonds instead of cash in settlement of obligations. See Singh, *Collateral and Financial Plumbing* (2nd edn, Risk Books 2016) for a detailed account of the use of bonds as money for this purpose.

### 4.4.6 Central bank money

4.41 There is one final class of central bank money which must be considered, since it forms the vast majority of that commodity. This is the class of deposits held with the central bank. In general, central banks do not permit anyone other than other banks[33] to hold deposits with them, so these deposits are in practice the money with which the banking system settles its debts. Unlike banknotes, central bank deposits clearly are credit claims on the central bank, and function in the same way as any other form of money. Central bank deposits are in practice almost indistinguishable from government bonds—in both cases a customer gives money to a government entity and receives in return a promise of payment and may or may not receive interest on the money deposited.[34] However this also gives rise to the government bond problem that 'redemption' simply consists in exchanging one claim for another on the same person in identical terms. There is an interesting debate to be had as to whether a central bank deposit is in fact a credit claim at all, since in principle a person seeking to withdraw money from such an account would be exchanging a claim on the central bank for another claim on the same central bank, and it is arguable that a claim is only a credit claim if it is a claim for something different from itself—indeed, pursued to its logical conclusion, this line of reasoning would take us to the conclusion that a claim which is only a claim for itself is not in fact a claim at all. However once again this legal knot is unravelled by the social observation that upon the redemption of a government bond or the withdrawal of a deposit made with the central bank, the exchange is not like-for-like, since what is received is unquestionably regarded by society as money whereas what is surrendered is unquestionably not.

## 4.5 Money as a Risk-free Asset

4.42 If money is not a credit claim, then the only thing that it can be is a quasi-commodity; a store of value. This idea has been roundly criticised—Keynes pointed out that, in principle, the idea of using physical money as a store of value was absurd:

---

[33] This is not quite true—for example, the Bank of England has expanded access to its deposits to non-bank payment institutions—but the broad principle that only institutions involved in the payment system may have direct access to central bank deposits remains true in almost all jurisdictions.

[34] It is therefore possible in this regard at least to recognise that one of the fundamental premises of modern monetary theory—that there is no functional difference between issued currency and government bonds—is no more than the observable truth. Unfortunately, this observation cuts both ways, and in the same way that demand for government bonds is restricted by the credit appetite of the real economy, demand for government money is restricted in the same way. Put simply, the credit requirements of the real economy are met by endogenous credit money, and the real economy's appetite for exogenous government money will not be affected by the supply of that money. If appetite exceeds supply then there will be a shortfall, leading to extended periods of low official interest rates, and if appetite falls short of supply there will be inflation (i.e. the economy will bid down the price of government IOUs). However, appetite is the given and supply the irrelevance.

For it is a recognized characteristic of money as a store of wealth that it is barren; whereas practically every other form of storing wealth yields some interest or profit. Why should anyone outside a lunatic asylum wish to use money as a store of wealth?[35]

However, the point about money is that it derives its value from the possibility of immediate use. Ownership of government bonds is useless if you want to buy a cup of coffee—it is money, in some form or other, which you need in order to actually purchase. In the short term, therefore, money is not so much a store of value as the thing which creates the possibility of expenditure in the very near future.

4.43 As regards that immediate future, therefore, money is a useful store of short-term value, even though, as Keynes says, it may make no sense to hold it for any very long period. It should also be noted that money may be a useful store of long-term value in the absence of any better option—the coin hoards which have been found dating from every period of historic turbulence are eloquent testimony to the fact that in sufficiently adverse circumstances physical coin may be the best safe store of value available.

4.44 It should be noted at this point that this behaviour of treating actually risky assets as risk-free money has been widely observed throughout history. Writing at a time when private banknotes issued by a wide variety of banks with an equally wide variety of credit standings were in circulation, Thornton[36] made the point that these notes circulated widely and were treated by their holders as carrying their face value 'for the time during which they intend to hold it is very short, and their responsibility will cease almost as soon as they shall have parted with it'.

4.45 This observation is the key to most of the logic behind the treating of money as risk-free. Gorton observed that 'There are two ways to produce safe debt: back the debt with the government's taxing power or use collateral'[37] and many people seem to have reasoned backwards from this proposition to the argument that because money is collateralised it must be backed with the government's taxing power in order to perform its function. However, there is a third way to render an asset risk-free, and that is to reduce to zero or near-zero the expected holding period of that asset. Money, in theory, can be exchanged for anything else at any time—it is only owned in order to be spent. Thus the holders of private banknotes of whose improvidence Thornton disapproved were acting perfectly rationally in disregarding the credit risk position as regards the banknotes which they owned, because they believed that the very short holding period which they expected rendered the notes information-insensitive *to them*. The paradox which this presents – that a thing which circulates rapidly may be perceived by every one of its holders as low-risk despite the fact that the risk which it poses to them in aggregate is high-risk—is not new, and indeed is familiar to historians of sub-prime securitisation paper.

---

[35] Keynes, *The General Theory of Employment*, Quarterly Journal of Economics, Vol. 51, No. 2 (February 1937) 209–23 at 216.
[36] Thornton, *An Enquiry into the Nature and Effects of the Paper Credit of Great Britain* (1802) at 172–3.
[37] Gorton, *The History and Economics of Safe Assets* (National Bureau of Economics Research Working Paper Series 2016), Working Paper No. 22210 at 8.

4.46   It is suggested that the terms 'money' and 'risk-free asset' are in practice synonymous. The risk-free asset literature, properly regarded, can be interpreted as an analysis of which assets, in which circumstances, can be regarded as functionally indistinguishable from money. A necessary implication from that is that money, in order to be money, must itself be a risk-free asset. However, the risk-free asset literature insists (correctly) that for this purpose 'risk-free' is simply synonymous with 'information-insensitive'—if there is a piece of information which could plausibly be held by one party to a transaction in an asset but not another, and that piece of information would affect the price at which the other party would be prepared to deal, then the asset is not information-insensitive and is therefore not risk-free. This brings us to the question of the information-insensitivity of money.

### 4.5.1 Information insensitivity of money

4.47   What does it mean to say that money is a risk-free asset. One answer is that money has many of the characteristics of natural numbers—the unit of counting exists, every unit is equal to every other unit, and all units have a non-zero value.[38] However, the more important issue is that money has these characteristics across time—a pound tomorrow is confidently expected to be the same as a pound today. These characteristics are in some respects a definition of information-insensitivity.[39] This is in one respect to say no more than that money is treated as the measure of things, not as a thing in itself. It is also notable that people actively seek out things to use as money which are information insensitive—for example, Gorton argues that a preference for bank money over physical money in the era of metallic coin can be explained by reference to the fact that physical coins are not completely information insensitive, since their weight and fineness may vary and can only be established by detailed investigation.[40]

4.48   This is to some extent irrational—money can change in value, and there are well-known and recent instances of its having done so. However, the issue is not that people believe money to be information insensitive, but that information insensitivity is a necessary characteristic of anything purporting to be money. Different assets can only be priced using a common metric, and money is that metric. Since a variable measure is an inefficient measure, economic efficiency is achieved by the adoption of a social convention by which the measure is invariant. This can best be characterised as a collective agreement to treat money as an information-insensitive, or 'safe', asset.[41] Since it must be clear that it is not the sovereign which makes assets

---

[38] Mathematicians refer to these as the Peano Postulates—Peano, *Arithmetices principia, nova methodo exposita* [*The principles of arithmetic, presented by a new method*] (1889).
[39] See Holstrom, *Understanding the Role of Debt in the Financial System* (BIS January 2015) Working Paper No. 479, for the connection between risk-free asset and information insensitivity.
[40] Gorton, *The History and Economics of Safe Assets* (National Bureau of Economic Research Working Paper Series 2016) Working Paper No. 22210.
[41] There is a large economic literature on safe assets, and a burgeoning legal literature. For a useful recent contribution, see Gelpern and Gerding, *Rethinking the Law in 'Safe Assets'* in Buckley, Avgouleas, and Arner (eds), *Reconceptualising Global Finance and its Regulation* (Cambridge University Press 2016).

safe (the sovereign cannot effectively improve the quality of its own obligations,[42] in the same way that I cannot effectively guarantee my own debt), that safety must be derived from social acceptance.

4.49 There is a logic here which is impeccably Austrian. If value is simply what people will give for an asset, and the value of what they will give for it is exclusively determined (as it is with money) by their estimation of what they will get for it, then we rapidly create a self-reinforcing valuation mechanism, in which the consensus as to treatment of money as risk-free results in the money actually becoming risk-free.

4.50 The idea of money as being information-insensitive is subject to one very significant caveat. There is one piece of information which, alone and without more, can destroy any currency; that being the information that the producer of the currency is about to substantially increase the amount of currency in circulation. Currency derives its value from its relative rarity, and any increase in supply necessarily destroys its value by precisely the amount of that increase. Where the amount of that increase is not known, then the destruction of faith in the currency will be greater, and if the amount of the increase is potentially infinite, then the currency will simply cease to function at all.

4.51 This is, of course, the banner which Copernicus and Locke fought under. One of the most important functions of a metallic standard is that it limits the extent to which the sovereign can create money, and it is that very limitation which forms the basis of confidence in the currency. Locke, Newton, and other upholders of the gold standard have been subject to vitriolic criticism over the years for failing to realise that money supply should adjust itself to economic demand, and not vice versa, and that criticism is to some extent justified. However, the point which they sought to advance, that to permit an increase in the money supply without any accompanying change in the economy would result only in an increase in price levels, with accompanying dislocation costs but for no social benefit, should not be completely dismissed. Government currency has this in common with all credit claims; that if the value of the claim is expected to fall, then the value of that credit claim will fall proportionately.

4.52 It is this credit issue which seems to have led so many of the proponents of what is sometimes referred to as 'modern monetary theory' into error. Their basic proposition is that the state can order its citizens to accept its specie as payment without limit, and should therefore do so, since by that device it can expand its expenditures without borrowing. The reason that this does not work (it is not as if it has not been tried—Germany in the 1920s provides an instructive example) is that the citizen has as much concern for the credit of the state as he does for any other counterparty with whom he deals. He will accept the currency issued by the state to a certain extent, but his appetite for its credit is as limited as his appetite for any other credit, and the state's power to compel acceptance of a rapidly depreciating currency will rapidly run up against self-interest on the part of its citizens. Again, there is a fundamental

---

[42] Technically, of course, it can, by giving security over them. However, that would be a change to the form of the obligation, not a change in the value or treatment of the same obligation.

confusion here between the state as lawgiver and the state as simply the largest participant in its own economy. The acceptability of currency issued by a state is a function of the state's willingness to accept it in payment, but this is no different from the position of a mill worker in nineteenth-century Yorkshire who accepts the local mill owner's tokens in payment because he can use them to purchase goods from the mill owner's shop. He may well also be able to exchange those tokens for value with other workers in the same mill, but if the mill owner doubles the number of tokens in circulation, all those concerned will simply receive a brief (and possibly painful) reminder of the doctrine of money neutrality. The mill owner may have a monopoly of the provision of the tokens, but he cannot mandate the value at which they circulate.

### 4.5.2 The unit of value as risk-free

4.53   The key point about money in everyday use is that it is an ideal—a unit of account. If I say that I will sell a thing for £5, I am not envisaging five £1 coins, one £5 note, one virtual currency unit of the value of £5, or indeed any specific mode of payment—what I mean is that I will exchange the thing for any mechanism, howsoever constituted, which delivers to me £5 of value. In the context of sale, price must necessarily be abstract, otherwise the transaction is not sale but barter, and if price must be abstract, then the unit of price must also necessarily be abstract.[43]

4.54   In order to function as money, currency *requires* abstraction. The point here is that when a price is named, it is named in abstract rather than concrete units, and when it is discharged the units to be used must correspond to an abstract standard. In eras where adulteration or clipping have caused faith in physical currency to be reduced, a common response has been to deal through central settlement mechanisms precisely in order to avoid this issue. This is most clearly seen in the development of the deposit banks of northern Europe in the first half of the seventeenth century.[44] In a world where confidence in physical currency was being challenged by repeated debasement, the creation of these banks represented what was in effect a payment clearing house. Merchants who wished to trade with each other could trade by transferring notional currency on the books of the banks, without having to involve physical currency in the transaction. The result of this was that bank money traded at a premium to physical coins, with Adam Smith reporting that the agio, or premium, varied from 5 per cent in Amsterdam to nearly 15 per cent in Hamburg.[45] This is an interesting example of a market having a preference for an asset with no intrinsic value over an identical asset with some intrinsic value, and although some small part

---

[43] If I were to take the position that I would exchange the thing for a specific £5 note but not for any other unit of currency, the transaction would no longer be sale, but barter.

[44] Kindleberger, *Currency Debasement in the Early Seventeenth Century and the Establishment of Deposit Banks in Central Europe* in *Essays in History: Financial, Economic, Personal* (Ann Arbour, University of Michigan Press 1999).

[45] Smith (ed.), *The Wealth of Nations* (1776). For a more detailed account see Quinn and Roberds, *The Bank of Amsterdam and the Leap to Central Bank Money*, American Economic Review, Vol. 97, No. 2 (2007) at 955–78, and by the same authors *How Amsterdam Got Fiat Money*, Journal of Monetary Economics, Vol. 66(C) (2014) at 1–12.

of this premium may be attributed to ease of settlement, the vast bulk of it must be the fact that by eliminating the 'lemons' problem the deposit banks returned money, for their users, to the status of a non-information-sensitive transaction medium.[46]

### 4.5.3 The riskiness of near-money

Instruments which can easily be exchanged with a high level of confidence for money are treated as near-money. They are not money, since in general they cannot be used to discharge debts directly, but the fact that they are close substitutes means that they participate in the certainty of money status to the extent that they can confidently and easily be exchanged for a specified amount of it. This is generally most true of foreign currency circulating in an economy. A UK supplier selling goods to a US customer priced in sterling may well be prepared to accept payment in US dollars at almost exactly the nominal exchange rate, since he knows that these can be immediately exchanged for sterling. The same may be true for payment in physical gold, or a number of other types of asset—in each case, the question which he must answer is whether this particular thing is either capable of being either deployed as money (if, for example, he has US suppliers who he must pay in dollars, then this will be automatic), or of being immediately and reliably converted into something which can be immediately deployed as money. The riskiness of near-money is simply an expression of the likelihood that it cannot be either used as money or converted into money. 4.55

### 4.5.4 The riskiness of virtual currency

The problem with virtual currency for many commentators is that it does not have a taxing authority behind it. What gives a fiat currency value is not a 'promise to pay' by a central bank issuer, since the central bank has nothing to pay with except the thing that the claimant already has. What gives it its value is acceptance by a taxing authority of that thing in discharge of tax liabilities. Thus, if there is no taxing authority, virtual currency per se is deprived of the mechanism which renders sovereign currencies risk-free. 4.56

This is not, of course, an obstacle to the circulation of virtual currency as payment. There are a number of instruments in any economy which are widely accepted as currency but which cannot be used directly to discharge tax liabilities. The question for any payee in respect of any virtual currency unit will remain as it has always been—can I rely on others accepting this thing from me in payment and, if not, how easily can I convert it into something that I am certain that they will accept? 4.57

---

[46] The agio is sometimes attributed to the fact that the deposit banks took great care to ensure that only high-quality coins could be deposited with them in exchange for account credit. However, as Schnabel and Shin (*Money and Trust: Lessons from the 1620s for the Digital Age* (BIS February 2018) Working Paper No. 698) point out, this cannot be the whole story. The real benefit to customers of the arrangement was the standardisation of the unit of account—'even if the coins backing the deposits were of uncertain quality, such uncertainty affected all account holders equally and symmetrically' at 21.

His assessment of the risk that either or both of these may not be possible may be christened quasi-currency risk.

4.58 Virtual currency risk is not credit risk, and should not be confused with it. Virtual currencies do not have issuers in the way that bonds have issuers, and it is generally entirely wrong to regard a virtual currency as a credit claim on an issuer. A unit of a virtual currency, once created, is a freestanding thing which does not embody a credit claim on any other person. Equally, whereas a holder of state issued monetary units can expect to have a liability to that state which will in due course require to be discharged, there is no equivalent to this with virtual currency—the holder of virtual currency absolutely does not expect to incur a further obligation to the virtual currency issuer. Thus, virtual currency risk is currency risk in its purest form—it is simply the risk that the currency will not be accepted at its assumed value by others. This risk has more in common with market risk for traded goods than anything else—if you have bought something in order to sell it, your risk is generally not that the thing itself will deteriorate, but that the market for the thing will move significantly against you after you have bought it but before you succeed in selling it. What this does mean, however, is that information asymmetry is not a useful approach to valuing virtual currency. In general, there is no asymmetry of information about any particular virtual currency, and there is no reason why any such unit should trade in the way that a bond trades.

# 5

# The Rise of Private Payment Instruments

| | |
|---|---|
| **5.1 Private Payment and Book Credit** | 5.02 |
| 5.1.1 The shortcomings of book credit | 5.03 |
| 5.1.2 Private payment instruments | 5.04 |
| 5.1.3 Private payment instruments in the form of physical tokens | 5.05 |
| 5.1.4 Private payment instruments in the form of bills and notes | 5.07 |
| 5.1.5 Foreign currencies as private payment instruments | 5.10 |
| **5.2 Private Banknotes and Bank Cheques** | 5.11 |
| 5.2.1 Banknotes as private payment instruments | 5.13 |
| 5.2.2 Limitation of the power to create private banknotes | 5.15 |
| 5.2.3 Banknotes and cheques compared | 5.18 |
| **5.3 Virtual Currency Issued by Banks** | 5.20 |

For a surprisingly large part of the history of the United Kingdom, private monies of one form or another have circulated. However, it is important to distinguish between private money in the form of book credit and private money in the form of private tokens. Private money in the form of book credit is unquestionably older than sovereign money, and its continued existence throughout the period of existence of sovereign money should not be a surprise. Equally, private monetary tokens have at times circulated alongside sovereign money, sometimes as a supplement to it and sometimes as a substitute for it. Although it is quite clear that the long-term trend of early social development was from credit to coin, it is equally clear that from time to time this trend has gone into reverse.

## 5.1 Private Payment and Book Credit

Debts which cannot be paid in money must be paid in some other way. Historically, the primary mechanism for debt repayment amongst mutual creditors was a 'reckoning', whereby multiple obligations between parties were set off and cancelled, with only the net balance being settled[1]. Reckoning is, of course, a mechanism for

---

[1] Usually either by the delivery of cash or of a sealed bond (effectively a non-negotiable promissory note).

private payment. However, it is an extremely inefficient one, since it requires all those trading to have mutual commercial relations either with each other or at least with a single central counterparty.

### 5.1.1 The shortcomings of book credit

5.03 Mutual credit can be an effective settlement mechanism where it operates between established citizens of a particular place who are known to each other to be of good credit standing. However, that is a fairly small percentage of the population. Alternative solutions are required for the transient, impoverished, or otherwise uncreditworthy part of society. Thus, where the state did not provide public tokens, private tokens were created to fill the gap.

### 5.1.2 Private payment instruments

5.04 The simplest private token is a transferable IOU. In principle, a debt is owed to a person, and the debtor is obliged to pay that person and that person only. However, if the debtor creates an acknowledgement of a debt and promises to pay that debt to any person who presents that acknowledgement to him for payment, the acknowledgement suddenly becomes a form of payment which can be used by the creditor. This is one of the earliest and most important of the developments of financial technology, in that it enables the debtor materially increase the value of the thing which he gives to the creditor without increasing the amount which he has to pay. This particular everyday miracle is capable of being invented in many different contexts, and we would therefore expect to find payment instruments being made transferable almost as soon as we find payment instruments. This appears to be the case—as far back as AD 162 we find payment instruments circulating in Dacia which have been made transferable. The important thing about these instruments is that the mechanism used to render the instruments transferable is the addition of a six-letter abbreviation.[2] This seems strong evidence that the process was familiar and established, and probably widespread. It is also interesting that this particular note was for the sum of 240 stertius—not a large sum, and further evidence that credit money was used for the discharge of small sums as a matter of course. Of course, the relative usefulness of a transferable promissory note to the holder was primarily a function of the identity of the creditor, and a transferable note issued by a pauper was most unlikely to be of any greater value than the promise of that pauper. But a transferable note issued by a citizen known to be rich and prominent, or in military service, or otherwise easily findable, was another matter altogether. Such instruments are very likely to have circulated as payment instruments.

---

[2] E.a.q.e.r.p.—*eive ad quem ea res pertinavit*—a phrase which could loosely be translated as 'pay to bearer'. See Fontes Iuris Romani Anteiustiniani no. 122; Inscriptiones Daciae Romanae i. 35.

### 5.1.3 Private payment instruments in the form of physical tokens

The next stage on is the creation of private tokens which are not promises to pay money but simply things that can be exchanged for other things. There is no shortage of precedents for these. F. S. Jones[3] recounts the stories of manufacturers and others effectively obliged to create their own tokens with which to pay workers and suppliers due to the chronic shortage of official coinage. In eighteenth-century England, at a time when 'The mint had been deprived of copper coinage, silver coinage was dead; and gold minting was only undertaken on a small scale',[4] manufacturers, employers, and others used paper notes to pay large bills, but were forced to create metal tokens to pay workers and small creditors. Typically, these arrangements involved providing workers with tokens which could be redeemed in company shops. As Glyn Davies[5] observes:

5.05

> Because of its later abuses, the whole of the truck system has been given a bad name ... But there were legitimate and honest reasons for many of the early company shops set up in industrial areas remote from established towns and villages, and for the issue of tokens and notes by many desperate and helpful employers.

The first large-scale issue of tokens in the United Kingdom appears to have been in 1787, with the Angelsea Copper Company creating a 'penny' which could be exchanged at any of its shops or offices for money value. Davies estimates that by 1800 the total supply and circulation tokens of this kind 'very probably exceeded those of the official coin of the realm'. The boom in copper tokens in the years running up to 1800 was succeeded by a boom in silver tokens in 1811–12, which appears to have worried the government rather more, for an Act to Prevent the Issuing and Circulating of Pieces of Copper and other Metal usually called Tokens was passed in 1817.

These tokens did not enter circulation because their issuers ordered people to accept them—the issuers did not have that power. The issuers were, however, the most important economic actors in the relevant region, and as a result they were locally accepted in payment for exactly the same reason that sovereign coins were accepted in payment. There should be no doubt that these arrangements were regional—as Davies says:[6] 'The currency of most tokens was restricted to their own localities, and they were subject to an increasing discount with distance.' There can also be little doubt that the average token circulated within the territory in which the dominant economic actor was the firm which issued the token. The reason for this is reasonably straightforward—if currency is that which can be used for economic transactions, the fact that it is known that the owner of the factory shop will accept that token as payment will be enough to render the token valuable to a large number of people—especially if the factory shop is the primary or only source of necessary goods.

5.06

---

[3] *Government, Currency and County Banks in England 1770–1797* in South African Journal of Economics, Vol. 44, No. 3 (1976).
[4] Craig, *The Mint; A History of the London Mint from AD 287 to 1948* (Cambridge University Press 1953) at 255.
[5] Davies, *A History of Money* (4th edn, University of Wales Press 2016).   [6] Ibid. at 308.

### 5.1.4 Private payment instruments in the form of bills and notes

5.07 As the nineteenth century progressed, the supply of coins increased and the problem of shortage of coin abated. However, by that time the expedients which had been created to avoid the consequences of the shortage of coin had by then taken on a life of their own. We know that in the later part of that century private bills of exchange were the principal circulating medium of exchange in Lancashire[7] and Pressnell quotes a Manchester banker giving evidence to a House of Lords committee looking into the circulation of promissory notes that he had seen bills that had been indorsed by fifty or more people as they circulated: 'I have seen slips of paper attached to a bill as long as a sheet of paper could go, and when that was filled another attached to that.'[8]

5.08 Banknotes issued by private banks also featured largely in this regard. Since a banknote, unlike a bill of exchange, does not require to be endorsed when it is transferred, there is no equivalent of the list of signatures that will tell us how often banknotes were in fact transferred. However, given that the sole purpose of their creation was precisely to facilitate their rapid and reliable transfer, it does not seem unreasonable to suggest that they largely performed that function.

5.09 It should also be pointed out that the English experience in this regard is not only typical, but in many respects conservative. In the United States, President Andrew Jackson, for reasons which are still not entirely clear decided in 1833 to abolish the central bank of the United States.[9] By the 1860s, the United States had more than 8,000 different private currencies in issue, issued by everything from railroad companies to department stores, along with the thousands of different notes issued by local banks of all kinds.[10] However, it is notable that in both England and the United States, the result was a differentiation of payment instruments but not of units of account. A seller would price goods in 'US Dollars', but might then pick and choose which dollar bills from which issues he would accept as 'dollars' for this purpose.

### 5.1.5 Foreign currencies as private payment instruments

5.10 Finally, it should be noted that there was no particular rule that only instruments issued by the English sovereign could be legal tender in England. Prices in England were denominated in the units prescribed by Pepin and Offa—twelve pennies to a shilling, twenty shillings to a pound—but could be paid in a dazzling array of

---

[7] Ashton, *Bill of Exchange and Private Banks in Lancashire* in Pressnell, *Country Banking in the Industrial Revolution* (Clarendon Press 1956) at 170–80; Edwards, *The Growth of the British Cotton Trade 1780-181* (Manchester University Press 1967) at 218–19.

[8] Ashton, ibid. at 173.

[9] The generally accepted explanation is that this was because the bank sought to remain independent whilst Jackson demanded that it make advances to his political allies—see Kahan, *The Bank War: Andrew Jackson, Nicholas Biddle and the Fight for American Finance* (Westholme 2016), for a very readable account of this curious episode. However, a goodly part of the thinking behind the abolition seems to have been an idea that the more banks, the more money, and the more money, the more prosperity—see Calomiris and Haber, *Fragile by Design* (Princeton University Press 2014) Ch. 6.

[10] See Maurer, *How Would You Like to Pay?* (Duke University Press 2015) for a short and readable overview.

currency instruments. In particular, foreign coins were sometimes ascribed sterling values by royal proclamation, so that you could pay a shilling using a variety of non-English coins, each of which had a prescribed English value.[11]

## 5.2 Private Banknotes and Bank Cheques

We live in a world where private banknotes have largely disappeared, and it is therefore important to take a few moments to explain the concept. 5.11

In a survey of banks and banking undertaken in 1839, the American author George Tucker drew a distinction between Continental European banks, which he described as 'deposit banks' and Anglo–US banks, which he described as 'circulation banks'.[12] The difference, in short, was that continental deposit banks held deposits, and could be drawn on by their customers for payment. Anglo-Saxon banks, by contrast, delivered banknotes in exchange for money paid to them, and those banknotes were themselves intended to be private payment instruments. The difference between the two was not in practice as absolute as it appears, since a holder of banknotes could in theory go to the bank of issue and demand sovereign currency to the value of the banknote, in the same way that he could with a cheque. Equally, both a banknote and a cheque are transferable instruments created by a bank acknowledging the bank's indebtedness. A cheque (at least in its original incarnation[13]) is a transferable instrument drawn on a bank creating the bank's indebtedness. Viewed from this perspective, the two seem so similar as to be indistinguishable. However, there is a particular legal issue which appeared at a very early stage. A cheque does not purport to be a means of payment—it is merely a mechanism by which the holder can obtain payment from the person on whom it is drawn. A banknote, however, is intended to function as a payment mechanism in its own right. 5.12

### 5.2.1 Banknotes as private payment instruments

Early 'banknotes' were receipts issued by goldsmiths, and in some respects resembled warehouse warrants. The question of whether goldsmith's notes were in fact treated as money—that is, were accepted in final payment of the obligation in respect of which they were tendered—is surprisingly unclear. The issue was the same as that which distinguishes a banknote from a cheque; a banknote is intended to be treated as a payment instrument whose delivery extinguishes liability; a cheque is 5.13

---

[11] Thus, for example, on the accession of James I a royal proclamation was issued to the effect that the Scottish Mark should have a value of thirteen-and-a-half pennies—English Proclamations 3, James I (8 April 1603). The group of foreign coins given English values had a cosmopolitan composition, where Portuguese, French, German, and Spanish coins were, at times, all circulating in England with ascribed English values in payment of sterling debts—see Challis, *The Tudor Coinage* (Manchester University Press 1978).
[12] Tucker, *The Theory and of Money and Banks Investigated* (A. M. Kelly 1964, reprint of 1839 edn).
[13] For this purpose, we disregard crossings and markings, and envisage the cheque in its original form as simply a bill of exchange drawn on a banker payable on demand (Bills of Exchange Act 1882, s. 73).

an instrument which enables the recipient to obtain payment, but is not itself payment. In *Ward v Evans* (1702),[14] Lord Holt declared that goldsmith's notes were cheques rather than banknotes—that is, that the delivery of a goldsmith's note in payment of a debt did not discharge that debt, but functioned only as a conditional payment, and payment itself happened only when the holder presented the note to the relevant goldsmith and received payment. However, it is clear from the judgement itself that this was a controversial ruling - Lord Holt observed that his ruling was made 'notwithstanding the noise and cry, that it is the use of Lombard Street, as if the contrary opinion would blow up Lombard Street'.[15] What this tells us is that in practice goldsmith's notes seem to have been regarded as payment instruments in their own right, and this seems to have continued after the decision in *Ward v Evans*. The basis of this continuation was not that Lord Holt was either disregarded or overruled (perish the thought), but that two other rules became established whose effect was to largely eliminate the problems that he had caused. One of these was to the effect that a payment by delivery of a note should be regarded as absolute rather than conditional where the note was delivered directly in exchange for the goods concerned—in other words, for an immediate payment a goldsmith's note was as good as cash. The other was that the conditionality of a note fell away if the holder did not seek payment from the goldsmith issuer 'in convenient time'.[16]

5.14   Although banknotes were negotiable, it is clear that they were not always negotiated or intended to be negotiated. Early notes came in two types; notes which promised to pay the bearer the whole of a particular deposit (an irregular sum), and notes which promised to pay the bearer a round sum.[17] Notes of the first type would typically purport to entitle the bearer to the payment of *l*.1 *s*.5 *d*.4 or some such sum. There are only two possible explanations for notes of this type—one is that that was the amount which the bearer happened to have on him when he went to the bank, and the other is that the note, like a cheque, was created to settle a specific transaction. In either case, the designation of the note effectively barred transferability in practice, and suggests that its only practical function was as a means to obtain other notes and coins.

### 5.2.2  Limitation of the power to create private banknotes

5.15   As governments came to issue notes themselves, the ability of banks to create their own banknotes was progressively circumscribed by legislation. In the United States, the imposition of a substantial tax on private banknote issuance in 1865 (as part of the introduction of a Federal currency) had the effect of forcing US banks out of note issuance and into becoming deposit banks. In the United Kingdom, the squeeze was more prolonged. The origins of the problem went back to the English currency crisis of 1695–98. This reduced confidence in Bank of England notes. To shore up confidence, in 1704 the government passed laws making promissory notes

---

[14] (1702) Ld. Raym. 928.    [15] Ibid.
[16] See the discussion in Geva, *The Payment Order of Antiquity and the Late Middle Ages* (OUP 2011) at 478ff.
[17] Clapham, *The Bank of England, A History* 2 *Vols* (CUP 1944) Vol. 1, at 21–3.

legally enforceable. This was a great benefit to bankers everywhere, but did not prevent a crisis and run on the Bank of England in 1707. In response, in 1708, parliament passed an Act[18] prohibiting private companies with more than six partners from issuing promissory notes anywhere in England, thereby fortifying the Bank of England's monopoly and seeking to compel acceptance of its notes. In 1720, in response to the South Sea Bubble, the Bubble Act[19] prohibited the formation of joint-stock companies without a royal charter. The Banking Act was clarified and reinforced in 1742,[20] and goldsmith's notes had more or less completely disappeared by 1750.[21] The cumulative impact of all this was that England was reduced to a single, note-issuing joint-stock bank in the form of the Bank of England, operating alongside a myriad of small, private partnership banks which accepted deposits but which did not issue notes in London. Outside London, however, there was still a plethora of country banks which issued notes.[22] The result of all this was that banknotes—both Bank of England notes and country banknotes—became a circulating medium.

This process left Bank of England notes in possession of the field as far as the UK was concerned. The position of these notes was recognised in 1758 in *Miller v Race*,[23] in which Lord Mansfield said of Bank of England banknotes:  5.16

> Now they are not goods, nor securities, nor documents for debts, nor are they so esteemed: but are treated as money, as cash, in the ordinary course and transaction of business, by the general consent of mankind; which gives them the credit and currency of money, to all intents and purposes. They are as much money, as guineas themselves are; or any other current coin, that is used in common payments, as money or cash.[24]

Banknotes were extremely unpopular with those who sought to place the pound on a gold-backed basis, since they appeared to constitute irresponsible and unconstrained creation of money substitutes. Adherents of this view (known as the currency school) debated vigorously in the 1820s and 1830s with their opponents (known as the banking school), who argued that the economy, left to its own devices, would determine the appropriate amount of money required and create it.[25] The triumph of the currency school was the Bank Act 1844, which required that the total note issue of the Bank of England should be limited by reference to its holdings of physical gold. This meant that the supply of money to the economy from official  5.17

---

[18] 7 Anne, c. 7.   [19] 6 Geo. 1, c. 18.   [20] 15 Geo. 2, c. 15.
[21] Lawson, *History of Banking* (2nd edn, Richard Bentley 1855) at 213.
[22] The power to issue notes was restored to country banks by the Country Bankers Act 1826, which provided that country banks might issue banknotes provided that they did not conduct business within 65 miles of London and that every member of the firm was to be fully liable for debts under its demand notes. The boom in country banking seems to have been enormous—Burke observed that when he arrived in England in 1750 there were not more than a dozen banks outside London, whereas by the end of the nineteenth century there seem to have been up to 400—Pressnell, *Country Banking in the Industrial Revolution* (Clarendon 1956) at 4.
[23] (1758) 1 Burr 452.
[24] Ibid. at 457. Note that at this point Bank of England notes were not legal tender—they were made such nearly eighty years later by the Bank of England Act 1833.
[25] See Goodhart & Jensen, *Currency School vs Banking School: An Ongoing Confrontation*, Economic Thought, Vol. 4, No. 2 (2015) 20–31 for an explanation as to how this debate has governed the development of banking regulation between that day and this.

sources was constrained at a time of substantial economic growth and (importantly) before the development of the South African gold mines came on-stream to facilitate an increase in gold holdings. The result was succinctly described by Keynes:[26]

> Up to 1844 bank notes showed a tendency to become a formidable rival to gold as the actual medium of exchange. But the Bank Act of that year set itself to hamper this tendency, and to encourage the use of gold as the medium of exchange as well as the standard of value. This Act was completely successful in stopping attempts to economise gold by the use of notes. But the Bank Act did nothing to hinder the use of cheques, and the very remarkable development of this medium of exchange during the next fifty years led in this country, without any important development in the use of money or tokens, to a monetary organisation more perfectly adapted for the economy of gold than any which exists elsewhere.[27]

### 5.2.3 Banknotes and cheques compared

5.18 One of the important aspects of banknotes as compared with cheques is that they make life much easier for the issuing bank. Once a banknote had been issued by a bank, its only further concern was authenticating it when it came to be presented. Whereas cheques involved the palaver of payment and collection, and more importantly verification that the drawer had the funds available in his account when the cheque was presented, banknotes were effectively self-transferring without any involvement by the bank of issue, and could be cashed immediately against presentment. Admittedly, a banknote carried with it the credit risk of the bank, but then again so did a cheque drawn on that bank. Indeed, from a bank's perspective a banknote is a more efficient and less expensive version of a cheque.

5.19 Thus, the movement from banknotes to bank cheques was the substitution of a weaker and more expensive method for a simpler and more effective one in the name of a then-fashionable ideology.

## 5.3 Virtual Currency Issued by Banks

5.20 The reason for the extended discussion of this now largely defunct form of instrument is that if modern banks were to create their own forms of virtual currency, the result would be very similar to the recreation of traditional banknotes in modern form. Modern banks find the payment and collection of debits and credits from current accounts as onerous as their forbears—indeed, in the race between the technology which simplifies such measures, and the demand from the economy for ever-greater payment volumes, it is not always clear which is winning. However, the idea of bank-specific virtual currencies—electronic banknotes—creates the possibility of the creation of instruments which, to the extent that they can circulate without the involvement of the bank concerned, have the potential to restore the idea of private banknotes to the realms of the possible.

---

[26] Keynes, *Indian Currency and Finance* (1913, Cambridge University Press 2013).
[27] Ibid. at 12.

# 6
# Banking, Payments and Money

| | |
|---|---|
| 6.1 Payment in a Modern Economy | 6.02 |
|     6.1.1 Commodity and Credit money | 6.08 |
|     6.1.2 The role of central bank money | 6.10 |
|     6.1.3 Exogenous and endogenous credit money | 6.13 |
|     6.1.4 The form of Private Bank Money | 6.14 |
|     6.1.5 Virtual currency within the monetary system | 6.17 |
| 6.2 Why Bank Money? | 6.20 |
| 6.3 Are private Money and Deposit-taking Interdependent? | 6.27 |
|     6.3.1 Payment, deposit-taking, and credit creation | 6.29 |
|     6.3.2 Instruments of Payment | 6.34 |
|     6.3.3 Ownership of deposited money | 6.37 |
| 6.4 Transfer and Negotiability of Private Payment Instruments | 6.45 |
|     6.4.1 What does transfer of a payment instrument actually transfer? | 6.49 |
|     6.4.2 Private payment in virtual currency | 6.51 |
| 6.5 Commercial Bank Credit Money as Private Money | 6.54 |
|     6.5.1 The state and bank credit money | 6.58 |
|     6.5.2 Payment in commercial bank credit money | 6.60 |
|     6.5.3 Virtual currency as commercial bank money | 6.61 |

There is a common illusion (sometimes extending even to economists) that there is a fixed amount of money in the economy which is provided by the state through its central bank. This is, of course, nonsense. State money has coexisted with private money for as long as it has existed. State money does a specific job, but the monetary jobs which need to be done across an economy generally require a wide variety of different types of instrument, and there is no reason why sovereign-issued money should seek to perform all of those functions.

## 6.1 Payment in a Modern Economy

The trouble with sovereign money is that there are some jobs for which it is too big, and others for which it is too small. The common denominator of the international corporation financing oil exploration and the legal researcher buying law textbooks

6.03 In broad terms, this is done through a mixture of transferable credit instruments and third-party payments intermediates by 'paymasters' (we are indebted to Geva[1] for this last term since the term 'banks' has proved altogether too charged and too misleading for everyday use). By a paymaster we mean nothing more than a person who provides payment services—that is, who, when instructed, makes a payment to another on the basis that he either has or will recoup the value from the person who has instructed him to make the payment. A provider of such payment services may well be—or become—either a deposit-taker or a lender: A paymaster will be a deposit-taker if he takes and holds funds from customers on the basis that he is looking after those funds until they decide who to pay them to; and he will be a lender if he makes a requested payment out of his own funds and seeks repayment from the customer after the event. A bank, as will be easily seen, is simply a person who provides all three of these services.

6.04 The structure of the modern economy involves a hierarchy of paymasters - the central bank acts as paymaster to commercial banks and payment service providers, and those commercial banks and payment service providers act as paymasters to the rest of the economy. Thus, the easiest way to understand the monetary system of any modern economy is to divide it into three components. These can be represented as shown in Figure 6.1:

6.05 This picture is broadly derived from Keynes, *A Treatise on Money*,[2] although a helpful exposition will also be found Moore's *Horizontalists and Verticalists*.[3]

6.06 The dimensions of Figure 6.1 are unrepresentative. In order to give some approximate orders of magnitude, the Bank of England Annual Report to 28 February 2017 indicated for the UK economy the total amount of commodity money in circulation was £73 billion, whilst the total of balances held with the bank (fiat money) was £415 billion. This compares with a total UK economy of roughly £2 trillion, which suggests that the size of the credit money segment of the graph is approximately £1.5 trillion.

6.07 One way of looking at this diagram is that it demonstrates that the real economy rests on a foundation of money provided by the central bank, and in some respects this is correct. The money provided by the central bank to the economy is in two

---

[1] Geva, *The Payment Order of Antiquity and the Late Middle Ages* (Hart 2011) at 3.
[2] *A Treatise on Money: The Applied Theory of Money* (CUP for the Royal Economic Society 1978), Chapters 1–3.
[3] Moore, *Horizontalists and Verticalists: The Macroeconomics of Credit Money* (Cambridge University Press 1988). A useful summary of current thinking as regards the interrelation between private money, public money, and central bank policy can be found in Palley, *Horizontalists, Verticalists and Structuralists: The Theory of Endogenous Money Reassessed* (Dusseldorf, IMK 2013) Working Paper No. 121. Also, see Geva, *The Payment Order of Antiquity and the Middle Ages: A Legal History* (Hart Publishing 2011) at 647.

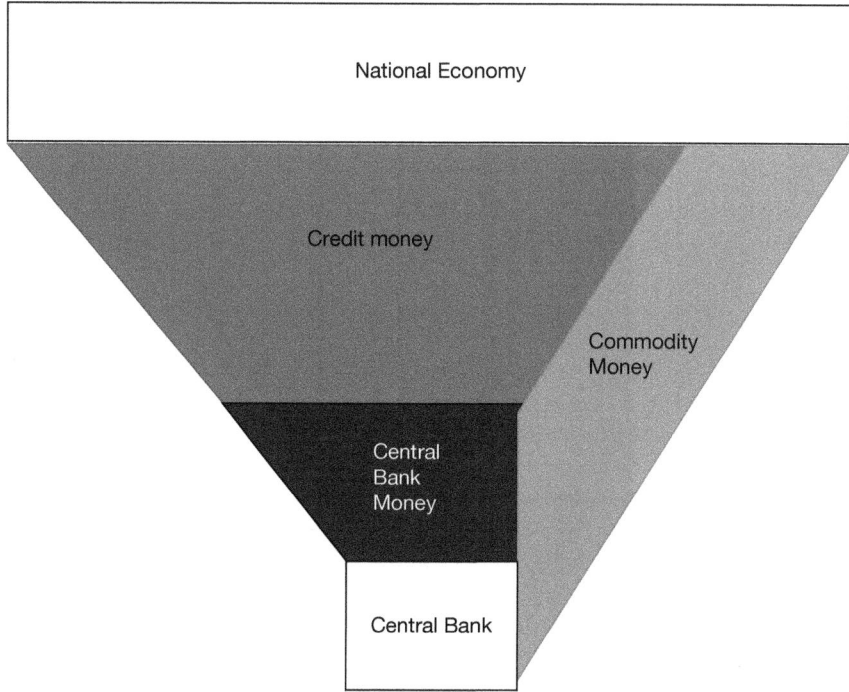

**Figure 6.1** The monetary system of a modern economy divided into three components.

forms: notes and coins (commodity money), and deposits maintained with the central bank. These are together referred to as the 'monetary base'.

### 6.1.1 Commodity and Credit money

Physical cash is a physical asset, not a financial claim.[4] It is perfectly liquid, so represents immediately available purchasing power, carries no credit risk, pays no interest, and is capital certain. Once it has entered the economic system there is no way for it to leave, save by wear, loss, physical export (only really relevant in the case of gold coins), or a wilful intent to destroy wealth.  6.08

Credit money, in contrast, is that set of financial claims on financial institutions making up the total liabilities of all institutions issuing transaction deposits. Credit money is the liability of the bank that creates it, and central bank credit money is the credit money created by the central bank. In general, real economy participants other than banks do not have accounts directly with the central bank, and therefore do not have access to central bank credit money. Real economy transactions  6.09

---

[4] For historical reasons UK central banknotes purport to be a liability of the central bank. They are not, since there is no way that such 'liabilities' can be discharged.

are therefore only able to be settled using either commodity money or private bank credit money.[5] Banks, by contrast, transact with each other in central bank money, in the form of balances maintained with the central bank.

### 6.1.2 The role of central bank money

6.10 The monetary base is (to some extent) under the control of the central bank. It is these balances which are the subject of the legal theory which is known as the 'institutional theory of money'. The basis of this idea is that 'money … is no more than credit against an obligor, whose acceptance as a store of value and as a means of payment by the public is dependent on a comprehensive legal framework that ensures stable purchasing power, its availability even in times of banking stress and its functional capability to settle monetary obligations'.[6] Thus, under this theory money is: (a) a claim against a central bank; (b) which can be used by the public as a means of exchange and a store of value; and (c) represents a claim which is originated by a central bank in a manner which preserves its availability, functionality, and purchasing powers. This definition clearly applies to the monetary base. It equally clearly does not apply to credit money—indeed, the institutional theory is nothing more than the theory of those aspects of the monetary system which are directly connected with the central bank.

6.11 However, if the same system is considered from the perspective of the real economy, the point which is immediately apparent is that participants in the real economy have no direct interaction with the central bank at all save for the use of notes and coins. There is an optical illusion which sometimes arises to the effect that, since participants in the real economy settle their debts by the transfer of claims on commercial banks, and commercial banks settle their debts by transfers through the central bank, this somehow means that all of these transactions are ultimately settled through the central bank. This is absolutely not the case. The central bank could be removed from the depiction above without affecting the position of the end-users in any way—as indeed it was in the United States from the mid-nineteenth to the early twentieth century.

6.12 It should be noted that there is no reason why the central bank should necessarily take this minimalist stance. A maximalist central bank could prohibit private banking, require that all transactions were settled through its books, and thereby assert complete control over the monetary (although not the credit) system. Since the advent of virtual currency makes this for the first time a practical policy choice, we consider below in section 8.2 how such a a system might operate. However, for this purpose it is sufficient to note that the current structure of the payment system, and in particular the role of private actors in its structure, is a policy choice and not an economic inevitability.

---

[5] It is possible in some jurisdictions for some non-bank real economy participants to have accounts with the central bank directly, but this is ignored for this purpose.
[6] Sáinz de Vicuña, *An Institutional Theory of Money* in Mario Giovanoli and Diego Devos (eds), *International Money and Financial Law: The Global Crisis* (OUP 2010) Chapter 25 at 517.

### 6.1.3 Exogenous and Endogenous credit money

If the monetary base is created by central banks, who creates credit money? The answer, unsurprisingly, is that credit money is created by the real economy itself.[7] This is why credit money is described as 'endogenous' to the economy, whilst the monetary base is described as 'exogenous'—credit money is created as a result of the operations of the market, whereas central bank money is created through the will of the central bank.[8] It is noteworthy that credit money obligations are generally denominated in the unit of currency of a state—thus domestic bank deposits in the United Kingdom are denominated in pounds sterling—but this does not mean that their existence owes anything to the role or the activity either of the government or of the central bank. The government provides a unit of reckoning, and banks and their customers denominate their claims on each other in that unit, but the fact that those claims are denominated in that unit does not mean that their existence is in any way dependent on any service, obligation, or liability of the entity which prescribed that unit.

6.13

### 6.1.4 The Form of Private Bank Money

The idea of a private payment instrument is relatively common. A private payment instrument is simply an instrument created by a person other than a state, which is accepted as payment by persons who in turn intend to use it in payment, and is not a simple proxy for fiat money.[9] Robert Owen's labour bank, the private coinages of the eighteenth century, and some virtual currencies, are all examples of private payment instruments.

6.14

The key distinction between private payment instruments and traditional e-money and voucher schemes is that private payment instruments circulate—in that they are transferred from person to person—whereas traditional e-money is created in order to be redeemed. Thus, with a store gift voucher or pre-paid transport card money is transferred 'on to' the voucher or card, but its only subsequent movement is to be transferred back to its creator. Private payment instruments, by contrast, are created for the purpose of being transferred multiple times between different economic actors.

6.15

There is no clear dividing line between private payment instruments and money. This is because many private payment instruments can be used to obtain money, and are valued primarily for that purpose. A simple example is a traditional cheque. In their earliest incarnation cheques could be passed on from hand to hand, and a person accepting a cheque in payment of a debt was as likely to negotiate the cheque as he was to present it for payment. At this point, the cheque functioned as

6.16

---

[7] It is sometimes said that credit money is created by banks, but that is to get the cart before the horse. Economic activity itself creates both a demand for and a supply of payment services. We can choose to call those suppliers 'banks', but if we tried to abolish banks the result would simply be the creation of alternative suppliers of the same product. 'Banks' is simply the name we choose to give to these suppliers.
[8] See Hicks, *A Market Theory of Money* (OUP 1989) for a good short introduction to the process.
[9] For example, a gift token.

a private payment instrument. However, later cheques were created and issued by banks with crossings endorsed. This meant that they could not be used for payment, and their only practical use was to be presented to the relevant bank in exchange for bank money.

### 6.1.5 Virtual currency within the monetary system

6.17　The fact that virtual currency does not have the imprimatur of a government absolutely debars it from the status of central bank money, or from forming part of the monetary base. However, that fact is irrelevant to the question of whether it can perform the function currently performed by bank credit money. Since bank credit money performs the function which it is created to perform by reason only of the fact that it exists to perform that function, there is no reason why the real economy should not produce other mechanisms for doing the same job, and the creation of those mechanisms is no more dependent on the cooperation or consent of the central bank or the government of an economy than is bank credit money today.

6.18　This takes us to the question of whether central banks should care about the creation of cybercurrencies and other forms of private payment instruments. Historically, central banks were extremely concerned about the creation of new forms of money,[10] since there was a perception that if new forms of payment instrument were created by non-bank private sector entities, this could result in central banks losing control of the money supply.

6.19　The basis of this concern was a belief that the creation of credit within the banking system was to some extent controlled by bank regulators, and a significant movement of credit creation outside the banking system would therefore result in a significant reduction in that control. This extent to which this was correct in practice even in 1998 is a subject for debate. However, what is clear is that economic theory provides no support for the argument. The monetary base is exogenous, credit money is endogenous. If the supply of credit money is controlled by banks and is endogenous, then rising and falling prices will have no tendency to adjust interest rates to equilibrate supply and demand—money will simply be created and destroyed in order to reflect the current demand. Increases in aggregate demand drive an increase in aggregate bank credit, and decreases in demand a decrease in bank credit. The rate of increase in credit money and the rate of expansion of aggregate demand are closely correlated, and an increase in the supply of credit money necessarily equals an increase in the supply of bank credit. Changes in the demand for bank credit translate into changes in the quantity of credit money supplied, which in turn results in changes in the quantity of money demanded. Thus, increase in bank credit necessarily results in an increase in bank deposits. Another way of looking at this is that central banks can control the supply price of credit money, but not its quantity. If this is correct, then central banks should be indifferent as to whether private credit money is created by banks, e-money institutions, or website operators.

---

[10] See, e.g., the European Central Bank's *Report on Electronic Money* of August 1998.

## 6.2 Why Bank Money?

There is a recursive definitional problem within the question of the origin of bank money—specifically, are banks the producers of money because of their credit creating function, or do they have their credit creating function because they are producers of money? We consider this in more detail in section 6.3, but it is necessary to say here that the short answer seems to be neither—it is perfectly possible for an entity to be a producer of money without being a credit creator, and it is perfectly possible for an entity to be a credit creator without being a producer of money. However there is a convenience factor in performing the two functions within the same entity which seems to create a sort of commercial centripetal force, drawing the two together. The problem that this creates in practice is that the credit creation function of banks is important for economic analysis, whereas the payment function is almost irrelevant for that purpose. Consequently economists tend to see banks primarily, if not exclusively, as credit creators.

6.20

It is, however, a serious intellectual error to forget about the payment service function of Banks. The key point here is that the reason that we use commercial bank deposits as stores of value is that the only reason for holding money is to spend it, and the most efficient way of making a payment to another person in a modern economy is by instructing a bank to make that payment. Hence keeping money 'in the bank' is simply another name for having money prepositioned so that it can be spent as easily as possible. If we look at the question posed by Keynes as to 'Why should anyone outside a lunatic asylum wish to use money as a store of wealth',[11] the answer—as applied to commercial bank money at least—is that the utility of money rests entirely on the fact that it may be spent, and the opportunity (or desire) to spend it may arise, at an unpredictable time. If it must be kept somewhere, the rational place to keep it is in a situation where it may be disbursed with the smallest amount of effort—in other words, with a paymaster.

6.21

The usefulness of this function can be easily understood by hypothesising an alternative—in an economy where all expenditure involved metal coins, the sheer effort involved in moving around large volumes of heavy metal in order to insure their availability upon demand would have been sufficient to ensure that an alternative would rapidly have been developed. This issue of the weight of metal leads us to the fundamental problem with silver and gold coinage. In today's money, we may carry around with us sufficient specie to buy lunch, but we do not carry sufficient to buy a car. If it were necessary to buy cars in specie, the specie that existed would be designed so that the amount of it needed to buy a car was capable of being carried. However, the necessary consequence of that would be that each individual coin would be valued in at least hundreds of pounds; a situation which would make it almost impossible to buy lunch. This is the problem with gold and silver currency

6.22

---

[11] Keynes, *General Theory of Employment, Interest and Money* (1936) (CUP for the Royal Economic Society 2012) at 216.

generally—there are some transactions for which it is too small, and others for which it is too big. In both of these cases, the market is forced to develop private alternatives to the use of sovereign money.

6.23 Beginning at the small end, matching the weight of gold and silver coins to the unit of account tends to point up the fact that the gold and silver coins this produced are too large to be used for anything other than commercial transactions. For most of the period when silver and gold coins circulated in England, the practical position was as it would be today if the smallest coin in circulation were worth £100. Attempts to produce lower-value coins were generally unsuccessful. The reason for this is partly that the seignorage on low-denomination coins is less than on large-denomination coins, so mints shied away from producing them, and partly because it was extremely difficult to produce a small coin which was actually physically worth less than its face value—this mattered because as soon as the intrinsic value of the coin exceeded its face value it tended to disappear from circulation.

6.24 The other main class of those denied the use of coin are those whose payments are too large to be made that way. This group probably includes most merchants engaged in international trade—the size of any cargo worth shipping probably meant that an unfeasibly large amount of metal would be required to pay for it. These two facts, without more, make clear that a proportion of economic activity which was at least non-trivial was certainly not settled with coin issued by the mint under royal proclamation.

6.25 In the context of the relative ease of using money, it is probably as well to point out that it is in this area that private credit money can provide the greatest utility as regards commodity money. The well-known story of the stone money of Yap,[12] which involved stone discs with diameters ranging from feet to yards (helpfully equipped with a hole in the middle to facilitate transportation) is an interesting manifestation of the awkwardness of commodity money.[13] However, a more interesting example arises in the context of classical money. W. V. Harris[14] draws attention to the scene in the film *Spartacus* where Charles Laughton hands two bags of coins to Peter Ustinov, explaining that the sacks contain 2 million sesterces. In practice, 2 million sesterces would have weighed 965 kg, or just under one imperial ton. The likelihood of anyone discharging any debt through the delivery of a ton of metal can be roughly set at zero in all circumstances. However, we know that transactions of this kind were not unusual—Cicero is known to have paid three-and-a-half million sesterces for his

---

[12] Furness, *The Island of Stone Money, Uap of the Carolines* (JB Lippincott Co. 1910) at 96–8, and see Einzig, *Primitive Money* (2nd edn, Pergamon Press 1966) pp48ff. The prominence of the story of the stones of Yap is due to Milton Friedman, who used Furness's account in a well-known paper *The Island of Stone Money* (1991, Hoover Institution, Stanford University, Working Papers in Economics) Working Paper No. E-91-3.

[13] It appears that on some of the stones, which were too big to move, transfer was effected simply by chiselling the name of the new owner onto the stone, as a result of which some of the older stones have the appearance of the backs of traditional bills of exchange (Einzig, ibid. at 48).

[14] *The Nature of Roman Money*, in Harris (ed.), *The Monetary Systems of the Greeks and Romans* (Oxford University Press 2008).

house on the Palatine;[15] a price equal at that time to three-and-a-half tons of coin. At the other end of the scale is the situation described by Ovid in the Ars Amatoria[16]—a pedlar comes by the house, an importunate girlfriend sees something that the pedlar has, and wants him to buy it for her as a present. When he argues that he cannot, because there is no money in the house, the girlfriend replies that he can simply provide a 'littera'. The key features about this transaction are that it is unlikely to be for a very large amount, but the pedlar is clearly to be presumed by the reader to be happy to accept the littera in payment.

Both of these situations make clear that some payment mechanism other than the delivery of physical money must in practice have been in use. This appears to be the case—as noted above,[17] as far back as AD 162 we find payment instruments circulating for small sums. However, a payment mechanism involves a payer—a 'paymaster' in the language of Benjamin Geva[18]—and in general a paymaster will not pay unless he has been put in funds to make the payment, or unless he has an enforceable claim to recover the relevant amount from the principal. Thus, the existence of payment mechanisms of this kind seems necessarily to imply the existence of deposit-takers, lenders, or both, of some form or description. 6.26

## 6.3 Are Private Money and Deposit-taking Interdependent?

The question to be addressed here is as to whether money creation and deposit-taking are necessarily interdependent—put simply, does a money-creator (or a paymaster) have to be a deposit-holder—and therefore a credit creator—i.e., a bank? Interestingly, we can approach this question by looking at the historical precedents. There is no doubt about the antiquity of deposit-taking—even towards the beginning of recorded western writing, we have Hesiod debating the relative merits of keeping savings at home or 'abroad'.[19] However, this sort of deposit-taking must immediately be sub-divided into two: custody and bailment-type transactions[20] where the very thing that was deposited must be returned, and lending for consumption,[21] in which the depositary agrees to give back different things which are nonetheless equivalent to those given to him (tantundem).[22] Only the latter constitutes 'deposit-taking' in the form with which we are concerned here. The difference must be emphasised—if I give you a priceless family heirloom to keep for me, what I expect back is that thing and no other; if I lend you a cup of sugar, I assume without further consideration that the sugar that you return to me will not be the same as that which I lent you. Loans of money, except in the most extraordinary circumstances, are of the second type.[23] Thus, the majority of deposits of money are and have always 6.27

---

[15] Epistulae ad Familiares 5.6.2. This is by no means the largest payment we know of—Clodius paid Scarus 14.8 million. Schatzman, *Senatorial Wealth and Roman Politics* (Brussels 1975) at 22–4.
[16] Ars Am. 1. 428.   [17] Para 5-04 above.
[18] Geva, *The Payment Order of Antiquity and the Middle Ages: A Legal History* (Hart Publishing 2011).
[19] Hesiod, *Works and Days* (Oxford World's Classics 2009) 364–5.   [20] Depositum.
[21] Mutuum in the case of goods, depositum irregular in the context of money.
[22] See *Justinian's Digest* 16.3.25.1.   [23] Ibid. at 19.2.31.

been on what we would call a banker–customer basis rather than on a mere custodian basis—indeed it is hard to see that the inconvenience of doing it any other way would have had any visible benefit for anyone.

6.28 At this point, it becomes too easy to jump ahead to the conclusion that since deposits of money were meant to be used, and the recipients of those deposits seem to have used them, that we have discovered fully-fledged banks; and, in particular, credit-creating banks. We have not. As Harris cautions, looking for modern institutions in antiquity is a trap. In particular, the modern bank combines three distinct and separate functions within its business model—it is a provider of access to payment services, a transformer of liquidity for profit, and is an investor in credit assets. These are not three separate business lines, but three different characteristics of the business model of modern banks. However, as Andreu points out, in Rome these three activities were separated out and performed by different actors. In particular, the activity of making loans (and assuming credit risk) was engaged in by feneratores, who are best considered as specialist credit investors.[24] Roman deposit-takers (known as argentarii) seem to have been simply deposit-takers and payment service providers who, when they wanted to invest their cash balances, lent them either to professional feneratores or to their clients. Some argentarii became coactores argentarii, who appear to have been deposit-takers who collected debts and effected other transactions for their clients in exchange for a commission on the amounts handled (a role not dissimilar to old English merchant banks).[25] The existence of private deposit-taking does not equate to the existence of bank-created money, and the existence of private money does not demonstrate the fact of commercial deposit-taking and credit creation.

### 6.3.1 Payment, deposit-taking, and credit creation

6.29 However the fact that the services of deposit taking and payment service provision are not necessarily interlinked does not affect the fact that they are generally encountered together, and although it is true deposit taking and credit creation are equally not necessarily interlinked, it is equally true that they are also generally encountered together. There are a number of reasons why a depositor might make a deposit. One is because he does not want the nuisance of physically safeguarding piles of coins, and would like someone else to take on that risk. Another is because he wishes the deposit-taker to assume an obligation to a third party on his behalf. However, there is a third, important, motive, which is a desire to make a profit through the receipt of interest. Deposits of this kind were characterised by the roman jurists as not 'true' deposits, but rather as loans to the banker concerned.[26] There is, however, no easy way to distinguish between loans to a banker and deposits with a banker. In

---

[24] The term fenerator seems to have been prejudicial—most senators or knights would acknowledge without embarrassment that they were lenders at interest, but would deny that they were feneratores—see Cato the Elder *De Agricultura*. Pr. 1.

[25] In order to confuse matters, there is a further class of actor known as numularii who originated as coinage specialists, acting as assayers and money-changers. The numularii appear to have become deposit bankers over time.

[26] Andreau *Banking and Business in the Roman World* (CUP 1999) at 42.

particular, it is not the case that the depositor always has, when he makes his deposit, a unique purpose. He may intend to go to the banker to collect small amounts of specie from time to time, or he could go to the banker with his creditor and instruct payment to the creditor, or he could effect the same result through writing. Finally, he may have intended none of the above, but simply for his payments to be effected by book transfer in the books of the banker where the person with whom he dealt was a client of that same banker.[27]

6.30 It is clear from the foregoing that one of the most important consequences of having one's money held by a payment service provider is precisely that one can give an instruction to that provider to make a payment on one's behalf. Another way of looking at this is that the customer can order the banker to make payment, and that order, if refined in a document, can have real existence. Thus, the paradigmatic situation as regards such instruments is that the customer owes his creditor money, and an instrument instructing the paymaster to pay to the creditor is created for the benefit of, and transferred to, the creditor.

6.31 The question of what is achieved by the handing over of such an instrument is at the heart of the question of what constitutes money. One possibility is to say that the instrument itself constitutes payment, and that the handing over of the instrument constitutes payment—in which case the instrument constitutes money. Another would be to say that the handing over of the instrument constitutes a promise of payment, such that the obligation is only in fact discharged when the instrument is honoured by person to whom it is addressed. In this case the instrument does not—and cannot—constitute money. This issue—of whether delivery constitutes an absolute and immediate discharge of a debt obligation—is the acid test of money-ness.

6.32 There has been extensive litigation over instruments of this kind—specifically in the context of the payment of commercial debts with cheques and other payment instruments. The approach which the courts have taken has generally been to enquire what the agreement between the parties may have been. There are a number of possibilities:

(1) The creditor has agreed under the contract that the delivery of the instrument itself will constitute payment. If this is the case, then the payment obligation which arises under the contract is discharged when the instrument is received by the creditor. If the instrument is subsequently dishonoured, the creditor must sue on the instrument, and can no longer sue on the underlying debt, since it has been discharged by payment.

(2) The creditor has stipulated for payment, but has subsequently accepted an instrument. In this case the creditor delivers the instrument to his bank to collect as his agent. The debt is discharged when the bank receives payment as agent for the creditor.[28]

---

[27] Andreu 43 fn 49.
[28] For the first two of these propositions, see *Ward v Evans* (1702) 2 Ld. Raym. 928 and *Hill v Lewis* (1709) 1 Salk 132. See also Holden, *The History of Negotiable Instruments in English Law* (University of London, The Athlone Press 1955, repr. 1993) at 85–6 and 109–11.

(3) The creditor has stipulated for payment, but has agreed that the balance will be settled by inter-bank transfer. In this case, the instrument is a bilateral instruction by the payer to the paymaster to make payment. In this case payment is made when the transfer is completed and funds have been credited to the account of the payee.[29]

6.33 The point here is that the question of whether the instrument is a form of money (case 1), a payment mechanism (case 2) or a mere instruction to make payment (case 3) is a matter of construction of the contract and of the surrounding facts.[30] However, such agreement may be signified by non-contractual means— thus, for example, a garage which displays a sign to the effect that it is prepared to accept a particular charge card is in effect offering to contract on terms that the proffering of that charge card will discharge the payment obligation that would otherwise arise.[31]

### 6.3.2 Instruments of Payment

6.34 We can say a great deal about the normal position regarding instruments of payment at English law since it is largely codified.[32] The default assumption as regards such instruments is that they are a form of conditional payment. This means that where a creditor is given a payment instrument in payment, the debt is suspended. If the instrument is presented for payment and is paid, the obligation is suspended—if not, it revives.[33] Merely creating an instrument instructing a person to pay does not of itself make that person liable to pay—that liability only arises if that person formally accepts the liability. However delivery of such an instrument may still suspend the payment obligation.

6.35 In the law of bills and notes, every instrument creates a separate autonomous obligation. If A orders goods from B and pays with a cheque, B can sue A on the cheque regardless of any other contractual dispute. Thus, in the situation where A is dissatisfied with the goods which he receives from B and cancels the cheque, B now has two options—the obligation to pay under the contract has revived, so he can sue under that, or he can sue on the cheque itself. The difference between the two, of course, is that the action for the price under the contract is likely to be met with a counterclaim based in the customer's dissatisfaction with the goods, whereas the action on the cheque is—in theory—absolute. Interestingly, this is not quite the case. If the underlying property has been rejected completely, then the holder is

---

[29] *The Chikuma* [181] 1 WLR 314, but query given HL obiter in *Mardorf Peach & Co v Attica Sea Carriers Corp of Liberia* [1977] AC 850. *Vogrie Farms v Revenue and Customs Commissioners* [2015] UKFTT 531 (TC) is recent authority that where a person is paid by a debtor instructing his bank to make payment is only 'paid' when the money is actually received into his account.
[30] *Goldshede v Cottrell* (1836) 2 M. & W. 20; *Re Boys* (1870) LR 10 Eq. 467; *Re Romer and Haslam* [1863] 2 QB 286; *Palmer v Bramley* [1895] 2 QB 405.
[31] *Re Charge Card Services Ltd* [1989] Ch 497.
[32] Bills of Exchange Act 1882 and the Cheques Act 1957
[33] Holden, *The History of Negotiable Instruments in English Law* (1955, repr. 1993) at 85–6 and 109–11. See also *Ward v Evans* (1702) 2 Ld. Raym. 928 and *Hill v Lewis* (1709) 1 Salk 132.

entitled to sue for the return of the price. This is a liquidated damages claim, which is capable of being set off against the obligation to pay the price.[34] However, if the buyer merely asserts a counterclaim based on defects in the goods, this will be an unliquidated claim, and as such requires to be heard and determined. It therefore cannot be a defence to payment on the instrument, either as a substantive defence or as a set-off.[35]

A creditor who has accepted such an instrument in payment is effectively barred from subsequently suing the debtor for payment until the instrument matures.[36] However, if the instrument is dishonoured then the debt revives, and the creditor can sue as if the instrument had never existed. This has the interesting consequence that a creditor who has accepted a negotiable instrument in part payment of a debt cannot seek judgement in default of appearance for the full amount claimed unless the cheque is dishonoured.[37]

6.36

### 6.3.3 Ownership of deposited money

This is a difficult issue. A preliminary point which must be addressed is that the creation of a payment instrument does not constitute a transfer of ownership of deposited money. If I have £5 deposited with my bank, and instruct the bank to pay £5 to you, and the bank accepts the instrument so as to be bound by it, the effect of the instrument is not to transfer the ownership of my £5 deposit to you. The only thing that you acquire through the instrument is a right to sue the bank for £5. This is clear[38]. However, the core issue remains as to who owns what in the context of intervening wrongdoing. This question can best be summarised as follows. Let us assume that A owes money to B. C, a fraudster, convinces A that he has B's mandate to claim payment of the money from A. A is taken in by the deception, and pays money to C. A then informs B that his debt to him has been discharged, at which point B protests vigorously. What is the legal position?

6.37

First and foremost, the fact that C has defrauded A has no impact at all on B's claim on A. The money that C has obtained from A may well continue to belong to A, but it does not and cannot be said to belong to B—particularly where B can establish that his claim on A remains intact. C may have been enriched, but B has not been impoverished, and the only remedy which is required is the remedy of A against C—if he can be found.

6.38

Now let us assume that there is something in the facts which gives rise to an argument that B is to some extent responsible for the success of C's deception. We will hypothesise that B had a token of some form which A was accustomed to see

6.39

---

[34] *Thoni GmbH & Co KG v R.T.P. Equipment Ltd* [1979] 2 Lloyds Rep 282, applying *Forman v Wright* (1851) 11 CB 418.
[35] *James Lamond v Hyland Ltd (No. 2)* [1950] 1 KB 585, *Cebora S.N.C. v SIP (Industrial Products) Ltd* [1976] 1 Lloyds Rep 271.
[36] *Chitty on Contracts* (32nd edn, Sweet & Maxwell 2016) para 21-075.
[37] *Bolt & Nut Co (Tipton) Ltd v Rowlands, Nicholls & Co* [1964] 2 QB 10.
[38] See Geva 'Bank Money': the Rise, Fall and Metamorphosis of the Transferrable Deposit in Fox and Ernst (eds), Money in the Western legal Tradition (OUP 2016)

used to authenticate payment instructions, and that through his negligence he lost this token, and had failed to alert A to the fact of the loss. In circumstances of this kind, it is entirely plausible that the contract between A and B might provide that A could (in effect) recoup his loss by writing down his obligation to B. If this were the case, would this have any impact on the proprietary analysis of money in the hands of C?

6.40 The starting point here remains that C has—in effect—stolen the money from A. The fact of his theft has caused a detriment to B equal to the value of the money stolen, and B will unquestionably be able to recover from C on the basis of an unjust enrichment claim—if C can be found. However, the question that we are asking here is as to whether the money in the hands of C can be, on this fact pattern, said in any meaningful form to belong to B. It is clear that there are remedies which, if pressed, could give rise to this conclusion—a remedial constructive trust would be an example—but this is a remedy imposed after the event in the interests of justice, and as such is not relevant to the issue which we are discussing here, which is the proprietary position *ab initio* before the invocation of remedies.

6.41 It is clearly true that there are fact patterns which would affect this analysis—for example, if C was acting as a fiduciary agent of B at the time when he received the money from A, then it is entirely possible that when the property passed into C's hands in the first place it might have arrived impressed with a trust of some kind in favour of B. However, unless we are to conclude that all fraud constitutes a breach of trust of some kind, then we must accept that in at least some cases there is no proprietary analysis which connects the money received by C with the money lost by B. This is no more than the observation of Lord Herschell in *London Joint Stock Bank v Simmons*, to the effect that

> The general rule of the law is, that where a person has obtained the property of another from one who is dealing with it without the authority of the true owner, no title is acquired as against that owner, even though full value be given, and the property be taken in the belief that an unquestionable title thereto is being obtained, unless the person taking it can shew that the true owner has so acted as to mislead him into the belief that the person dealing with the property had authority to do so. If this can be shewn, a good title is acquired by personal estoppel against the true owner.[39]

6.42 If we go further and ask about the position of a second depositary—D—with whom C seeks to deposit the property so obtained, there are a number of answers depending on the nature of the property—and in particular, according to whether what C had obtained from A was: (a) currency; (b) a cheque; (c) a direct payment instruction; or (d) some other form of property, such as gold bars or virtual currency. If the answer was (a) currency, then the principle in *Miller v Race*[40] applies, and D will take good title to the money if he took it 'fairly and honestly upon a valuable and bona fide consideration'. If the answer was (b) a cheque, section 29(1)(b) of the Bills of Exchange Act will apply, and D will be a holder in due course of the cheque if it is

---

[39] [1892] AC 201, 222.   [40] (1791), 1 Burr 452.

negotiated to him with no notice of any 'defect in title' of C,[41] provided the notice is actual and not merely constructive.[42] If the answer was (c), it is by no means clear that there is any scope of the application of any defences. However, the rule *nemo dat quod non habet* would seem here to have no application. There is no doubt that A owned the property, there is no reason why D's title to what he received should be impeached by the fraud of C on B, and the position is therefore that A's remedy is to attach C's claim on D. If the answer was (d) the answer would seem to be exactly the same as it would be as for (c)—that is, if the fraud is discovered after the transfer is complete, there is nothing to impeach D's claim to the property, and the only way that the transaction can be challenged is through the attachment in some way of C's claim of D resulting from the transfer.

In equity, the position is more straightforward. The basic remedy in knowing receipt is based on A's claim that C has received money, and that it is unconscionable for him to retain the money.[43] However, again, this is an after-the-fact approach, which seeks to design the correct end-state rather than analysing the precise proprietary position. 6.43

The conclusion from all this is that the only person who owns my deposit is me. There are circumstances in which I may lose it, in the sense that the bank may be excused from repaying me. However, there are no circumstances in which ownership of it can be transferred to someone else. Thus, a payment instrument does not and cannot effect a transfer of ownership of money, or of ownership of a claim to payment of money. What can be transferred, however, is the payment instrument itself. 6.44

## 6.4 Transfer and Negotiability of Private Payment Instruments

A private payment instrument does not have to be transferable to be useful—a written instruction to one's banker to pay money to X is of value to X, even though X cannot transfer it to anyone. However, there is no doubt that it is of considerably more value to X if it can be transferred, and of more value still if it gives the transferee a claim which is an independent free-standing right not dependent on the performance of the contract in respect of which the payment obligation was owed in the first place. This last characteristic—loosely, 'negotiability'—is a significant commercial technical advance, and much of the work on the development of private payment instruments consists of analyses of how it arose, how it developed, and what the legal bases were for it. However, it cannot be over-emphasised that useful as negotiability 6.45

---

[41] In this case the defect in title is not as regards C's ownership of the cheque (which is clear), but the fact that the cheque is voidable.
[42] *May v Chapman* (1847) 16 M. & W. 355, 361 per Parke B, *London Joint Stock Bank v Simmonds* [1892] AC 201, 221 per Lord Herschell. Fox, *Property Rights in Money* (OUP 2008) asserts that this actual notice standard is in practice equivalent to the good faith requirement.
[43] *Bank of Credit and Commerce (Overseas) Ltd v Akindele* [2001] Ch 437. In this regard, the courts have accepted that 'unconscionability' depends on context, and have retreated from the traditional five-point classification set out by Peter Gibson J in *Baden v Société Générale pour Favoriser le Developpement du Commerce et de l'Industrie de France SA* [1993] 1 WLR 509 at 575–6.

6.46 However, it is important not to confuse negotiability with simple transferability. At its simplest, transferability does not even require transferability. The heart of this paradox is that if I am owed £100 by X, it is a relatively simple matter for me to make an agreement with Y that when I receive the £100 from X I shall pay it over to Y. If this arrangement is made known to X, such that X agrees (for example) that he will not pay £100 to me without telling Y first, we have between us created 90 per cent of the functionality of a transferable instrument without ever having heard of transferability. However, the utility of formal transferability increases the larger the group becomes—if Y wishes to transfer the instrument to Z in due course, his task is considerably harder, and Z's task in transferring it to A is harder still. However, the mere non-existence of a legal concept of transferability is no barrier to the development of transfer in practice.[44]

6.47 It therefore seems likely that the lack of evidence in early legal codes for a doctrine of negotiability bears little or no relevance to the issue of whether negotiable instruments were used in that society. Thus, it seems that treasury tallies in the United Kingdom were effectively used as mechanisms for the transfer or liabilities from the earliest time,[45] despite the absence of any concept of negotiability in the law of that period.

6.48 It is important, however, not to underplay negotiability too much. Negotiability turns a commercial receivable into quasi-money. Negotiability, at its simplest, is the characteristic which an instrument has when it can be transferred to a third party on terms that the third party may sue as if he were the original recipient without reference to any failure of performance by the original party. Thus, if I buy ten cartons of goods from you and issue you a negotiable instrument for £100 in exchange, you may transfer (negotiate) it to another person, and that person may sue me for £100 regardless of what was in the cartons, or indeed if there were ever cartons at all. Negotiability is a peculiar form of legal magic, created to facilitate the use of commercial obligations as money in a world where commercial requirements were growing considerably faster than the supply of state money.

### 6.4.1 What does transfer of a payment instrument actually transfer?

6.49 This question does, however, need be asked separately in respect of the claim which the instrument embodies. Although the recipient of a cheque may regard it simply as a vehicle by which a claim to money is transferred to him, the 'money' which he receives is a credit claim on the payer's bank, which is transformed into a credit claim on his bank. That claim may be denominated in pounds, but it is not in any

---

[44] For a good explanation of how payment mechanisms can develop based on simple transfer without a formal concept of negotiability see Rogers, *The Early History of the Law of Bills and Notes* (Cambridge University Press 1995).
[45] See Moore, *Score it Upon My Taille; The Use (and Abuse) of Tallies by the Mediaeval Exchequer*, Reading Mediaeval Studies, Vol. 1 (2013) at 24.

meaningful sense a transfer of pounds. Even for larger payments, where the transfer of credit between banks is matched by a transfer within the settlement system (such as CHAPS in the United Kingdom[46]) it is not the case that money belonging to the payer is delivered to the payee—in effect, a payer pays his bank to transfer an amount to the payee's bank on the basis that that bank in turn will credit an equivalent amount to the payee's account with it. Thus, when we ask what, in modern society, is meant by having 'money', the answer is having a claim on a financial institution.

It is worth pausing to examine this situation in a little more detail. Although the balance on the customer's account with his bank is denominated in money units, it is actually no such thing—there is no money anywhere which is actually owned by the customer. The only money involved in the process is owned by the bank. What the customer has is the right to instruct the bank to transfer money to someone else—in other words, what he has in law is no more than a right to give instructions to a person who is under a legal obligation to act on those instructions. This sounds odd, but only because we have the intellectual habit of conflating ownership and alienability. This conflation can be dissolved when considering money because of the fundamental nature of money. Money is unique in that it is of no use in itself, but its only purpose is to discharge obligations owed to others; consequently, the core characteristic which anything must have in order to be able to function as money is unrestricted transferability. It follows from this that *ownership* of money is an irrelevance—if I have the power to instruct a particular person to transfer a specified amount of money to another, it is irrelevant to me whether I am said to own it or whether he is said to own it, provided that my right to have it transferred is valid. 6.50

### 6.4.2 Private payment in virtual currency

The reason for emphasising this point is that when we come to look at the position of virtual currency in modern society, we should not compare it with physical notes and coins, but with credit claims on banks. This simplifies matters, in that we are at least comparing intangibles with other intangibles. However, this comparison emphasises the differences as well as the similarities between the two. In particular, the essence of the claim on the bank is precisely that it is a claim on a person—if a customer were to sue for his account balance, the question of what he was suing for might be unclear, but the question of who he should sue would be entirely clear. With virtual currency, by comparison, not only is the question of what is being sued for unclear, but the question of who might be sued for it is even more unclear. However, the core of the structure within which the virtual currency unit is created is precisely a mechanism which facilitates its transferability. The performance of a particular series of actions in a particular way will result in a transfer, and the value of the transfer and the identity of the transferee may be specified (indeed must be specified) before any transfer takes place. The difference between the two situations is that whereas the holder of a bank deposit relies on a promise by the bank to transfer upon 6.51

---

[46] https://www.bankofengland.co.uk/payment-and-settlement/chaps.

instruction, the holder of a virtual currency unit relies on the transfer functionality which is built into the structure of the unit which he owns. A simple analogy might be between registered shares and bearer shares—a person who holds registered shares relies on the registrar performing his duty in order to transfer them, whereas a holder of bearer shares relies on the legal structure of the share itself in order to transfer it—thus a registered holder can sue the registrar if a transfer fails, whereas the holder of a bearer share has no one to sue. Nonetheless, if the shares are issued by the same company and rank *pari passu* with each other, these are unlikely to be regarded as material differences between what is fundamentally the same instrument.

6.52    The only remaining question in this regard is as to how much difference it makes that the claim on the bank is almost certainly denominated in a state currency, whereas the virtual currency unit is its own denomination. The answer, for this purpose, is that it makes no difference at all. As a starting point, consider why the bank account is denominated in existing currency. If a bank agrees to make 100 of any currency unit available to a customer, it will in general require 100 of that currency to be delivered to it. Thus, although your bank will probably open an account for you in any currency in the world, in order to open a US$ account for you it will require the delivery to it of US$, in order to open a GB£ account it will require the delivery of GB£, and so on. Your bank would almost certainly be happy to open an account for you in virtual currency X if you were to deliver to it the relevant value of that virtual currency. Assume that it is, and that you have done so. Now assume that you owe someone a debt denominated in virtual currency X, and you wish to pay him. What legal difference in this case could there be said to be between payment through a bank transfer of £100 and payment through a bank transfer of 100 virtual currency units. The issue of legal tender is (again) irrelevant—the fact that US$ are not legal tender in the United Kingdom is irrelevant to the question of whether a debt denominated in US$ can be paid through a US$ transfer in the United Kingdom through a UK bank. It seems impossible, in this scenario, to believe that such a payment would be subject to any legal obstacle based solely on the fact that the currency unit employed was not created by a sovereign state.

6.53    If this is the position for payments where the virtual currency unit is transformed into a claim on a financial institution, it is difficult to see that the outcome could or should be any different if the virtual currency unit is withdrawn from the financial institution and transferred directly using its own inherent transfer mechanism. Again, there is a useful comparison between paying a bill with a cheque and paying it with a banknote—the fact that the transfer mechanism used is different should not have any impact at all on the legal analysis of the position as between the parties.

## 6.5 Commercial Bank Credit Money as Private Money

6.54    In order to understand the interaction of virtual currency with the existing money, banking, and payment systems, it is necessary to say a little about those systems. As noted earlier, part of the problem with banking is the extent to which neither bank customers nor, from time to time, either bank users or the courts have engaged with the actual structure of the bank payments. It is therefore necessary to spend some time explaining how this system actually works.[47]

As a matter of law, it is clear that when a customer gives money to a bank, that money becomes the property of the bank. Not only does the customer not expect that specific money back again, the money (in the sense of money being owned by him) ceases to exist.[48] At the most basic level, the transaction is similar to a loan of anything that is to be consumed in the ordinary course of events—if I lend a friend a packet of cigarettes, I do not expect the precise cigarettes lent to be returned. This sort of deposit of consumables is known as commodatum in Roman law, and is characterised in the *Digest of Justinian* as an 'irregular deposits'[49]—irregular, because the law tends to presume that where a thing has been lent, the very same thing must be returned, and it is only deposits of this latter kind which are classified as 'regular'. However, 'regular' deposits are almost never encountered in finance—even where a deposit is of (say) shares in a company, provided that the shares are all equal the depositor is only concerned that he obtains the same *number* of shares back; he will not care *which* shares he gets back. Where what is handed over is currency, then the deposit is necessarily irregular. Absolute ownership of the currency passes to the recipient on delivery, since the currency is effectively exchanged for a claim on the deposit-taker. Thus, any currency redelivered to the depositor will necessarily be legally different to the amount deposited, even if it constitutes the same notes and coins.

6.55 This is true *a fortiori* if (as is almost invariably the case) the relevant funds are transferred to the bank electronically. In the typical situation of an employee receiving wages from his employer, the employee's bank will receive an electronic notification from the employer's bank to the effect that money is due to its customer. This creates a minor problem, in that the employer is obliged to pay the money to the employee. The position is therefore analysed as that the employee's bank will collect the payment from the employer's bank as agent for the employee. Thus, if the bank were receiving physical currency, it would collect it as agent for its customer. There would therefore be a *scintilla temporis* in which the customer owned the notes and coins through its agent, and a point thereafter in which the bank appropriated the notes and coins itself in exchange for crediting the customer's account, in exactly the same way that it would have done if the customer had paid the currency in over the counter. However, this again is a fiction, since the employee's bank unquestionably did not receive notes and coins from anyone. What it received was an electronic notification from the employer's bank to the effect that the employer's bank recognised that it was indebted to the employee's bank. What the employee's bank therefore almost certainly did in

---

[47] The major work on this topic remains Malek and Odgers (eds), *Paget's Law of Banking* (14th edn, LexisNexis 2014) and Brindle and Cox (eds), *The Law of Bank Payments* (5th edn, Sweet & Maxwell 2018), along with Geva, *Bank Collections and Payment Transactions* (OUP 2001) although in this regard an important contribution is Fox's *Property Rights in Money* (OUP 2008). I am indebted to that work for much of what follows.

[48] *Foley v Hill* (1848) 2 HLC 28 at 36; *London Joint Stock Bank Ltd v Macmillan* [1918] AC 777 at 814 (HL), *Joachimson v Swiss Bank Corp* [1921] 3 KB 110 (CA); *Libyan Arab Foreign Bank v Bankers Trust Co* [1989] QB 728 at 784.

[49] Dig. 19.2.31; 16.3.7.2–3.

real life was to recognise in its accounts a debt due to it, and to increase its indebtedness to the employee by increasing the balance recorded on his account.

6.56 Money itself has thus largely disappeared from the system. The process involves a number of banks crediting and debiting accounts between themselves. When one bank has a net surplus with another, it may settle that surplus through the central bank. However, what is settled is a net balance, and not the specific individual payments which have been effected. Even with systems such as Faster Payments, what happens is a debiting and crediting of accounts, with settlement of net balances following along some time later.

6.57 This reflects the structure discussed above, and in particular the distinction between endogenous and exogenous money. Endogenous money is created by the banking system as required by the economy, and is completely separate from the exogenous money created and supplied by the central bank.[50]

### 6.5.1 The state and bank credit money

6.58 It should be evident at this point that endogenous commercial bank money is created by commercial banks inter se, and is an entirely different form of property from central bank money or notes and coins. However, the common feature is denomination. A bank depositor whose account is in credit does not own any sort of currency of any form, whether notes and coins or central bank reserves. All that he owns is a claim on a commercial bank. However, that claim is denominated in sterling. It need not be—it would be perfectly possible for a bank to create an entirely new value unit of its own and operate an account by reference to that unit, and it is also perfectly theoretically possible for that unit to be a virtual currency unit, a commodity (such as gold[51]) or indeed anything else. However, because of the strong social necessity for a common unit of value, in practice such arrangements are vanishingly rare, and accounts are generally denominated in national currencies.

6.59 This fact creates the illusion that the account balance is somehow 'composed of' currency units issued by the state. This is simply wrong—as noted above, a bank account balance is a bilateral thing between the bank's customer and the bank, and the state is not involved. What the state does have, however, is an absolute right to prescribe what at any given time is meant by 'sterling'. This is the 'principle of nominalism'. Nominalism is sometimes presented as an unusual doctrine unique to money, but in fact it is nothing of the kind. If I contract to sell you a new Fiat 500 in twelve months' time, what I am contracting to sell you is whatever the Fiat company choses to market under that label at that time. In effect, what we have agreed between us is that the subject matter of the contract between us shall be defined by a third party, and

---

[50] Moore, *Horizontalists and Verticalists, The Macroeconomics of Credit Money* (Cambridge University Press 1988). A useful summary of current thinking as regards the interrelation beween private money, public money, and central bank policy can be found in Palley, *Horizontalists, Verticalists and Structuralists: The Theory of Endogenous Money Reassessed* (Dusseldorf, IMK 2013) Working Paper No. 121.

[51] This is exactly how unallocated gold deposits do operate.

the terms of that determination shall become part of the contract. Thus, if I contract to deliver sterling to you at a point in the future, and the UK government chooses to change its definition of sterling at some point prior to the obligation falling due, my obligation is to deliver whatever the UK government chooses to define as pounds simply because that is what the contract between us provided for. There is no special magic of monetary law involved. Equally, there is nothing difficult about the two of us contracting out of the UK government's definition of a pound and substituting another of our own if that is what we wish to do. This practice used to be widespread in the era of high inflation, and this was the function of 'gold clauses' in contracts. A typical gold clause provided that an amount payable in a currency should be payable at the value in gold of that currency on the day of contracting—thus, if the obligation was for N pounds sterling, the clause might provide that on the payment date the obligation should be to whatever amount of sterling would amount to the worth in gold of N pounds at the contract date; the aim being to protect the seller against depreciation of sterling by the UK government in the period between contract and payment. Although there has been some judicial murmuring about whether or not clauses of this form are compatible with monetary sovereignty,[52] it is clear from the House of Lord's decision in *Feist v Société Intercommunale Belge de L'electricite*[53] that such clauses are entirely compatible with English law.

### 6.5.2 Payment in commercial bank credit money

The basic question is therefore as to what is meant by 'payment' in this context. The fundamental principle is that if you pay me money through the banking system, I can be said to have been paid at the moment when I become unconditionally entitled to deal with the money credit to my account with my bank. It should be noted that this is entirely unconnected with the transfer of any actual money, exogenous or endogenous, physical or electronic. Indeed, it is not necessary that money should move from the payer—if, through inadvertence, your bank forgets to debit your account with money which has been credited to mine, the validity of the payment (from my perspective) is unaffected. This lack of connection means that it is entirely wrong to think of any sort of title to anything being transferred when an electronic payment is made. When a bank credits a customer's account with an amount, it is bringing into existence a new right which did not previously exist, and has no legal connection to any other pre-existing right. It is this, rather than the rules relating to the loss of title through mixture, which explains why there is no possibility of tracing legal title to money through electronic bank systems. It is important to understand this point. Even in a situation where a transferor has a balance with his bank, and instructs his bank to pay the whole of that balance to an empty account in the name of another, he will have no legal title claim at all to the resulting balance.

6.60

---

[52] See per Denning LJ in *Treseder-Griffin v Co-Operative Insurance Society* [1956] 2 QB 127 at 145.
[53] [1934] AC 161, and see *Multiservice Bookbinding Ltd v Marden* [1979] Ch 84, in which a provision whereby the amount of sterling due under a contract should be calculated by reference to the value of the Swiss franc was held to be valid.

### 6.5.3 Virtual currency as commercial bank money

6.61  Translated into the world of virtual currency, this becomes complex. Because of the nature of distributed ledgers, there are two ways in which an intermediary can curate virtual currency units for a customer, and these correspond fairly well to the old Roman distinctions. It is possible for an agent in this context to operate simply as a custodian for his principal—that is, he will pass through instructions to the operator(s) of the ledger as agent of the customer, but the customer will remain the owner of the virtual currency units concerned. Conversely, he may take title to the units himself, such that what the customer has is a claim on the intermediary for the delivery of virtual currency units, but ownership of those units is vested in the intermediary. This latter situation will also bring into account questions of trustee status—the mere fact that legal title (in the form of registration in the register) is in the name of the intermediary will not of itself determine the question of whether beneficial title vests in the client or in the intermediary.

6.62  Interestingly, this takes us back to the question of mixtures. If an intermediary is registered as the legal owner of virtual currency units which initially belonged to a number of his clients, the question which is likely to arise is as to whether those clients collectively have a proprietary interest in the underlying assets. If the underlying assets are not money, then there is a developed body of law which will answer this question.[54] However, if the underlying assets are money, then the presumption that title passes on transfer will be deployed, and the investors will have nothing more than a debt claim on the intermediary.

6.63  This is, of course, the problem which the Financial Conduct Authority client money rules have been developed to overcome. The easiest way of thinking about these rules is that they govern the situation where money is transferred to a non-bank (usually, but not invariably, a securities intermediary) by a client of that non-bank pursuant to an exemption from the rules on deposit-taking.[55] The basis of these rules is that clients should not be expected to exchange cash balances for a claim on a possibly thinly capitalised intermediary. Consequently, they require that where monies are transferred to a non-bank intermediary in this way, they are required to be held with a bank in a segregated account in such a fashion that if the intermediary were to fail, the clients would have a direct claim on the balance maintained in that account. Similar rules apply (in a more limited way) to securities held for clients. The challenge for regulators will be to determine whether client money rules will—or should—be applied in respect of virtual currency units managed by intermediaries for clients.

---

[54] The most comprehensive summary of the law of custody is to be found in Yates and Montagu, *The Law of Global Custody* (Bloomsbury 2013).

[55] Securities intermediaries are effectively required to handle cash on behalf of their clients pursuant to their normal activities. They are permitted under the regulatory system to do this without being subject to the ordinary bank regulatory regime—see Walker, Purves et al., *Financial Services Law* (4th edn, OUP 2018) at paras 18-233 to 18-241.

# 7

# The Legal Character of Money

| | | |
|---|---|---|
| 7.1 | **Legal Definitions of 'Money'** | 7.02 |
| | 7.1.1 Characterisation as 'money' | 7.03 |
| | 7.1.2 The argument that only sovereign currency is 'money' | 7.06 |
| | 7.1.3 How free are the courts to recognise private intention as determinative of money status? | 7.12 |
| | 7.1.4 Are different characterisations in different circumstances permissible? | 7.15 |
| | 7.1.5 Case-by-case versus once-and-for-all characterisation | 7.17 |
| | 7.1.6 Impracticality of once-and-for-all determination | 7.21 |
| | 7.1.7 Hard and soft boundaries in legal classifications | 7.23 |
| 7.2 | **The Attributes of Money** | 7.26 |
| 7.3 | **Currency** | 7.29 |
| | 7.3.1 Currency and negotiability | 7.36 |
| | 7.3.2 Virtual currency as currency | 7.40 |
| 7.4 | **Abstraction** | 7.46 |
| 7.5 | **Untraceability through Mixtures** | 7.49 |
| 7.6 | **Tender** | 7.53 |
| | 7.6.1 Legal tender | 7.54 |
| | 7.6.2 Determination of the value of the thing tendered | 7.56 |
| | 7.6.3 The *Case de Mixt Moneys* | 7.58 |
| | 7.6.4 Divergence of common and civil law | 7.61 |
| | 7.6.5 Practical significance of legal tender legislation | 7.62 |
| | 7.6.6 Tender and the discharge of debts | 7.65 |
| | 7.6.7 Discharge of debts—Can the debtor unilaterally discharge a debt? | 7.67 |
| | 7.6.8 Discharge of debts—Can the creditor unilaterally discharge a debt? | 7.68 |
| | 7.6.9 Contractual provisions regarding payment | 7.69 |
| | 7.6.10 Tender through the provision of a payment mechanism | 7.72 |
| | 7.6.11 The relevance of tender | 7.74 |
| | 7.6.12 Tender of money and tender of goods | 7.76 |
| | 7.6.13 Tender of virtual currency | 7.78 |
| 7.7 | **Payment** | 7.84 |
| | 7.7.1 What is a 'sale'? | 7.86 |
| | 7.7.2 The two elements of payment | 7.88 |
| | 7.7.3 Methods of payment | 7.91 |
| | 7.7.4 Payment in virtual currency | 7.93 |

7.01 The law regards money as a species of property with unique characteristics.[1] The most important issue is that claims for money (debt claims) are regarded in law as different from claims for any other thing. It is important to emphasise here that this is not, as is sometimes said, a hangover from the old forms of action[2]—the reason that the law treats a claim for money as fundamentally different from a claim for things is that this reflects the way in which people think about such claims in practice. The fundamental issue (which has been with us since the earliest times[3]) is that if you owe me money, and fail to pay it, my action against you is an action in debt, and the remedy I seek is an order requiring you to pay me that sum (plus interest if appropriate). If you are obliged to deliver goods to me, but fail to do so, my action against you is an action for damages—that is, for compensation for the harm which I have suffered as a result of your breach of your obligation.[4] Thus, the question of how much you must pay is decided by measuring the damage I suffered. This may be very different from the value of the goods not delivered—it may be less (if I could reasonably have been expected to mitigate the loss or it may be more (if your breach caused me to suffer other foreseeable losses). Only in the most unusual circumstances will a court order the seller to perform his obligation to deliver things. If a person breaches an obligation to pay money, however, the remedy is an order to pay that amount of money. The question of how much damage (if any) the payee has suffered through the refusal to pay is simply irrelevant,[5] and concepts like mitigation, remoteness, or foreseeable damage have no place in this system—the remedy for a failure to pay £100 is an order to pay £100. Thus, in an action in relation to virtual currency today, the basic question of whether the virtual currency should be treated as 'money' or not for this purpose is largely determinative as to the potential remedy available.

## 7.1 Legal Definitions of 'Money'

7.02 The existence of this sharp distinction between actions for debt and actions for damages is a problem, because there is no legal definition of the term 'money' at English law. There are a number of cases in which the meaning of the term is considered, and a number of statutes in which the term is partially defined, but these do not add up to a workable definition. As a demonstration of the diversity in practice, it may be

---

[1] See *First National Bank of Chicago v Customs and Excise commissioners* (C172/96) [1999] QB 570 ECJ (Fifth Chamber), to the effect that trading in foreign exchange with a customer is to be regarded as a service and not a sale of goods since money is not tangible property.
[2] It is a frequent complaint that some aspects of English law are as they are because the old system, in which different types of claims were governed by different procedures and rules, has been inadvertently carried over into the new—this is the essence of Maitland's famous observation that 'The forms of action we have buried, but they still rule us from their graves' (Lecture 1, *The Forms of Action at Common Law* (1909)).
[3] See Baker, *An Introduction to English Legal History* (2nd edn, Butterworths 1979) at 266–8.
[4] *Johnson v Agnew* [1980] AC 367, *The Golden Victory* [2007] UKHL 12.
[5] This is not quite true—there are some circumstances where damage which was foreseeable under the rule in *Hadley v Baxendale* [1854] 9 Exch 341 can be recovered. However, these are rare.

helpful to consider two fairly extreme cases in this regard, both of which consider the status of near-money items. On the one hand, we have *In re Hodgson*,[6] where a nurse, asked to make her will within two days of her death and having in her case by the side of her bed some 800l. in cash and 600l. in savings certificates, left all her 'money' to a named beneficiary. She left no next-of-kin, and it was held that the savings certificates passed to the crown *bona vacantia*, since they did not constitute 'money'. At the other extreme there is *Perrin v Morgan*,[7] a will case in which the court was called upon to construe the meaning of a bequest of 'all monies of which I die possessed'.[8] Since the deceased's estate consisted almost entirely of securities, the House of Lords accepted that 'money' in this context could include these securities.

### 7.1.1 Characterisation as 'money'

How, therefore, should an English court decide what is money and what is not? This can be rephrased as a question as to whether the law can properly regard anything as money per se unless it has the backing of a sovereign state? This is an entirely separate issue from the question of the origin of money per se—it is a question about how the law characterises things. 7.03

English courts regard English money as money because English law tells them to.[9] However, they also regard foreign money as money, despite the absence of any law telling them to. Consequently, a sale of goods in exchange for foreign currency is treated as a sale and not a barter, and an exchange of English money for foreign money is not treated as a sale of goods.[10] Sadly, there is no particular definition which can be used to decide which foreign moneys are in fact money. 7.04

The courts are also—clearly—prepared to recognise private payment instruments as money. However, it is important to draw a distinction in this regard between private instruments which purport to create a claim *for* money, and private instruments which claim to *be* money. In general, the courts do not have difficulty with instruments of the first type—cheques, bills of exchange, promissory notes, etc.— and this lack of difficulty is likely to be continued as regards electronic versions of these instruments. However, true virtual currencies, which claim to be money, are a different matter. Whether or not the very large number of virtual currency units currently in circulation should be treated as currency is the question which this work is intended to address; the fact that they are created for that express purpose is not open to question. Hence the question of whether they are money cannot be entirely avoided by pretending that they are mere payment instruments facilitating the payment of sovereign money. 7.05

---

[6] [1936] Ch 203.   [7] [1943] AC 399.
[8] [1943] AC 399 HL at 406–7 per Viscount Simon and followed in *Re Barnes Will Trust* [1972] 1 WLR 587 Ch D and *RSPCA v Sharp* [2011] 1 WLR 980.
[9] Section 1(1) of the Currency and Bank Notes Act 1954 for banknotes and s. 2(1) of the Coinage Act 1971 for coins.
[10] See Chapter 7 of Bridge, Gullifer McMeel, Worthington, *The Law of Personal Property* (2nd edn, OUP 2018), esp. at 7-033.

### 7.1.2 The argument that only sovereign currency is 'money'

7.06 A simple answer to the question of whether virtual currency units can be regarded in law as money could be provided by asserting that there is an absolute rule of law that only instruments created by governments can be recognised in law as money.[11] Unfortunately, there is no legal basis for any such rule.[12] Those who contend for such a rule are obliged to base their arguments on public policy and presumed intention rather than extant laws and decided cases. It is possible that such a rule may at some point be formulated, but we can say with some certainty that it is not decided law today.

7.07 As perhaps befits the common law, the assembled cases have almost nothing to say about what money is; only about the function which it performs in the immediate case. In this regard the courts have followed the economists since, as noted above, from the perspective of an economist money is simply something which does the job of money. The locus classicus of this position is the observation of F. A. Walker[13] that money is simply 'that which passes freely from hand to hand throughout the community in final discharge of debts and full payment for commodities, being accepted equally without reference to the character or the credit of the person who offers it and without the intention of the person who receives it to consume it or apply it to any other use than in turn to tender it to others in discharge of debts or payment for commodities'. This definition was cited with approval by Darling J in *Moss v Hancock*.[14]

7.08 The academic authorities have followed a very different path. Darling J's approval of Walker's dictum excited the rage of F. A. Mann, the leading authority on the law of money in his lifetime, who strongly took the view that this interpretation was too broad to be useful for lawyers. Mann therefore suggested that in law the quality of money is to be attributed to all chattels 'which, issued by the authority of the law and denominated with reference to a unit of account, are meant to serve as universal means of exchange in the state of issue'. This is an articulation of the state theory of money promulgated in Knapp's *State Theory of Money*.[15] Its unfortunate consequence is that bank credit money—that is, the primary and almost exclusive medium of payment in the real economy—is excluded from the definition of money.[16] It seems likely that Mann reached this conclusion by backwards reasoning from the principle of nominalism—if, as the nominalistic

---

[11] This was the view of the leading English legal commentator—Mann, *The Legal Aspect of Money* (4th edn, OUP 1982) at 13. For a modern restatement of the position see Zimmermann, *A Contemporary Concept of Monetary Sovereignty* (OUP 2013).

[12] Mann's argument that 'to permit the circulation of money that is not created or at least authorized by the state would be tantamount to a denial of the state's monetary prerogative' (ibid. at 14) is stronger on rhetoric than rationality. The position in the United States may be different, in that UCC s. 1-201(24) defines 'money' as 'a medium of exchange currently authorized or adopted by a domestic or foreign government'.

[13] *Money, Trade and Industry* (London 1882).   [14] [1899] 2 QB 111 at 116.

[15] Trans. Lucas and Bonar (Macmillan 1924).

[16] See Gleeson, *Personal Property Law* (FT Law and Tax Law 1997) and Brindle and Cox, *The Law of Bank Payments* (4th edn, Sweet & Maxwell 2010) para 2.1.

principle asserts, the attributes of money are exclusively determined by the state of issue of that money, then it seems hard to say that anything which is not an emanation of that state should be money, since it is hard to see that an instrument which is purely privately created and is not an emanation of state power can be subject to the nominalistic principle in this way.[17] It is also largely incompatible with Knapp's views—he seems to have accepted that anything which the state is prepared to accept at its pay-offices as money,[18] and the modern state accepts private payment instruments such as bank credits in payment of a wide variety of obligations.

7.09 To take a recent example, imagine a depositor holding a deposit of French francs with a US bank immediately prior to the creation of the euro. If the depositor were to go to the bank the day after the adoption of the euro and say 'repay me my French francs', the response he would get from the bank would be that the term of the agreement between them was that the bank should pay to the customer whatever 'counted' as a French franc, and if the government of France had proclaimed (as it had) that henceforth the franc was to become the euro, then the obligation of the deposit-holding bank was to repay euros, and only euros. The point is that although the claim may be a private claim between private parties, the claim is for the thing defined by the sovereign as such, and both parties effectively agree that the question of what is meant by the term 'French franc' is up to the French government to determine.[19] It should be noted that there is no reason why the parties should not contract out of this arrangement, or indeed as between themselves define the term 'French franc' to mean anything they please at any time that they please. However, where two parties contract in the currency of a country, the assumption is that what they mean by that currency is what the government of the country says it means. This can be a hard position for statists to accept—the idea that currency is created by the exercise of state power is a common illusion (although largely unsupported by fact), and the reality—that currency is a convenience provided by the state for private use—involves considerably less grandeur. However, this position is no different from the position as it was settled by the United Kingdom in the *Case de Mixt Moneys*[20]—in that case again the issue was a private contract between private individuals, with the point at issue being little more than the construction of that agreement, and yet the case is frequently cited as authority for the strong form of the nominalistic principle.

7.10 Charles Proctor, the current editor of *Mann*,[21] puts forward a weaker definition intended to address the exclusion of bank credit money (and other forms of payment such as e-money) from the definition put forward above. Proctor's definition is that money is any claim which has the following three characteristics:

---

[17] At least this seems to be the view of the current editor of Mann: see Proctor (ed.), *Mann on the Legal Aspect of Money* (7th edn, OUP 2012) at para 1-18.
[18] *The State Theory of Money*, trans. Lucas and Bonar (Macmillan 1924) at 51.
[19] The principle of Lex Monetae—see *Mann on the Legal Aspect of Money* (7th edn, OUP 2012) paras 6.24–6.33 for an overview of the legal issues which arise where one currency is replaced by one or more others.
[20] (1604) Davis 18.
[21] *Mann on the Legal Aspect of Money* (7th edn, OUP 2012) at para 1.168.

(1) it must be expressed by reference to a name and denominated by reference to a unit of account which, in each case, is prescribed by the law of the state concerned;

(2) the currency and unit so prescribed must be intended to serve as the generally accepted measure of value and medium of exchange within the state concerned; and

(3) the legal framework for the currency must include a central bank or monetary authority responsible for the issue of the currency, and including appropriate institutional provisions for its management through the conduct of monetary policy and the oversight of payment systems.

7.11 The third element of this definition cannot stand, as there are too many difficulties associated with it. Some of these are historical—it means that the United States did not have a currency at all for most of the nineteenth century—and some contemporaneous—it would mean that any currency operated on a pure currency board basis (such as the Hong Kong dollar today) was not a currency—and some again purely logical—is it really suggested that if bitcoin were to become the predominant global currency employed in the settling of debts and to acquire all of the characteristics set out by Walker above, that the mere fact of the non-existence of a bitcoin central bank would forever debar it from the legal status of money? However, if this element is discarded, the remaining elements of the definition strongly suggest that the term 'money' means 'any private claim denominated in the units prescribed by a state'. Thus, for example, Robert Owen's time-based currency issued out of his National Equitable Labour Exchange, exchangeable for goods in the company store, could never acquire the status of money.[22]

### 7.1.3 How free are the courts to recognise private intention as determinative of money status?

7.12 One of the more difficult socio-legal issues in any system is as to the extent to which actual social practice is a source of law. This has always been a difficult issue, not least because since modern enacted law is frequently intended to vary social practices, it is hard to think of social practice as a source of law without apparently creating an irreconcilable conflict. However, this may be to confuse social practice, as regards obedience to authority, with social practice as regards interactions between citizens.

7.13 The point here can best be explained by highlighting the distinction between a *private agreement* that X should be Y and a *common understanding* that X should be Y. Private parties cannot, simply by agreement, make a commodity money—if you and I agree to exchange sheep for goats, and one of the terms of the contract is that as between the two of us the goats shall be regarded as money, that will not be sufficient to make a court treat my action against you for goats as an action in debt. However, if you and I agree to exchange sheep for goats in a society in which goats are widely

---

[22] Although since they definitely were exchanged for goods, one must wonder at the legal characterisation of that exchange if it was not a sale.

regarded as money,[23] it would be perverse for the courts to regard the goats as anything other than money, since that was the common basis on which the parties contracted. In such a case, it is difficult to see how a court could do anything other than accept the common understanding within the society concerned as constituting the basis of the understanding between any two members of it.

7.14 It should be noted that this is nothing more than a restatement of the basic proposition that the law's purpose is to give effect to agreements, not to frustrate them. A comparison may be drawn with what is sometimes called the reception of the *lex mercatoria* into English law under the direction of Coke LJ in the seventeenth century.[24] This is sometimes erroneously pictured as the reception into English law of a complete alternative legal system. This belief seems to be based on the fact that special statutes were put in place to provide that, as between merchants, the 'law merchant' should apply.[25] However, the idea that there was an identifiable sovereign legal system called the law merchant appears to be a legal fiction. In reality, 'modern scholars have tended to reject the traditional, rather romanticized, view of the mediaeval English law merchant as a separate corpus of law'[26] and to regard it instead as 'the factual matrix within which certain types of contract are made'.[27] This is a complex way of saying that where the law confronts a body of activity which is conducted amongst a group on the basis of a common orthodoxy, the starting point should be to recognise and enforce that orthodoxy.

### 7.1.4 Are different characterisations in different circumstances permissible?

7.15 This creates an immediate difficulty, in that it appears to revive the idea of different laws applicable to different people on the basis of status—the idea that contracts between merchants should be judged according to different principles to contracts between non-merchants—and this appears inimical to everything we believe about equality before the law. It does not. The starting place of analysis on this point is one of the relatively few surviving relics of the special treatment of merchants at English law—the Factors Act 1889. This has the effect that a 'mercantile agent' gives good title to goods that he sells, even if he does not have title to them himself. The policy behind this section is intuitive—if a merchant sells goods, their buyer is entitled to assume that he is entitled to sell them, whereas if a private person sells goods, the buyer should at least wonder whether the goods are the seller's to sell.[28] The point here is that we are not dealing with a peculiarly status-based law (freemen have

---

[23] Common in a number of parts of the world—see, e.g., Kenyatta, *Facing Mount Kenya—The Tribal Life of the Gikuyu* (London 1938).
[24] See Holdsworth, *A History of English Law*, 17 vols (7th edn, Sweet & Maxwell 1956–72) Vol. IV.
[25] Statute of Merchants (also known as the Statute of Acton Burnell) 1283, 11 Edw I, as amended by the Statute of Merchants 1285, 13 Edw 1; Statute of the Staple.
[26] McKendrick (ed.), *Goode on Commercial Law* (5th edn, Butterworths 2016).
[27] Baker, *The Law Merchant as a Source of English Law* in Swadling and Jones (eds), *Essays in Honour of Lord Goff* (OUP 2000) at 26.
[28] See McKendrick (ed.), *Goode on Commercial Law* (5th edn, LexisNexis 2016) at 462.

different legal rights from slaves), but the idea that a person may act in a capacity which is recognised by society, and to which society attaches different significance. The key point about the mercantile agent is that such a man does not acquire his special status by virtue of his person, but by virtue of the capacity in which he acts. In his capacity as a market participant he has unlimited power to pledge goods in his possession, and his pledges are protected at law.[29] However, if, on his way home from the market, he pledges his partner's watch to buy a drink, at that point he is acting as a private citizen, and that pledge is subject to the ordinary laws of the land. The point here is that there are multiple capacities in which a man can act, and in considering each action we begin by enquiring which capacity he was acting in.

7.16 The same logic applies to any transaction. Where two merchants deal with each other in a market in which they are accustomed to deal, neither they nor anyone else should dispute that they are subject to the customs of that market. Equally, the law should be very ready to accept that the customs of that market should be the first port of call in determining the rights and liabilities of the two merchants inter se. This means that the outcome of a legal dispute between those two merchants on particular facts may be significantly different to the outcome that would pertain on identical facts between two private persons operating outside that market. That is not a problem; it is simply the legal system seeking to deliver the intended outcome of human interaction. This issue has a devil's tail, in that even if the position is clear as between merchants, and clear as between private parties, it may still not be perfectly straightforward where one party is a merchant and the other is not. In cases of this kind, the question is basically as to where the transaction took place—that is, was it a market transaction (i.e. did the customer come to the market and deal with the merchant as such), or was it a private transaction (i.e. did the merchant come and deal with the customer without giving any indication that he was anything other than a private individual). However, this is not a boundary with which the courts are unfamiliar,[30] and to suggest that the outcome of a particular transaction should be different according to the status of the parties in this regard is no more than to accept the fact that different transactions, undertaken in different contexts, should properly have different outcomes.

### 7.1.5 Case-by-case versus once-and-for-all characterisation

7.17 What follows from this is that there is no reason why the question of whether a particular instrument is money or not should be a once-and-for-all determination that applies to all persons in all circumstances. It is entirely possible to envisage a transaction between two technologically active parties in which it is the clear common intention of both that virtual currency should be a payment medium, whereas in a similar transaction between unsophisticated investors, it may well be the case that virtual currency units are the subject matter of, rather than the

---

[29] Factors Act 1889, s. 2(1).
[30] See *Bentley (Dick) Productions Ltd v Harold Smith (Motors) Ltd* [1956] 1 WLR 623 for a magnificent illustration of a case on exactly this borderline.

payment medium in, the transaction. This is consistent with the approach taken in *Moss v Hancock*,[31] in which the question was whether a particular (ceremonial, presentation) £5 gold piece should be regarded as money or not. The court's approach was in effect to consider, on the basis of evidence, the intention and state of mind of those involved in the transaction, and to answer the question of whether the rules relating to money should be applied to the transaction by reference to that evidence. Thus, in *Moss v Hancock*, the fact that the relevant £5 coin had been treated as a thing rather than as money (it had been held in a presentation case, and never used as currency—presumably because it was worth considerably more than its face value of £5) was held to be determinative, since the court held that it was 'Permitted to draw inferences from the facts stated to us . . .'.[32] This principle provides a sensible and effective basis for deciding the proper treatment for virtual currency in contracts.

7.18 This, however, raises a further question. Assuming we have a clear basis on which to make a determination as to what is money and what is not, the question is as to whether we are characterising a thing as money *once-and-for-all purposes*, or whether we are asking whether a thing should be regarded as money in the context of the particular circumstance before the court.

7.19 The difference between the two can be illustrated by a simple example. The question of whether an arrangement to hold the property of another constitutes the regulated activity of deposit-taking depends on the nature of the property—if the property is money, then holding it for another constitutes deposit-taking and the holder must be a regulated bank;[33] if the property is not money, then no such consequence follows. Assume that there exists a binding judicial precedent that the holding of exactly the virtual currency concerned is a form of banking, and that therefore, by necessary implication, the virtual currency concerned is money for the purposes of the banking legislation. Is that authority determinative of the question of whether the virtual currency concerned should be regarded as 'money' for the purposes of deciding whether an action for its non-delivery is an action in debt or an action in damages?

7.20 This question can only be answered by asking whether there is a single concept of 'money' for all purposes at law, or whether references to 'money' in different contexts should be interpreted in the context of that legislation in order to give the most rational effect to that legislation.

### 7.1.6 Impracticality of once-and-for-all determination

7.21 If we are basing our approach on a social/purposive analysis, then the initial question should be whether the parties treated the particular thing as money in the context of the particular transaction in which they actually engaged. If this is our starting point, then the idea that a once-and-for-all determination can be made

---

[31] [1899] 2 QB 111.   [32] Ibid. per Darling LJ at 116.
[33] Or otherwise exempt from the requirement to be authorised to take deposits.

about a particular instrument which will be true at all times for all parties seems insupportable. Consider, for example, the famous case of the circulation of cigarettes as a form of money in prisoner-of-war camps described in Radford's account of their economics.[34] Had litigation been possible in such a context, it seems reasonably clear that it would produce a surprising and perceptibly unjust outcome to rule that a single rule should be selected and applied indiscriminately to a failure to make a payment denominated in cigarettes and a sale of cigarettes for the purposes of smoking. If the same rule is applied in both cases, manifest injustice will be done in one or other. This must take us to the conclusion that the answer to the question 'should this be treated as money' is to ask how the parties to the contract intended it to be treated.

7.22    It may be objected at this point that this extends too much liberty to the parties—parties to a contract may make what commercial terms they like, but must contract within the framework of the law—thus, for example, the parties to a contract for the sale of land cannot agree privately that the rules relating to the conveyancing of land will not apply as between them. Some legal rules can be contracted out of, others cannot. The question is as to which category the classification of a thing as 'money' falls.

### 7.1.7  Hard and soft boundaries in legal classifications

7.23    Another way of asking this question is to ask which legislative categories have hard boundaries and which soft. Hard boundaries are generally encountered in the field of policy-driven legislation—thus the question of whether an investment arrangement is a regulated scheme, whether an arrangement in respect of housing is a lease, or whether an arrangement in respect of the supply of services constitutes employment, is interpreted solely by reference to the relevant legislation, and the intentions of the parties are disregarded. Conversely soft boundaries—such as whether particular Sale of Goods Act terms are implied into a contract of sale, or whether an arrangement in respect of property is a trust—are left almost entirely to the parties to determine. In the context of money, it was the case—at least in some areas—that the definition of money was a 'hard' definition—for example, for many years only an obligation to deliver the legal currency of the realm could constitute a debt obligation, and an obligation to deliver any money other than English money could not be sued for in debt, but was required to be treated as a claim for breach of a contract to deliver a thing. This was swept away in the 1960s, and thereafter it was clear that the English courts would treat as money anything that was regarded in some other part of the world as money, even if it was not legal tender in the United Kingdom. However, the court did not consider—because there was no reason to do so—whether this concession should be regarded as extended to any sort of asset whatsoever provided that it was treated by the parties

---

[34] Radford, *The Economic Organization of a P.O.W. Camp*, (Economica November 1945).

as money, or whether it was confined to those assets which were recognised as money by statute in some part of the world or another. How hard or soft is the classification today?

7.24 The question can perhaps best be answered by asking why 'hard' boundaries are hard. The answer is usually either to protect third parties, or to prevent undue advantage being taken of unequal bargaining positions. In the case of a sale of land, for example, the reason that the formalities relating to land transfer cannot be contracted out of is to ensure that a subsequent purchaser of the land can determine with certainty whether the vendor actually owns the land he is purporting to sell. In the case of the lease/licence distinction, the assumption is that the protections afforded to tenants should not be capable of being contracted out of because of the assumed unequal bargaining power between the two parties. There are a number of other reasons why legal categories should be made 'hard' rather than soft, but we can take these two as a starting point. The third party argument falls away immediately—if determination is made on a case-by-case basis according to the intention of the parties, the characterisation of a thing as 'money' in one transaction will not necessarily affect its characterisation in the next transaction in which it is used. Equally, the party protection arguments do not apply—there is no reason to assume *a priori* that either party will be advantaged or disadvantaged by classification of a thing as 'money' or 'non-money'. Other similar arguments can be made in respect of other principles, to the extent that we are left with the conclusion that there is no strong policy justification in this context for adopting either a hard or a soft definition.

7.25 This takes us to the basic argument for hard law—predictability. It is arguable that an 'intentions of the parties' test results only in legal uncertainty, and thereby harms economic activity and tempts injustice in cases where different parties can be shown to have had different understandings of the transaction into which they entered. There is force in all of these arguments. However, the doctrine of legal certainty is only of any use in contexts of this kind where the certain rule is well-known and has been broadly absorbed into the behaviours of society. The idea of beginning with the idea of certainty, creating it in silence, and then waiting for society to begin to transact before unveiling the certain rule, is an approach which cannot be supported. In this context, there is a clear analogy with the 'certainty' which prevailed for some years over the construction of the word 'money' in probate cases. In this regard, as per the speech of Lord Simon LC in *Perrin v Morgan*:[35] '... the judiciary has waged a long fight to teach testators that "money" means "cash", but as the ordinary testator who makes his own will does not study the law reports, he persists in constantly using the word in a wider sense'. The consequence, as Meredith J said in *Re Jennings*,[36] was that 'For two centuries the Courts have been endeavouring to force testators to use the word "money" in the sense of "cash". They have signally failed ... It is time to hoist the white flag'. It is submitted that the same principle

---

[35] *Perrin v Morgan* [1943] AC 399 at 415.
[36] *Re Jennings, Caldbeck v Stafford* [1930] IR 196 at 200.

should be applied in the case of the characterisation of new varieties of payment instrument as money. Legal certainty should support social consensus, but is a very poor tool with which to try and create that consensus.

## 7.2 The Attributes of Money

7.26 Money itself is not a unique or legally distinct type of property—it is a species of personal property to which the law attributes certain characteristics.[37] However, although money must be property, it is a special type of property—there are some attributes which property has but money does not have. The most important of these is that the transfer of money can only be done through a mechanism appropriate to it. Thus, although title to personal property generally passes by a legal act (e.g. under the Sale of Goods Act a mere mutual intention to pass title to goods is sufficient to effect that transfer[38]), this is not the case for currency—a contract for the sale of physical currency would not transfer title to that currency in the absence of physical delivery.[39]

7.27 We therefore need to establish those attributes which the law accords to the species of property known as money. As Fox says:

> the full complement of characteristics is more likely to be found in money than in ... other related kinds of property. This corresponds to the way that the definition of money (as opposed to other kinds of asset which may serve as media of exchange) is a matter of degree arising out of social usage. There is no absolute and clearly delineated distinction of type between them.[40]

7.28 The characteristics are: *currency*,[41] in the sense that a fresh and indefeasible legal title is created in the transferee when the asset is transferred; *abstraction*, in the sense that a debt obligation, howsoever arising, exists independently of the contract, statute, or other arrangement by which it came into being; *untraceability through mixtures*, in the sense that mixtures of money are subject to different rules than mixtures of other physical things; and *tender*, in the sense that an offer of money which is legal tender in payment of a debt will effectively estop the creditor from suing for the debt. None of these are absolutely unique to money, but money is the only thing which has all of them.

---

[37] Fox, *Property Rights in Money* (OUP 2008) at 18. Bridge Gullifer et al. *Personal Property (Sweet & Maxwell 2013)* at 8.
[38] Sale of Goods Act 1979, s. 17: 'Where there is a contract for the sale of specific or ascertained goods the property in them is transferred to the buyer at such time as the parties to the contract intend it to be transferred.'
[39] In the same way Fox, *Property Rights in Money* (OUP 2008) at 86 speculates—almost certainly correctly—that it would not be possible to transfer title to physical currency by deed.
[40] Ibid. at 18.
[41] This characteristic is commonly encountered in finance, particularly with regard to bills of exchange, but is by no means a uniquely financial concept. A purchaser of property from a receiver, for example, receives the same sort of fresh indefeasible title to that property.

## 7.3 Currency

7.29 At law, money is a thing which has the characteristic of currency. It should be emphasised that the concept of currency is distinct from the concept of legal tender—it is perfectly possible for an asset to have the characteristic of currency without being legal tender (this is true of foreign money currency) and it is possible—although rare—for an asset to have the characteristic of legal tender without being currency.[42]

7.30 Currency is simply another word for negotiability. It was initially an attribute of physical coins, and referred to the fact that the transfer of money falls outside the application of the rule that *nemo dat quod non habet*.[43] When a thief spends stolen notes and coins, the payee receives good title to those notes, regardless of the fact that the person who transferred them had none, in exactly the same way that he would do if he had received a stolen bill of exchange. More importantly, where money is received by an agent for the account of a principal, the money itself becomes the property of the agent absolutely, and the principal cannot sue for conversion of it.[44]

7.31 The old cases relate to physical coins,[45] but are clear that once a coin has been spent—that is, has been passed by delivery to a person who has obtained possession of it honestly and good faith—then the rule of *nemo dat quod non habet* does not apply, and that coin (or its value) cannot be recovered. This was explained in *Wookey v Pole* as being inherent in the purpose for which money was provided to perform 'by the use of money, the interchange of all other forms of property is most readily accomplished. To fit it for its purpose, the stamp denotes its value and possession alone must decide to whom it belongs'.[46] Interestingly, it was also held in *Wookey v Pole* that the rules which applied to physical coins must necessarily also be applied to 'the representation of money which is made transferrable by delivery only'.[47]

7.32 This was a simplification of Lord Mansfield's 'currency' theory as set out in *Miller v Race*:[48]

> The true reason is upon account of the currency of it; it cannot be recovered after has passed into currency. So, in the case of money stolen, the true owner cannot recover it, after it has been paid away fairly and honestly upon a valuable and bona fide consideration, but before money has passed into currency, an action may be brought for the money itself...

7.33 Thus, if a thief steals five £10 notes from your wallet, and you immediately apprehend him and can identify the specific notes, the £10 notes are still yours, but if he can get to a shop and spend them before you catch him, you cannot recover them from the shopkeeper even if you can prove that the notes handed to the shopkeeper were in fact your notes. There are needless to say some interesting cases on what is

---

[42] See below 7.67.
[43] *Mann on the Legal Aspect of Money* (7th edn, OUP 2012) at para 1.72, *Crossley Vaines on Personal Property* (4th edn, Butterworths 1967) at 155.
[44] *Orwell v Mortoft* (1505) CP 40/972, M 123.
[45] *Higgs v Holiday* Cro Eliz 746; *Miller v Race* (1758) 1 Burr 425.
[46] *Wookey v Pole* (1820) 4 B & Ald 1 at 7.  [47] Ibid. at 1.  [48] (1758) 1 Burr 452.

meant by bona fide in this context.[49] The position was summarised by Haldane LC in *Sinclair v Brougham*:[50]

> In most cases money cannot be followed. When sovereigns or bank notes are paid over as currency, so far as the payer is concerned, they cease ipso facto to be the subject of specific title, as chattels. If a sovereign or bank note be offered in payment, it is, under ordinary circumstances, no part of the duty of the person receiving it to inquire into title. The reason for this is that chattels of such kind form part of what the law recognises as currency and treats as passing from hand to hand in point, not merely of possession, but of property.

7.34  The usefulness of this proposition is based on the fact that the person accepting the notes is entitled to rely on a legal presumption that the possessor of money is the legitimate true owner.[51] However, this defence can be rebutted, either by actual knowledge or where the money is not handed over for a commercial purpose.[52] Thus, 'where money or notes are paid bona fide, and upon a valuable consideration, they never shall be brought back by the true owner; but where they come mala fide into a person's hands, they are in the nature of specific property; and if their identity can be traced and ascertained, the party has a right to recover'.[53]

7.35  What is not clear from these cases is how the courts arrived at the decision as to what was 'money' for this purpose and what was not. There are no cases of the period dealing with private tokens, and by the time banknotes appear in the litigation there already seems to be judicial notice taken of the fact that they are created and used as currency.

### 7.3.1 Currency and negotiability

7.36  Some assistance may be derived in this regard from the law of bills of exchange. Contrary to common perception, the Bills of Exchange Act 1882 was not a wholesale creation of new law but a codifying act which was intended to reflect the law as it then stood.[54] Thus, section 31 of the Bills of Exchange Act, which establishes the negotiability of bills of exchange, is simply a codification of the common law rule as stated in *Crouch v Credit Foncier of England Ltd*,[55] that 'where an instrument is by the custom of trade transferable like cash, by delivery, and is also capable of being sued upon by the person holding it, it is entitled to the name of a negotiable instrument, and the property in it passes to a transferee who has taken it for value and in good faith'. There was a good deal of discussion in *Crouch* as to how this state of affairs might legally be brought about, with the starting point being that the parties could

---

[49] See *R v Curtis ex p. A-G* (1988) 1 Qd R 546; also, *Grant v the Queen* (1981) 147 CLR 503.
[50] [1941] AC 398 at 418.
[51] *King v Milsom* (1809) 2 Camp 7; *Solomons v Bank of England* (1810) 13 East 136; *Wyer v The Dorchester and Milton Bank* (1833) 11 Cush (65 Mass) 51.
[52] See *Lipkin Gorman v Karpnale Ltd* [1991] AC 584, in which money passed to a gambling club was held not to have passed into currency.
[53] Per Lord Mansfield in *Clarke v Shee* (1774) 1 Cowp 197.
[54] See paras 1-003 to 1-005 of Gleeson (ed.), *Chalmers & Guest on Bills of Exchange and Cheques* (Sweet & Maxwell 18th edn, 2017).
[55] (1873) LR 8 QB 374.

not, by private contract between themselves, bring about a result which was contrary to the common law.⁵⁶ However, the House of Lords subsequently affirmed that a basis for any such arrangement could be found in 'any custom or usage prevailing generally in the particular [trade]. By this process, what was before usage only, unsanctioned by legal decision, has become engrafted upon, or incorporated into, the common law, and may thus be said to form part of it'.⁵⁷ This line of authority has been followed in subsequent English decisions.⁵⁸

Perhaps most importantly for the current issue, it is clear that in discussing the issue the relevant courts were not drawing a distinction between 'negotiability' as it applied to securities or bills and negotiability as it applied to currency—indeed in *London and County Banking Co v London and River Plate Bank Ltd*,⁵⁹ Lindley and Bowen LJJ explicitly relied upon 'the doctrine in *Miller v Race*' in order to find that certain securities were negotiable. 7.37

We should also note at this point that the idea that negotiability arrived fully formed into English law through the incorporation of an established body of 'commercial law' is now generally rejected. As Rogers says: 7.38

The task that the judges and lawyers faced in the seventeenth and eighteenth centuries was not to adopt ready-made rules from some source outside the ordinary English law. Rather, new commercial transactions had to be fitted within the categories of the existing legal system; or perhaps more accurately, the categories of the system had to be reworked so that they would accommodate new economic conditions. What the English judges incorporated into the common law was not commercial law but commercial practice; by doing so they composed commercial law.⁶⁰

It would be difficult to find a better summary of the challenge which the development of virtual currency poses to the legal system today.

It is therefore suggested that the correct test for any instrument to acquire the status of 'currency' in this regard is simply as to whether that instrument is generally regarded as having the status of money or near-money in the context in which it is transferred. Context here is important—an instrument which is negotiable in one respect when transferred within one market may not be regarded as negotiable when transferred in a different way in a different market (the classical example is a banknote sold to a collector as a rarity—such a sale would not constitute a negotiation of the note, and it could be recovered if it could be identified from a subsequent purchaser under the ordinary application of the *nemo dat* rule). 7.39

---

⁵⁶ In this case depriving an assignee (who was *ex hypothesi* not a party to the contract) of his right to assert his title against a bona fide purchaser for value acquiring the debenture from an intervening thief.
⁵⁷ Per Cockburn CJ (1875) LR 10 Ex 337 at 352, affirmed by the House of Lords in (1876) 1 App Cas 476.
⁵⁸ *Bechuanaland Exploration Co. v London Trading Bank Ltd* [1898] 2 QB 658, QBD, *Edelstein v Schuler & Co.* [1902] 2 KB 144, Com Ct.
⁵⁹ (1888) 21 QBD 535.
⁶⁰ Rogers, *Early History of the Law of Bills and Notes* (Cambridge University Press 1995), and see generally McKendrick (ed.), *Goode on Commercial Law* (5th edn, LexisNexis 2016) at paras 1.06–1.09.

### 7.3.2 Virtual currency as currency

7.40 Thus, as regards virtual currency, the question of whether a virtual currency can acquire the status of currency is one which is answerable purely by reference to the market which develops for that virtual currency. If it can be demonstrated that units of virtual currency satisfy the *Goodwin v Robarts* test that the fact that they circulate as units of payment is a 'custom or usage prevailing generally' amongst persons of the kind. Part of the reason that this is an appealing outcome is that it corresponds closely with the analysis set out above as to what we mean by money in the first place. In principle it is entirely appropriate for a court, in examining the status of a particular instrument which has been used for payment, to look at the context in which it was used, and in particular to derive from that a doctrine of the common expectation of the parties.

7.41 An issue which is sometimes urged in this regard is the fact that, with sufficient cryptographical skill and computing power, it is possible to trace any individual virtual currency unit through any number of transformations. This produces the argument that it cannot be possible to treat virtual currency as currency, since it can always be traced. Consequently, it is argued that virtual currency units cannot be compared with metal coins in this way—whereas it is true that metal coins are untraceable, virtual currency units are.

7.42 The difficulty with this argument is that the same is true of banknotes. Each banknote (in the United Kingdom, and in many other countries) has a unique identifying number which in theory enables it to be traced. The difference, of course, is that whereas a banknote's number enables the identification of the banknote, it tells us nothing about how many hands it has passed through (and whether it has 'passed into currency') between leaving the hands of one person and entering the hands of another. In theory, distributed ledger technology is very different, in that it would—to a person with perfect access to the ledger—be entirely possible to establish which hands the unit passed through at what point. Hence, it is argued, a virtual currency unit can never pass into currency.

7.43 This is wrong for two important reasons. First, no examination of the ledger can reveal whether the transferee of a unit was a purchaser for value without notice. Without that information, the fact of transfer tells us nothing about the eventual proprietary claims on the unit. The principle enunciated in *Kynaston v Moore*[61]—that where money is found in the hands of a person, it is presumed to have been negotiated to him for value unless the contrary can be proved—is as true for virtual currency units as it is for individual identifiable banknotes. As was said in *Wookey v Pole*:[62] 'It is not because the loser cannot know his money again that he cannot recover it from a person who has fairly obtained the possession of it; for if his guineas or shillings had some private marks on them by which he could prove that they had been his, he could not get them back from a bona fide holder.'

---

[61] (1627) Cro Car 89 at 114.   [62] (1820) 4 B & Ald 1 at 6 per Best J.

7.44 Given that the electronic ledger is by definition silent on this matter, the challenge for pleaders will be the same as it has always been—assembling facts which can challenge the presumption.

7.45 The second major problem with this argument is that information which would be revealed to an omniscient party with complete access to all of the relevant public and private keys is irrelevant if no such party exists. The point is not dissimilar to the argument that parties can only reasonably have expected to have known those things which he could reasonably have found out—a true fact which could not have been discovered with reasonable diligence by the parties to an action is simply irrelevant to that action. This point extends to permissioned ledgers. The mere fact that the ledger operator could have established certain facts is not relevant between parties which could not by themselves have established those facts, and did not have the power to require the ledger operator to establish and communicate to them those facts.

## 7.4 Abstraction

7.46 The principle of abstraction is simply the principle that once a claim for a sum of money has arisen, it can be pursued independently of the contract or arrangement under which the payment obligation arose in the first place. This is to some extent simply a restatement of the fact that an action for debt is a freestanding thing in itself, and the existence and value of a debt is determined—and can be recovered—independently of other factors affecting the performance of the contract under which the debt was created.

7.47 The reason that money claims are different in this way is precisely in order to ensure that a debt claim on a person has a fixed, predictable value which does not vary according to the identity of its owner, and this in turn is because it is the policy both of the legislator and of the courts that debt claims are and should be an object of commerce. As regards claims for commodities, however, the opposite is the case, and the old rules of champerty and maintenance still lie for attempts to trade claims for damages.[63]

7.48 This takes us to a point which has often been regarded as a quirk of the law of cheques (and is not generally known by lawyers outside the specialised sphere of bank payment litigation). If a seller takes a bill of exchange (including a cheque) in payment of a debt, in the event of non-payment of the bill an action immediately arises against the person liable on the bill.[64] This action—the action on the bill—is effectively a free-standing action, in that it is distinct from the original obligation to pay and can be pursued even if the original obligation falls away. Thus, if I sell you a car and you pay me by cheque, I can sue you on the cheque even if the contract for the sale of the car is void. The reason for this is straightforward—in order for an obligation to be capable of being made an independent obligation by reason of its

---

[63] Although the crime and tort of champerty were abolished by the Criminal Law Act 1967, the common law prohibition continues—see *Arkin v Borchard Lines Ltd* [2005] EWCA Civ 665.

[64] Bills of Exchange Act 1882, s. 47(2).

## 7.5 Untraceability through Mixtures

7.49 The difference between money and non-money as regards mixtures is simply that where non-money fungible items (such as oil or grain) belonging to different people are mixed together, the consequence is that the owners of the individual components become the owners in common of the bulk.[65] Their ownership interest in their own goods is extinguished by the act of mixing, and their ownership rights attach to the resulting bulk.

7.50 There is no such joint ownership when money is mixed.[66] Instead, the owner of money which has been mixed with other money acquires a right over it which is closely allied to a lien—in effect, a proportionate ownership right to a defined amount of money secured by a right to the mixture.

7.51 The common law rule that money cannot be followed into a mixture is longstanding. Fox provides an explanation of this,[67] and points out that before the decision of the Court of Appeal in *Re Hallett's Estate*,[68] this rule applied in equity as much as it did at common law—that an adverse interest in money was unenforceable, and, for all practical purposes, extinguished, once the money was mixed by the recipient.[69] The basis of this approach was what is known as the 'earmark' theory, which asserted that money could not be followed because it 'had no earmark'.[70] What this translated into in practice was an irrebuttable presumption that once physical money had 'passed into currency' that it could no longer be identified. This doctrine did not, however, apply to promissory notes or bills of exchange, since such instruments were clearly identifiable.[71] Thus, in *Miller v Race*,[72] Lord Mansfield effectively laid down a new rule of common law to the effect that an owner of paper money could not sue to enforce a legal title to money once it was 'paid away fairly and honestly upon a valuable and bona fide consideration'.[73] This rule was applied to paper notes which 'are treated as money, as cash, in the ordinary course and transaction of business, by the general consent of mankind; which gives them the credit and currency of money, to all intents and purposes. They are as much money, as

---

[65] McKendrick (ed.), *Goode on Commercial Law* (5th edn, LexisNexis 2016) at para 8.38ff.
[66] Although Lionel Smith (*The Law of Tracing* (OUP 1997) at 163–4) complains that this is irrational.
[67] Fox, *Property Rights in Money* (OUP 2008) at paras 7-34ff.    [68] (1880) 13 Ch D 696.
[69] See *Whitecomb v Jacob* (1710) 1 Salk 160, *Burdett v Willett* (1708) 2 Vern 638; and Fox, *Common Law Claims to Substituted Assets* [1999] RLR 55.
[70] Per Lord Mansfield in *Miller v Race* (1758) 1 Burr 452 at 457, and see Fox, *Bona Fide Purchaser and the Currency of Money*, Cambridge Law Journal, Vol. 55, No. 3 (November 1996) at 547–65.
[71] *Ex parte Dumas* (1754) 1 Atk 232, and see Richards *The Evolution of Paper Money in England*, Quarterly Journal of Economics, Vol. 41, No. 3 (1927) at 361.
[72] (1758) 1 Burr 452.    [73] Ibid. at 457.

guineas themselves are; or any other current coin, that is used in common payments, as money or cash.'[74] Consequently, banknotes mixed with other banknotes cease to be the property of the original owner. However, his lordship made clear that this was not true of 'securities, or documents for debts'.

This raises the interesting question of what the position would be as regards a unit of payment which did not fit easily into the category of banknotes. The rules that relate to goods are reasonably straightforward—where goods belonging to different persons are mixed together, the result is a tenancy in common in proportionate shares of the resulting mass,[75] and this produces an outcome which is not necessarily all that different from the outcome produced in *Re Hallett*[76] where all of the owners of the mixed property are innocent of any wrongdoing in respect of the mixing.

## 7.6 Tender

Tender is an entirely different thing from both 'legal tender' and payment. 'Legal tender' is the rule which prohibits tender of particular items being rejected in particular circumstances, and payment is a transaction, in which money is delivered in exchange for the extinction of an obligation.[77] If a thing is tendered, it is proffered in discharge of an obligation. The doctrine of tender applies equally to money and things – thus if I am obliged to deliver tins of peaches to you, I can tender those tins. However, in the case of debt obligations, tender is a complete defence to any action in debt.[78] If money is proffered to a creditor in respect of a debt owed to him, then the creditor loses his right to sue for the debt, and is thus in effect debarred at law from seeking payment in any other medium. However, tender does not and cannot constitute payment—payment can only occur when the creditor has accepted the money tendered.

### 7.6.1 Legal tender

As noted above, there is no necessary identity between the ideas of currency and legal tender. There are numerous examples of legislatures declaring assets other than fiat money to be legal tender. In ancient Rome there are instances of laws providing for *datio in solutum necessaria*, by which debtors became entitled to pay off their debts by the delivery of certain specified commodities.[79] The same type of provision was made during the French Revolution[80] and has been encountered elsewhere—in 1783, for example, the South Carolina state legislature made 'property of every kind'

---

[74] Ibid.
[75] *Indian Oil Corporation v Greenstone Shipping SA* [1988] 1 QB 345; *The Ypatianna* [1988] QB 345, and see McKendrick, *Goode on Commercial Law* (5th edn, 2016) at 243ff.
[76] Smith, *Law of Tracing* (OUP 1997) at 163–4.
[77] Fox, *Property Rights in Money* (OUP 2008) at 28; see also *Jowett's Dictionary of English Law* (4th edn, Sweet & Maxwell 2015).
[78] *Dixon v Clarke* (1848) 5 CB 365 (CP) per Wilde CJ at 377.
[79] Steiner, *Datio in Solutum* (Beck 1914) at 161.
[80] Decrees of 16 Frimiaire, Year 2, 28 Thermidor, Year 2, 2 Thermidor, Year 3.

legal tender.[81] However, it is not suggested that in any of these cases the property so designated thereby became money,[82] and the correct position is that an asset can be legal tender without being money.[83] This is the correct classification of the commemorative coin in *Moss v Hancock*.[84] An even more interesting example is the US 'trade dollar'. The trade dollar was a US silver dollar produced for the benefit of US–China trade, and was intended to be exported to China, where more importance was attached to the silver content of coins than in the United States. It was created under the Currency Act 1873,[85] which declared it to be legal tender in the United States. In 1876, the statutory legal tender status of the trade dollar was removed, but the number in circulation nearly doubled in the following year[86] and it continued to circulate in the United States until 1887.

7.55 The point of legal tender laws is, of course, that they provide that if a specific thing is proffered in payment, they must be treated as having a specified value. Legal tender laws do not mandate the creditor to accept the things tendered in payment—there is no legal mechanism which positively requires a creditor to accept a thing in discharge of the debt owed to him. However, what the law does say is that a creditor who rejects legal tender cannot sue for the debt in any other way, and cannot invoke any of the remedies to which he would have been entitled on non-payment.

### 7.6.2 Determination of the value of the thing tendered

7.56 The key to this is the fact that the common law of legal tender specifies not only the thing to be accepted, but also the value at which it must be valued. To understand how radical a proposition this is, it is helpful to consider the state of the civil law authorities. These can best be approached through the classical quaestiones of the Bolognese bushel and the Luccan creditor. The hypothetical fact pattern of the Bolognese bushel is as follows: Titius leases his Bolognese farm to Seius for a rent of a specified number of bushels of corn. The Bolognese pass a law changing the size of a bushel, and enact a penalty if anyone measures by any other standard of measurement. Can Titus sue for the originally agreed amount of corn? The Glossators answered yes—the terms of a contract should be interpreted as they were at the time and in the place where the contract was made, and the Bolognese law could not vary the terms of that contract. This argument was carried through in quaestio of

---

[81] *Edwards v Kearzey*, 96 US 595, 24 L.Ed 793 (1877).
[82] Indeed, it is arguable that no circulating commodity can ever become money. Mitchell Innes makes this point succinctly with respect to Adam Smith's example of dried cod being used as money in Newfoundland—'A moment's reflection shows that a staple commodity could not be used money, because ex hypothesi the medium of exchange is equally receivable by all members of the community. Thus, if fishers paid for their supplies in cod, the traders would equally have to pay for their cod in cod, an obvious absurdity.' Innes, *What is Money? The Banking law Journal* (May 1913) 377–408 at 377–8.
[83] Contrary to the oft-quoted dictum in *Vick v Howard*, 136 Va. 101, 109,116 SE. 465 (1923) that 'All legal tender is money, but not all money is legal tender'.
[84] [1899] 2 QB 111 (QB).
[85] At the last minute, and because of the lobbying of the silver interest.
[86] Rolnick and Weber, *Gresham's Law or Gresham's Fallacy?*, Journal of Political Economy, Vol. 94 (1986) at 185-185-99.

the Luccan creditor, described as the Glossator's central achievement in the field of money.[87] If Luccan coins are given as a loan, and before the repayment date Lucca debases its coin, can the lender demand payment in old coins or is he forced to accept new debased coins? The conclusion of the Glossators was that in the case of a loan of money, the borrower should not be able to repay something which is qualitatively different from what he received.[88]

The essence of these positions was that a coin, once placed in circulation, was a thing like any other, and once it had left the hand of the authority which created it, it might be dealt with by the parties as they chose. Ernst[89] (undoubtedly correctly) characterises this as a triumph of the *ius commune* (the idea that money should be valued at the value that society as a whole gave it) over the sovereign power (the nominalist idea that money was worth exactly and solely what the sovereign who issued it prescribed). It is interesting to note that in this area, where the civil and common laws divided sharply, the civil law took its stand against the absolute power of princes in favour of the commercial reality, whereas in the *Case de Mixt Moneys; Gilbert v Brett*[90] the common law took its stand in favour of royal absolutism regardless of commerce. Seldom have archetypes been so sharply rebutted.

### 7.6.3 The *Case de Mixt Moneys*

The *Case de Mixt Moneys; Gilbert v Brett*[91] settled the position of English law as regards money for several centuries. It has been exceptionally analysed by David Fox,[92] to whose work the reader is referred for a full treatment. The context is that the English crown had sought to debase the currency of Ireland whilst retaining the gold content of the currency of England. This led to the manufacture of an 'Irish pound' whose nominal value was the same as an English pound, but whose metal content was very significantly lower. There was no doubt that at English law a pound was a pound if statute declared it to be a pound, regardless of its metal content, and this had remained the position through the spectacular debasements of Henry VIII and Edward II.[93] The facts were that Brett (an Irish merchant) had entered into a bond to pay Gilbert (a London merchant) a sum of money in 'sterling', described as the 'lawful money of England'. The proclamation declaring the debasement of Irish coinage, and requiring them to be accepted as sterling, was issued after Brett had entered into the bond. The relevant royal proclamation was to the effect that:

---

[87] See Ernst in Fox and Ernst, *Money in the Western Legal Tradition* (OUP 2016) Ch. 7 at 118.
[88] The strong form of this argument, which prevailed as a matter of commercial law for some centuries, was that a loan of gold coins could not be repaid in an equivalent value of silver coins, but must be repaid in coins of the same weight and denomination as those borrowed.
[89] Ernst in Fox and Ernst, *Money in the Western Legal Tradition* (OUP 2016) Ch. 7 at 118.
[90] (1604) Davies 18; 2 State Trials 114.   [91] (1605) Davis 18, 80 (KB).
[92] Fox, *The Case de Mixt Moneys* in Fox and Ernst, *Money in the Western Legal Tradition* (OUP 2016).
[93] See Gould, *The Great Debasement* (OUP 1970).

> Her majesty ... doth hereby publish and make known to all men to be from henceforth ... her coin and moneys established and authorised to be lawful and current ... and doth expressly will and command ... That they nor any of them shall not, after the day of publishing hereof refuse, reject or deny, to receive in payment ... any of the said monies, but that they shall receive and accept the same at such values and rates as they are coined for.[94]

7.59 The proclamation also provided that any person who refused to accept a tender of the relevant coins was in contempt of the sovereign power and liable to imprisonment or other sanction.

7.60 On the payment date, Brett delivered Irish currency to Gilbert, who refused it and demanded English coins in payment. The Privy Council held that this was a breach of the law—that Brett was entitled to deliver to Gilbert whatever English law regarded as currency, and that it was the Queen's prerogative to assign sterling values to currency.

### 7.6.4 Divergence of common and civil law

7.61 This decision constitutes the cleanest possible break with the civil law rule of the time. It is questionable whether this was the intent of the court—although the civilian authorities were cited, the citations are partial and incomplete,[95] and it is not entirely clear that the judges fully understood the extent of their divergence from what was then mainstream European law. However, what is clear is that they were in absolutely no doubt that the crown's power was not only over the physical units of currency, but over the idea of that unit. It was not the case that the crown placed coins in circulation and the parties then agreed what value to give them—the crown could determine the very essence of the unit of account itself, such that where any two parties contracted with each other in pounds, they necessarily and implicitly agreed between themselves that the term 'pound' meant at any particular time whatever the Queen of England determined it to mean. This doctrine (known as 'nominalism') remains the basis of the modern analysis of currency obligations.

### 7.6.5 Practical significance of legal tender legislation

7.62 Legal tender laws—in the sense of laws prohibiting demand for payment in anything other than designated currency—are still sometimes encountered, although they should not be confused with the laws prohibiting transactions in anything other than a specific currency which are sometimes encountered as part of exchange control regimes. However, the concept of legal tender laws considered as laws requiring certain contracts to be conducted in certain currencies has broadly disappeared from modern law—it is broadly accepted in most jurisdictions that citizens may contract in whatever currency they wish. This is largely because the ineffectiveness of such

---

[94] Irish Proclamation 20, Elisabeth I (20 May 1601).
[95] Fox and Ernst, *Money in the Western Legal Tradition* (OUP 2016) at 240–2.

laws has been amply demonstrated over time, but is also in part due to the experience of the twentieth century that such laws perform no useful legal function.

7.63 It may also be, to some extent, a result of the dramatic demonstrations that the twentieth century has provided that such laws do not work. We have already noted that the Chinese laws described by Marco Polo which prescribed death for anyone refusing imperial paper as payment were ineffective in respect of the exchange of such paper for silver and gold coins.[96] This demonstration of the fact that even government cannot buck the market is unremarkable. However, it demonstrates a wider point, that law cannot compel the acceptance of a medium that is not socially acceptable except in extreme cases. It is also worth mentioning in this context that the twentieth century also provides one of the most dramatic possible demonstrations of the uselessness of legal tender designation in the form of the history of the German Rentenmark during the fightback against the great inflation of the 1920s.

7.64 In an era where currencies were expected to be gold backed, the collapsed Reichmark had to be replaced with another currency. However, since Germany had no gold or equivalent, the replacement currency had to be backed by something other than gold. Hence the replacement currency, the Rentenbankscheine was backed by (in effect) real estate receivables. This put the authorities in what they clearly regarded as the difficult position of putting into circulation an asset intended to be treated as currency but which they feared would not be so treated because of its lack of gold backing. Their response was to create the idea of 'public receivability'. Rentenbankscheine were not declared to be legal tender, but the government declared that it would accept the relevant instrument at its face value. As noted above, if the state accepts an asset in discharge of x worth of taxes, and that asset is transferable, then it will rapidly become worth x as a medium of exchange The result of this, as should have been expected, was that Rentenscheine became the de facto currency of Germany in a very short space of time, and the public seem to have been completely indifferent to the legal tender issue.[97] This constituted a demonstration of the proposition advanced by Knapp in his 'state theory of money' that the key to money status was in fact the extent to which the relevant unit was accepted by the state in satisfaction of obligations owed to the state,[98] and that legal status was not relevant to the question.

### 7.6.6 Tender and the discharge of debts

7.65 We have already established that tender is not payment. However, tender is a legal process which is a preliminary to the extinguishment of a debt. A debt cannot be—and is not—extinguished merely by tender. Debts are only extinguished when the creditor agrees that they are extinguished. More importantly, 'no creditor is under

---

[96] *The Book of Ser Marco Polo, The Venetian*, edited and translated by Henry Yule, Book II Chapter XXIV.
[97] See Fergusson *When Money Dies* (William Kimber 1975) for a very readable account of this fascinating period in monetary history.
[98] Knapp, *The State Theory of Money* (1924) at 154.

any positive, legal duty to accept payment, nor can the debtor effectively force payment upon the creditor'.[99] If the creditor rejects a valid tender, this (semble) does not per se constitute a breach of an underlying contract by the creditor.

7.66 It should be noted that the term 'tender' has a slightly different meaning in Equity. The common law rules on tender create a defence to an action for payment; whereas the equitable rules on tender determine when interest should stop running against a mortgagor who tenders repayment of a mortgage debt. *Shearer v Spring Capital*,[100] on tender, is a good account of the difficulties of determining whether tender has been properly made. In that case, borrowers had borrowed money at a very high interest rate and wanted to repay the money early. However, in order to make repayment they had to procure a release of the charges on certain assets charged to the old lenders. The new lenders would only advance the money once the securities were granted, and the old lenders would not release the securities until the debt was actually discharged. It was held that the fact that the borrowers had done everything that they could to discharge the debt, and were being prevented only by the actions of the lenders from doing so, did not constitute tender.

### 7.6.7 Discharge of debts—Can the debtor unilaterally discharge a debt?

7.67 The answer to this question is a clear no. *Canmer International Inc v UK Mutual S.S. Assurance Association (Bermuda) Ltd (the 'Rays')*[101] is authority that a successful plea of tender does not discharge the debt: 'a creditor accepts payment either by expressly declaring its unconditional assent to payment, or by acceptance, or by treating the money as its own (e.g. by intermingling it with its own money or lending it out)'.[102]

### 7.6.8 Discharge of debts—Can the creditor unilaterally discharge a debt?

7.68 It is clear that discharge is accomplished by a bilateral act whereby tender by the debtor is accepted by the creditor. It is an interesting issue as to whether a creditor can unilaterally extinguish a debt by accepting a payment directly from a non-party without the sanction of the contractual counterparty. There is authority that this is not permissible—in other words that discharge is a mutual act which requires the cooperative assent of both parties, such that the creditor cannot determine that he will accept in settlement an amount received from a non-party without the sanction of the debtor.[103] However, the academic commentary rejecting this conclusion is stronger than the reasoning the decision itself,[104] and it is submitted that the true

---

[99] Mann on the Legal Aspect of Money, ed. Proctor, (7th Ed OUP 2012) at 7.08.
[100] [2013] EWHC 3148.
[101] [2005] EWHC 1694 (Comm), [2005] 2 Lloyds Rep 479.
[102] See *TSB Bank of Scotland v Welwyn Hatfield District Council* [1993] 2 Bank LR 267 at 272–3.
[103] *Owen v Tate* [1976] QB 402.
[104] See Birks, *In Defence of Free Acceptance* in Burrows, Essays on the *Law of Restitution* Ch. 5 (Oxford Clarendon Press 1991); Beatson, *Use and Abuse of Unjust Enrichment* (Oxford Clarendon Press 1991) at 177ff, Burrows, *The Law of Restitution* (3rd edn, OUP 2011) at 449–52 and Virgo, *The Principles of the Law of Restitution* (3rd edn, OUP 2015) at 243–5. However, there remains a degree of unease at the idea that a third party could discharge a debt over the active objection of the debtor.

position is that if a creditor elects to treat himself as discharged, that election is binding on him, and valid under the contract. The argument here is that although the debt itself is created under the contract, once it is created it is a free-standing obligation in its own right, and like any obligation can be waived by the obligee at his discretion. This argument is supported by the fact that a debt obligation which arises under a contract does not necessarily have the characteristics of that contract—for example, a contract under one law can create a debt obligation governed by a different law, and if it does so then the debt obligation is extinguished according to the rules of the law applicable to it, not the law applicable to the contract.[105]

### 7.6.9 Contractual provisions regarding payment

7.69 A contract may, of course, make any provision it likes as to the mechanism by which the payment obligation must be discharged—thus, as regards a contract which provides for payment to be made in a particular currency, payment must be made in that currency and cannot be made in any other way.[106]

7.70 This takes us to the issue of the connection between the unit of account and the unit of payment. The idea of a unit of measurement is entirely independent of the medium of exchange which is used to settle obligations expressed in that unit. This is as clear in law as it is in monetary theory—Denning LJ in *Woodhouse AC Israel Cocoa Limited v Nigerian Produce Marketing Ltd*[107] made clear that the two are unconnected, and if a contract denominated in currency A provides that it should be settled in currency B, an attempt to settle by tendering currency A will be ineffective.

7.71 Unless he has agreed otherwise, a creditor is not bound to accept payment in the form of anything other than legal tender,[108] and chattels can be constituted as legal tender either by statute[109] or by royal proclamation (as in the *Case de Mixt Moneys*). Since, in general, modern contracts have nothing to say about payment beyond identifying the denomination of the payment obligation, this is not as helpful as it may first appear.

### 7.6.10 Tender through the provision of a payment mechanism

7.72 Debate in this area is generally the result of arguments as to what constitutes tender. In certain circumstances, the law answers this question—thus, the law provides that Bank of England banknotes are legal tender for any amount, and coins are legal tender for certain amounts.[110] However, despite some antique cases in which the

---

[105] *In re British American Continental Bank, Lisser & Rosenkranz's Claim* [1923] 1 Ch 276.
[106] *Marrache v Ashton* [1943] AC 311. Note, however, that if an English law contract designates a unit of account but is silent as to unit of payment, English law presumes that the debtor has an option to pay in sterling—McKendrick (ed.), *Goode on Commercial Law* (5th edn, Butterworths 2016) at para. 37.95.
[107] [1971] 2 QB 23 (CA) at 54.   [108] *Gordon v Strange* (1847) 1 Exch. 477.
[109] The Coinage Act 1971 in respect of coins and the Currency and Bank Notes Act 1954 in respect of banknotes.
[110] Currency and Bank Notes Act 1954 and Coinage Act 1971.

courts ordered debtors to pay in banknotes,[111] and some rather more modern cases in which courts have held an obligation to pay 'in cash' to mean exactly that,[112] it is hard not to sympathise with the view expressed in the current edition of Mann that a modern debtor who had specified payment of an amount in sterling without specifying a particular payment mechanism would get extremely short shrift from the English courts if he were to seek to reject a tender of (say) a cheque and demand banknotes instead.[113] The modern rule is as expressed by the court of appeal in *The Brimnes*,[114] that 'payment in cash' in a modern commercial contract should be interpreted as meaning any commercially recognised method of transferring funds the result of which is to give the transferee the unconditional right to use the funds transferred.[115]

7.73 The classical example is the situation where a debtor has provided the creditor with an instrument which enables him to obtain payment (such as a cheque) rather than physical notes and coins. An interesting example is in *Weldon v SRE Linked Life Assurance*,[116] where a debtor had provided his creditor with a direct debit mandate entitling the creditor to take certain sums from his bank account on a regular basis. It was held that sufficient tender had been made in respect of each instalment, even though the creditor had not in fact exercised the right to withdraw the funds.

### 7.6.11 The relevance of tender

7.74 If it is true that it is the acceptance of the creditor which discharges the debt, then the question may be asked as to whether the legal concept of tender really performs any useful function at all. The answer to this appears to be that the concept is useful in one context and one context only; that being where the creditor seeks to set up non-payment by the debtor as a breach entitling him to exercise other remedies under the contract. This is the topic of *Mardorf Peach & Co v Attica Sea Carriers Corp of Liberia*[117] and is interesting in itself. The facts were that a shipowner, having chartered a vessel to a charterer, wished to break the charter. The charterer was scheduled to make a payment on a day which was a Sunday. The charterer consequently made the payment on the next day. However, the shipowner was held to be entitled to break the charter on the basis of non-tender of payment on the specified date. The fact that the notice of termination was sent after the payment was held not to be a relevant consideration—any failure to tender the specified amount on the specified date constituted a breach of contract. Critically, there is nothing in the decision

---

[111] *Blumberg v Life Interests and Reversionary Securities Corp* [1897] 1 Ch 171, aff [1898] 1 Ch 27, in which an amount of £463 (equal to around £28,000 in today's money) was held to be required to be paid with notes and coins, and that a cheque for this amount did not suffice as tender.
[112] *Pollway Ltd v Abdullah* [1974] 1 WLR 493.
[113] Proctor, *Mann on the Legal Aspect of Money* (7th edn, OUP 2012) at 182 fn. 19.
[114] *Tenax Steamship Co v Reinante Transoceania Navegacion SA, The Brimnes* [1975] QB 929 (CA).
[115] At first instance [1975] 1 WLR 386 at 400, approved by the CA [1975] QB 929 at 948, 963, and 968.
[116] [2000] 2 All ER 914 (Comm).     [117] [1976] QB 835.

which suggests that the position would have been any different at all had the tender been made by the presentation of banknotes constituting legal tender.

What this demonstrates is that a payer cannot, simply by making a payment, compel a recipient to accept it, and this is as true of the presentation of paper notes as it is of the making of a bank transfer.  7.75

### 7.6.12  Tender of money and tender of goods

Finally, and importantly, it seems that there is no significant distinction between the rules relating to tender of money in payment of a debt and tender of goods as delivery under a contract of sale (aside from the fact that whereas money can be paid into court, goods cannot). This was made clear in *Startup v Macdonald*:[118]  7.76

> Now, it may be observed, that in every contract by which a party binds himself to deliver goods, or pay money, to another, he in fact engages to do an act which he cannot completely perform without the concurrence of the party to whom the delivery or the payment is to be made. Without acceptance on the part of him who is to receive, the act of him who is to deliver or to pay, can amount only to a tender. But the law considers a party who has entered into a contract to deliver goods or pay money to another, as having, substantially, performed it, if he has tendered the goods or money to the party to whom the delivery or payment was to be made, provided only that the tender has been made under such circumstances that the party to whom it has been made, has had a reasonable opportunity of examining the goods, or the money, tendered, in order to ascertain that the thing tendered really was what it purported to be. Indeed, without such an opportunity an offer to deliver or pay does not amount to a tender.

Thus, it seems that the rules which apply to tender of money in payment of a debt are in effect identical to the rules which apply to tender of goods. There is one practical difference between the two; that being that under the UK Civil Procedure Rules (CPR) a defence of tender can only be maintained if the amount which is purported to be tendered is paid into court.[119] Tender is only available for a claim for delivery of specific goods or payment of a specified amount of money—it is not available for unliquidated damages.[120]  7.77

### 7.6.13  Tender of virtual currency

This takes us to the interesting question of what the position would be if an obligor who had contracted to pay a specified number of identified virtual currency units were to try and advance a defence of tender. *RSM Bentley Jennison (A Firm) v Ayton*[121] confirmed that defence of tender remains limited to debt actions, and there can be no defence of tender to a claim for unliquidated damages. Consequently, the  7.78

---

[118] (1843) 6 M. & G. 563 at 609. See also *Isherwood v Whitmore* (1843) 11 M. & W. 347 (tender of goods in a closed box is good), *Dixon v Clark* (1848) 5 CB 365, 377 (tender of part is bad).
[119] CPR Part 37.2.   [120] *John Laing Construction v Dastur* [1987] 1 WLR 686.
[121] [2015] EWCA Civ 1120, CA.

answer to this question would be determined by asking whether the virtual currency units were money or goods?

7.79 There is in fact a large amount of authority on this issue, mostly as regards foreign currency. The approach of English law to foreign sovereigns (that they are basically private actors) means that foreign currency, not being British currency, was for many years regarded as not being currency at all.[122] This position was reversed by the British courts in *Camdex International v Bank of Zambia*,[123] in which the Court of Appeal rejected the old line of authorities to the effect that foreign money at English law should be regarded as a commodity, and held that any sum of money, whatever currency it was denominated in 'retains its character as a medium of exchange'.[124] Thus, although foreign money is not legal tender in the United Kingdom, the better view is that obligations denominated in currencies other than sterling are treated under English law as monetary obligations.[125]

7.80 The facts of *Camdex* highlight the difference between payment in a medium considered to be currency and a medium not considered to be currency. Where an obligation to deliver property is breached, the value of the breach is calculated as at the date of the breach, and any writ issued in the English courts must be endorsed with the sterling value that that claim had at that date. However, where an obligation to pay money is breached, the writ should be endorsed with a claim for that amount of money, and judgement can be delivered in that amount.

7.81 It should be clear that this is a significant issue for virtual currencies. If the parties are using a virtual currency as a payment medium, it is overwhelmingly likely that they would expect judgement for the amount of virtual currency units due. However, if the parties were—for example—an investor in virtual currency and a broker who had undertaken to supply that investment—then it is likely that the proper approach should be that judgement for the investor should be for the virtual currency units as at the date of breach. The difference between the two cases is that in the first case the parties have agreed as between themselves to disregard fluctuations between the value of the virtual currency unit and other currency units, whereas in the second case the existence of those fluctuations is the primary reason for entry into the contract. It is by no means beyond the scope of the probable that conflict between the parties in such a case may turn—inter alia—on precisely this issue of how the currency units were intended to be regarded as between the parties.

7.82 It is of course the case that this is by no means the only distinction between the two treatments. More important in many cases may be the basic attribute of currency that if a person accepts non-money property in payment of a debt, he is vulnerable to any claimant of the property which was delivered to him on the basis of a prior claim of a third party presented through the medium of *nemo dat*.[126] This raises the unpleasant spectacle of a plaintiff being forced to elect between pleading

---

[122] *Marrache v Ashton* [1943] AC 311.   [123] [1997] EWCA Civ 798.
[124] Per Phillips LJ. See also *The Halcyon the Great* [1975] 1 WLR 515 at 520, in which Brandon J said that the term 'money' included money in foreign currency as well as sterling.
[125] *Mann on the Legal Aspect of Money* (7th edn, OUP 2012) at para 1.89.
[126] Ibid. at para 1.73.

that virtual currency is currency, and thereby foregoing a claim to the true value of that currency at the date of action, and pleading that it is not currency, in which case other currency units that he already owns may become vulnerable to litigation. It is hard to think of a better demonstration of the fact that these issues must be separated and decided by reference to the intention of the parties in the light of commercial and social context—a single rule which is applied for all purposes is almost a guarantee of injustice in some cases.

If virtual currency units were regarded as goods, in principle a claim in respect of them would be a claim for unliquidated damages. It is entirely possible that the question could turn on the form of endorsement of the writ. If the writ purported to be a claim for money—that is, for judgement to be given in the number of units of the relevant virtual currency—it is very hard to see how the plaintiff could reject a tender if such were made—since he has in effect elected to treat the relevant virtual currency units as money in his pleading, it would be curious to say the least if he were able to argue that the units should not be regarded as money for the purpose of court procedure. Conversely, if the writ were endorsed as a claim for a commodity—that is to say, for the value of the units in sterling (or some other currency), it would seem that tender would be impossible, since the claim would be for unliquidated damages. There is a further complexity to this, in that a plea of tender can only be made out under the CPR if payment is made into court. Whether a court would be able to accept a payment in virtual currency units is an interesting administrative issue, and gives rise to the further interesting question of what the position should be if the defendant were to seek to make a plea of tender, proffering the relevant units to the court service, which found itself unable to accept them. 7.83

## 7.7 Payment

Payment is a surprisingly difficult legal concept. It can be described as the extinguishment of a debt in exchange for the receipt of money, but Goode[127] points out that this is the wrong way around—the question of what is money is a subdivision of the real question, which is what constitutes payment, since a good working definition of money for legal purposes is that which, when tendered and accepted, extinguishes an obligation.[128] This follows Mann's definition that 'payment in the legal sense must connote any act offered and accepted in performance of a money obligation without changing the essential nature of the original obligation'.[129] However, again this is slightly less than helpful. It is unquestionably the case that anything accepted by the creditor as payment discharges the payment obligation—for example, where a buyer trades in a car with a car dealer for a newer model, the transfer of the old car is accepted by the dealer in satisfaction of part of the payment obligation. 7.84

---

[127] McKendrick (ed.), *Goode on Commercial Law* (5th edn, LexisNexis 2016).
[128] Ibid. at 490.   [129] Ibid. at para 7-04.

7.85    It may well be felt that at this stage that the distinction between 'payment by delivery of money' and 'payment by delivery of something which the seller has agreed to accept in payment' may be a purely notional distinction. It is not. It has been with us since the earliest times—in Justinian's *Digest* it is provided that:

> a material was selected which, being given a stable value by the state, avoided the problems of barter by providing a constant medium of exchange. That material ... demonstrates its utility and title not by its substance as such but by its quantity, so that no longer are the things exchanged both called wares, but one of them is termed the price. And today it is a matter for doubt whether one can talk of a sale when no money passes, as when I give an outer garment to receive a tunic. Nerva and Proculus maintain that it is barter, [and this view] is the sounder [since] in such an exchange one cannot discern which party is the vendor and which the purchaser.[130]

And it is with us today in the Sale of Goods Act 1979.

### 7.7.1 What is a 'sale'?

7.86    The definition of a 'sale' for the purpose of this Act is a contract by which the seller transfers or agrees to transfer the property in goods to the buyer for a money consideration, called the price.[131] A similar definition is used in section 5 of the Consumer Rights Act 2015, which provides that a contract is a sales contract if under it the trader transfers or agrees to transfer ownership of goods to the consumer and the consumer pays or agrees to pay the price. This means that a simple dichotomy is presented by the act—transfers of goods in exchange for 'money' are covered by it, transfers of goods in direct exchange are not, since there is no money price. This has led to some fascinating tergiversations on the question of what happens where a payment obligation is satisfied partly in money and partly in goods. A short summary of these is as follows:

(1) When goods are simply exchanged for other goods, there is no sale because there is no price.[132] The same is true where goods are provided in exchange for services.[133] Consequently these transactions fall outside the Sale of Goods Act.

(2) When the buyer and the seller agree a money price for goods, and the price is discharged—in whole or in part—by the delivery of other goods, the result is a sale.[134] This is why where a customer returns goods to a store and receives new goods in exchange for the returned goods, the result is a sale of the new goods.[135]

---

[130] D. 18.1.1-2.    [131] Sale of Goods Act 1979, s. 2.
[132] See also *O'Dea v Merchants Trade-Expansion Group* (1938) 37 AR (NSW) 410 (provision of goods for trading stamps not a sale).
[133] *Garey v Pyke* (1839) 10 Ad & El 512.
[134] *Robshaw Brothers v Mayer* [1975] Ch 125, *Simpson v Connolly* [1953] 2 All ER 474. This doctrine has an ancient and respectable pedigree—in *Aldridge v Johnson* (1857) 7 E & B 885, an exchange of thirty-two bullocks valued at £192 for 100 quarters of barley valued at £215, difference to be paid in cash, was held to be a sale.
[135] *Flynn v Mackin* [1974] IR 101.

(3) Where two parties specify a price for their goods and each supplies goods to the other, with the resulting mutual balances written off, there are two sales, since the delivery of each parcel of goods discharges the money obligation to the other.[136]

It is interesting to note that the confining of the law of sale to exchange of goods for money was not regarded as an inherent and necessary feature of the law of sale—the original draft of the sale of goods act contained a provision applying its terms *mutatis mutandis* to barter transactions, but this was removed during the course of the passage of the act by the select committee.[137] This removal is somewhat mysterious since the pre-existing law on pure barter, as set out in *Le Neuville v Nourse*,[138] approached barter on a pure *caveat emptor* basis and declined to imply any terms at all, holding that the only remedies available in a barter transaction would arise from 'express warranty or direct fraud'. It is notable that when the Law Commission produced its 1979 report on implied terms in contracts for the supply of goods, none of the responders could see any reason for the obligations implied into a contract of sale to be any different from those to be implied into a contract of barter.[139] Consequently, the Supply of Goods and Services Act 1982 was created to rectify the position, and extended some (but not all) of the provisions of the Act to any contract for the transfer of goods 'whatever is the nature of the consideration for the transfer or agreement to transfer'.[140] However, there are still a number of cases in which the rights of the parties are determined by reference to the question of whether the transaction between them is a 'sale' in the Sale of Goods Act sense.

## 7.7.2 The two elements of payment

It should therefore be clear that there are two elements here—the agreement on the price, and the discharge of that obligation. The two can be interconditional, in the sense that it may be agreed that the sale will take place only if the seller agrees that the price will be paid in a particular form. Thus if a customer goes to buy a car from a car dealer, he may well agree that he will buy a new car for a specified price, but only if the dealer agrees to accept his existing vehicle in discharge of x per cent of that price.[141]

It should be noted that the determination of a price need not be accompanied by any actual intention to transfer money. Companies may trade on open account with each other for very extended periods of time, and as between such companies

---

[136] *Davey v Paine Brothers (Motors) Ltd* [1954] NZLR 1122.
[137] Parliamentary Papers 1893–4 (374) XV 11. Note that this distinction is not made in the US Uniform Commercial Code, where the price may be paid in money or goods—if it is paid in goods, each party is a seller as regards those goods—UCC s. 2-304(1); Uniform Sales Act, s. 9(2).
[138] (1813) 3 Camp 351.   [139] Law Com No. 95 HMSO paras 48–55.
[140] Supply of Goods and Services Act 1982, s. 1(3).
[141] The fact of conditionality does not affect the status of the contract under the Act—Sale of Goods Act 1979, s. 2.

it is well-known that there will never be—nor is there intended to be—any money settlement of the obligations thus created. However, this does not prevent the contracts being sales, since the establishment of a price is clear in each case, and the mode of discharge of the obligation this created is immaterial to the issue of whether the goods concerned are sold for a price.

7.90 For this purpose, therefore, we can conclude that a payment obligation has been created where the parties have agreed on a price which is reckoned in money, whether or not it is intended that that price should be settled in money.

### 7.7.3 Methods of payment

7.91 When payment is made by the handing over of physical currency, the payment is effected by the transfer. However where payment is made through a payment system, there may be no connection between the time when the payer's account is debited and the time when the seller's account is credited. In this case, payment occurs when the seller's account is credited. This is true even where the payer and the payee have accounts with the same branch, such that the transfer is accomplished by nothing more than an account entry in the books of the branch concerned.[142] Thus, if the subject matter of the book entry is money, then the making of the book entry constitutes payment.

7.92 In *The Chikuma*[143] it was held that an electronic transfer constituted a payment for this purpose from the moment that the recipient was able to apply the relevant amount without reservation in the discharge of its own obligations—thus, a person whose bank account is credited with funds in an unconditional manner (in other words, where there is no prospect of any other person being entitled to reverse the transaction and recall the funds) is in the same position as a person who has taken possession of physical currency.

### 7.7.4 Payment in virtual currency

7.93 This takes us to the fascinating question of the position of a person who has accepted virtual currency in payment for goods delivered by him under what he believed to be a contract of sale. It is entirely plausible that a supplier being challenged for inadequacy of supplied goods might seek to argue that the contract between them was a contract of barter. The determining issue here is likely to be the unit of account. If the transaction was priced and executed in virtual currency units, it seems difficult to argue that the arrangement could be characterised as anything other than a purchase for money's worth—if the seller has priced his goods in a particular unit, it seems hard for him to argue that he regarded that unit as anything other than 'money'.

---

[142] *Momm v Barclays Bank* [1976] 3 All ER 588 (QB) and see *Libyan Arab Foreign Bank v Manufacturers Hanover Trust Co* [1989] 1 Lloyds LR 608 (QB).
[143] [1981] 1 WLR 314.

## The Legal Character of Money

The position is more complex where the goods are priced in a fiat money unit— 7.94
say US dollars—but the seller accepts virtual currency units in exchange for the
goods. In this position, the question of whether the transaction is a sale or a barter
of goods for goods is much more complicated. In a case of this kind, it seems likely
that the facts which a court would take into consideration would be the way in
which the seller held out the transaction to potential buyers. Here again, it seems
highly likely that what the seller would want would be a combination of the benefits
of a money claim—no *nemo dat* risk and certainty of entitlement—alongside the
relative freedom of the constraints of the Sale of Goods legislation resulting from
characterisation as barter. The key point here is that a court is most unlikely to allow
this outcome—in effect, the seller is likely to be put to his election at an early stage
in the proceedings as to whether he accepts the transaction as a sale or not, and if he
does not, he will have to suffer the consequences of his claim for the relevant virtual
currency units being a claim for property rather than money.

What then is the remedy available to a disappointed buyer who has paid virtual 7.95
currency units in exchange for goods which are defective or possibly non-existent.
The starting point here is that 'There is reasonable agreement among the authorities that it is not open to a disappointed party who has parted with his goods
without receiving the expected return to sue for the value of the goods delivered as
a price'[144]—his remedy is to sue in damages for breach of contract, or possibly for
unjust enrichment, and this is true even if the goods have been valued for the purpose. Conversely, a person who has paid money but received nothing at all in return
has an action which is in effect a debt action for repayment of the money that he has
paid over.[145]

It seems that in cases of this kind the courts are prepared to take an expansive view 7.96
of what counts as currency of this purpose, and in particular to regard the transfer of
private payment instruments as 'money'. In *Davies v Customs & Excise*,[146] a transfer
of goods in exchange for a trading cheque[147] was a sale for value.

There is an interesting line of value added tax (VAT) cases in this regard. Item 1 7.97
of Group 5 of Schedule 9 to the Value Added Tax Act 1994 (VATA 1994) provides
an exemption from VAT for 'The issue, transfer or receipt of, or any dealing with,
money, any security for money or any note or order for the payment of money'. This
has from time to time raised the question of the position where a person receives
legal tender and gives the payer in return something which can be used to purchase
services. This seems to have been the conclusion on vouchers which entitled the purchaser to the services of a lap dancer[148] and on vouchers which entitled the bearer

---

[144] *Benjamin's Sale of Goods* (9th edn, Sweet & Maxwell 2014) para 1-035; *Read v Hutchinson* (1813) 3 Camp 352; *Harrison v Luke* (1845) 14 M. & W. 139.
[145] *Moses v Macferlan* (1760) 2 Burr 1005, and see Burrows, *The Law of Restitution* (3rd edn, OUP 2011) and Virgo, *The Principles of the Law of Restitution* (3rd edn, OUP 2015) at 308–9.
[146] [1975] 1 WLR 204.
[147] Trading cheques were a primitive form of gift voucher—a device used by retailers, whereby the retailer created an instrument which he would accept in payment for purchases made in his shop.
[148] *Wilton Park Ltd v The Commissioners for Her Majesty's Revenue and Customs* [2015] UKUT 0343 (TCC).

to spend money in a supermarket.[149] These authorities all tend in the direction of the conclusion that if what the parties intended was a transfer of ownership of goods (or, in the case of the lap dancers, the supply of services) in exchange for something which was not itself an asset requiring independent valuation, then that something is 'money' to the extent that its delivery constitutes payment.

---

[149] *Coinstar v The Commissioners for Her Majesty's Revenue and Customs* [2016] UKFTT 0610 (TC).

# 8

# Private and Public Virtual Currency

| | |
|---|---|
| 8.1 **Private Virtual Currency** | 8.02 |
|     8.1.1 A taxonomy of private virtual currencies | 8.04 |
| 8.2 **Central Bank Digital Currency (CBDC)** | 8.05 |
|     8.2.1 CBDC compared with other payment instruments | 8.10 |
|     8.2.2 Designs for CBDC | 8.12 |
|     8.2.3 CBDC as a replacement for commercial bank money | 8.17 |
|     8.2.4 CBDC as a control mechanism for commercial bank money | 8.21 |
|     8.2.5 A centralised banking model | 8.26 |
|     8.2.6 Economic consequences of the adoption of a centralised money model | 8.33 |
|     8.2.7 Interaction of central bank digital currency and private virtual currency | 8.38 |

There are two broad classes of virtual currency: private and public. The public variety at the moment remain entirely speculative, but remain of great interest. We shall consider each in turn.    8.01

## 8.1 Private Virtual Currency

Modern private payment instruments are generally electronic. This is not invariably true—the Bristol pound in the United Kingdom[1] is a good example of a private payment instrument which exists in physical form as well as in electronic form—but the recent burst of activity in this area has been based on the fact that developments in computing technology—in particular distributed ledger technology—have enabled the construction of secure internet-based programmes which facilitate transaction settlement without involvement of existing payments or settlements systems. The key point here is that the functionality of existing currency is composed of two elements—one is its acceptability as payment, and the    8.02

---

[1] See https://bristolpound.org/.

other is the facility with which it can actually be transferred. As regards real (physical) money, the latter is accomplished by transfer of physical possession, an exceptionally simple and straightforward purpose. However, the inconvenience of holding large amounts of value in the form of physical money has meant that since the earliest times money has been held with third party custodians. The ease of dealing with such balances must then be set off against the greater difficulty involved in transferring them. This difficulty is a major reason for the existence of modern banks, one of whose primary services to their customers is access to payment systems which enable money held in a bank account to be easily and quickly transferred. It was really only with the creation of a technological solution to this problem that the existence of virtual currency outside the banking system (and therefore outside existing payment systems) became possible, and distributed ledger technology was the key which unlocked this possibility.

8.03 When we speak of a virtual currency, what we mean is a unit registered in a publicly accessible register in the name of a legal person. The effect of the way in which the register is created is that there is (or should be) only one identifiable owner of each unit, and that identifiable owner has an absolute right to manipulate the register so as to change the identity of the registered owner of that unit. Strictly speaking this is not a transfer of property, but in practice it has that effect. There are a number of different ways of thinking about these units. In principle, they are free-standing items with no necessary connection to any other item of property. However, like any other item of property which can be bought and sold, a market may develop within which an exchange rate may be discerned, so that X units may be obtained for Y dollars.

### 8.1.1 A taxonomy of private virtual currencies

8.04 It is, however, an error to assume that the classical virtual currency—the 'Bitcoin' model—is the only possible way that this technology can be used. In practice there are four broad models which can operate, of which the bitcoin model is only one.[2] These models are as follows:

   1. 'Currency tokens'. These tokens are intended to function as direct substitutes for money and—importantly—have no other purpose or characteristics. Such

---

[2] There are a number of taxonomies of virtual currency in existence, but these generally address the functional characteristics or background creation of the unit concerned, and are of limited use for legal purposes. See the ECB's *Virtual Currency Schemes* (October 2012) and *Virtual Currency Schemes— A Further Analysis* (February 2015). The analysis below is broadly congruent with those put forward in Rohr and Wright, *Blockchain-Based Tokens Sales, Initial Coin Offerings, and the Democratization of Public Capital Markets* Cardozo Legal Studies Research Paper 572, University of Tennessee Legal Studies Research Paper 338, as refined by Hacker and Thomale in *Crypto-Securities Regulation: ICOs, Token Sales and Cryptocurrencies under EU Financial Law*, available on SSRN at https://papers.ssrn.com/sol3/papers.cfm?abstract_id=3075820. See also FATF Report *Virtual Currencies Key Definitions and Potential AML/CFT Risks*, 2014 FATF/OECD.

a token is constituted solely by a register. An 'owner' of a cybercoin has no claim on anything or against any person arising out of his 'ownership' of the coin—what he has is a mere right to instruct that the register be changed such that some other person's name should be entered in place of his own. The legal paradox thus created—that it is possible to transfer something which does not at first glance appear to be capable of being owned—is at the heart of much of the current discussion of the law relating to virtual currency. These are referred to as 'currency tokens'.

2. 'Utility tokens'. These are tokens which are intended to confer some benefit or right on the bearer other than by payment for goods or services. An example is a service like Filecoin,[3] in which investors purchase coins and then 'spend' them to acquire data storage capacity. There are also hybrid products such as Etherium, where users can use Etherium tokens either as currency units or to purchase access to the Etherium decentralised computing and smart contract platform.

3. 'Investment tokens'. These are transferable tokens which promise the holder a return based on some kind of underlying asset. These fall into two separate subcategories:

   a. 'money-backed tokens'. Tokens of this kind purport to be 'backed' in one way or another by fiat currency, and have a value expressed in monetary units. Some examples of this have been created by pure non-bank actors,[4] but a number of banks (and some central banks) are considering the creation of such units.

      i. 'Bank money-backed tokens'. For tokens created by individual banks, each unit is likely to be capable of being presented to the relevant bank at any time and exchanged for an account credit denominated in fiat money. Thus, bank issues bankcoin which can be exchanged for money in a current account at the rate of one bankcoin for one pound. The primary objective of a system of this kind would be for the bank concerned to persuade its customers who were suppliers to accept bankcoins in payment of debts directly, thereby reducing the cost of operation to the bank of processing the payment. A system of multiple bankcoins would be effective and would operate in much the same way as the paper cheque market operates—retailer who banks with Bank 1 accepts a bankcoin created by Bank 2, delivers that bankcoin to Bank 1, which then either presents it to Bank 2 for settlement in money, or simply holds it as a liquid asset equivalent to

---

[3] See https://filecoin.io/.
[4] For example, Tether (see https://tether.to/) is a virtual currency which purports to be backed one-to-one by US dollars, such that one Tether coin represents $1.

an overnight deposit with Bank 2. An instrument of this kind is most closely akin to an electronic promissory note.

ii. 'Non-bank money-backed tokens'. An example of these is the 'Utility Settlement Coin' or USC model.[5] This is defined as follows: 'USC is an asset-backed digital cash instrument implemented on distributed ledger technology for use within global institutional financial markets. USC is a series of cash assets, with a version for each of the major currencies (USD, EUR, GBP, CHF, etc.) and USC is convertible at parity with a bank deposit in the corresponding currency. USC is fully backed by cash assets held at a central bank. Spending a USC will be spending its paired real-world currency.' In a structure of this kind, the primary objective is the reduction of transaction costs. This is intellectually similar to the immobilisation of securities. In the early days of automation of the securities industry, it was clear that it would not be possible to move straight from paper-based processing of securities transactions to electronic processing. An intermediate step of 'immobilisation' was therefore created. In an immobilisation structure, the paper securities were transferred to a transferee which issued electronic instruments which created rights to those securities. Thus, when an owner of an immobilised security sold that security, he settled his obligation by transferring to the buyer the electronic instrument which conveyed the right to the underlying security. In an immobilisation system, each electronic instrument reflects a claim to an underlying asset. Importantly, these instruments are simply reflections of the underlying assets. The reason for doing this is simply that settlement in such units may incur considerably smaller (or no) transaction costs compared with the use of existing payment systems—in this regard a comparison with global depositary receipts may be appropriate.

b. 'Asset-backed tokens'. Tokens of this kind confer an investment return of some kind based on the performance of some identified asset, project, business, or other factor. With tokens of this kind the token-holder generally does not have any property or other claim to the underlying assets, but the terms on which he acquired the token will provide for some benefit to accrue to him in the event that an underlying investment made with the proceeds of the token offering is successful.

4. 'Warrant tokens'. Tokens of this kind operate in a manner equivalent to depositary receipts or warehouse warrants. They can take two forms: those

---

[5] See UBS News Release, 24 August 2016 *Utility Settlement Coin concept on blockchain gathers pace*. This project is under way but incomplete at the time of writing. Its interest in this context is derived not from the instrument itself, but from the ideas that underpin it.

where an individual identifiable unit relates to an individual identifiable item of property (e.g. if the underlying property were individually numbered bags of coffee in a warehouse, it would be possible for each individual unit to be linked to a specific bag); and those where the underlying is an undistinguished mass (e.g. if the underlying property were a pool of shares, each individual unit would entitle the holder to a delivery of a number of shares out of that mass).[6]

## 8.2 Central Bank Digital Currency (CBDC)

8.05 This issue has received a large amount of attention recently at the highest levels of macroeconomics, and a merely mechanical analysis cannot compete at this level. However, there are some points which might usefully be made.

8.06 One of the issues which the invention of virtual currency has brought into sharp focus is the possibility of disintermediating the entire banking sector. It is probable that such an idea is some way away from technical feasibility, but the theoretical possibility deserves some consideration.

8.07 The proponents of this idea generally look back to the Chicago Plan. This proposal, advanced by a number of US economists at the height of the Great Depression, envisaged the separation of the monetary and credit functions of the banking system, by requiring 100 per cent reserve backing for deposits—effectively, that commercial banks should pass all of the deposits which they received directly to the central bank. Irving Fisher (1936) claimed the following advantages for this plan: (1) much better control of increases and contractions of bank credit and of the supply of bank-created money; (2) complete elimination of bank runs; (3) dramatic reduction of the (net) public debt; and (4) dramatic reduction of private debt, as money creation no longer requires simultaneous debt creation.[7] The question of whether these claims are plausible or not is well beyond the scope of this work, but it should be clear that for those who believe in the desirability of the effective replacement of private banking with state-controlled banking, public virtual currency would provide a magnificent tool with which to implement this policy. Consequently, the issue deserves consideration.

8.08 The Estonian government has famously suggested that the nation could launch a new currency, known as 'estcoin';[8] there have been continuing suggestions that

---

[6] The distinction between this class of token and the class identified above, where the underlying is fiat money, is not structural, but simply to do with the fact that the nature of the underlying—fiat money—is itself sufficient to justify differentiated treatment of the instrument. A claim for a thing and a claim for money are legally very different.

[7] Fisher, *100% Money and the Public Debt*, Economic Forum, Spring Number (April–June 1936) at 406–20. For a recent appreciation of the Chicago Plan see Benes and Kumhof, *The Chicago Plan Revisited*, (IMF Working paper August 2012).

[8] Blogpost by Kaspar Korjus, head of the Estonian e-residency programme, August 2017 at https://medium.com/e-residency-blog.

the US Federal Reserve is considering a 'Fedcoin';[9] and the Swiss recently put to a referendum the question of whether private bank money should be abolished and replaced with central bank money ('Vollgeld'). These proposals were met with concern by the relevant central banks.[10] The Finnish proposal also met with a predictable backlash from the European Central Bank (ECB), to the effect that a member of the Euro (which Estonia is) must retain the Euro as its currency, and cannot have a parallel currency in circulation. However, this proposition is questionable—when the state of California fell into economic difficulties in 2009 it created 'IOUs' which circulated as money and were used to pay state government debts, and this does not appear to have caused difficulties with the US Federal Reserve[11] (although the US Securities and Exchange Commission (SEC) did determine that the IOUs were securities[12]). However, the issue of whether or not a central bank could issue virtual currency either alongside or in substitution for its own currency has been the subject of significant debate.

8.09 The Bank of England, in particular, has focused on central bank digital currencies (CBDCs), and this was set out as a focus area in its 2015 research agenda,[13] and recent speeches by the governor[14] and other senior members of the court[15] have discussed in some detail the possible responses of central banks to the development of virtual currencies.

### 8.2.1 CBDC compared with other payment instruments

8.10 A useful architecture for thinking about CBDCs is provided in Bech and Garrett's *Central Bank Cryptocurrencies*.[16] They suggest that money-like things can be classified in four dimensions: (a) issuer (central bank or other); (b) form (electronic or physical); (c) accessibility (universal or limited); and (d) transfer mechanism (centralised or decentralised). Thus, the current position of the two types of current central bank money (physical cash, and cash balances held with the central bank (such as cash settlement balances maintained in the Bank's Real Time Gross Settlement System (RTGS)) is as follows in Table 8.1:

---

[9] See *Should the Fed Create 'FedCoin' to Rival Bitcoin? A Former Top Official Says 'Maybe'*, New York Times May 18 2018.and see *Fedcoin: A Central Bank-issued Cryptocurrency*, Koning (R3 Reports 2016).

[10] For the Swiss central Banks response see the announcement of the Chairman of the Governing Board at https://www.snb.ch/en/mmr/speeches/id/ref_20180503_tjn and for the Estonian Central bank see the interview with Madis Muller, deputy governor, on the bank's website at https://www.eestipank.ee/en/press/articles-and-interviews/crypto-assets-bubble-or-future.

[11] See https://www.federalreserve.gov/newsevents/pressreleases/bcreg20090702b.htm.

[12] See SEC investor alert at https://www.sec.gov/investor/pubs/californiaiou-alert.htm.

[13] See Bank of England, *One Bank Research Agenda* (2015).

[14] See https://www.bankofengland.co.uk/speech/2018/mark-carney-speech-to-the-inaugural-scottish-economics-conference.

[15] Ben Broadbent, Deputy Governor for Monetary Stability, https://www.bis.org/review/r160303e.pdf and Andy Haldane, Chief Economist,https://www.bankofengland.co.uk/speech/2015/how-low-can-you-can-go.

[16] BIS Quarterly Review, September 2017.

Table 8.1 The current position of the two types of current central bank money

|  |  | Physical cash | Central bank balances | Bitcoin | Central bank digital currency |
|---|---|---|---|---|---|
| Issuer | Central bank | √ | √ |  | √ |
|  | Other |  |  | √ |  |
| Form | Electronic |  | √ | √ | √ |
|  | Physical | √ |  |  |  |
| Accessibility | Universal | √ |  | √ | ? |
|  | Limited |  | √ |  | ? |
| Transfer mechanism | Centralised |  | √ |  | ? |
|  | Decentralised | √ |  | √ | ? |

Table 8.1 neatly highlights the issue which arises in considering the design of CBDCs. The first two boxes are reasonably straightforward—the issuer has to be the central bank, and a digital currency is unlikely to take a physical form. However, it is not at all clear whether a CBDC should circulate freely, or whether its use should be confined either to those who already have access to central bank balances such as banks (in which case its utility is in some doubt), or whether it should be permitted to compete with private bank money as a payment medium (a development which would be roughly equivalent to the central bank expanding into private banking in competition with commercial banks). This is connected to the issue of the available transfer mechanism. In particular, the question of who should be allowed access to CBDCs may be of limited relevance if it can subsequently be freely transferred over a decentralised register.

### 8.2.2 Designs for CBDC

The point that this brings out is that there are a number of possible design philosophies for a CBDC. These are broadly classified in a recent Bank of England Research paper by Kumhof and Noone.[17] Their classifications are as follows.

*Financial institutions only access*: Access to CBDCs is limited to banks and non-bank financial institutions (NBFIs). CBDCs can then be thought of as being similar to the reserve assets currently used within the Bank of England's RTGS system.[18]

8.11

8.12

8.13

---

[17] Kumhof and Noone, *Central Bank Digital Currencies—Design Principles and Balance Sheet Implications* (March 2018) Staff Working Paper No. 725.
[18] The Bank of England's RTGS infrastructure is designed to facilitate the settlement of electronic sterling transfers. In the United Kingdom, banks and a few other types of financial institutions (such as central counterparties) can hold accounts in RTGS for holding reserves or settling net obligations. Since mid-2017, non-bank payment service providers have also been able to apply to hold settlement accounts in the RTGS system; the first non-bank payment service providers are expected to join RTGS during 2018.

Banks and NBFIs would be able to interact directly with the central bank to buy/sell CBDCs in exchange for eligible securities.

8.14 *Economy-wide access*: Alongside banks and NBFIs, households and firms also have access to CBDCs. CBDCs can therefore serve as money for all agents in the economy. The central bank does not provide retail services to all holders of CBDCs—only banks and NBFIs can interact directly with the central bank to buy or sell CBDCs, while other users must use a CBDC exchange to buy and sell CBDCs in exchange for money. It would in theory be possible to expand this still further, so that households and firms could directly trade CBDCs with the central bank.

8.15 *Financial institutions intermediated access*: CBDC access is limited to banks and NBFIs. Within the NBFI sector there is at least one financial institution that acts as a narrow bank, providing a financial asset to households and firms that is fully backed by CBDCs but that does not extend credit. That is, they provide households and firms with an asset that has the risk profile of central bank money, rather than a risk profile linked to the financial institution and of its borrowers. Holders of this asset can transact amongst themselves in this narrow bank money (termed indirect CBDCs, or iCBDCs). The narrow bank or banks that provide this service are termed indirect CBDC providers (iCBDCPs). iCBDCPs do not need access to reserves and to RTGS to operate,[19] and (interestingly) are not credit institutions for EU purposes and may well not be deposit-taking institutions for UK purposes.

8.16 This taxonomy gives some structure to the various proposals from what might be described as the radical wing of the commentariat for the abolition of the banking system and its replacement with either centralised record-keeping or central bank money. These come in two broad classes: those which seek to abolish money altogether, and those which seek to abolish private money.[20]

## 8.2.3 CBDC as a replacement for commercial bank money

8.17 The first of these is the more coherent but the less practical. It can be viewed as an attempt to restore the economy to an Arrow-Debreu state. It is quite clear that in theory the existence of money is not essential to the functioning of an economy, provided that some sort of scorekeeping mechanism exists to keep track of and balance exchanges of value. It would therefore be perfectly possible to create a single central register of payment obligations, thereby dispensing with the necessity for the transfer of money. This could be regarded as a nationwide giro system, with every member of the population as a member.

8.18 Technological development is bringing ideas such as this out of the realms of fantasy and towards (albeit not yet into) the realm of reality, so it deserves some consideration as a policy proposal.

---

[19] The paper's authors accept that a narrow bank fully backed by cash is unlikely to be a profitable going concern—indeed, given the non-interest-bearing nature of cash and its storage cost, the narrow bank would need to charge a negative interest rate or a fee to cover costs.
[20] These issues arise in the context of a broader debate about the causes of and appropriate regulatory responses to the global financial crisis of 2008–11 which are well beyond the scope of this book.

The first point to make about such a system is that it turns out in reality to be   8.19
little more than reorganisation of the system which already exists. If the existing
private banks were to be pooled together into a single private legal entity to provide
such services, this objective would be largely achieved, and once full coverage of the
population had been effected the abolition of notes and coins would be an irrelevance. However, the relationship between the central bank and the private legal entity would be identical to the relationship between the central bank and the current
private banking system today—save for the fact that the private entity would have
greater negotiating power.

Thus, the idea can be reversed by assuming that instead of recruiting private   8.20
entities as its agents to perform certain functions, the central bank could simply
expand to perform those functions itself. Again, there is nothing philosophically
untenable about the idea of the central bank being the sole provider of cash management, deposit, and payment services—indeed there are arguments that a market in
which all payments were settled in central bank money would be more robust than
one which was dependent on private institutions. In order to effect this proposal,
the central bank would in effect have to acquire all of the private commercial banks
operating in its territory, since their account management and payment capabilities
would be required in order to manage the flow of payment all of which would not
flow through the central bank.

### 8.2.4 CBDC as a control mechanism for commercial bank money

A modern economy settles its obligations in private bank money. Central banks provide   8.21
central bank money to commercial banks, and those banks provide money to
the economy. This appears to some to be an appalling inversion of the natural order
of things. They therefore argue for a reversion to what they perceive as the good old
days in which governments are the providers of payment instruments directly to
the economy (and can therefore control the total value of instruments within that
economy).[21] The mechanism which is suggested to accomplish this is full reserve
banking.[22] The idea is that if all deposit banks are required to hold balances with
the central bank equal to 100 per cent of the amount of deposits received, they will
effectively be conduits between the private economy and the central bank. Thus,
private banks will continue to provide payment services, but they will no longer be
able to create credit beyond the limits of the amount of central bank money to be
made available to them by the central bank.

The first thing to say about this idea is that it is neither novel nor impossible. In   8.22
1985, Charles Goodhart considered the practicalities of a 100 per cent reserve banking
system and determined that there was nothing in the proposal which was unfeasible.[23]

---

[21] Martin Wolf's *The Shifts and the Shocks* (Penguin 2015) is the most eloquent articulation of this argument.
[22] See, e.g., Tobin, *Financial Innovation and Deregulation in Perspective*, Bank of Japan Monetary and Economic Studies, Vol. 3, No. 2 (1985).
[23] Chapter 7 of *The Evolution of Central Banks* (MIT Press 1988).

However, he correctly identified the inherent problem with the arrangement. The current arrangement of banking is that private banks take deposits, lend out the money deposited, and then deliver the profits of that lending activity to customers, either in the form of interest-bearing deposits or in the form of a subsidisation (or, more usually in the United Kingdom, elimination) of bank charges. Since central banks do not pay interest on balances maintained with them, this would mean that banks would cease to be able to offer interest on deposit accounts and would have to pass on to customers the full costs of payment services provided to them. The likely economic effect of this would be the redirection of customer savings and surplus cash balances to non-bank (and generally unregulated) vehicles which were not obliged to hold their balances in return-free form, which could invest their cash balances with the aim of making a profit from the assumption of credit risk, and which could therefore offer a substantial return to their investors. Goodhart envisaged these vehicles as cash funds investing in high-quality, near-cash products, thereby predicting the development of money market funds some years before their florescence.

8.23 The difficulty which this proposal presents, however, is that banks in practice do not invest only in high-quality near-cash instruments, but are the major providers of credit to the economy. Even those who do not believe that banks should be engaging in this sort of high-risk activity must presumably accept that someone should be doing it. Thus, if the aim is to confine banks to holding highly secure investments, it will become necessary to create some sort of vehicle to hold the less secure investments.

8.24 This is the point at which difficulties arise. Goodhart again, anticipating by twenty years the debate over constant versus variable net asset value figures for money market funds, correctly identifies the problem that for the vast bulk of users of the financial system, their primary aim is to put £1 in a place where they are reasonably sure that when they ask for it back they will receive £1. From the perspective of an ordinary everyday investor or saver, an offer of an account on terms that he comes to spend the contents of the account it may be £110 or it may be £90 is highly unattractive—he has probably invested that portion of his assets which he has free to invest, and his primary concern for the remainder is that it should be roughly in the same state when he spends it as it as when he deposited it. Put simply, he does not want an investment, he wants access to payment capability in the amount initially deposited.

8.25 If the position is that depositors want access to payment services, and the banking system sneakily commits their deposited funds to long-term investment without their knowledge, that may well argue for a restructuring of the banking system. However, if we assume that no such restructuring will happen in the short term, then we are left with the question of how 100 per cent reserve banking would actually work in practice.

### 8.2.5 A centralised banking model

8.26 Surprisingly, this takes us back to well-trodden ground. This is broadly the economic architecture of the Soviet Union, whose operation is well-described by Conway in a paper entitled 'Currency Proliferation: The Money Legacy of the Soviet Union'.[24] In particular, Gosbank, the central bank, was the only bank for the entire economy,[25] and government obligations were the chief asset for the entire financial system. When a business purchased inputs, the invoice was presented by the purchaser to Gosbank, who automatically credited the supplier with the value of the goods provided. If there was insufficient credit to the account of the purchaser, further credit was granted. A substantial cash economy existed—in general transactions between individuals took place in cash, transactions between business in the books of Gosbank, with little overlap between the two.

8.27 This system worked whilst the Soviet Union was in a period of financial repression. Because there was a severe shortage of goods of all forms throughout the period, and transactions with persons outside the rouble area were heavily discouraged or illegal, holders of cash balances effectively had no choice but to hold surplus cash balances with Gosbank. These balances effectively financed the large and growing budget deficit of the soviet government.

8.28 The essence of this system was that Gosbank's approach to the creation of credit was entirely passive—when more credit was demanded, it was automatically supplied, provided that the demand was backed by a commercial invoice. Within the soviet system this was not as irrational as it may appear—Gosplan was charged with planning the economy, and Gossnab (the supply ministry) with deciding what goods were required where. Gosbank existed simply to facilitate these plans, so arguably had no choice but to create credit upon request. Further, the fact that credit was created only upon the presentation of an invoice resulted in a system not unlike that advocated by supporters of the real bills doctrine in nineteenth-century England—a doctrine which was advocated specifically to reduce the supply of excess credit.

8.29 There are a number of problems involved in transplanting the Gosbank system to a modern economy. The first, and most important, is that in the current western system private bank deposits are used to finance commercial lending. If the central bank were the only entity able to advance such finance, it would be obliged to take on the Gosplan and Gossnab functions, deciding where in the economy required credit and directing credit to those areas. It seems highly arguable that this is likely to be well beyond the capabilities of any central bank (or, as the soviet experience shows, any government) and is probably best left to the private sector. It would of course be possible for a central bank within such a system to leave the advancing of credit to the private sector, and to apply the deposits placed with it to the making of loans to those banks. This would result in a system where private banks took in deposits, advanced them to the central bank, and then bid to borrow those funds back from the central bank again.

8.30 It is at this point that the proponents of this scheme identify what they perceive to be one of its most significant advantages. If the system were to work in this way, the central bank would be able to control the flow of funds to private banks and thereby to

---

[24] Essays in International Finance No. 197 (Princeton June 1995).
[25] In 1997, Gosbank was formally divided into a group of smaller banks, but these remained under the control of the central Gosbank leadership.

the economy—if they felt that there was too much money in the system they could reduce the amount of funding redistributed to private banks (presumably by increasing the cost charged to banks for that funding), although this could also be done by absolutely reducing the amount of funding available, and if they felt there was too little they could increase the supply (presumably by reducing the cost of such funding).

8.31   Another advantage of the scheme, propounded by advocates such as Rogoff,[26] is that it would facilitate the imposition by the central bank of negative interest rates on the economy. If all deposits are required to be maintained with the central bank, then the central bank can impose a charge for handling those deposits; in effect a negative interest rate, which cannot be avoided.

8.32   It may well be that this aspect of these various schemes—the tightening of government control over the economy—would be advantageous in economic terms—that is beyond the scope if this work. However, that advantage will only accrue if the nationalisation of deposits is completely effected. We must therefore think about how this might be done and what its consequences might be.

### 8.2.6 Economic consequences of the adoption of a centralised money model

8.33   As noted above, the principal problem with the idea of routing all transactions through the central bank is that it turns the central bank into an economic planning ministry,[27] required to exercise overall control of the supply and allocation of credit. However, advocates of this abolition of banking argue that the problem is imaginary. Their position is that deposit-taking banks should not be taking credit risks of this kind in the first place. The specific point is that it is wrong (and arguably dishonest) for banks to promise to repay deposits at their nominal value unless they invest the money received in risk-free securities. Thus, for example, King observes that 'it is [the current banking] structure, in which risky long-term assets are funded by short-term deposits, that makes banks so hazardous. Yet many treat loans to banks as if they were riskless. In isolation, this would be akin to a belief in alchemy—risk-free deposits can never be supported by long-term risky investments in isolation. To work, financial alchemy requires the implicit support of the tax payer.'

8.34   This is of course a condemnation of the way in which the banking industry has operated since its inception—indeed, many would say that the core function of a banker, and the trait by which a bank can be most clearly identified, is the accepting of money placed on deposit for transactional purposes and the investment of surplus balances in credit investments. The way in which this operates can be seen in Figure 8.1.[28]

---

[26] Rogoff, *The Curse of Cash* (Princeton 2016).
[27] It is difficult not to note in passing that the economic consequences of a policy based on government command and control of credit in the Soviet Union had outcomes which were considerably worse for its citizens than the free-market policies pursued by the west, even despite the western financial crises which occurred during the period of the soviet experiment.
[28] Derived from Bank of England aggregate data and reproduced from the speech by Ben Broadbent at fn 15.

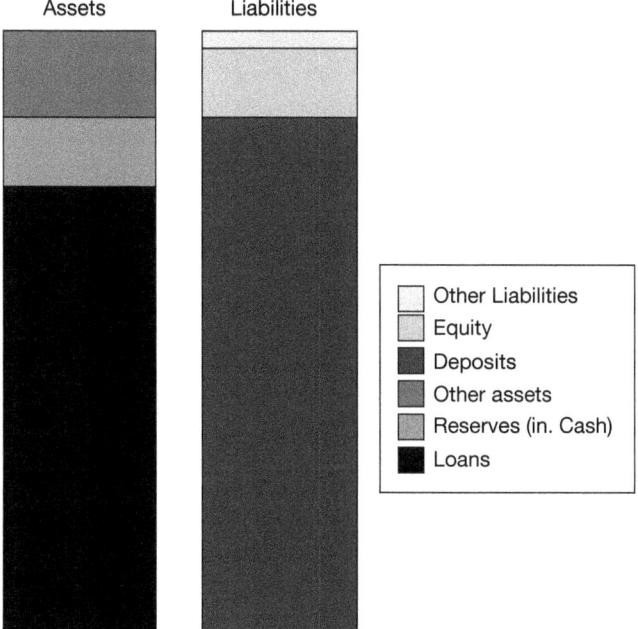

**Figure 8.1** Commercial banks' assets liquid assets smaller than deposit liabilities

In general, those who argue in this way suggest that bank depositors be forced to confront the riskiness of their banks, by dividing their deposits between a risk-free deposit payment account backed by the central bank (and costing a reasonably large amount of money—the proponents of these schemes are generally united in their opposition to 'free banking'), and an explicitly risky investment account which is subject to credit risk but presumably either carries a positive investment return or is at least cheaper to operate than the full-fee payment account. Proponents of this model often suggest that the result of this separation is that the bank effectively divides itself into a payment service provider (frequently but misleading referred to as a 'narrow' bank) whose only assets are claims on the central bank or the relevant government, and an non-bank financial institution (NBFI) which performs broadly the function of a credit investment fund.

If the system could be organised in this way, a number of things would seem to follow. First, deposit balances would drop sharply across the system, since balances of this kind would be expensive to operate. It is important to understand that the greater the drop in balances, the higher usage fees would become for the remaining users of the system—the payment system is effectively a fixed cost for banks, and their costs of operating it are distributed across the balances of their payment customer base. Thus, the smaller this base becomes, the higher fees will become as a proportion of the value of that base. Second, if King is correct, there would be a sharp decline on the aggregate amount of credit made available by the banking system to the real economy. Third, since the money withdrawn from the payment system would have to go somewhere, it would likely find a home with NBFIs.

8.37    The question which arises is as to how stable this system would be. The major criticism of this proposed architecture is that it should be assumed that in normal economic times, investors would wish to hold as large a proportion of their cash balances as they could reasonably manage with NBFIs in order to maximise returns. More importantly, a group which contained both a payment service provider and an NBFI would be incentivised to make 'switching' between NBFI units and payment account balances as painless as possible. In a downturn, however, customers could be expected to switch out of NBFI units and into deposit account balances to preserve capital values. This would create a run on NBFIs, resulting a severe and immediate withdrawal of credit from the real economy (also, since the NBFIs are intended to invest almost exclusively in long-term loans rather than short-term cash balances, resulting in their failure through liquidity pressures). Thus, it is argued, this architecture creates a significant financial stability risk which would not exist if the two activities were contained in a single legal entity. It is fair to point out that the introduction of CBDCs into any system on terms that CBDCs can be owned by non-banks increases the run risk to some extent (since it significantly facilitates a run on the banking system as a whole, with bank customers able to switch from bank or NBFI deposits into CBDCs; effective running from the private banking system to the central bank). It is fair to point out that Kumhof and Noone have considered these issues and conclude that the risks are low, but this is on the assumption that CBDC is only issued against high-quality collateral (mostly government securities). If this constraint is removed, the picture becomes more complex.

### 8.2.7   Interaction of central bank digital currency and private virtual currency

8.38    A system which divided up the existing banking model in this way would seem to provide the ideal breeding ground for virtual currencies. The NBFIs envisaged above would seek to offer as near as possible the service previously provided by the banking system—that is, a unit which could be regarded as a proxy for currency, which would be widely accepted in the discharge of debts, and which did not carry significant holding or usage charges. This would seem to be the ideal environment for the rapid development of virtual currencies, which in this fact pattern could rapidly displace conventional banking as the preferred mechanism for value storage and payment.

8.39    Finally, a question which is substantially debated as regards CBDCs—and for that matter virtual currency generally—is whether and to what extent Gresham's law would operate upon their introduction. Gresham's law[29]—'bad money drives out good'—states that where there are two different payment media in circulation with different perceived values, the more valuable one will tend to be hoarded whilst the less valuable one will be used—thus, the more valuable unit will disappear from circulation. It should be clear that this is relevant to CBDCs, which are by definition of a higher credit quality than private bank money issued by the banks of the territory for which the CBDC issuer is the central bank.

---

[29] See para 4.3.1 above.

# 9

# Virtual Currency and the Law

| | |
|---|---|
| 9.1 Virtual Currency as Property | 9.04 |
| 9.1.1 Property in an entry in a distributed ledger | 9.08 |
| 9.1.2 Ownership or mere right to transfer? | 9.12 |
| 9.1.3 Transfer of ownership of virtual currency | 9.17 |
| 9.1.4 Virtual currency and nominalism | 9.21 |
| 9.2 Virtual Currency and Set-off | 9.30 |
| 9.2.1 The rules of set-off | 9.35 |
| 9.2.2 What can be set-off—common law? | 9.39 |
| 9.2.3 What can be set-off—equity? | 9.44 |
| 9.2.4 Set-off and virtual currency | 9.45 |
| 9.3 Virtual Currency, Transferability, and Negotiability | 9.46 |
| 9.4 Taking Security Over Virtual Currency Units | 9.49 |
| 9.4.1 Virtual currency unit balances maintained with a bank | 9.53 |
| 9.5 Repo of Virtual Currency | 9.57 |
| 9.6 Recovery of Misappropriated Virtual Currency | 9.62 |
| 9.6.1 Proprietary and possessory remedies | 9.63 |
| 9.6.2 Personal restitution | 9.67 |
| 9.7 Situs of Virtual Currency | 9.70 |
| 9.8 Loan of Virtual Currency Units | 9.84 |
| 9.9 Claims for Payment in Virtual Currency | 9.87 |
| 9.9.1 Foreign money and virtual currency | 9.88 |
| 9.9.2 Consequences of treatment of money as a commodity | 9.90 |
| 9.9.3 Recognition of non-UK currency as money | 9.92 |
| 9.9.4 Deciding the relevant currency of a contract | 9.97 |
| 9.9.5 Virtual currency and obligations | 9.109 |

The law in general has little difficulty dealing with things which do not physically exist. Loans, patents, payment obligations, and service contracts create a complex matrix of intangible but identifiable and enforceable legal obligations. It may therefore be thought that simply adding another intangible to this mix will cause no great difficulty.

However, although it is wrong to think of property as a bundle of rights, property—particularly intangible property—is defined by the way in which it is protected in law. Different types of property are entitled to different types of protections, and it can be argued that a property right is defined by the rights which confers on the property owner to resist interference with the property. Different types of property trigger different types of protections—for example, interference with physical property is protected under the law of trespass, whereas the doctrines of trespass do not apply to intellectual property.[1]

9.03 It follows from this that in considering the legal position in respect of any particular thing, identifying it as a form of property is the beginning rather than the end of the legal analysis. It is not enough to say 'this is property'—we must go on to decide what sort of property it is, and this determination in turn is made largely by considering how it can be transferred, what remedies are available for its misappropriation, and how certain issues relating to it will be dealt with.

## 9.1 Virtual Currency as Property

9.04 Is virtual currency property at law? Here, at least, we do have a legal rule of recognition. In *National Provincial Bank v Ainsworth*[2] Lord Wilberforce summarised the basic rule of law relating to the identification of a thing as property as follows:

> Before a right or an interest can be admitted into the category of property, or of a right affecting property, it must be definable, identifiable by third parties, capable in its nature of assumption by third parties, and have some degree of permanence or stability.

9.05 The things which are 'property' may be defined as things which have actual existence and can be owned.[3] Some things have existence but cannot be owned; these are not property,[4] but something which could be transferred were it not for a statutory prohibition on its transfer is nonetheless property.[5] Something which is inherent in a person but cannot be transferred is not property.[6] Other things have no incidents of existence apart from their ownership; these are nonetheless property.[7] It is therefore clear that there is no clear rule of law which answers the question of what is, and what is not, property. However, the general trend of the law—and in particular decide cases—is clear; as the US 5th Circuit Court of Appeals said in *First Victoria National Bank v United States*:[8]

> 'Property' evolves over time. It can be described as the bundle of rights attached to things conferred by law or custom, or as everything of value which a person owns that is or may be the subject of sale or exchange. Both of these definitions contemplate the possibility that law or custom may create property rights where none were earlier thought to exist.

---

[1] See Mossoff, *The Trespass Fallacy in Patent Law*, Florida Law Review, Vol. 65, No. 6 (2013) for a discussion of this point.
[2] [1965] AC 1175 1247–8, HL.   [3] Gleeson, *Personal Property* (Sweet & Maxwell 1997).
[4] For example, at common law a dead body cannot be owned (3 Co Inst 110 at 203; *Haynes' Case* (1614) 12 Co Rep; *Handyside's Case* (1750) East PC 652; *Doodeward v Spence* (1908) 6 CLR 406).
[5] For example, an office of profit held under the crown.
[6] For example, natural or human rights.
[7] For example, an Advowson—see Co Litt 17b.   [8] 620 F. 2d 1096.

9.06 The court considered the development in the United States of the 'right of publicity', which has been held in the United States to be a property right,[9] and observed that 'the courts have realised that the tag "property" expresses a legal conclusion rather than an independent meaning'. It is submitted that this is the correct approach for common law courts generally to adopt. In particular, the fact that there is no precedent for a newly created right to be recognised as a property right should not be permitted to determine the court's determination of the appropriate legal consequences of a dealing with that right.

9.07 It is therefore necessary to consider the question of whether virtual currency is property in more detail.

### 9.1.1 Property in an entry in a distributed ledger

9.08 The essence of distributed ledger technology is precisely that it is a ledger. When we speak of someone 'owning' a bitcoin, what we mean is that they are registered in an identifiable and verifiable register as being the person entitled to transfer a particular item (strictly speaking the ledger is a record of transactions and not ownership interests, but that can be disregarded for this purpose). However, what this means is that they do not have the core characteristic which enables English law to recognise intangibles. In general, at English law what can be owned is a chose in action—that is to say, an intangible right which can be enforced by litigation. Thus, for example, a share in an English company does not have physical existence, and a shareholder becomes a shareholder only by virtue of being registered in the company register as such. However, the consequence of a person's acquiring the status of shareholder is that he acquires enforceable rights against both the company and against other shareholders, and it is that bundle of rights which enables the law to see him as the 'owner' of a chose in action. Equally, a cheque is a chose in action on the basis that it creates a right against its issuer which in theory is capable of being enforced in an action.

9.09 The fact that the law struggles when confronted with species of property which are not enforceable by action against any person is well-known. There is some misleading but elderly authority to the effect that this distinction is binary—in particular the observation of Fry LJ in *Colonial Bank v Whinney*[10] that 'all personal things are either in possession or in action. The law knows no tertium quid between the two.' Taken literally, this would suggest that there can be no ownership of an intangible thing which does not constitute a right against a third person. However, it is now clear from statute that an intangible thing can be property without being a chose in action,[11] and there is authority that rights under a government licence[12] do

---

[9] *Haelan Laboratories v Topps Chewing Gum*, 202 F 2d 866, *Factors etc. Inc v Pro Arts* 579 F. 2d 215 at 221.
[10] (1885) 30 Ch D 261 at 285.
[11] Patents Act 1977, s. 30(1) provides that 'Any patent or application for a Patent is personal property (without being a thing in action) …'.
[12] *Attorney General of Hong Kong v Nai-Keung* [1987] 1 WLR 1339, PC.

not constitute things in action (since there is no person against whom they can be litigated) but nonetheless constitute property. Thus, for example, in *Armstrong DLW GmbH v Winnington Networks Ltd*[13] it was held that carbon trading units were not things in action but were nonetheless intangible property.[14]

9.10 The best way of regarding these rights may well be as a species of the classification of rights put forward by Goode[15] as a right 'ad rem' as opposed to a right 'in rem'. A right ad rem is a right which is not a right of ownership but a right which, when exercised, will result in ownership being transferred—an example is the right of a buyer of goods to have the purchased property delivered to him.[16]

9.11 A further issue is that not all existing rights are transferable. Leaving aside rights which either cannot be transferred by statute or as a matter of policy, in *Investor Compensation Scheme Ltd v West Bromwich Building Society*, it was held that a right to rescind a mortgage is unassignable per se, since it is a right which only has any real relevance between the two parties concerned. Lord Hoffman said:

> what is assignable is the debt or other personal right of property. It is recoverable by action, but what is assigned is the chose, the thing, the debt or damages to which the assignor is entitled. The existence of a remedy or remedies is an essential condition for the existence of the chose in action but that does not mean that the remedies are property in themselves, capable of assignment separately from the chose. So, for example, there may be joint and several liability; a remedy for the recovery of a debt or damages may be available against more than one person. But this does not mean that there is more than one chose in action. The assignee either acquires the right to the money (or part of the money) or he does not. If he does, he necessarily acquires whatever remedies are available to recover the money or the part which has been assigned to him.[17]

### 9.1.2 Ownership or mere right to transfer?

9.12 It is important here to distinguish between the concepts of 'ownership' and of 'transfer right'. This issue was recently examined by the House of Lords in *Tasarruf Mevduati Sigorta Fonu v Merill Lynch Bank and Trust Company (Cayman)*.[18] The point at issue in the case was that a debtor had settled assets on trust for others in a Cayman trust, but retained a power to revoke the trust, such that if he were to exercise that power, those assets would revest in him. The creditor sought to have a receiver appointed over the power to revoke the trust, and was resisted on the grounds that a receiver could only be appointed over an asset, and a mere power over assets did not constitute property in those assets for this purpose.[19]

---

[13] [2012] EWHC 10 (Ch), [2013] Ch 156.    [14] Ibid. at para 61.
[15] McKendrick (ed.), *Goode on Commercial Law* (5th edn, LexisNexis 2016) at 29.
[16] It should be noted that there is some dispute as to whether this class of rights is really a separate class of right (see Bridge, Gullifer, et al, *The Law of Personal Property* (Sweet & Maxwell 2013)).
[17] Per Hoffman LJ at 117.    [18] [2011] UKPC 17.
[19] *Ex Parte Gilchrist: Re Armstrong* (1886) 17 QBD 521 is long-standing authority that there is a fundamental distinction between a power over property and an ownership interest. The fact that s. 3 of the Bankrupt Laws (England) Act 1822 (now s. 130(5) of the Insolvency Act 1986) had been introduced in order to allow trustees in bankruptcy to appropriate and exercise such rights was argued to imply that there was statutory recognition that in other cases there could be no property remedy arising in respect of a mere power.

The basis of this defence was the longstanding principle articulated in *Ex Parte* 9.13
*Gilchrist: Re Armstrong*[20] that there is a fundamental distinction between a power over property and an ownership interest in that property. In *Gilchrist* Fry LJ said: 'The power of a person to appoint an estate to himself is, in my judgement, no more his "property" than the power to write a book or to sing a song. The exercise of any one of those three powers may result in property, but in no sense which the law recognises are they "property".'

In *Tasarruf* the Supreme Court decided that this was overly absolute. In particular, 'There is no [21]invariable rule that a power is distinct from ownership. Nor ... is there an invariable rule that any departure from the distinction between power and property is effected solely by legislation'. The Court also cited with approval Upjohn J's observation in *Re Triffitt's Settlement*[22] that 'where there is a completely general power in its widest sense, that is tantamount to ownership'. 9.14

These cases address the position where there is a power to instruct the disposition of an item of property, and consider whether the holder of that power might be said to be the owner of the underlying property. However, it is submitted that the order actually made in *Tasarruf* in respect of the appointment of receivers was not an appointment over the underlying assets owned by the trust, but over the power to revoke the trust. This latter order could only have been made if the court had concluded that the power of revocation itself was an item of property. Thus, it seems that a power of appointment is per se an item of property. This takes us to the conclusion that even if a unit of virtual currency could be said to have no legal existence at all, a pure and unconstrained power to instruct that it be transferred to another person is capable of being a property right. It is therefore not wrong to describe the person in whom that power is vested as an owner of property. 9.15

It should be noted that the above applies to unconstrained powers—that is, the position where a person has sole and undisputed control of a private key to a particular pool of virtual currency, and as a result has unlimited power to dispose of it. In particular, it was emphasised in *Tasarruf* that although an absolute and unconstrained power to dispose of property could constitute an equitable ownership interest, this would not necessarily be the case if there were constraints on that power—thus, for example, if the defendant had owed fiduciary duties in respect of his exercise of the power, the power would potentially not have constituted an ownership interest.[23] Thus, it does not follow that mere possession of a key to a virtual currency necessarily constitutes ownership of that currency—it is perfectly possible, for example, that A might have entrusted his key to B in circumstances where B may only use the key on the instructions of A—in such a case the property right will not vest in B. 9.16

---

[20] (1886) 17 QBD 521.   [21] Per Lord Collins at para 60.
[22] [1958] Ch 852 at 861.   [23] At para 62.

### 9.1.3 Transfer of ownership of virtual currency

9.17 Another important point regarding the status of virtual currency as property is as to how and when it is transferred. The currency aspect of money really only applies to physical transfers, and in practice the transfer of virtual currency operates in the same way as the transfer of bank credit money; that is, that an entry is made in a ledger to reflect the elimination of one entitlement and the creation of another, with nothing really being transferred. The starting point for this is that the ledger entry is probably no more and no less relevant in this regard than the equivalent entry which is made in respect of a bank payment—in reality it is the law relating to the transaction in respect of which the payment is made which will determine the legal rights of the parties.

9.18 If we begin by assuming that virtual currency units are a form of property, the rules are themselves bifurcated, in that there are in effect two sets of rules relating to the transfer of property which is neither real estate nor money—one of these arises through the provisions of the Sale of Goods Act 1979, the other through the ordinary rules of common law. The principle of the Sale of Goods Act is straightforward—property passes when the parties intend it to pass (section 17(2)). The common law rules are more complex.

9.19 The basic common law rule for the passing of property is that a mere agreement to transfer is not sufficient to transfer ownership—the transferor must either deliver possession or utilise some other mode of transfer recognised by law.[24] In addition, the common law only recognises a transfer of ownership by a person who is the owner at the time of the transfer—unlike equity, common law does not recognise the possibility of a transfer of after-acquired property.[25]

9.20 In the context of virtual currency, this creates some difficulties. If virtual currency is not currency, these rules must apply to its transfer. In principle, this is straightforward within a distributed ledger system—presumably the giving of instructions to transfer units to another person would constitute the necessary transfer, provided that the units were in the account at the time of the transfer. Technically, however, if the sequence of events were reversed—that is, the instructions to transfer were given before the relevant virtual currency units were received into the relevant account—then it is arguable that there would be no valid transfer of the units at common law.

### 9.1.4 Virtual currency and nominalism

9.21 The creation of a new currency unit almost necessarily gives rise to the creation of a new unit of account. By and large, anything can be priced in anything—you could value your house in Lamborghinis, or your Labrador in tins of dog food—but special problems arise where the thing being used for valuation is explicitly created for

---

[24] Oral transfer may be sufficient—*Flory v Denny* (1852) 21 LJ Ex 223, 7 Exch 581—but there must be a separate and identifiable act of transfer—McKendrick (ed.), *Goode on Commercial Law* (5th edn, LexisNexis 2016) at para 2.31.

[25] *Lunn v Thornton* (1845) 1 CB 379.

the purpose of payment. In this case, the question arises as to who decides what the relevant unit actually is.

As noted above, as regards currency the doctrine of nominalism is more or less undisputed in English law—a contract which is denominated in sterling is denominated in whatever the government of the United Kingdom determines to be sterling at the relevant time. However, this is not simply a doctrine which applies to English currency within English contracts, but is part of a broader doctrine (the 'lex monetae'), by which the determinations of a state in respect of its currency are recognised by other states as a matter of international law.[26] In principle, the lex monetae has two aspects to it—an internal aspect, which permits the state to determine how the currency issued by it shall be determined, and an external aspect, which permits the state to impose exchange restrictions on that currency.[27] The second of these has been subject to considerable discussion, and it is generally held that where state purports to place limitations on dealings with its currency, those restrictions will be disregarded by the courts of other countries as extraneous to the contract and constituting an unjustified attempt to enforce a prerogative right.[28] This will be true even if the obligation concerned falls to be performed in a place to which the relevant foreign exchange rules apply—under English law a contractual obligation is not rendered unenforceable merely by virtue of the fact that it would be contrary to the law of the place where it falls to be performed.[29]

9.22

The position is more complicated as regards the first aspect. In principle, if state X reorganises its monetary system, it will do so in the exercise of its sovereign power, which is non-justiciable before the courts of any other state.[30] Consequently, if under an English contract I am obliged to pay German marks on a particular date, what I must pay on that date is what the German government says is that amount. This doctrine has from time to time been challenged as the enforcement by English law of the prerogative powers of foreign state, but the English courts have in general respected the lex monetae doctrine. Thus, in *Re Chesterman's Trusts*,[31] an obligation was due from a UK payer to a Dutch bank under an English law agreement payable in German marks. The obligation was held to be payable in whatever German law determined to be marks, regardless of the position under other applicable laws. The Dutch banks argued that their claim against a UK defendant could not be affected by a German law, but the court of appeal rejected this argument.

9.23

---

[26] Proctor, *Mann on the Legal Aspect of Money* (7th edn, OUP 2012) Ch. 13. Lastra, *Legal Foundations of International Monetary Stability* (OUP 2006) at 16, points out that although this sovereignty is generally recognised and accepted, it is not explicitly stated in any international law instrument.
[27] This is the right which is recognised in Art. VIII(2)(b) of the Articles of Agreement of the IMF—however, the treaty only explicitly recognises restrictions which are 'imposed consistently with this Agreement'. The position in other cases is discussed in Mann Ch. 16.
[28] *Government of India v Taylor* [1955] AC 491 for the general principle of unenforceability of the prerogative rights of other countries under UK law—this principle is frequently expressed as confined to tax law, but it applies to any exercise of a prerogative right, of which exchange control is one—see Dicey, Morris, and Collinson, *The Conflict of Laws* (15th edn, Sweet & Maxwell 2017) paras 5-030–5-037.
[29] *Kalaher v Midland Bank* [1950] AC 24 at 51 (HL).
[30] *Buttes Oil & Gas Co v Hammer (No 3)* [1982] AC 888.  [31] [1923] 2 Ch 466, CA.

9.24 How, in this context, can we think about virtual currency units? For as long as we do not accept them to be money the problem does not really arise—the lex monetae is unique to money. However, the idea that virtual currency units are not subject to any governing authority is somewhat uncomfortable. One question which arises is as to what happens where the community which operates a virtual currency decided to make a fundamental change in the structure of that currency. Historically, operations of this kind have resulted in 'forks', whereby a single unit is separated into two new units. It should be emphasised that in a true distributed ledger system such forks are not mandated by a single issuing entity, but are the result of consensus-building amongst the community which operates the unit—in particular the miners and exchange operators who provide the infrastructure for the unit. This does mean that where such a unit changes its structure, a court will not be asked whether it should recognise a decision by a creator of the currency. This does, however, create difficulties where a contract entered into before the fork is expressed to be settled in the unit prior to the fork. Thus, for example, in August 2017 the bitcoin unit forked into two new units, Bitcoin Cash and Bitcoin Classic. It is by no means clear what the position would have been had a seller contracted to sell goods for a price payable in bitcoins prior to that date and without knowledge of the impending fork.

9.25 The position becomes more interesting, however, if we contemplate virtual currency units created by private actors using permissioned ledgers. If a bank, for example, were to create a virtual currency unit using a proprietary system of its own, it seems highly likely that the courts would take the view that the bank would be in the same position relative to that unit as a state would be in relation to its own currency. Thus, if X bank were to create a virtual currency unit 'Xcoin', and parties were to contract and specify payment in Xcoin, it seems very likely that the courts would take the view that a party who agreed to accept Xcoin in payment at a future time was agreeing to accept Xcoin as Bank X determined it to be at that time.

9.26 A further issue arises here as to the relationship between Xcoin and the state where Bank X is based. That state could clearly validly impose payment and exchange control restrictions on its fiat currency, with some hope of having them recognised internationally. Would that state be able to impose equivalent restrictions on Xcoin, such that those restrictions would be binding on transactions executed between persons outside the state? The easiest way to think about this is to apply the facts of *Re Chesterman*—assume Bank X is a German bank, the obligation between the parties was denominated in Xcoin, and the German legislature had passed a law redenominating Xcoin as well as the German mark. What would the position have been as between two non-German parties to an English law contract?

9.27 The starting point for this analysis would seem to be *Metliss v National Bank of Greece*[32] in which it was held that a change in foreign law will not affect the terms of an English contract as between private parties. Thus, if the effect of the German law concerned was—for example—to prohibit delivery of Xcoin, then the German law would be disregarded as between the non-German parties. However, if the

---

[32] [1959] AC 509.

effect of the German law were—for example—to decree that an Xcoin tomorrow is worth half of what it was yesterday, the position might become more complex. Nonetheless, it is difficult to come up with a legal theory which would suggest recognition of such a law.

9.28 The conclusion which seems to flow from this is that such privately created units are outside the lex monetae of the state concerned. This conclusion flows from the degree of connection between the units and the state, and is not affected by the question of whether the units are regarded as 'money' or not by the state where the contract falls to be determined.

9.29 Thus, it would appear that a government in this position seeking to control the use of a virtual currency unit created by a private actor in its territory would be required to do this by issuing orders to the private actor rather than by exercise of its sovereign power.

## 9.2 Virtual Currency and Set-off

9.30 One of the most important questions relating to any financial asset is as to when and where claims in respect of it may be set off against other claims. This is a particularly interesting issue as regards virtual currency units. The question at its simplest is what happens if I owe you sterling and you owe me virtual currency units?

9.31 The vast majority of the set-offs in the world are governed by contract—in financial transactions, where the issue is most likely to arise, it is standard practice in almost all relevant documentation to provide for set-off of sums due in either direction in order to produce a single net obligation. However, the issue is still regularly litigated, and requires examination.

9.32 It is worth explaining at this stage why it matters. If I owe you £5 and you owe me £10, the substantive question is as to whether there exist mutual debts, or whether the two are in fact combined into a single claim. Assuming both parties are solvent and there are no relevant contractual provisions, there are three possible states of the world which could be found to exist:

(1) The two claims continue to exist and can both be separately litigated. This will be the case as between solvent opponents where the two debts are completely unconnected.

(2) The two claims continue to exist, but any attempt to litigate the one will result in a counterclaim for the other. The two proceedings must, as a matter of law, be joined, and only a judgement for a single amount can be delivered. This will be the case where either common law or equitable set-off apply.

(3) The two claims have ceased to exist, and only a single claim for the balance exists and can be litigated. This occurs in transactional set-off, where claim and cross-claim are so closely connected that it would be unjust to allow one claim to be enforced without the other being taken into account.[33]

---

[33] *Geldof Metaalconstructie NV v Simon Carves Ltd* [2010] EWCA Civ 667.

9.33 Thus, if we revert to our initial enquiry—what happens if I owe you sterling and you owe me virtual currency units—the question that we really need to have answered is which of these is the most likely to be applied. There are of course two further questions that need to be answered—what if one of us is insolvent, and what can we write into the contract between us that would address the issues—but we will begin by assuming solvency and no applicable contractual terms.

9.34 Set-off issues under English law are based on a jurisprudence which has disappeared as a matter of law, but lives on in substance in rule 16.6 of the Civil Procedure Rules 1998 (CPR). The rule as drafted makes broad provision for the recognition of set-off as a defence to a claim, and apparently applies whether or not the claim would satisfy the criteria for common law or equitable set-off are met.[34] However, courts have in practice been guided by the rules on common law and equitable set-off in determining whether litigation set-off is available.[35] Although the CPR has been recently rewritten, the previous rule was in almost identical terms, so cases decided under it are still prima facie applicable.

### 9.2.1 The rules of set-off

9.35 The rules of solvent set-off at English law have been fairly described as 'lacking logic and sense',[36] and it is true to say that they are probably well overdue for review.

9.36 Solvent non-contractual set-off at English law can be divided into statutory set-off and equitable set-off. Set-off in English law appears to have begun life as an equitable remedy,[37] but the easiest way to explain the current state of English set-off is to begin with the common law statutes of set-off.

9.37 The Statutes of Set-off were enacted in 1729 and 1735. The title of the first statute, 'An Act for the Relief of Debtors with respect to the Imprisonment of their Persons', suggests that their purpose was to assist debtors who were liable to be sent to debtors' prison for non-payment of debts, although Willes CJ, not long after their enactment, considered that they were designed to avoid circuity of action and multiplicity of suits. The first statute provided that:

> [W]here there are mutual Debts between the Plaintiff and Defendant, or if either Party sue or be sued as Executor or Administrator, where there are mutual Debts between the Testator or Intestate, and either Party, one Debt may be set against the other, and such Matter may be given in Evidence upon the General Issue, or pleaded in Bar, as the Nature of the Case shall require, so as at the Time of his pleading the General Issue, where any such Debt of the Plaintiff, his Testator or Intestate, is intended to be insisted on in Evidence, Notice shall be given of the particular Sum or Debt so intended to be insisted on, and upon what Account it became due, or otherwise such Matter shall not be allowed in Evidence upon such General Issue.

---

[34] See the White Book, 2017, commentary on CPR 16.6.1 at 574.
[35] See *Re Kaupthing Singer and Friedlander Ltd (In Administration)* [2009] EWHC 740 (Ch).
[36] *Axel Johnson Petroleum AB v MG Mineral Group AG* [1992] 1 WLR 270 at 274, and see Gleeson, *Personal Property Law* (Sweet & Maxwell 1997) at 154–8.
[37] See *Jeffs v Wood* (1723) 2 P Wms 128, where an injunction in equity was granted to restrain proceedings for a debt in the common law courts on the basis of a contractual agreement to set off.

Statutory set-off is thus a purely procedural remedy—its only effect is to provide 9.38
that where mutual debts exist, they must be heard together such that they are fused
in a judgement for a single amount.[38]

### 9.2.2 What can be set-off—common law?

The question of what counted as a 'debt' for the purpose of the statute was not al- 9.39
together clear, and there was debate in particular as to whether simple debts and spe-
cialty debts could be combined into a single claim. Therefore, by the 1735 Statute (8
Geo II, c 24, section 4), it was provided that mutual debts could be set off notwithstanding that in law they were deemed to be of a different nature.

Slightly oddly, although repealed, these statutes are effectively still in force. 9.40
Technically, they were repealed in 1879 by section 2 of the Civil Procedure Acts
Repeal Act, but this section preserved any 'jurisdiction or principle or rule of law
or equity established or confirmed, or right or privilege acquired', and this has been
interpreted by the courts as preserving the rule of common law set-off.[39]

Our starting point is as regards the availability of common law set-off. The basic 9.41
principle is that set-off is concerned with money claims.[40] For this purpose, the term
'debt' seems to be narrowly construed—a claim for the return of goods cannot be
set off in this way,[41] and it has been suggested that a liability to repay a preferential
payment in a liquidation is not a 'debt' for this purpose.[42]

The question of what constitutes a 'debt' for this purpose is therefore not clear. It 9.42
seems clear that the term is not confined to those claims which could have been the
subject of the old action of debt.[43] Rather, as Cockburn CJ said in *Stooke v Taylor*,[44]
the plea of set-off under the Statutes 'is available ... where the claims on both sides
are in respect of liquidated debts, or money demands which can be readily and
without difficulty ascertained'.[45] Thus, common law set-off is available where each
demand is capable of being liquidated or ascertained with precision at the time
of pleading.[46] The modern rule is as set out by Lord Hoffmann in *Stein v Blake*[47]
that claims must be 'either liquidated or in sums capable of ascertainment without

---

[38] Per Hoffman LJ in *Stein v Blake* [1995] 2 All ER 961 at 964.
[39] *Re Daintrey* [1900] 1 QB 546, 548. See now the Senior Courts Act 1981, s. 49(2) and CPR 16.6: *Re Kaupthing Singer and Friedlander Ltd* [2009] EWHC 740 (Ch).
[40] Derham, *Set-off* (4th edn, OUP 2010) at 1.01, citing *Tony Lee Motors Ltd v M S McDonald & Son (1974) Ltd* [1981] 2 NZLR 281 at 288; *Hamilton Ice Arena Ltd v Perry Developments Ltd* [2002] 1 NZLR 309 at 311.
[41] *Green v Farmer* (1768) 4 Burr 2214, 98 ER 154.
[42] *Re Luxtrend Pty Ltd* [1997] 2 Qd R 86, and see *In the matter of One. Tel Pty Ltd* [2014] NSWSC 457.
[43] *Morley v Inglis* (1837) 4 Bing (NC) 58, 71.    [44] (1880) 5 QBD 569 at 575.
[45] This constituted a significant broadening of the right, which was previously believed to be available only where the agreement was such that an action for indebitatus assumpsit would lie—see per Hill
J in *Crampton v Walker* (1860) 3 El & El 321 at 330–1, referring to Tindal CJ in *Morley v Inglis* (1837)
4 Bing (NC) 58 at 72.
[46] *Morley v Inglis* (1837) 4 Bing (NC) 58 at 71; *Henriksens Rederi A/S v THZ Rolimpex (The Brede)*
[1974] 1 QB 233, 246; *Axel Johnson Petroleum AB v MG Mineral Group AG* [1992] 1 WLR 270, 272;
*Courage Ltd v Crehan* [1999] 2 EGLR 145, 155.
[47] [1996] AC 243 at 251.

valuation or estimation'. Thus, for example, in *Axel Johnson Petroleum AB v MG Mineral Group AG*,[48] a set-off was permitted where A agreed to buy from B all of the oil that B bought from C at a mark-up of US$1.00 per tonne. The Court of Appeal held that the price payable by the plaintiff under the arrangement was liquidated, and accordingly could give rise to a defence under the Statutes so as to entitle the defendant to leave to defend.

9.43 The question is therefore whether we are dealing with a claim for a 'sum capable of ascertainment without valuation or estimation'. The better view[49] is that this includes not only the old indebitatus counts, including claims in quantum meruit and quantum valebat, where work had been performed or goods sold without a price having been agreed.[50] It may also include a demand that strictly sounds in damages.[51] For our purposes, the most important illustration is as regards liquidated damages clauses. It was settled in the eighteenth century that the obligation pursuant to a clause in a contract for the payment of liquidated damages in the event of a breach gives rise to a debt for the purpose of the Statutes,[52] despite the fact that it is clearly a claim in damages. This takes us back to the problem of valuation—as discussed in para 7.86 above, the important difference for this purpose is that whereas a money claim can be pleaded as such, a claim for non-money must be pleaded at the valuation as a the date of breach. However, since both are clearly liquidated amounts, the issue should be irrelevant for the purpose of determining whether set-off is available.

### 9.2.3 What can be set-off—equity?

9.44 This takes us to equitable set-off. This permits liquidated and unliquidated claims to be set off against liquidated claims where they 'flow out of and are inseparably connected with the dealings and transactions which also give rise to the subject of the assignment'.[53] It was made clear in *Geldof Metaalconstructie v Simon Carves*[54] that this test replaces the old 'impeachment of title' test in *Rawson v Samuel*. It should be emphasised that this is not a blanket permission for all set-offs[55]—it was emphasised in *Esso Petroleum v Milton*,[56] where Simon Brown LJ observed that 'for equitable set-off to apply, it must therefore be established, first that the counterclaim is at least closely connected with the same transaction as that giving rise to the claim, and second that the relationship between the respective claims is such that it would be manifestly unjust to allow one to be enforced without the other'.

---

[48] [1992] 1 WLR 270 at 272.
[49] See Derham, *Set-off* (4th edn, OUP 2010) at para 2.19 and per Hirst LJ in *Aectra Refining and Marketing Inc. v Exmar NV* [1994] 1 WLR 1634 at 1647.
[50] See the discussion by Farwell LJ in *Lagos v Grunwaldt* [1910] 1 KB 41 at 48 in relation to the meaning of the expression 'debt or liquidated demand', referred to in *Aectra Refining and Marketing Inc. v Exmar NV* [1994] 1 WLR 1634 at 1647.
[51] See per Leggatt LJ in *Axel Johnson Petroleum AB v MG Mineral Group AG* [1992] 1 WLR 270 at 272.
[52] *Fletcher v Dyche* (1787) 2 TR 32, 100 ER 18.
[53] *Government of Newfoundland v Newfoundland Railway Co* (PC) (1888) 13 App Cas 199.
[54] [2010] EWCA Civ 667.   [55] (1841) Cr and Ph 161.   [56] [1997] 1 WLR 938.

## 9.2.4 Set-off and virtual currency

As applied to a cross-claim for virtual currency units, the issue which arises is as to what the position is if the court concludes that a claim for the units is a claim in damages rather than a claim in debt. Imagine that two parties have two unconnected claims, one denominated in virtual currency units and the other in sterling. If the common law analysis is that the claim for virtual currency is not a money claim capable of being set off under existing equitable jurisdiction which could be invoked to remedy a shortcoming of the common law, the question for the equitable jurisdiction is whether it can be invoked at all. If we conclude that the claims are not in fact connected (and it seems necessarily true that if claims are not in fact connected with each other under the 'manifestly unjust' head, the mere fact that one of them is denominated in virtual currency rather than fiat money, will not of itself be sufficient to change that conclusion), then the question is whether there is an equitable jurisdiction separate from the existing equitable jurisdiction that could be invoked. The best one can say about this is that it is by no means obvious that such a jurisdiction exists, or what its basis could be. However, it should be noted that the bare words of rule 16.6 do not rule out any such decision by a court. Consequently, in the event that a person is sued on a debt who is owed an amount of virtual currency by the claimant, it would be open to the court to permit the virtual currency counterclaim to be brought into the action as a defence of set-off.   9.45

## 9.3 Virtual Currency, Transferability, and Negotiability

It seems unlikely that an ordinary virtual currency unit could qualify as a negotiable instrument, either under the Bills of Exchange Act or at common law, since in general these instruments do not embed a money claim on an issuer. However, as noted earlier, some virtual currency units are deliberately created to embed a claim to money, and it is at least theoretically possible that these might fall within the class of promissory notes under Part IV of the Bills of Exchange Act 1882. This is not entirely implausible. Section 83 of the Act requires a promissory note to be 'in writing', and section 2 provides that 'written' includes printed, and writing includes print. This takes us to the Interpretation Act 1978, section 5, which is to the effect that 'Writing includes typing, printing, lithography, photography and other modes of representing or reproducing words in a visible form, and expressions referring to writing are construed accordingly'.   9.46

It is argued in *Chalmers*[57] that a bill or promissory note could by this definition be issued by purely electronic means provided it could be reproduced in visible form (e.g. by being capable of being printed out or displayed on a screen). The problems for the Bills of Exchange Act arise from the fact that it is difficult to see how such an instrument could be 'signed' by the drawer of a bill or the maker or indorser of   9.47

---

[57] Gleeson (ed.), *Chalmers & Guest on* Bills of Exchange and Cheques (18th edn, Sweet & Maxwell 2017) at para 2-011.

a promissory note. It is true that section 7 of the Electronic Communications Act 2000 provides that an electronic signature incorporated into or logically associated with a particular electronic communication or electronic data is to be admissible in evidence (though not conclusive) in any legal proceedings in relation to any question as to the authenticity or integrity of the communications or data, and there is authority that an electronic signature can satisfy both the requirement of writing for a contract of guarantee[58] and the requirements of section 4 of the Statute of Frauds.[59]

9.48 It should be noted in this regard that the amendments to the Bills of Exchange Act in respect of electronic presentation of cheques made by the Small Business, Enterprise and Employment Act 2015—the insertion of a new Part 4A relating to electronic presentation of instruments—apply only to the presentation of cheques for payment between banks, not to their creation.

## 9.4 Taking Security Over Virtual Currency Units

9.49 At first sight, the question of whether security can be taken over virtual currency units appears to be of relatively little interest—a grant of security constitutes a grant of a proprietary right over an asset, and there is no obvious reason why a virtual currency unit should be treated differently from any other asset in this regard. However, the question is considerably more complex than this.

9.50 The question of whether an asset can be made the subject of a security interest is often confused with the question of whether a property interest in the asset can be transferred. The linkage is valid where the security is a mortgage, since the definition of a mortgage is a transfer of a proprietary interest in the security asset from the debtor to the creditor which can ripen into full ownership through foreclosure.[60] However, it is not a necessary component of a charge. This is because the essence of a charge is that a particular asset is to be appropriated to the repayment of an obligation. A charge does not transfer any existing property interest in the charged property to anyone, and a chargor has complete legal and equitable title to the charged property.[61] It should also be noted that the chargor and chargee need not be debtor and creditor at the time when the charge is created.[62] What the charge receives from a charge is a right to compel the owner of the asset to realise it (or to consent to its realisation), and then to have the proceeds resulting from the use of the asset applied in a

---

[58] *Mehta v J. Pereira Fernandes SA* [2006] EWHC 813 (Ch); [2006] 2 Lloyds Rep 244 at [28].
[59] *Golden Ocean Group Ltd v Salgaocar Mining Industries Pvt Ltd* [2012] EWCA Civ 265; [2012] 1 Lloyds Rep 542.
[60] See Bridge, Gullifer, McMeel and Worthington, *The Law of Personal Property* (2nd edn, Sweet & Maxwell 2013) at 153 and Gleeson, *Personal Property* (Sweet & Maxwell 1997).
[61] *National Provincial and Union Bank of England v Charnley* [1924] 1 KB 431, *Carreras Rothmans v Freeman Matthews Treasure* [1985] Ch 207.
[62] Bridge, Gullifer, McMeel and Worthington, *The Law of Personal Property* (2nd edn, Sweet & Maxwell 2013) at 182.

particular way. What this means is that what the charge acquires is a series of newly created rights, which rights are quite distinct from either legal or equitable ownership or possession.

This point about title means that it is quite possible for a charge to be taken over property which cannot be transferred. For example, it is clear that a right to draw down under a loan cannot be assigned.[63] However, it is common for a charge over the assets of (for example) a project company to include a charge over the undrawn portion of loans, and it is clear that a receiver appointed under such a charge would have the right to draw down under such loans in the same way that the borrower himself would. 9.51

Where assets are charged, it is important that those assets be identifiable. Thus, in *TXU Europe Group Plc*[64] and *Flightline v Edwards*,[65] assets had to be held in the form of some identifiable fund before it could be held that a charge could exist. Assets which are simply held as general assets of the borrower will not have this level of specificity, even if they are identifiable. Thus, for example, in *Swiss Bank Corp v Lloyds Bank*,[66] a loan was made to a person in order to enable that person to purchase certain securities. The agreement between the parties contemplated that the dividends on the securities should fund the payment of interest on the loan, and that the sale of the securities should fund the repayment of the principal amount of the loan. However, it was held that this arrangement did not give rise to a charge in favour of the lender on the assets. It therefore seems likely that a commitment to transfer virtual currency units will not be sufficient to grant a charge over those units. However this seems to take us back to *Tassaruf*[67] (see paragraphs 9.12–9.15 above), as regards what items of property can be the subject of an ownership interest and what cannot, since although it is clear that a property interest is not necessary for the creation of a charge, it is clear that a charge can be granted in any circumstances where a property interest could be transferred between the parties. 9.52

### 9.4.1 Virtual currency unit balances maintained with a bank

When cash is delivered to a bank, the depositor loses his title to the cash delivered to the bank and acquires a right of action against the bank in respect of an equivalent sum.[68] This is arguably a necessary consequence of cash passing into currency when it is transferred for value—technically, I could not retain title to particular money paid by me to the bank even if both of us wanted to achieve that aim. That is not necessarily true of virtual currency, so it would probably be possible for a bank to hold virtual currency units for a customer on the basis that the customer retained title to those units. However, if the virtual currency units were held by 9.53

---

[63] See *Guest on The Law of Assignment*, ed. Liew Sweet & Maxwell 2018 Assignment
[64] [2003] EWHC 3105 (Ch).   [65] [2003] 1 WLR 1200, CA.   [66] [1982] AC 584.
[67] *Tasarruf Mevduati Sigorta Fonu v Merill Lynch Bank and Trust Company (Cayman)*. [2011] UKPC 17.
[68] *Foley v Hill* (1848) 2 HLC 28.

a banker in the course of the provision of banking services to the customer concerned, a more convenient structure for all parties would unquestionably be an arrangement whereby title to the units passed to the bank in the same way as money does.

9.54 This raises the further question of how security over such a balance might be taken. It is not entirely clear whether a claim on a banker in respect of an obligation to deliver virtual currency units would constitute a cash balance. However, note that the Financial Collateral Arrangements (No. 2) Regulations 2003[69] apply to 'cash, financial instruments or credit claims', and this could include claims for virtual currency units. However, recital 18 to the Directive from which the UK regulations are derived provides that 'cash refers to only to money which is represented by a credit to an account, or similar claims on repayment of money (such as money market deposits), thus explicitly excluding banknotes'. This is unhelpful as regards near-cash claims.

9.55 Yeowart and Parsons[70] suggest that for this purpose cash cannot simply mean all claims for the repayment of money, since such a definition would swallow up and render redundant the reference to other credit claims.[71] They also say that in order to qualify under any of the heads of the Regulation, the claim must be a claim for the payment of money narrowly defined—a claim under a commodity futures contract, a commodity futures option, or a similar contract which does not amount to a claim for payment of money would not be 'cash' for this purpose.[72] However, they base this on the observation in the Law Commission's report on Company Security Interests,[73] which refers to exposures of these kinds as examples of exposures which may not fall within the scope of the Directive. However, it seems that the argumentation behind the Law Commission's position in this issue is that contracts of this kind are generally 'contracts for differences', and constitute synthetic holdings of an underlying commodity which is not itself cash. It is not clear the extent to which the expression of view would continue if the underlying asset were cash-like—thus, for example, a futures contract over a money market deposit might well qualify as 'cash' for this purpose.

9.56 It may be noted that the European Central Bank, like a number of other central banks, has forcibly expressed its view that cryptocurrencies are not 'money' within the legal meaning of the word.[74] However, this approach is based on the proposition that such coins are not legal tender, neither are they denominated in currencies which are legal tender, which to some extent prejudges the issue to be discussed.

---

[69] (2003/3226) the Financial Collateral Directive (2002/47/EC).
[70] *The Law of Financial Collateral* (Elgar Financial 2016) at 52.
[71] Citing Ho, *The Financial Collateral Directive's Practice in England*, Journal of International Banking Law & Regulation, Vol. 26 (2011) at 151, 156.
[72] *The Law of Financial Collateral* (Elgar Financial 2016) at 54.
[73] Law Com No. 296 (31 August 2005) at para 5.29.
[74] European Central Bank, *Virtual Currency Schemes* (October 2012) and *Virtual Currency Schemes—A Further Analysis* (February 2015).

## 9.5 Repo of Virtual Currency

The question of whether virtual currency can be used in repo transactions is strangely illuminating. This is because a repo (and its cousin, the securities lending transaction) are exchanges of money for things. In both transactions, ownership of a financial asset (usually securities) is exchanged for money, on terms that at a future time equivalent assets will be returned in exchange for repayment of the money.[75] These agreements are probably best characterised as two connected transactions, with an immediate sale accompanied by a future resale.[76] The fact that the redelivery obligation is to deliver equivalent assets, rather than the same assets, means that there is no continuing interest in the securities delivered over the life of the repo. For the purposes of this chapter we will call these the asset leg and the money leg.   9.57

There are two broad questions which can be asked here—what is the position if it is sought to treat virtual currency as the asset leg in this context—in other words, if a party seeks to acquire virtual currency units in exchange for money—and what is the position if it is sought to treat virtual currency as the money leg—in other words, if a party seeks to acquire securities by paying virtual currency?   9.58

The issues which arise if virtual currency is to be the asset leg of the transaction is that the transaction may well become an exchange of money for money. There is nothing difficult about money-for-money transactions per se,[77] but the use of repo documentation for such transactions forces consideration as to whether an exchange of money for money can be correctly characterised as a sale within the meaning of normal repo documentation. More importantly, a sale of money for money is arguably not a sale at all at common law[78] but a mere barter. The reason that this is problematic is that the ordinary rules of sale do not apply to barter; thus, it is not clear when property passes, what the rights of the parties are or when risk passes.[79]   9.59

The issues where virtual currency is the money leg are broadly the mirror image of the asset considerations. In this case, the risk is that the exchange is asset-for asset, which again falls outside the basic characterisation as a sale and into the questionable territory of barter.   9.60

The legal position where money is exchanged for other money is not as clear as it might be. In the United States there is authority to the effect that a sale of money is   9.61

---

[75] The difference between the two is that in a repo the amount of money advanced is fixed, and the value of securities delivered as collateral may be increased or reduced to maintain a constant value of cover. In a stock loan the amount of stock is fixed, and the value of cash delivered as collateral may be varied.

[76] See the ICMA Global Master Repo Agreement 2011, Art. 1(a) and accompanying guidance notes on the ICMA website for detail of the mechanisms used in these transactions. See also *Mercuria Energy Trading v Citibank* [2015] EWHC 1481.

[77] See the International Foreign Exchange and Currency Option Master Agreement (June 2005) and its legal guide published by the Federal Reserve Foreign Exchange Committee and others.

[78] *R v Grimes* (1752) Fost 79n; *R v Leigh* (1764) 1 Leach. 52, and see *Benjamin's Sale of Goods* (ed Bridge, 10th edn, Sweet & Maxwell 2017) at para 1-084.

[79] See *Benjamin's Sale of Goods* ibid. at paras 1-034–1-038 on the legal uncertainties created by the classification of a contract as not a contract of sale.

a sale like that of any other currency, such that an unpaid vendor who has delivered currency but has not been paid may recover the property.[80] However, the position at common law is considerably less clear, since it is not open to a disappointed party who has parted with goods without receiving the expected return to sue for the value of the goods delivered as a price[81]—his remedy is a claim for unliquidated damages for non-delivery of the goods promised in exchange, or possibly to sue the other party in tort on the basis that the property has passed.

## 9.6 Recovery of Misappropriated Virtual Currency

9.62 The development of English law as regards the recovery of stolen goods has led to a significant (and arguably unhealthy) focus on whether the claim to be protected is proprietary or not. To the uninitiated, this is not a material consideration—if I can be proved to have stolen £100 from you, and have £100 in my possession, it is not always easy to see why the intervening chain of events should be a material factor in a court's decision to order me to return £100 to you. However, the difficulty is that the point involves a conflict of two very powerful legal principles—one being that misappropriation of property should be remedied, but the other being that good title to property should not be interfered with except in an identifiable number of defined cases. In broad terms, the remedy for interference with the right of constructive possession is a restitutionary action of some form or other.[82] However, there is debate about whether the basis of the remedy arises from a 'pure' claim created in order to reverse the relevant unjust enrichment, or whether it rests on an assertion of the claimant's ownership rights[83] (generally referred to as 'vindication').

### 9.6.1 Proprietary and possessory remedies

9.63 In *Foskett v McKeown* the House of Lords decisively adopted a vindication approach.[84] However, there was considerable academic support for the idea that an approach based on a pure unjust enrichment analysis was valid,[85] and in a situation where a vindication approach was not available on the basis of an absence of an ownership right, the better view must be that this approach would be taken in preference to leaving an unjust enrichment in place. However this is a distinction with a very significant difference. Whereas a vindication approach will be complete once

---

[80] *In re Koreag, Controle et Revision S.A.* 961 F. 2d 341, criticised in Wardrop, *The Dual Personality of Money and the Legal Nature of Foreign Exchange Transactions Settled by Wire Transfers*, Banking and Finance Law Review, Vol. 15 (1999) at 61.
[81] *Read v Hutchinson* (1813) Camp. 352; *Harrison v Luke* (1845) 14 M. & W. 139.
[82] *Foskett v McKeown* [2001] AC 102; *MacMillan Inc v Bishopsgate Investment Trust Plc (No. 3)* [1995] 1 WLR 978.
[83] See Bridge and Gullifer et al. *Personal Property Law* (OUP 2013) at 1-042 for discussion.
[84] 110 (Browne-Wilkinson), 115 (Hoffmann), 127 (Millett).
[85] Burrows, *The Law of Restitution* (OUP 3rd edn, 2011) at 118–19, 121–2, 169–71, and Mitchell et al., *Goff and Jones: The Law of Unjust Enrichment* (Sweet & Maxwell 8th edn, 2012) at paras 8.83–8.93.

title has been demonstrated, an unjust enrichment approach leaves the beneficiary subject to a general defence of bona fide purchase as well as change of position.[86] Vindication is clearly the better option for the plaintiff. However, a vindication approach relies on being able to demonstrate a continuing right of ownership, and this is extremely problematic for most financial assets.

The action for recovery of physical goods is an action in tort for conversion or trespass,[87]. These actions do not require any demonstration of ownership; merely of the better right to possession. In general theft or misappropriation of physical notes and coins or bearer securities is generally pursued via these routes. However, an action in conversion fails when the property ceases to be the property of the claimant, and thus an action for conversion of money fails where the money passes into currency or is mixed with other money.[88] It should be noted in this regard that the Torts (Interference with Goods) Act 1977 'excludes things in action and money' from its scope (section 14(1)).[89]  9.64

Conversion does not lie for any sort of intangible, including intangible money.[90] Thus, although the action in conversion has been a staple of cheques litigation for many years (on the basis of the fiction that where a fraudulent cheque is presented, it is the paper cheque itself which is converted[91]), it is of no application as regards transfers made otherwise than by a paper instrument.  9.65

There is a final issue which arises out of the question of whether, if virtual currency units are held to be money, it is possible for a court to order specific units to be delivered. The point here is that it is generally assumed that there can be no specific performance of an order to pay money—the argument that money is money has the necessary corollary that damages are always an adequate remedy for a failure to pay money.[92] However, the proposition itself is an oversimplification—although it is unlikely that damages will not be considered an adequate remedy in a case of non-payment, the mere fact that an obligation is classified as a monetary obligation does not mean that there is no possibility of specific performance.[93] Thus, it would be permissible for a court to hold that virtual currency units are money but to order delivery of specific units in an appropriate case.  9.66

---

[86] *Lipkin Gorman v Karpnale Ltd* [1991] 2 AC 549, HL.
[87] Conversion is an appropriation of property sufficient to deprive the true owner of it completely—it lies against any possessor, whether or not they know of the existence of the superior title (*Kuwait Airways Corporation v Iraqi Airways Co (Nos 4 and 5)* [2002] UKHL 19, [2002] 2 AC 883, paras 38–43 per Lord Nicholls). Trespass is an interference with ownership short of complete deprivation—it is only committed by the immediate interferer, and not by any subsequent person: *Fouldes v Willoughby* (1841) 8 M. & W. 540, *Penfolds Wine Pty Ltd v Elliot* (1946) 74 CLR 204.
[88] *Jackson v Anderson* (1811) 4 Taunt 24.
[89] Fox (*Property Rights in Money* (OUP 2008) at 308) suggests that this is not intended to disapply the act from actions for the recovery of physical money, but merely to reflect the old common law rule that conversion would not lie to enforce a debt expressed in fungible money.
[90] *OGB v Allan* [2007] UKHL 21.
[91] *Morrison v London County and Westminster Bank Ltd* [1914] 3 KB 356, 365 per Lord Reading.
[92] *Co-operative Insurance Society Ltd v Argyll Stores (Holdings) Ltd* [1998] AC 1 at 11, and see *Chitty on Contracts* (32nd edn, Sweet & Maxwell 2015) at paras 27-05ff.
[93] *Beswick v Beswick* [1968] 1 AC 58 and Brindle and Cox, *The Law of Bank Payments* (Sweet & Maxwell 5th edn, 2017) at 39.

### 9.6.2 Personal restitution

9.67 The old action for money had and received forms the basis of the modern law of recovery of money. The remedy is an order that one person should pay money to another because they received it mala fide. The essence of the action was set out by Lord Mansfield in in *Clark v Shee*:[94]

> Where money or notes are paid bona fide, and upon valuable consideration, they shall never be brought back by the true owner; but where they come mala fide into a person's hands, they are in the nature of specific property; and if their identity can be traced and ascertained, the party has a right to recover … Here the plaintiff sues for his identified property, which has come into the hands of the defendants iniquitously and illegally, in breach of the Act of Parliament. Therefore they have no right to retain it; and consequently the plaintiff is well entitled to recover.

9.68 This formed the basis of the house of Lord's decision in *Lipkin Gorman v Karpnale Ltd*.[95]

9.69 Personal restitution is one of the relatively few areas in which the distinction between money and non-money is of relatively little significance. The authorities are clear that where a person has received a benefit wrongfully, the benefit can be recovered whether it is in the form of money or of non-money, provided that the benefit is a definite benefit that can be readily assessed in money.[96]

## 9.7 Situs of Virtual Currency

9.70 In dealing with rights to any particular thing, the first step is to identify the legal system under which those rights arise. Unfortunately, as a matter of common international agreement, this is generally done by seeking to identify the situs of the asset.[97] The issue here is not the nature of the asset (that is a matter of physical fact), but the way in which the asset itself is characterised as a matter of law, and the way in which rights in respect of it can be created, transferred, and extinguished.

9.71 The problem with the rule of situs is that although it is broadly applicable to tangible things, it is entirely artificial as regards things which have no physical existence. Consequently, when we speak of the situs of an intangible, what we are actually describing is a series of legal fictions which ascribe situs to an intangible based on a set of assumptions. There are good authorities for the entirely sensible proposition that an intangible has no situs,[98] but these have been broadly overruled,[99] and it seems

---

[94] (1774) 1 Cowp 197 at 200–1.   [95] [1991] 2 AC 548.
[96] *Phillips v Homfray* (1883) 24 Ch D 439, and see *Chitty on Contracts* (32nd edn) at paras 29-148–29-152.
[97] Dicey, Morris, and Collins, *The Conflict of Laws* (15th edn, Sweet & Maxwell 2017) paras 22-002 et seq.
[98] *Lee v Abdy* (1886) 17 QBD 309.
[99] *English, Scottish and Australian Bank v IRC* [1932] AC 238. It has not helped that most of these issues were considered in the context of taxing statutes where the ascription of situs to an intangible was a necessary preliminary step to taxing it.

to be a current rule of English law that all assets must have a situs ascribed to them regardless of their nature.

The general rule for a chose in action is that its situs is the country in which it can be enforced;[100] however, as Dicey somewhat drily notes, 'problems arise where, as is not infrequently the case, this can be done in several countries'.[101] More importantly, situs cases are frequently decided on the basis of tax policy, and it by no means always follows that the determination of situs which provides the correct outcome in tax cases will also provide the correct outcome in other cases. Consequently, as Dicey also notes, 'it does not follow that if a particular type of chose is regarded for one purpose as situate in a particular country it will be held there situate for another purpose'.[102]

9.72

As noted above, a chose in action implies a right against a person, and the rule that where a right can only be enforced by suing a person, the situs of that right is the place where that person is to be found makes broad sense.[103] Where the debtor is a corporation with business activities in multiple countries, this would seem to lead to the conclusion that a debt owed by that corporation has multiple situses.[104]

9.73

This leads us to the difficult issue as to the proper treatment of a right which is not immediately dependent on enforcement against a third party. In *Re Helbert Wagg & Co.*[105] the position was considered where a creditor had a debt which was not yet due for payment. Although clearly an item of property, that debt was not immediately enforceable anywhere, and was said not to have a situs. However, in *Kwok Chi Leung Karl v Commissioner of Estate Duty* the opposite conclusion was arrived at with regard to a non-negotiable promissory note which was not yet due for payment.[106]

9.74

The rules set out in the Recast Brussels I Regulation[107] and the Lugano Convention radically change the position as regards the enforceability of debts by adopting the principle that the obligor must be sued in his member state of domicile.[108] However, this rule is only relevant in cases where an obligation must be enforced by taking action against a person.

9.75

---

[100] Dicey (Fn. 97) Rule 129 at para 22R-023, and see *New York Life Insurance v Public Trustee* [1924] 2 Ch 101 (CA); *Alloway v Phillips* [1980] 1 WLR 888 (CA).
[101] Ibid. at 22-025.
[102] Ibid. and see *Braun v The Custodian* [1944] 3 DLR 412, 422 (Exch Ct of Can), affd [1944] 4 DLR 209 (Sup Ct Can), *Brown, Gow, Wilson v Beleggings-Societeit NV* (1961) 29 DLR (2d) 673, 691 (Ont).
[103] This is the rule for debts—see Dicey 22-026.
[104] See *Kwok Chi Leung Karl v Commissioner of Estate Duty* [1988] 1 WLR 1035 (PC). However, it is arguable that if the debt is not expressed to be payable in any specific place, it should be payable where it would be paid in the normal course of business *Jabbour v Custodian of Israeli Absentee property* [1954] 1 WLR 139 at 146.
[105] [1956] Ch 323 at 339–40.
[106] Dicey points out that *Helbert Wagg* was cited in argument but not referred to in the judgment, so its authority remains unclear.
[107] Regulation (EU) No. 1215/2012 of the European Parliament and of the Council on Jurisdiction and the recognition and enforcement of judgements in civil and commercial matters, given effect in the United Kingdom by the Civil Jurisdiction and Judgements Order 2001 (2001/3929) as amended for the recast Brussels I by the Civil Jurisdiction and Judgements (Amendment) Regulations 2014 (2014/2947).
[108] Art. 4 of the Recast Brussels I Convention, Art. 2 of the Lugano Convention.

9.76　　Negotiable instruments and securities which can be validly and effectively transferred by delivery are sited in the place where the physical paper which constitutes the instrument or security is to be found.[109] However, for stocks or other instruments where transfer occurs otherwise than by delivery, the presence of certificates or other paper evidencing ownership is not determinative, and the claim is held to be sited in the place where the obligor can be sued.

9.77　　The position relating to immobilised securities is more interesting. In the case of immobilised securities, a physical bearer security is held by a depository for a clearing system (Euroclear and Clearstream in the international bond markets), and the clearing system records in its books the identities of the persons for whom it holds the security and in what proportions.[110] The situs of the physical bearer security is the place where it is held by the depositary. However, the better view is that for conflicts purposes the situs should be taken to be the place of business of the clearing system. This conclusion seems to be based on the argument that a holder wishing to sue the issuer of the bond would have to go to the operator of the clearing system and request him to take the necessary steps; so that in effect the place where the holder's rights must be executed, and the person against whom they must be executed, is the clearing system operator.[111] Thus, the situs of the holder's rights is (or may be) different from the situs of the depositary's rights. This arrangement has the advantage that the holder's rights are all in one place, so that if a holder holds a portfolio of different bonds issued by companies in different countries, he can grant security over those rights on the basis that they are all subject to the laws of the place of business of the clearing system operator, without having to perfect the security over each bond under the laws of the place of incorporation of the issuer.

9.78　　This argument, however, is heavily based on a principle of private international law based on the law of companies. As regards shares in companies, it is established that the law of the place of incorporation of a company determines how shares in the company may be transferred, and if they are regarded as being capable of transfer only by registration, they will be taken to have their situs at the place where the register is kept.[112] However, this is itself a development of the rule of company law that an interest in a company is subject to the law of the place of incorporation of the company, which governs all matters concerning the constitution of the company.[113] It follows from this that if the law under which the company is incorporated permits a share register to be maintained outside that country, then the situs of the shares so issued will be the country in which the register is maintained. However, the law of

---

[109] *A-G v Bouwens* (1838) 4 M. & W. 171.
[110] See Yates, *Law of Global Custody* (4th edn, Bloomsbury Professional 2013); Ooi, *Shares and Other Securities in the Conflict of Laws* (OUP 2003).
[111] Dicey para 22-043.
[112] *A-G v Higgins* (1857) 2 H. & N. 3-39; *New York Breweries Co. v A-G* [1899] AC 62, *Commissioners of Inland Revenue v Maple & Co Ltd* [1908] AC 22. If transfer is not by registration (as in the case of bearer shares), situs is the place of incorporation of the company—*Macmillan Inc v Bishopsgate Investment Trust Plc (No. 3)* [1996] 1 WLR 387 (CA).
[113] Dicey Rule 175(2).

the place of incorporation of the company must always be able to override any such arrangements.[114]

9.79 A relevant issue arises as regards interests in entities which are not formally established by statute. Thus, for example, a share in a partnership is situated in the country in which the business is carried on.[115] There appears to be no authority on the position where the business of the partnership is carried on in multiple jurisdictions.[116]

9.80 Intellectual property and other trademarks are a difficult case. However, the general principle is that since they are by and large protections granted by statute, their situs is the jurisdiction to which that right applies[117]—thus, for example, an Australian trademark is situated in Australia. This becomes complex as regards protection arrangements which cover multiple jurisdictions, such as the European Community Trademark, which are created under European law,[118] however, even here a provision of the relevant EU regulation has the effect that where a person with no relevant connection with an EU state is granted a trademark, that trademark is treated as a Spanish trademark since the relevant EU entity is established in Spain.[119]

9.81 Part of the reason that the difficulty of establishing the situs of an investment has not caused more trouble in the last fifteen years has been the development of EU legislation designed, not to solve the problem, but to bypass it. By the Financial Markets and Insolvency (Settlement Finality) Regulations 1999[120] it is provided that where securities are provided as collateral to certain persons, and those securities are accounted for in a register, account, or centralised deposit system located in the EEA, the rights of the security taker in relation to those securities is governed by the law of the EEA state where the account or centralised deposit system is located.[121]

9.82 It is of course the case that a payment obligation almost never exists in isolation. Mann[122] discusses the extent to which the nature of a payment obligation may help to determine the governing law of a contract,[123] but we are concerned here with the opposite problem—the relationship between the governing law of the payment obligation created under the contract and the governing law of the contract itself.

9.83 By convention, payment in a currency is deemed to be settled in the country where that currency is issued. The basis of this convention is that such payments are ultimately settled within the relevant central bank. This triggers the provisions of Article 12(2) of the Rome I Convention, which provides that 'In relation to the manner of performance and the steps to be taken in the event of a defective

---

[114] *Secretary of State for Canada v Alien Property Custodian* [1931] 1 DLR 890 at 913–14 (Sup Ct Can); *Braun v The Custodian; Brown, Gow, Wilson v Beleggings-Societeit NV*, and see Mann, International & Comparative Law Quarterly, Vol. 11 (1962) at 497–500.
[115] Dicey 22-049; *In the Goods of Ewing* (1881) 6 P.D. 19 at 23; *Laidly v Lord Advocate* (1890) 15 App Cas 468.
[116] Dicey 22-049.  [117] *Re Usine de Melle's Patent* (1954) 91 CLR 42 at 48.
[118] Council Regulation (EC) 207/2009.  [119] Ibid. Art. 16.
[120] SI 1999/2979, implementing Directive 98/26/EC.  [121] Reg. 23.
[122] Mann on the Legal Aspect of Money, ed. Proctor, OUP 2012 at 115.
[123] A short summary is that it doesn't—the payment of money is never a characteristic performance, since payment is common to almost all contracts—thus, the fact that the price under a contract must be paid in a particular place or in the currency of a particular state is not material to the determination of the governing law of the contract.

performance regard shall be had to the law of the country in which performance takes place'. The use of the term 'have regard to' is weak,[124] but is at least an indication that as regards a payment obligation, the question of whether the obligation has been properly discharged should be considered in the light of the laws of the country where the relevant currency is issued.

## 9.8 Loan of Virtual Currency Units

9.84 There are two very substantial questions which fall to be determined if a loan is made of virtual currency—what is the nature of the initial transaction, and what is the nature of the repayment obligation.

9.85 A loan of virtual currency units will presumably have to take the form of a commodatum—that is, a loan where the borrower can deal with what he has borrowed as absolute owner, and return equivalent units. However, as regards virtual currency units this raises many of the same issues which so troubled the glossators as regards loans in the civil law. In particular, the issue as to whether it was permissible to repay a loan of silver coins in gold and vice versa would immediately reappear as regards whether it was permissible to repay a loan of one virtual currency unit in the equivalent value of a different currency unit,[125] or indeed in fiat currency.

9.86 This is another area where the characterisation of the virtual currency is critical to determining the rights of the parties. If the claim for return of the amount borrowed were to be characterised as a claim for the delivery of things as opposed to money, then the borrower's obligation would not be to redeliver the amount borrowed, but to compensate the lender for the loss suffered by him as a result of the borrower's failure to perform his obligation under the contract. This could be either a higher or lower amount than the value of the virtual currency due under the loan agreement, but the resulting uncertainty would of itself be sufficient to discourage lenders from lending in this way. This suggests that if a bank wished to lend virtual currency units to a borrower, the best way of doing so might be to lend the borrower fiat currency and then enable him to exchange that currency immediately with the bank as a purchase of virtual currency units. This would guarantee that the bank's claim for repayment was a debt claim for a specified amount of fiat currency.

## 9.9 Claims for Payment in Virtual Currency

9.87 For the English courts, virtual currency and foreign money have potentially the same characteristic—that they are used in English-law-governed transactions as

---

[124] See commentary on the measure in the Giuliano-Lagarde Report, to the effect that this gives the relevant court a 'discretion whether to apply [that law] in whole or in part so as to do justice between the parties'.

[125] See Ernst, *The Legists Doctrine on Money and the Law* in Fox and Ernst (eds), *Money in the Western Legal Tradition* (OUP 2016).

methods of payment, but they are not formally recognised as money under English law. The position of the English courts on foreign money has developed over the years—from a starting point of regarding all non-English money as a commodity, it has developed over time towards its current position under which all non-English money can potentially be accepted as money, depending on the nature of the transaction. By considering the development of English law as regards foreign money, we can therefore learn a great deal about the potential treatments of virtual currency. In particular, if virtual currency is not treated as money, the older cases regarding the consequences of a breach of an obligation to pay foreign currency give us a useful picture of the consequences of a breach of an obligation to pay virtual currency.

### 9.9.1 Foreign money and virtual currency

Litigation in the English courts over debts due in other currencies is probably as old as the court system itself. There is a case report from 1355 in the year books over a bond for 1,000 French ecus,[126] and as is so often the case, it seems clear that there was nothing particularly remarkable about the court being asked to deal with a debt due in a currency other than sterling. However, it seems that for an English court, the question of the value of such foreign money was a matter of fact to be left to the jury. Courts could and did take judicial notice of the value of English money,[127] but an obligation to deliver foreign money was in principle no different from an obligation to deliver bullion or any other valuable commodity, and the question of the valuation of that obligation was a matter of fact to be decided by the jury. The result of this was that pleadings in respect of foreign money obligations were frequently expressed in terms of the English money equivalent. Thus, a plaintiff suing for an amount of foreign currency would plead that the debt due amounted to a specified amount in English money,[128] and it would be up to the defendant to decide whether or not to counter the plea.

9.88

This was the position at English law for many centuries. In *Di Ferdinando v Simon Smits & Co. Ltd*,[129] it was held that a claim for damages for breach of contract in a foreign currency had to be converted into sterling at the rate of exchange prevailing at the date of the breach. This was confirmed as recently as 1961 in *Re United Railways of Havana and Regla Warehouses Ltd*,[130] in which it was held that where proceedings were brought in England as regards a foreign money obligation, the claim had to be expressed in sterling in the writ, judgment had to be given in sterling, and the correct date for converting the foreign currency was the date of the defendant's breach.[131]

9.89

---

[126] Pasch. 29 Edw III fo.19. See generally on this subject Fox, *The Structures of Monetary Nominalism in the Pre-Modern Common Law*, Journal of Legal History, Vol. 34, No. 2 (2013) at 139–71.
[127] See *YB* (1455) Mich. 34 Hen VI, pl 23, fo.12a and *Bagshaw v Playn* (1595) Cro. Eliz. 537.
[128] *Ward v Ridgwin* (1625) Latch 84; *Bagshaw v Playn* (1595) Cro. Eliz. 536.
[129] [1920] 3 KB 409.   [130] [1961] AC 1007, HL.
[131] *Rastell v Draper* (KB (1605)), was followed in *Manners v Pearson* [1898] 1 Ch 581 as authority that an English court cannot give judgment in anything but sterling. Lindley MR observed that the courts of this country cannot give judgment in anything but sterling (ibid. at 587) however, the court decided that the sterling value should be calculated at the date of the judgment. Vaughn Williams J

This was on the basis that (a) foreign money was a commodity, therefore debt did not lie, and there was no possibility of an order for specific performance (since delivery of a commodity is the paradigm of a case where damages are generally an adequate remedy) and (b) on the non-delivery of a commodity under a contract, damages should be assessed by reference to the market price of the relevant currency at the breach date.[132]

### 9.9.2 Consequences of treatment of money as a commodity

9.90  The most important consequence of this rule is that the risk of change in the value of the currency is reallocated. Consider, for example, the facts of *Gilbert and Brett*. In that case, the debt from the Irish buyer to the English seller was denominated in sterling. When by royal proclamation the Irish currency was devalued, the English seller had no defence to the Irish buyer's claim to be able to deliver devalued Irish coins at their face value in payment. Thus, the cost of the devaluation would have fallen on the seller. If the agreement had been with a Dutch buyer, by contrast, the English seller would have been able to quantify the claim at the moment of non-payment. Thus, if the Dutch currency had been devalued after that moment, the cost of that devaluation would have fallen on the buyer. It should be noted that this is bilateral—if the value of the Dutch currency had appreciated substantially against sterling in the period between breach and judgment, the benefit of that appreciation would have inured for the benefit of the buyer and not the seller. However, the key point is the asymmetry which this rule produces—for obligations in English currency, the risk of currency movement between breach and judgment is on the seller, for obligations in other currencies, the risk of currency movement between breach and judgment is on the buyer.[133] This rule was also applied to liabilities in breach of contract[134] and tort.[135]

9.91  The effect of this, as Mann observed,[136] was that the institution of legal proceedings changed the nature of the obligation between the parties. The widespread dissatisfaction with this position was the subject of a great deal of discussion in the commercial world, and the subject of some successful lobbying—for example, in 1965 the Council of Europe was prevailed upon to set up a committee of experts which in 1967 proposed a European Convention on Foreign Money Liabilities[137]

---

dissented, holding that the conversion should be at the date of the breach, applying a pure commodity theory (ibid. at 593). This was upheld by the House of Lords in *Havana Railways*.

[132] But see Denning LJ's dissent in *Owners of Turbo Electric Bulk Carrier Teh Hu v Nippon Salvage Co Ltd (the Teh Hu)* [1970] P. 106 CA (Civ Div) for a protest as to the consequences of this approach.

[133] There is a valuable discussion of this point in Black, *Foreign Currency Claims in the Conflict of Laws* (Hart Publishing 2010) at Ch. 1.

[134] *Ottoman Bank v Chakarian (No. 1)* [1930] AC 277.

[135] *The Volturno* [1921] 2 AC 544.

[136] Mann Ch 8 'Legal proceedings and their effect on monetary obligations', 7th ed at 231 et seq.

[137] Council of Europe Treaty No. 060.

### 9.9.3 Recognition of non-UK currency as money

The first breach in this rule was the 1974 case of *Jugoslavenska Oceanska Plovidba v Castle Investment Co Inc*.[140] That case concerned an arbitrator's award. The Court of Appeal held that since the purpose of an arbitral award was to enable the injured party to recover the same amount as they ought in the first place to have received, it would be wrong to apply procedural rules which would cause the effect of the award to have a different consequence.[141] It is clear from the judgment that the collapse of the *Bretton Woods* agreement and the subsequent extraordinary volatility in the international markets had highlighted the extraordinary potential unintended consequences of the application of the breach-date rule, and were a material factor in the court's decision.   9.92

The next step was the decision in *Schorch Meier v GmbH v Hennin*.[142] In that case, Denning LJ in the Court of Appeal declined to apply the breach-date rule in respect of a claim in German Deutschmarks on the basis of European law. The kindest thing that can be said about the *Schorch Meier* decision is that its conclusions were eminently satisfactory from a commercial perspective. However, the legal analysis by which those conclusions were reached can best be described as questionable.[143]   9.93

This point was finally authoritatively decided in *Miliangos v George Frank (Textiles) Ltd*.[144] The essence of the House of Lords position is best summarised by Mann as that the creditor in respect of a foreign currency denominated debt is both entitled and obliged to seek judgment in the currency concerned.[145] A creditor retains the right to pay his debt either in the currency in which the judgment debt is denominated or in sterling at the conversion rate on the date of actual payment, but in both of these cases the risk of currency fluctuation remains with the creditor. In *Miliangos* itself, the obligation was in Swiss francs, but sterling collapsed between the breach date and the judgment date, so the plaintiffs amended their pleading to demand the nominal value of Swiss francs on the basis of *Schorch Meier*.   9.94

The point at issue in *Miliangos* was as regards contractual obligations, but the doctrine has subsequently been expanded so that it applies to claims for unliquidated   9.95

---

[138] See the *Explanatory Report to the European Convention on Foreign Money Liabilities* Paris, 11.XII.1967. The treaty is still in existence, although its substance has been overtaken.
[139] Per Denning LJ in *The Teh Hu* [1970] P 106, 124. Mann notes, possibly unkindly, that the force of this criticism is somewhat muted by the fact that Denning was one of the judges who had confirmed this rule in *United Railways of Havanah*.
[140] [1974] QB 292.
[141] The power of an arbitrator to make an award in any currency was subsequently confirmed in the Arbitrators Act 1996, s. 48(4) (which does not, however, define the term 'currency'), and see *Lesotho Highlands Development Authority v Impreglio SpA* [2005] UKHL 43.
[142] [1975] QB 416.
[143] See per Lord Wilberforce in *Miliangos*, and see further White, *Judgements in Foreign Currency and the EEC Treaty*, Journal of Business Law, Vol. 7 (January 1976).
[144] [1976] AC 443, HL.   [145] 7th ed at 234.

damages in contract and to claims in tort[146] and to claims where payment is to be made in foreign currency under contracts governed by English law.[147] Note, however, that this is not a universal rule—in insolvency, for example, claims are converted as at the date of the winding-up.

9.96 The decision in *Miliangos* brought a welcome clarity to the position in front of the English courts. However, given the complexity of the fact patterns arising from international trade, it raised a whole new set of issues as to how damages should be calculated where there were multiple considerations in play. The most challenging of the immediate issues were heard by the House of Lords in the conjoined cases of *The Despina R* and *The Folias*.[148]

### 9.9.4 Deciding the relevant currency of a contract

9.97 In both of these cases a loss was sustained in one currency by a plaintiff whose business was conducted in a different currency. The court therefore had to consider whether judgment should be given in the currency in which the loss was immediately sustained—the contractual currency—or in the currency in which the loss was effectively suffered—the operating currency of the plaintiff, or whether to simply apply the sterling equivalent, either at the time the losses occurred or at some other date.

9.98 The basis of the approach was to try and establish an expressed or implied agreement as to which currency should be used for payment in the event that there was a breach of contract. If there was a clear understanding that, in the event of a breach, payment was to be made in a particular currency, then that is the currency in which the judgment would be awarded. In the absence of any such agreement, damages should be calculated in the currency in which the loss was actually felt by the plaintiff or which most truly expresses his loss.

9.99 The easiest way of understanding the application of this principle is to look at the facts of one of these cases. In *The Folias* a cargo was shipped from Spain to Brazil by the French charterers of a Swiss vessel. The cargo was damaged, and the French charterers were obliged to pay damages to the Brazilian consignees in Brazilian cruzeiros. The charterers claimed against the shipowners to recover their loss. However, the charterers sued in French francs, on the basis that that was the currency in which they carried on their business. However, the practical reason for this was that the cruzeiro had collapsed in value in the intervening period, and a judgment against the shipowners for the value of the cruzeiros paid out at the day of judgment would have been worth a small fraction of the value of the payment actually made to the consignees.

9.100 At first instance, it was held that because their loss had been experienced in cruzeiros, their compensation claim must also be in cruzeiros. However, the Court of Appeal (upheld by the House of Lords) disagreed. In their view, the loss suffered by

---

[146] *The Folias* [1979] AC 685, HL.
[147] *Barclays Bank International Ltd v Levin Bros (Bradford) Ltd* [1977] QB 270 QBD (Comm).
[148] [1979] 1 Lloyds Rep 1.

the French charterers had been incurred in French francs. This was because the cost to them of paying the cruzeiro-denominated compensation had been incurred in French francs, since they had had to use French francs to purchase the cruzeiros due to the Brazilian consignees. The real point at issue here was where the risk should lie for currency volatility occurring between the payment of the original damages and the making of the claim for reimbursement.

A more recent example is *The Texaco Melbourne*.[149] A Ghanaian company had purchased a cargo of oil to be delivered to Takoradi in Ghana for 7.9m Ghanaian cedis—worth (at the time of the contract) US$2.8m. However, due to the collapse of the Ghanaian cedi, at the time of the hearing this would have been worth US$21,000. The suppliers refused to deliver, and the question was the amount of compensation due for their breach. 9.101

The contract did not provide for damages to be paid in any particular currency, so the court applied the principles set out in the *Despina*. However, since the plaintiff was a domestic Ghanaian company which operated only in cedis (and indeed was prohibited from dealing in US dollars; a privilege reserved for the Central Bank of Ghana[150]), the court had little choice but to hold that the loss must have been suffered in cedis, and that the payment of the amount of cedis specified in the initial contract must therefore be appropriate compensation.[151] 9.102

It should be noted in this context that this rule is not confined to commercial cases. In a personal injury case brought on behalf of a mother who had died in childbirth in an English hospital by her extended family (who would incur the costs of raising the child), the fact that the extended family lived in Italy and would incur those costs in Italian lire justified the making of an award in lire.[152] 9.103

*Miliangos* is one of the relatively rare cases which marks a sudden and substantial change in English law. One of the things which follows from this is that authorities which pre-date *Miliangos* on this issue should be regarded as of very doubtful authority.[153] 9.104

The final link in this chain is *Camdex International Ltd v Bank of Zambia (No 3)*.[154] In that case, the plaintiffs[155] sought a garnishee order in respect of amounts due from a Zambian company to the Zambian central bank in Zambian currency. 9.105

---

[149] [1994] 1 Lloyds Rep 473.
[150] It is possible that this fact was determinative in this case. In a very similar case involving a Nigerian oil importer, the fact that the importer in practice conducted its business in US dollars was held to justify an award in dollars: *Milan Nigeria Ltd v Angelika B Maritime* [2011] EWHC 892 at para 62. See also *The Mosconi* [2002] 2 Lloyds Rep 313.
[151] This outcome requires a word of explanation. It is clear that if the importer had purchased an alternative cargo from another source, he would have been able to claim the difference between the two costs as damages in the ordinary fashion. It is only because he did not do so that his claim was merely for the purchase price of the cargo.
[152] *Bordin v St. Mary's NHS Trust* [2000] Lloyds Rep Med 287.
[153] *Monrovia Tramp Shipping Co v President of India* [1978] 2 Lloyds Rep 193, affd [1979] 1 WLR 59, and see Morris, *English Judgements in Foreign Currency: A Procedural Revolution*, Law and Contemporary Problems, Vol 41, No. 44 (1977).
[154] [1997] 6 Bank LR 44 CA (Civ Div).
[155] Relying on *Re British American and Continental Bank, Re Lisser and Rosenkranz claim* [1923] 1 Ch 276.

9.106 The question that remains is whether the rule in *Miliangos* that the plaintiff may sue for the amount in the relevant foreign currency, or is it that he must sue in that currency and not in sterling. In principle, *Miliangos* is authority for the conclusion that the rule is procedural.[156] *Ozalid Group (Export) Ltd v African Continental Bank Ltd*[157] suggests that a plaintiff retains the right to elect to sue for a sum in sterling if he wishes; however, the weight of both commentary[158] and authority seems now to be against this principle.

9.107 It should be noted that this is not a finding that foreign money in the United Kingdom is money for all purposes—in *A Ltd v B Bank*,[159] in the admitted slightly unusual context of a dispute over the right of a foreign state to prevent its banknotes circulating in the United Kingdom, it was held that foreign banknotes in England 'are not to be regarded as legal tender, but commodities or objects of commerce'.

9.108 This does of course raise the question of special damages. The basic rule of damages is that damages can be recovered in respect both of the loss suffered and in respect of any further loss suffered as a result of non-performance if that loss was specifically in the contemplation of the parties.[160] There may well be circumstances in which a failure to pay an amount in a particular currency has knock-on effects for the recipient which go beyond the simple loss suffered by the failure to deliver, and such losses will be recoverable in the same way as damages for any other failure to perform.[161]

### 9.9.5 Virtual currency and obligations

9.109 None of these cases—entirely unsurprisingly—has anything to say about what is meant by a currency. The nominalistic principle means that in respect of any particular instrument, the question to be asked is simply whether it is recognised by its government as its currency.

9.110 It should be clear from the foregoing that the essence of this question is simply as to how a UK court, if it were asked to give such a decision, would characterise the decision which it was being asked to give.

---

[156] Although *Rogers v Markel Corp* [2004] EWHC 2046 seems to suggest that the identification of the currency in which judgment should be given is a matter for the governing law of the contract rather than the procedural rules of the forum—see Mann 7th edn Ch. 8, fn 24.
[157] [1979] 2 Lloyds Rep 231 QBD (Comm) at 233–4.
[158] Goode on Payment Obligations in Commercial and Financial Transactions (Sweet & Maxwell 3rd ed. 2016), Mann 7th ed para 8.06.
[159] [1997] 6 Bank LR 85 CA (Civ Div).   [160] *Hadley v Baxendale* [1854] 9 Exch 341.
[161] *Re Lehman Brothers International (Europe) (In Administration)* [2015] Ch 1, aff [2016] Ch 50. The rules that apply to exchange losses arising on a breach of contract are the same as for any other type of damages (as per Lord Brandon in *President of India v Lips Maritime Corp (the Lips)* [1988] AC 395, HL) and can be recovered if they were specifically in the contemplation of the parties.

9.111 One possibility would be to hold that the virtual currency units concerned were simply commodities like any other. In this case, it seems extremely unlikely that specific performance would be awarded, and the order would simply be to pay damages. It seems highly likely that the ordinary rules would be applied, and that the order would be to pay the value of the virtual currency units concerned at the date of the breach. This would be an unexpected result for both plaintiff and defendant.

9.112 Another possibility would be for the UK court to recognise the virtual currency unit as a currency, and to give judgment in that currency. There would be considerable concern over this approach. It must be reasonably clear that a court cannot give judgment denominated in a commodity—it would not be possible, for example, for a court to give judgment for six bars of gold—such a judgment could only take effect as an order for specific performance. Consequently, the court would have to be satisfied that it was justified in regarding the virtual currency concerned as a currency. It seems likely that a court seeking to decide this issue would ask two broad questions; first, is this unit instrument generally treated as currency—that is, is there evidence of a market or social practice by which the units concerned are treated as money-like—and second, is it clear that the intention of the parties in making the contract was that the unit concerned should be regarded as money as between them? This latter point boils down to the issue of whether the intention of the parties was that the virtual currency unit was intended to be the unit of account of payment, or was merely intended to be the medium of exchange. Put another way, if the supplier of goods wished to obtain a specific number of a specific type of thing, the contract is simply one of barter, and there is no justification for giving judgment in the units concerned. However, if the units were intended by the parties to be a unit of account—that is, to designate a value rather than a thing—then the case for giving judgment in that unit is considerably improved. The fact pattern here is not dissimilar to the issues faced by medieval courts when considering payment obligations in particular coins. Where a debt was denominated in (say) guineas, there would have been a live question as to whether the obligation was for the payment of guineas at their nominal value (originally 20s) or their market value (which, because of their gold content, varied as high as 30s) in the period immediately after their appearance. Ultimately, this question would have been determined by asking whether the intention of the parties was to buy and sell physical things, or to deal in units of currency. It is submitted that the question is not different to the issues which arise where a party to a contract has provided a payment instrument—for example, a cheque or a letter of credit—in payment of debt. There are two possible constructions of such an arrangement; one being that the presentation of the instrument is itself sufficient to discharge the obligation, the other being that the instrument is a mere mechanism by which the recipient is enabled to obtain payment—in the first case the credit risk of the drawee of the instrument (or the issuer of the letter of credit) is transferred to the seller at the moment of transfer; in the second that risk remains with the buyer until the issuer/drawee actually performs their obligation under the instrument. The question of whether the delivery of the instrument constitutes payment—that is, whether the delivery of the instrument is the benefit bargained for, or whether the instrument is a mere mechanism by which the recipient can obtain the benefit bargained for—can, if not specified in the contract, only be addressed by consideration of all of the circumstances surrounding the transaction. This is in essence exactly the decision which a court is required to make in determining whether the delivery of a virtual currency unit should be treated as 'payment' for this purpose.

# 10
# Financial Regulation in the New World

| | |
|---|---|
| 10.1 Financial Regulatory Structures and Virtual Currency | 10.02 |
| 10.2 The Regulation of Investments | 10.10 |
|     10.2.1 Virtual currency and securities regulation | 10.13 |
|     10.2.2 Debt securities | 10.14 |
|     10.2.3 Public offering | 10.17 |
|     10.2.4 Receipts and units with underlyings | 10.19 |
|     10.2.5 Collective investment scheme regulation | 10.21 |
| 10.3 The Regulation of Deposits and Payment Systems | 10.29 |
|     10.3.1 E-money | 10.33 |
|     10.3.2 Payment services | 10.40 |
|     10.3.3 Lending and credit | 10.50 |
| 10.4 The Regulation of Virtual Currency | 10.51 |
|     10.4.1 Investment business | 10.51 |
|     10.4.2 Deposit-taking | 10.60 |
|     10.4.3 E-money | 10.62 |
|     10.4.4 Payment services | 10.63 |
| 10.5 The US Experience | 10.64 |
|     10.5.1 The CFTC—futures and derivatives regulation | 10.65 |
|     10.5.2 The SEC—securities regulation | 10.67 |

In a perfect world, the appearance of a new financial phenomenon would result in the construction of a new regulatory system to accommodate it, and there is a flourishing literature discussing how such systems should be structured. However, in general this does not happen—although there are new regimes being created to cope with the challenges posed to regulators by virtual currency,[1] the reaction of regulators and legislators to new developments is almost invariably to seek to accommodate them within existing regulatory frameworks. Consequently, until the arrival of the new world, it is necessary to examine how virtual currency units fit within the existing regulatory framework. 10.01

---

[1] See, e.g., the New York State Department of Financial Services' '*Bitlicence*' regulatory framework—23 NYCRR Part 200 Virtual Currencies.

## 10.1 Financial Regulatory Structures and Virtual Currency

10.02   The starting point for this analysis is that although financial regulation touches almost every aspect of the financial industry, the one thing that it carefully avoids regulating is the use of money itself. There are fairly obvious reasons for this. The basis of financial regulation is permissioning, accompanied by some sort of prohibition of non-permissioned persons engaging in the activities concerned. Since more or less everybody needs to use money on a regular basis, the use of money cannot be made a regulated activity. Thus, those items of virtual currency which are characterised as money will fall outside the scope of financial regulation altogether.

10.03   The problem, however, is that there are a number of different types of virtual currency unit, and these are by no means always clearly 'money' even for regulatory purposes. As noted above, a virtual currency can take one of three forms:

(1) A pure 'unit', which consists of nothing more than an entry on a register. Bitcoin is an example of a virtual currency of this type (*Type 1*).

(2) A token which carries an entitlement to a return derived from some sort of underlying asset. The digital token issued may represent a share in a firm, a prepayment voucher for future services. Most ICO offerings take this form (*Type 2*).

(3) A token which entitles the holder to a money claim. This may be either a claim on a bank or other payment provider, an entitlement to a pool of money held somewhere, or some other structure. Tether and Ripple are examples of this sort of concept (*Type 3*).

10.04   It should also be emphasised that the creators of many of these kinds of instruments are likely to think of their products as protocols rather than things—that is, in regulatory terms, they are providers of systems which are used by others rather than buyers and sellers of things. However, regulators are required by the laws within which they operate to force these products into the straightjacket of the existing regulatory classifications.

10.05   In general this classification involves asking four questions.

10.06   The first question is as to whether the virtual currency unit is an 'investment' or not. If it is, a person dealing in it by way of business will be required to be an authorised firm, or to deal with or through an authorised firm. Regulatory customer protections must be applied by that authorised person in respect of any transaction in that product by the authorised person to the customer, and rules may apply to restrict the types of customers to whom the product may be sold at all. A subdivision of this analysis is the question of whether the virtual currency unit can be characterised as a 'security'—if it can, then its offering may require a prospectus. A further issue which arises from this classification is that if the virtual currency unit concerned constitutes an investment, then the establishment of a venue on which it can be traded may require authorisation as constitution establishing a regulated exchange or trading venue.

The second question relates to banking regulation. Holding money for another person constitutes deposit-taking, and since most virtual currency is held through service providers, the question of whether that service constitutes deposit-taking is an important one.  10.07

The third question is in relation to payment systems. The operation of a payment system is itself a regulated activity, and a system whereby virtual currency units are employed to discharge payment obligations can in certain circumstances require the operator to be authorised as an operator of a payment system.  10.08

The fourth question is in relation to the e-money regulatory system established during the dot-com boom. This schema remains in existence, and a creator of a virtual currency may be characterised as an issuer of e-money, and to require regulation on that score.  10.09

## 10.2 The Regulation of Investments

The basis of the investment regulatory structure of the United Kingdom is the definition of 'regulated activities'. This is set out in broad terms in section 22(2) and Schedule 2 to the Financial Services and Markets Act 2000 ('the FSMA'), and is given (substantial) further detail in the Financial Services and Markets Act 2000 (Regulated Activities) Order 2001[2] ('the RAO'). The architecture involves the definition of 'specified investments' and 'specified activities'—in broad terms, conducting one of the specified activities in relation to one of the specified products is a regulated activity. Engaging in a regulated activity in the United Kingdom without the appropriate authorisation is a criminal offence under section 21 of the FSMA.[3]  10.10

The RAO does not list money as a 'specified investment'. This means that the use or exchange of money is not per se a regulated activity. Even here, however, practical difficulties are posed—this exclusion means that dealers in foreign exchange do not require authorisation to engage in their business.[4]  10.11

The next limitation is that the regulatory system only applies to activities which are undertaken 'by way of business'.[5] In general, this is taken to mean on a commercial rather than a non-commercial basis—however, in practice, it is very unusual to encounter any arrangement regarding money which cannot be said to have at least some commercial purpose, and the only arrangements which this certainly excludes are those undertaken between friends and family for demonstrably non-commercial reasons.[6] A distinction which is of importance in this regard is the distinction between: (a) engaging in an activity 'carried on by way of business'; and (b) engaging  10.12

---

[2] SI 2001/544.
[3] There are a variety of other consequences of the conducting of unauthorised regulated business, including potential voidability of the contracts concerned.
[4] Most FX dealers are authorised, since in general it is necessary for them to enter into options, futures, and forwards as well as spot trades, and all of these latter are regulated products.
[5] Financial Services and Markets Act 2000, s. 22(1).
[6] See, e.g., *Rolls v Miller* (1884) 27 Ch D 71 at 81: Business means 'anything which is an occupation as distinguished from a pleasure—anything which is an occupation or duty which requires attention'.

in 'the business of engaging in an activity'.[7] In the first case, an activity is regulated if it is engaged in for a commercial purpose, even if it is a single standalone activity—thus the court is required to characterise the particular transaction. In the second case, the question is not as to whether a particular transaction has been entered into, but whether the person entering into it did so in the course of carrying on a business of engaging in transactions of that type—thus the court is required to characterise the business in the course of which the particular transaction was carried out. The best-known manifestation of this distinction is as regards dealing in investments—I can buy and sell investments as an investor without requiring authorisation because I am not engaged in the business of buying and selling investments; however, if I hold myself out as willing to buy and sell investments on a continuous basis I will be taken to be in the business of buying and selling investments, and will require authorisation.[8] Conversely, if I give someone investment advice on a commercial basis, even once, I will be engaging in a regulated activity, regardless of whether the giving of investment advice is my business or not.

### 10.2.1 Virtual currency and securities regulation

10.13   There are two broad regulatory categories into which virtual currency may fall. Type 3 virtual currency may fall within the class of debt securities (conventionally referred to in regulatory circles as debentures), and both type 2 and type 3 virtual currencies may fall within the definition of 'collective investment scheme'. However, there seems to be broad agreement on both sides of the Atlantic that type 1 virtual currencies are entirely outside the existing securities regulatory framework. Consequently, discussion of type 1 currencies is primarily as to whether a new regulatory regime should be constructed to catch such units.

### 10.2.2 Debt securities

10.14   Debt securities are regulated investments, and dealing in them is a regulated activity. The definition of a debt security (referred to in the RAO as an 'instrument creating or acknowledging indebtedness'[9]) is effectively any instrument which either creates or acknowledges a debt. On its own this would potentially catch a wide variety of private payment instruments, ranging from cheques to promissory notes. Consequently, some (but by no means all) private payment instruments are excluded from the definition.[10] However, more importantly, a lender who signs a loan agreement is not treated as doing regulated business,[11] and a borrower can generally rely on the argument that he is not dealing in his own debt. There has been recent

---

[7] See *Helden v Strathmore Limited* [2011] EWCA Civ 542.    [8] Art. 15(1)(a) RAO.
[9] Art. 77 RAO. The definition clearly draws on the judgement of Chitty J in *Levy v Abercorris Slate Co.* (1888) 37 Ch D 260 at 264.
[10] Notably cheques, bills of exchange, banker's drafts, banknotes, and letters of credit—see Art. 77(2) RAO.
[11] Financial Services and Markets Act 2000 (Regulated Activities) Order 2001, Art. 17.

Court of Appeal authority on the issue of when a document relating to an advance of money may be deemed to be a debenture and therefore an investment,[12] but this is generally regarded as inapplicable to transactions generally.

The first question which arises in applying this to virtual currencies is the question of whether a virtual currency can be said to be an 'instrument'. In general, the term 'instrument' connotes a piece of paper with writing on it, but it is clear that an 'instrument' can be created purely electronically.[13] However, this is only clear as regards electronic documents which are capable of being 'reproduced in a visible form',[14] and a virtual coin which exists only in the form of a distributed ledger entry does not appear to satisfy that test. However, it is submitted that in practice, if a virtual currency unit is structured so as to be legally identical to a debenture, the mere fact that it is not technically 'in writing' would not be sufficient to persuade either the securities regulators or the courts that it should not be treated as a debenture for regulatory purposes merely by virtue of the fact that it was not in writing.

10.15

The more difficult issue in this regard is the nature of the claim which the unit embeds. As noted above, a 'pure' (type 1) currency unit is not a debt security precisely because of the fact that it does not create or acknowledge indebtedness—it is of the essence of a pure token that it is not a claim on anyone. However, this becomes harder to establish when units are established by private entities using permissioned ledgers—if a person X creates his own virtual currency (Xcoin), on terms that people can acquire Xcoin by paying him money, and that he will accept Xcoins tendered to him in exchange for money, the question of whether Xcoins constitute his 'indebtedness' is not at all clear. In a way, what has been created here is a close equivalent of the private banknotes discussed in section 5.2 above, and it seems clear that such notes were not considered to be debentures under the laws of the time. However, article 77(2)(c) of the RAO explicitly excludes banknotes from the definition of debentures, and that exclusion could be taken to imply that instruments of that form would fall within the definition if they were not explicitly excluded. The only clear conclusion which can be reached in this area is that statutory updating is sorely needed.

10.16

### 10.2.3 Public offering

The offer of debentures (and indeed securities generally) to the public requires a prospectus.[15] There are broad exemptions to this requirement for offers which are confined to professional investors or which have high denominations, but since the

10.17

---

[12] *Fons HF (In liquidation) v Corporal Ltd* [2014] EWCA 304. This decision has been treated by banks, firms, the legal profession, and the FCA (see the letter of 17 July 2014 from the FCA to the Loan Market Association on the City Law Society website http://www.citysolicitors.org.uk) as confined to its particular facts.

[13] In the absence of statutory clarification, this point remains highly unclear—see the *Law Society and City of London Law Society Practice Note on Electronic Signatures* of July 2016 for the most recent thinking on this issue.

[14] As per the definition of 'writing' in s. 5 and Sch. 1 to the Interpretation Act 1978.

[15] Financial Services and Markets Act 2000, s. 85.

whole purpose of a virtual currency unit is to obtain broad circulation, these are unlikely to be relevant. More important is the fact that a prospectus requirement is only triggered where the offer is an offer of 'transferable securities'. The meaning of this term is not entirely clear—section 102A(3) of the FSMA defines it by reference to the EU Markets in Financial Instruments Directive (MiFID),[16] and MiFID defines it[17] as follows:

'transferable securities' means those classes of securities which are negotiable on the capital market, with the exception of instruments of payment, such as:

(a) shares in companies and other securities equivalent to shares in companies, partnerships or other entities, and depositary receipts in respect of shares;
(b) bonds or other forms of securitised debt, including depositary receipts in respect of such securities;
(c) any other securities giving the right to acquire or sell any such transferable securities or giving rise to a cash settlement determined by reference to transferable securities, currencies, interest rates or yields, commodities or other indices or measures.

10.18 There are a number of aspects to this. First, there is the requirement for transferability—it is hard to think of any virtual currency unit where this requirement is not satisfied, but there would be nothing difficult about structuring (say) an ICO on the basis that the units created were not transferable, and such an offering would clearly fall outside the scope of the definition of transferable securities, and therefore of the prospectus requirement. Second, the fact that the definition is confined to securities 'which are negotiable on the capital market'—in general virtual currency units are not dealt in on such markets, and this offers strong support for the proposition that they simply fall outside this definition and therefore do not trigger prospectus requirements. However, for reasons set out elsewhere in this chapter, some virtual currency trading venues are seeking to obtain regulated market status, and it may well be that in the future there is an identifiable pattern of market trading of virtual currency units. The third issue is that the definition excludes 'instruments of payment'. It seems reasonably clear that pure virtual currency units are intended to be instruments of payment, and as such these do seem to be clearly outside the scope of this definition.[18] However, it is not at all clear whether the sorts of tokens identified in the DAO case (see 10.67 below) would be classified as instruments of payment.[19] However, one of the key differences between the US and the UK regime is that whereas in the United States an 'investment contract' is simply a form of security, in the United Kingdom a unit in a collective investment scheme is not a

---

[16] Directive 2014/65/EU of the European Parliament and of the Council of 15 May 2014 on Markets in Financial Instruments and Amending Directive 2002/92/EC and Directive 2011/61/EU.
[17] Art. 4(44).
[18] This conclusion is supported by the ECJ's decision in *Hedqvist*, C-264/14 EU:C:2015:718 at para 55.
[19] It should be noted in this context that when the State of California issued IOUs in its financial crisis of 2009, the SEC responded with an investor alert to the effect that these IOUs were securities, and the offering of and trading in them was subject to federal securities laws—see https://www.sec.gov/investor/pubs/californiaiou-alert.htm.

transferable security. Consequently, it is only if a virtual currency unit falls into the definition of a debenture that a prospectus will be triggered.

### 10.2.4 Receipts and units with underlyings

Some virtual currency units function as receipts, entitling the holder to an identifiable underlying commodity or claim. This is distinct from the regulation of futures and options—we can disregard for the time being the idea of a virtual currency which confers on the holder the right to purchase property at a future time, noting only that such units would be regarded as investments under the provisions of the RAO relating to futures[20] and options.[21]

Instruments of this kind are touched in a number of ways by the regulatory system, but these fall within two broad classes. First, there is the specialised class which relates to those instruments whose underlyings are themselves investments. This includes the regime for 'instruments giving entitlement to investments'.[22] This catches any instrument which entitles the holder to subscribe for a share or debenture. More important is the regime governing 'certificates representing certain securities'[23] which catches any instrument which confers any right—whether proprietary or merely contractual—to shares, debentures, or government securities. Finally, there is the catch-all that any instrument which confers rights to any investment of any kind is itself an investment.[24] The second, and potentially more important class, arises within the definition of 'contract for differences'[25] (CfD). A contract for differences is any contract the purpose of which is to give one party economic exposure to fluctuations in the price or value of property of any description. Thus, an instrument can be a CfD, and therefore a regulated product, quite regardless of the identity of the underlying property—an arrangement whereby an investor will receive a gain by reference to the success of a business is likely to be a CfD. There are a number of exemptions from this classification, the most important of which is that it is limited to contracts which are settled by payment of money—any arrangement which the parties expect to settle by the delivery of underlying property is outside the scope of the CfD regime.[26]

### 10.2.5 Collective investment scheme regulation

The concept of the 'collective investment scheme' plays a major role in UK financial regulation.[27] This concept was designed to catch investment products structured as funds, and the rules are much as might be expected—a 'unit' in a 'collective investment scheme' is an investment, and dealing in it is a regulated activity.

The definition of a collective investment scheme for this purpose is set out in section 235 of the FSMA. This reads as follows:

---

[20] Art. 83 RAO.  [21] Art. 84 RAO.  [22] Art. 79 RAO.  [23] Art. 80 RAO.
[24] Art. 89 RAO.  [25] Art. 85 RAO.  [26] Art. 85(2)(a) RAO.
[27] It does the same job as the rule in *SEC v Howey Co.* 328 US 293 (1946) does in US regulation.

235 Collective investment schemes

(1) In this Part 'collective investment scheme' means any arrangements with respect to property of any description, including money, the purpose or effect of which is to enable persons taking part in the arrangements (whether by becoming owners of the property or any part of it or otherwise) to participate in or receive profits or income arising from the acquisition, holding, management or disposal of the property or sums paid out of such profits or income.
(2) The arrangements must be such that the persons who are to participate ('participants') do not have day-to-day control over the management of the property, whether or not they have the right to be consulted or to give directions.
(3) The arrangements must also have either or both of the following characteristics–
   (a) the contributions of the participants and the profits or income out of which payments are to be made to them are pooled;
   (b) the property is managed as a whole by or on behalf of the operator of the scheme.

The essence of this structure is that any arrangement is a collective investment scheme if it has the following characteristics:

(1) multiple investors;
(2) identifiable underlying property;
(3) participation by investors in the profits or income derived from that property;
(4) pooling of risks and returns by individual investors;
(5) separation of ownership and control, such that the relevant property is not directly managed by the investors, but is managed by a common manager.

10.23 The collective investment scheme definition has been given a very expansive scope over the years. This is because it is the regulators' weapon of choice to attack investment products structured to get around the regulatory system by purporting to offer investments in physical assets. Thus, for example, in *FCA v Asset Land*,[28] promoters seeking to raise funds from multiple investors in respect of an investment in a plot of land for development had proceeded by dividing the plot into individual sections, and purporting to sell each section to an individual investor whilst retaining overall control of the project as a whole. Their argument was that they had sold individuals land; and therefore did not require FSMA authorisation. The Supreme Court held that the entire arrangement was a collective investment scheme in respect of the land concerned and that the operators were engaged in the unlawful regulated activity of operating an unauthorised collective investment scheme.

10.24 The essence of the definition of a collective investment scheme is that there should be an identifiable pool of property (the 'scheme property') out of which investors will be repaid. However, this does not mean that only arrangements which involve identifiable underlying assets will be caught. This is clear from *FSA v Fradley*,[29] which involved an arrangement whereby contributor's money was pooled for the purpose of being bet on horse races. This arrangement was held to be a collective

---

[28] [2016] UKSC 17.   [29] [2005] 1 BCLC, [2006] BCLC 216 (CA).

investment scheme. It is illuminating in this regard to consider the trial judge's description of the arrangement in question:

Investors in the scheme would provide a minimum sum of £500, known as a 'betting bank', and were told that they stood a realistic chance of increasing their betting bank by a factor of 10 each year ... The mailshot included an application form for membership of 147, which contained a standing order mandate in favour of 147; and a form appointing TBPS the member's agent for the purpose of placing bets. It was not initially compulsory to use TBPS for bet placement: members would receive confidential information and could place bets themselves, but they were encouraged in the mailshot to use TBPS's services. Once accepted into the scheme, members were sent an acceptance letter; and if they had applied to use TBPS's services, they were also sent TBPS's terms and conditions. Those terms and conditions provided (among other things) that the member's betting bank would be held in TBPS's client account, out of which payments could only be made for the purpose of payments to bookmakers, repayment to the members, or payment to TBPS's management fee and 'placement levy'; and that clients' accounts would be updated daily and computerised accounts issued monthly.

The similarity of this arrangement to a modern ICO offering is striking.

10.25 In this arrangement there was no investment property—the money collected from the investors was applied for a particular purpose. Nonetheless, the court found that the arrangement was a regulated collective investment scheme, and that its operators were breaking the law by offering units in it to persons in the United Kingdom.[30]

10.26 It is of course the case that the definition of collective investment scheme catches (inter alia) most banks. Consequently, there is an exemption for arrangements in which the whole of each participant's contribution constitutes a deposit.[31] However, this is only available where the person accepting the deposit is either an authorised UK bank or has the benefit of a specific exemption from regulation as a bank. Thus, an arrangement whereby an unauthorised person accepts money from investors on terms that he will invest the proceeds but then return the money with interest derived from the investment is potentially both illegal deposit-taking and an illegal collective investment scheme.

10.27 It is worth pausing in this context to look at the consequences of an arrangement being characterised as a collective investment scheme under UK law. It is important to appreciate in this context that this is a definitional provision—the question of whether an arrangement falls within the UK definition of a collective investment scheme is not affected by the geographical location of the scheme. However, if an arrangement does fall within this definition, then there are certain activities which may not be performed with respect to it in the United Kingdom. These are:

(1) *Offering of units*. The general principle of UK law is that only regulated collective investment schemes may be offered to the general public in the United

---

[30] A similar conclusion was reached in *Broderick v Centaur Tipping Services* (2006) 103(34) LSG 32.
[31] Financial Services and Markets Act 2000 (Collective Investment Schemes) Order 2001, SI 2001/1062, Sch. 1, para 3.

Kingdom. Section 238[32] of the FSMA prohibits the offering of units in unregulated collective investment schemes to persons in the United Kingdom except to certain classes of investors—loosely professionals, high net worth and sophisticated investors.[33]

(2) *Arranging transactions in units, and dealing in units.* Since units in a collective investment scheme are always investments, dealing in them and arranging deals in them constitutes regulated activity, and can only be engaged in in the United Kingdom by a firm with the relevant regulatory permissions.

(3) *Establishing, operating, or winding up a collective investment.* Engaging in any of these activities constitutes regulated activity, and consequently it is an offence for an unauthorised person to engage in any of these activities in the United Kingdom. With arrangements which are deemed to be schemes, it is sometimes quite challenging to work out who the 'operator' of the scheme actually is.

10.28 The collective investment scheme issue is most likely to be relevant to type 2 and type 3 units, where the value of the unit is to some extent derived from some underlying asset or set of arrangements. In any arrangement where there are such assets—in other words, in any circumstances where the unit is not a 'pure' coin of the type 1 variety—there is a risk of recharacterisation as a collective investment scheme.

## 10.3 The Regulation of Deposits and Payment Systems

10.29 Once we have established that our virtual currency unit is not an investment, we next have to consider whether it constitutes money. The point here is that certain dealings with money (notably deposit-taking and the granting of consumer credit) are themselves regulated activities, and merely ascertaining that a particular unit is not an investment is by no means the end of the regulatory story.

10.30 The regulation of deposit-taking is the foundation stone of banking regulation. The way in which this is given effect in the United Kingdom is that 'deposits' are specified investments for the purpose of the RAO. However, a deposit is nothing more than an arrangement under which money is paid to a person on terms that it will subsequently be repaid—the formal definition is:

A sum of money paid on terms under which it will be repaid, with or without interest or premium, and either on demand or at a time or in circumstances agreed by or on behalf of the person making the payment and the person receiving it: and which are not referable to the provision of property or services or the giving of security.[34]

---

[32] Technically s. 238 applies only to authorised persons. However, an unauthorised person communicating a financial promotion of any kind will be caught by the identical prohibition contained in FSMA, s. 21.
[33] Identified in the Financial Services and Markets Act 2000 (Promotion of Collective Investment Schemes (Exemptions)) Order 2001, SI 2013/1388.
[34] Art. 5 RAO.

This definition is extremely wide, and covers anything from lending a friend his 10.31 taxi fare home through to borrowing money—in theory a loan by a lender to a borrower is a deposit placed by the lender with the borrower. In order to avoid these consequences, the scope of regulation is further narrowed, in that what requires regulation is not the taking of a deposit, but the taking of a deposit in the course of a 'deposit-taking business'. There are two limbs to this—one is the ordinary 'by way of business' test, but the other is a special test to determine whether a business is a deposit-taking business. This latter test is satisfied only where 'funds received by way of deposit are lent to others; or any other activity of the Issuer accepting the deposit is financed, wholly or to a material extent, out of the capital of or interest on money received by way of deposit'.[35] Consequently, a business which simply takes in and gives out money, but does not use that money at all whilst it has it, is not a deposit-taking business for this purpose. In addition to this, a conventional 'by way of business' test as described above is applied. Thus, it is not the taking of deposits which is regulated, but the taking of deposits 'by way of business'. Thus, the taking of deposits is only a regulated activity if the deposit-taker 'holds himself out as accepting deposits on a day to day basis'.[36]

In addition to regulating the taking of deposits, the UK regulatory system also restricts the provision of payment services. There are two aspects to this, the regulation of e-money and the regulation of payment services. 10.32

### 10.3.1 E-money

Electronic money means monetary value as represented by a claim on the issuer which is stored electronically, including magnetically; issued on receipt of funds; used for the purposes of making payment transactions;[37] and accepted as a means of payment by persons other than the issuer.[38] The concept is that e-money is basically a claim on an issuer stored in electronic form. The storage can be physical or electronic—thus, storage on a prepaid payment card, a personal computer, or a plastic card that uses magnetic stripe technology all fall within the definition. There is a general assumption that e-money schemes are card-based, but there is no legal basis for this—pure account-based schemes with no physical token involved at all are still capable of falling within the e-money definition.[39] 10.33

In order to be electronic money, a product must be capable of being used to make payments to persons other than the issuer. Consequently, gift vouchers and store discount cards are not e-money. 10.34

The definition of electronic money says that for a product to be electronic money, it must be issued on receipt of funds. Thus, any arrangement whereby the e-money 10.35

---

[35] Art. 5(1) RAO.
[36] Art. 2 of the Financial Services and Markets Act 2000 (Carrying on Regulated Activities by way of Business) Order 2001, SI 2001/1177.
[37] As defined in reg. 2 of the Payment Services Regulations.
[38] This definition is set out in the Electronic Money Directive.
[39] See recital 7 of the Electronic Money Directive.

issuer grants credit to the buyer (e.g. by agreeing to accept deferred payment for the e-money) is likely to involve the card issuer in acquiring a separate authorisation for consumer credit business. This is also why credit cards are excluded from the definition of electronic money.

10.36 The primary reason for the creation of the e-money regime was to police the border between e-money and bank deposit-taking. The point here is that an e-money arrangement looks very much like a deposit-taking arrangement, in that in both cases a customer gives money to a person on terms that when the customer incurs an obligation to a third party, the person discharges the obligation to the third party and debits the customer's balance. Legally, e-money institutions argued that they were not deposit-taking, but selling payment tokens to the customer, and that there was no element of deposit-taking involved in the transaction since it was a pure sale of choses in action. This argument was based on the definition of deposit-taking as money paid on terms *that it will be repaid*.[40] A necessary consequence of this was that e-money should not be capable of being redeemed for cash. This argument has been broadly accepted, and the current position as set out in recital 13 of the Electronic Money Directive is that the creation of electronic money does not constitute a deposit-taking activity 'in view of its specific character as an electronic surrogate for coins and banknotes, which is used for making payments, usually of limited amount and not as a means of saving'.[41]

10.37 An e-money institution may only engage in certain activities beyond its core e-money issuing function. These are:

(1) the provision of payment services;

(2) the provision of operational and closely related ancillary services, including ensuring the execution of payment transactions, foreign exchange services, safe-keeping activities, and the storage and processing of data; and

(3) the operation of payment systems, as defined at regulation 2(1); and

(4) business activities other than the issuance of electronic money.

10.38 Some firms do not create e-money, but do engage in the administration of electronic money schemes and the distribution of electronic money. Such firms do not fall within the scope of the e-money regulations, but may well fall within the scope of the payment services rules.

10.39 The basis of the regulation of e-money in the United Kingdom is the RAO. Article 9B of the RAO renders the issuance of e-money a regulated activity, such that banks must apply for a separate permission if they wish to engage in it,[42] and non-banks may not do so unless they have obtained authorisation as an e-money institution. By regulation 63 of the Electronic Money Regulations 2011,[43] the creation of e-money by any person other than a credit institution or an authorised e-money institution is

---

[40] Art. 5(2) RAO.  [41] Given effect in the United Kingdom in Art. 9AB RAO.
[42] For the difference between authorisation and permission generally, see Gleeson, *Regulatory Processes—Authorisation and Supervision* in Walker and Purves, *Financial Services Law* (4th edn, OUP 2018).
[43] SI 2011/99.

prohibited. It should be noted that the authorisation requirement applies solely to issuers—those who accept e-money in payment, or arrange for e-money to be paid, do not require authorisation under the e-money regulations. This does, however, raise the difficult question of whether or not those activities constitute payment services.

### 10.3.2 Payment services

10.40 Payment services in the United Kingdom are regulated under the Payment Services Regulations 2017,[44] which implement the Second Payment Services Directive.[45] This is a separate regulatory system which is not linked to the FSMA. Again, if a person who is not authorised under the regulations provides a payment service in the United Kingdom, they commit a criminal offence.[46]

10.41 The definition of 'payment services' is multivariant, and includes, amongst other things:

(1) services relating to the operation of payment accounts (e.g. cash deposits and withdrawals from current accounts and flexible savings accounts);
(2) execution of payment transactions;
(3) card issuing;
(4) merchant acquiring; and
(5) money remittance.

10.42 The rules are aimed at applying to a wide range of electronic payment media, including direct debit, debit card, credit card, standing order, mobile or fixed phone payments, and payments from other digital devices as well as money remittance services. They do not apply to cash-only transactions or paper cheque-based transfers. A separate regulatory regime is also created for payment intermediaries—that is, firms who provide holders of online payment accounts with payment initiation services and account information. Agents of payment institutions are also required to be registered with the FCA.

10.43 The regulations also apply in limited circumstances to non-payment service providers, if they provide a currency conversion service. Likewise, a non-payment services provider which imposes charges or offers reductions for the use of a given payment instrument is required to provide information on any such charges or reductions.[47]

10.44 The definition of payment services as set out in the Payment Regulations would catch almost all forms of financial activity, and there are therefore a series of detailed exemptions which reduce its scope. These are:

(1) payment transactions through commercial agents acting on behalf of either the payer or the payee;

---

[44] SI 2017/752.   [45] 2015/2366/EC.   [46] Reg. 138.   [47] Regs 58 and 141.

(2) cash-to-cash currency exchange activities (e.g. bureaux de change);

(3) payment transactions linked to securities asset servicing (e.g. dividend payments, share sales, or unit redemptions);

(4) services provided by technical service providers (which does not include account information services or payment initiation services);

(5) payment services based on instruments used within a limited network of service providers or for a very limited range of goods or services ('limited network exclusion'); and

(5) payment transactions for certain goods or services up to certain value limits, resulting from services provided by a provider of electronic communication networks or services ('electronic communications exclusion').

10.45 Also—and importantly—activities are only caught by these rules if they are entered into as a regular occupation or business activity. This means that a firm which provides payment services in a way which is purely ancillary to another business activity will not fall within the definition of payment services provider. Thus, people such as solicitors or brokers, who regularly handle cash payments on behalf of others, will not be required to register as payment service providers.

10.46 A payment institution may only hold money in an account in relation to payment transactions.[48] A 'payment transaction' for these purposes[49] is defined as 'an act, initiated by the payer or payee, of placing, transferring or withdrawing funds, irrespective of any underlying obligations between the payer and payee'. This means that a payment institution cannot hold funds for a payment service user unless accompanied by a payment order for onward transfer (whether to be executed immediately or on a future date). If funds are held indefinitely, the arrangement will constitute deposit-taking and not payment services.

10.47 The fact that a payment account operated by a payment institution can only be used for payment transactions distinguishes it from a deposit. A deposit can nevertheless be a form of payment account—a bank current account, for example, is both a deposit and a payment account.

10.48 Payment institutions have the benefit of the same exclusion from the deposit-taking rules as e-money institutions[50]—thus, money received by an authorised payment services firm in the course of the provision of payment services will not constitute a deposit. However, unlike e-money there is generally no argument that a payment services provider is merely selling a chose in action, and an unauthorised firm could well find itself in breach of both the deposit-taking and the payment services prohibitions.

10.49 Payment services for this purpose includes the creation of an electronic payment instrument, defined as any personalised device or set of procedures agreed between the service provider and the service user which are used by the service user to initiate a payment order. Examples of this include credit card and debit card issuers and

---

[48] Reg. 33 of the Payment Regulations.  
[49] Reg. 2 of the Payment Regulations.  
[50] Art. 9AB RAO.

electronic money institutions. Arrangements by way of telephone call with password, or online instruction or a mobile telephone application by which a payment order can be initiated could also amount to issuing payment instruments, depending on the service being provided.[51]

### 10.3.3 Lending and credit

In the United Kingdom there is no general regulation of lending per se—thus, a person can lend to another without requiring authorisation of any form, provided that the lending is not funded by deposits. However, there is a regulatory regime in place which covers the provision of credit to 'consumers'. A 'consumer' for this purpose is anyone acting outside the scope of their business or profession—thus, a commercial company can be a 'consumer' if the transaction it is entering into is not in connection with its business.[52] Perhaps surprisingly, credit in this regard is not limited to loans of money—the provision of any other form of financial accommodation falls within the scope of the provision of credit. Thus, in principle, selling property on terms that the buyer may defer the payment of the purchase price constitutes the provision of credit for this purpose.[53] Thus, if a virtual currency unit is created and delivered to a buyer before the buyer has paid, or if a buyer is asked to pay in advance of a unit being created, credit issue could potentially arise. It is also the case that a person lending virtual currency units would be in exactly the same regulatory position as a person lending fiat money.

10.50

## 10.4 The Regulation of Virtual Currency

### 10.4.1 Investment business

The FCA has confirmed that it does not regard 'pure' (type 1) virtual currency as an investment, and therefore does not consider it to be a security, a debenture, or a collective investment scheme,[54] although it is clear that futures, options, and CfDs which relate to virtual currency units are regulated investments. The FCA explicitly gives Bitcoin as an example of a virtual currency that it does not currently regulate.[55]

10.51

---

[51] See further the Court of Justice of the European Union decision in *T-Mobile Austria GmbH v Verein für Konsumenteninformation*, C-616/11.

[52] See Art. 60C(3) RAO. Note that this does not apply to loans of less than £25,000, which in principle are always regulated unless some other exemption applies.

[53] In practice, commercial agreements of this kind are almost all exempted by the provision that one-on-one agreements which have no or a low interest rate (loosely 1 per cent over bank base rate) are exempt agreements. However, a deferred purchase arrangement with a high or variable interest rate may well be a regulated credit agreement.

[54] Press Release 29 January 2018: https://www.fca.org.uk/news/press-releases/fca-warns-increased-risk-online-investment-fraud-investors-scamsmart and speech by Mary Starks, Director of Competition, FCA, on 26 April 2018: https://www.fca.org.uk/news/speeches/blockchain-considering-risks-consumers-and-competition.

[55] Interview with Andrew Bailey, Head of the FCA, 14 December 2017: http://www.bbc.co.uk/news/business-42360553.

10.52 The position becomes more nuanced where the virtual currency unit concerned has some sort of asset backing. If the unit is e-money issued by an authorised e-money institution (or constitutes the provision of a payment service), then it will not be a deposit. However, the issue of whether its structure constitutes a collective investment scheme needs to be addressed separately.

10.53 A collective investment scheme is, as set out above, defined as an arrangement by which investors share in the proceeds of an underlying investment. The sharing need not amount to complete economic ownership—any participation in the risks or rewards of an underlying asset is sufficient. There must be a real asset in existence, since a collective investment scheme is defined as an arrangement 'in respect of property', and if there is no identifiable property there can be no collective investment scheme. Thus, a public offering of a bond which offers investors a financial return calculated by reference to the performance of (say) the FTSE index is not a collective investment scheme, since there is no underlying property. However, if a bank purchased a portfolio of shares whose composition matched that of the FTSE, placed those shares in a designated account, and issued to investors bonds whose return was linked to the value of that specific account, then the result would be a collective investment scheme. The point which this illustrates is that an arrangement can be a collective investment scheme regardless of who owns the property of the scheme, and regardless of whether the investors have any specific claim on it. All that is necessary in this regard is the existence of identifiable property, and a return linked to that property.

10.54 In the context of virtual currency, this may be problematic. A classical ICO, whose terms are that the proceeds of the offering will be invested in something, and that that something will be used to support the value of the units, is likely to be a collective investment scheme, since the holders of the coins are in reality participating in the value of the underlying property. It is fair to point out at this stage that almost every possible legal device has by now been used in order to argue that the relevant assets are not really the property of the investors, and the fact that the investors derive comfort from the existence of those assets as regards the repayment of their investment is entirely fortuitous. Such arguments are generally unsuccessful—the courts will be assiduous to consider the impression which the investor was encouraged to form as to what was likely to happen when he made his investment, and will proceed to characterise the investment on that basis. The fact that the legal documentation may say something different is unlikely to be persuasive.[56]

10.55 Another important issue as regards virtual currency units which are characterised as investments is that the arranging of transactions in investments is itself a regulated activity. This activity has two broad branches; regulation of individual transactions and regulation of trading venues.

10.56 Arranging individual transactions in investments, referred to as broking, requires the broker to be authorised in the place where he is conducting the activity. If a particular virtual currency unit were to be characterised as an investment,

---

[56] *Asset Land v FCA* [2016] UKSC 17.

then arranging for a person to exchange such a unit either for money or for goods[57] would be a regulated transaction. Also, arranging for a person to issue or create an investment, or grant the rights of which the investment consists would be caught by the definition of selling,[58] so there is no defence based on the idea that the units are created and destroyed rather than bought or sold in the traditional sense.

10.57 The territoriality of brokerage rules varies—in the United Kingdom, for example, a transaction between two persons in the United Kingdom arranged by a broker who is entirely outside the United Kingdom is not subject to UK regulation,[59] whereas in some other countries the provision of broking services to persons in that country triggers a regulation requirement. Thus, persons in the United Kingdom using a website operated by a broker whose business was entirely outside the United Kingdom could legitimately deal in the unit without either they or the broker contravening UK law.

10.58 However, although UK law broadly does not prohibit unauthorised individuals from dealing in certain investment between themselves, this permission is limited. In particular, two unauthorised persons may not directly enter into futures, options, or contracts for difference (loosely 'derivatives') with each other—such business is prohibited unless it is either executed with or arranged by an unauthorised person. Consequently, although UK persons can deal in units for immediate delivery, if they deal either in units for delivery at a future date or in contracts that give them exposure to the value of the unit rather than immediate delivery of the unit itself, they are likely to be in breach of UK law.

10.59 The establishment of a venue on which transactions in investments can be effected, referred to as exchanges, also triggers a regulatory requirement. An exchange for this purpose is defined as a multilateral system which brings together multiple third-party buying and selling interests in investments in the system in a way that results in a contract in that investment.[60] Again, UK persons can deal on exchanges based entirely outside the United Kingdom without risk of illegality. However, if a UK person establishes a system within which people can buy and sell units, if the units are investments then that person will require authorisation to operate a trading venue, and will be in breach of UK law if he does not have such authorisation.

## 10.4.2 Deposit-taking

10.60 The purpose for which funds are transferred to the issuer of the virtual currency by buyers in connection with its issuance and how such funds may (or may not) be used by the issuer will determine the form of licence required by the issuer in the United Kingdom.

---

[57] The RAO is expressed to apply to 'buying and selling' of investments, but art 3 RAO defines buying as 'acquiring for valuable consideration' and selling as 'disposing of for valuable consideration'.
[58] Art. 3 RAO.   [59] See Art. 65 RAO.
[60] The regulatory system actually provides for three different types of trading venues—the different definitions can be found in MiFID 4(21) (regulated markets), 4(22) (multilateral trading facilities), and 4(23) (organised trading facilities).

10.61    Whether the receipt of funds by the issuer should be characterised as the regulated activity of 'accepting deposits' is determined by reference to whether there is a contractual obligation to repay money paid to the issuer.[61] It would be technically possible to create such an arrangement in respect of a virtual currency unit—for example, the issuer could enter into a unilateral contract or a deed of covenant promising to repay amounts advanced. However, absent such an arrangement, it is extremely unlikely that a virtual currency offering could constitute a deposit.

### 10.4.3  E-money

10.62    In general, a virtual currency unit seems to meet the criteria for e-money. It seems clear that it can be said to represent 'stored monetary value as represented by a claim on the [issuer]', and the whole point of a virtual currency unit is that it should be 'accepted by a person other than the Issuer'. Consequently, the primary consideration as to whether a virtual currency unit constitutes e-money depends on whether the funds are received 'for the purpose of making payment transactions'. In this regard, a 'payment transaction' means an act, initiated by the payer or on his behalf or by the payee, of placing, transferring, or withdrawing funds, irrespective of any underlying obligations between the payer and the payee.

### 10.4.4  Payment services

10.63    E-money is encompassed in the larger class of things created under the Payment Services Regulations of an 'electronic payment instrument'. Consequently, any electronic payment instrument created by a regulated payment services provider is excluded from the definition of deposit set out above. The position as regards unauthorised issuers is less clear.

## 10.5  The US Experience

10.64    The US authorities have (unsurprisingly) been forced to take a leading position in considering the regulation of virtual currency. It is therefore enlightening to consider the approaches which have been adopted as regards the issues considered above. Given the strong similarities between the legislative frameworks of the United States and the United Kingdom as regards financial regulation, it is not surprising that in some regards there are some clear lessons for the United Kingdom in the analysis accepted by the US courts.

---

[61] It is generally reckoned that the requirement for 'repayment' in art. 5 is only satisfied where there is a contractual obligation to repay—a trustee's obligation to return trust assets on the termination of a trust, for example, is not regarded as a repayment obligation in this sense.

## 10.5.1 The CFTC—futures and derivatives regulation

The United Kingdom regulates futures and derivatives as 'investments' under the common scheme of the FSMA. However, in the United States futures and commodities are regulated under a different regulatory jurisdiction by the Commodity Futures Trading Commission (CFTC). In the United States, it was the CFTC who took the lead on bitcoin trading regulation, establishing in 2015 that Bitcoin was a regulated currency in the United States.[62] This has recently been confirmed by the US courts in *CFTC v McDonnell*.[63] However, it is important to understand the scope of the CFTC's jurisdiction in order to see the relevance of this at English law. The basis of the CFTC's authority is its exclusive jurisdiction over 'accounts, agreements . . . and transactions involving swaps or contracts of sale of a commodity for future delivery'.[64] The definition of a 'commodity' for this purpose includes a long list of agricultural commodities, but ends 'and all other goods and articles . . . and all services, rights, and interests . . . in which contracts for future delivery are presently or in the future dealt in',[65] and it is established that 'commodities' for this purpose includes intangibles as well as goods.[66] This has two consequences. One is that derivatives and futures in commodities are regulated contracts, and must be effected on a regulated market. The other is that spot contracts are excluded from this requirement. However, the CFTC's anti-fraud jurisdiction extends to any dealing in a commodity which is the subject of regulated futures transactions. Thus, the CFTC does not have regulatory authority over spot transactions (defined as transactions that result in actual delivery within two days).[67] Thus, the CFTC can only regulate spot trades in a commodity if there is evidence of manipulation or fraud. The CFTC's interventions in this area have been founded on allegations of fraud in the spot trading of virtual currency units, which was the basis of the action in *McDonnell*.

10.65

The equivalent jurisdiction in the United Kingdom is less broad. The United Kingdom regulates futures and derivatives in much the same way as the United States, in that any contract for future delivery is a regulated investment contract unless it is entered into for commercial purposes. However, instead of the very broad US definition of commodities, the United Kingdom has a closed list derived from MiFID which does not include virtual currency.[68] This is backed up by a general provision relating to futures on 'property of any description',[69] but this does not apply to any contract entered into for a commercial purpose and settled by physical delivery of the underlying asset. Thus, a contract for the future sale of virtual

10.66

---

[62] *In the Matter of: Coinflip, Inc., d/b/a Derivabit, and Francisco Riordan*, CFTC Docket No. 15-29 (Sep 17, 2015). The CFTC has produced an extremely useful 'Primer' summarising the structure of cryptocurrencies, the regulatory issues posed, and their views on legal characterisation—see *A CFTC Primer on virtual currencies*, LabCFTC, October 17 2017, available on the CFTC website.

[63] *Commodity Futures Trading Commission v Patrick K. Mcdonnell, and Cabbagetech, Corp. D/B/A Coin Drop Markets*, No. 18-CV-361, 2018 WL 1175156, at *12 (E.D.N.Y. Mar. 6, 2018).

[64] Commodity Exchange Act 1936 (CEA), s. 2.   [65] CEA, s. 1(a)(9).

[66] See, e.g., *In re Barclays PLC*, CFTC No. 15-25 (May 20, 2015) (regulating fixed interest rate benchmarks as commodities).

[67] CEA, s. 2(c)(2)(C)(i)(II)(bb)(AA).   [68] Art. 84(1A)(1B) RAO.

[69] Art. 84(1) RAO.

currency by persons who intended the contract to result in the physical delivery of the virtual currency would be outside the scope of this regime.[70] Equally, the UK equivalent of the US anti-fraud jurisdiction, the market abuse regime is derived from the European Market Abuse Regulation[71] whose scope is confined to contracts actually traded in an EU-regulated market and to products which underlie such contracts. Thus, for as long as there is no regulated contract traded on an EU regulated market relating to a particular virtual currency unit, there is no regulatory jurisdiction to intervene in transactions in the underlying product on grounds of market abuse.

### 10.5.2 The SEC—securities regulation

10.67 The issues set out here are usefully illustrated by the enforcement action taken by the US SEC in respect of an organisation called 'the DAO'. The facts are set out in the SEC report:[72]

> The DAO is one example of a Decentralized Autonomous Organization, which is a term used to describe a 'virtual' organization embodied in computer code and executed on a distributed ledger or blockchain. The DAO was created by Slock.it and Slock.it's co-founders, with the objective of operating as a for-profit entity that would create and hold a corpus of assets through the sale of DAO Tokens to investors, which assets would then be used to fund 'projects.' The holders of DAO Tokens stood to share in the anticipated earnings from these projects as a return on their investment in DAO Tokens. In addition, DAO Token holders could monetize their investments in DAO Tokens by re-selling DAO Tokens on a number of web-based platforms ('Platforms') that supported secondary trading in the DAO Tokens.

10.68 The DAO had raised $150m through the sale of tokens in exchange for Ether (ETH) virtual currency. The idea was that projects would be proposed to the holders of tokens (through smart contracts held in the etherium blockchain[73]), and the holders would 'vote' through a purely electronic process on whether or not the funds so collected should be invested in any particular project. The returns to investors in the tokens would be in the form of 'rewards'. Tokens were traded on a number of electronic trading platforms, where there was substantial trading volume.

10.69 The SEC concluded, unsurprisingly, that the tokens were securities and therefore fell within the scope of the US securities laws. The basis for this conclusion was that the tokens were 'investment contracts'.[74] The concept of 'investment contract' in US law is broadly similar to the concept of 'collective investment scheme' in UK law—a US investment contract is an investment of money in a common enterprise with a reasonable expectation of profits to be derived from the entrepreneurial or managerial efforts

---

[70] Art. 84(5) RAO.   [71] 569/2014/EU.
[72] Report of Investigation Pursuant to Section 21(a) of the Securities Exchange Act of 1934: The DAO Release No. 81207/July 25, 2017.
[73] The express purpose of the DAO was 'To blaze a new path in business for the betterment of its members, existing simultaneously nowhere and everywhere and operating solely with the steadfast iron will of unstoppable code' (SEC report ibid. at 5)—no element of new age cyber mysticism was missing from the project.
[74] Under s. 2(a)(1) of the Securities Act and s. 3(a)(10) of the Securities Exchange Act.

of others.⁷⁵ The definition of an 'investment contract' was set out by the Supreme Court in *SEC v Howey*.⁷⁶ That test requires an investment of money in a common enterprise with an expectation of profit derived from the efforts of others. In *Howey*, a hotel operator sold interests in a citrus grove to its guests and claimed it was selling real estate, not securities. The deal offered to investors also included a service contract to cultivate and harvest the oranges. The purchasers could have arranged to service the grove themselves but, in fact, most were passive, relying on the efforts of Howey-in-the-Hills Service, Inc. for a return. In articulating the test for an investment contract, the Supreme Court stressed: 'Form [is] disregarded for substance and the emphasis [is] placed upon economic reality.'⁷⁷ So, the purported real estate purchase was found to be an investment contract—an investment in orange groves was in these circumstances an investment in a security. In the United States, as in the United Kingdom, an investment contract is regarded as an investment, and its offering is restricted by financial regulatory laws. Importantly, the SEC's approach was that the analysis should be at the level of the economic substance of the project and not its legal or technological form—since the marketing materials in relation to the tokens had promised investors returns based on the profits of the investments to be made, the fact that there was no formal promise of such returns could be disregarded. It was on this basis that in the case of the DAO the fact that token holders had voting rights in respect of proposed investments was not sufficient to negative the fact that there was a separate management determining the investment of the funds collected.⁷⁸

10.70 The same issue arose as regards the operators of the trading platforms. Under US law an organisation, association, or group of persons shall be considered to constitute, maintain, or provide 'a marketplace or facilities for bringing together purchasers and sellers of securities or for otherwise performing with respect to securities the functions commonly performed by a stock exchange', if such organisation, association, or group of persons: (a) brings together the orders for securities of multiple buyers and sellers; and (b) uses established, non-discretionary methods (whether by providing a trading facility or by setting rules) under which such orders interact with each other, and the buyers and sellers entering such orders agree to the terms of the trade.⁷⁹ The SEC concluded that the platforms had come within the scope of this definition by admitting the tokens to trading, and should therefore have been registered as securities exchanges.

10.71 The close correspondence of US and UK securities laws in this particular area means that it is hard to conclude that either of these issues would have been decided differently if the same facts had arisen in the United Kingdom.

---

⁷⁵ See *SEC v Edwards*, 540 US 389, 393 (2004); *SEC v W.J. Howey Co.*, 328 US 293, 301 (1946); see also *United Housing Fund, Inc. v Forman*, 421 US 837, 852–53 (1975) (the 'touchstone' of an investment contract 'is the presence of an investment in a common venture premised on a reasonable expectation of profits to be derived from the entrepreneurial or managerial efforts of others').
⁷⁶ *SEC v W.J. Howey Co.*, 328 US 293, 301 (1946). ⁷⁷ Ibid. at 298.
⁷⁸ Subsequent to this report the SEC has made cease-and-desist orders in relation to at least one proposed ICO offering on the basis that it was in breach of the Securities Act—see *In the matter of Munchee*, Securities Act Of 1933 Release No. 10445/December 11, 2017.
⁷⁹ Securities Exchange Act Rule 3b-16(a), which provides a functional test to assess whether a trading system meets the definition of exchange under s. 3(a)(1) of the Act.

# Index

abstraction 7.28, 7.46–7.48
appointment of receivers 9.15
Argentine Peso 1.49
Aristotle 1.06
Arrow-Debreu models 3.08
asset backing 10.52
  asset-backed tokens 8.04
attributes of money 7.26–7.28
  *see also* legal character of money

Babylonic economic activity 3.02
bank cheques *see* cheques
Bank of England 1.22, 1.26, 1.34–1.36,
  4.30, 4.38–4.39, 5.15–5.16, 7.36, 8.09
bank money
  central 4.41
    role of 6.10–6.11
  as imaginary property 1.30–1.33
  social perception of 1.27–1.29
  *see also* central banks
bank money-backed tokens 8.04
banking school 5.17
banknotes 1.27, 1.47, 2.32, 5.08,
  7.51–7.52, 7.72, 9.107
  bank cheques and 5.11–5.19
  central 4.38–4.40
  cheques vs 5.18–5.19
  English 4.30
  as PPIs 5.13–5.14
  private 4.36
    backed by assets 4.37
    limitation of the power to create 5.15–5.17
  rarity of 7.39, 7.42–7.43
bargaining power 7.24
barter 1.15, 2.07–2.08, 7.85, 7.87,
  7.93–7.94, 9.59–9.60
bills 5.07–5.09
  of exchange:
    payment by 6.34–6.36
bimetallism 2.40
bitcoin 1.11, 1.28, 1.32, 8.04,
  9.24, 10.01, 10.51, 10.65
blood-money 2.09
Bolognese bushel 7.56
*bona fide* purchase 9.63
bonds
  government 4.31–4.33
  international markets 9.77
book credit
  private payment through 5.02–5.09
  shortcomings of 5.03
book entry 3.25

bottomry 3.49
Brazilian cruzeiros 9.99
breach of contract 9.90
bright-line test 1.51
British currency 7.79
British pounds 8.02
brokerage rules 10.57
*bureaux de change* 10.44
business
  by way of business, definition of 10.12, 10.31
  credit and 3.14–3.15
  investment 10.51–10.59

cartalist theory 2.02, 2.04, 2.31, 2.33–2.34
*Case de Mixt Moneys* 7.09, 7.58–7.60
  *see also* tender
cash payment 1.17, 7.72
central banks 4.41
  deposits 4.41
  digital currencies (CBDCs) 8.09–8.11
    control mechanism for commercial
      bank money 8.21–8.25
    designs for 8.12–8.16
    indirect 8.15
    private virtual currency and 8.38–8.39
    replacement for commercial bank
      money 8.17–8.20
  role of 6.10–6.11
  virtual currencies 8.05–8.39
central counterparty (CCP) 3.21, 3.24
centralised banking model 8.26–8.32
centralised money model
  economic consequences of 8.33–8.37
CHAPS payment 6.49
characterisation of money
  'case-by-case' 7.17–7.20
  different, permissibility of 7.15–7.16
  as 'money' 7.03–7.05
  'once-and-for-all' 7.17–7.20
    impracticality of 7.21–7.22
characteristics of money 1.01–1.02,
  7.10–7.11
charge, components of 9.50
charterer of vessels 7.74
chattels 7.08
cheques 0.02, 1.21, 6.16, 9.08
  payment by 6.34–6.36
  private banknotes and 5.11–5.19
Chicago Plan 8.07
China, imperial 7.54
Cicero 6.25
circulation banks 5.12

# 218  Index

claim for the payment of money,
 definition of 9.55
classification of money 1.13
 *see also* legal classification
clearing houses
 as a substitute for money 3.20–3.22
Clearstream 9.77
clipped coins 2.31
coinage 2.13, 2.23–2.28
 free 2.28
 metal 1.41, 2.24
 pound 1.17, 1.34–1.36
 valuation of 2.39
 weight vs tale 2.29–2.31
collective investment schemes
 characteristics 10.22
 definition 10.13, 10.22, 10.24, 10.27, 10.53
 regulation 10.21–10.28
  arranging transactions in units 10.27
  dealing in units 10.27
  establishment 10.27
  offering of units 10.27
  operation 10.27
  winding-up 10.27
 *see also* financial regulation
colonisation 2.23
commercial bank money 0.10, 1.28
 CBDC as a control mechanism for 8.21–8.25
 CBDC as a replacement for 8.17–8.20
 commercial bank credit money:
  creation of 6.58–6.59
  payment in 6.60–6.61
 as private money 6.54–6.64
 Private Payment Instruments 6.01–6.64
 as a store of value 4.09–4.10
 virtual currency as 6.62–6.63
commercial exchange 2.10
commercial law 7.38
Commodity Futures Trading
 Commission (CFTC) 10.65
 futures and derivatives
  regulation 10.65–10.66
commodity of money 1.34–1.39
 commodity money, role of 6.08
 consequences of treatment 9.90–9.91
 definition of 'commodity' 10.65
 sovereign money 1.36–1.39
common law 9.39–9.43
company security interest 9.55
confidential information 1.14
consumer, definition of 10.50
contactless cards 1.22
contract for differences (CfD) 10.20
Copernicus, Nicolaus 4.28, 4.51
Court decisions 0.05, 1.51–1.52
cowrie shells 2.25
credit 2.21, 3.01–3.49
 business and 3.14–3.15
 claim 4.34–4.35

clearing houses as a substitute for
  money 3.20–3.22
 credit risk transfer 3.47–3.48
 discharge of credit obligations 3.30–3.49
 fluctuation in supply of 1.38–1.39
 girobank(s) as substitutes for
  money 3.23–3.24
 lending and 10.50
 mercantile agency as a substitute
  for money 3.25
 money:
  exogenous and endogenous 6.13
  role of 6.09
  vs 3.08–3.09, 3.16–3.19
 open vs closed systems 3.26–3.27
 origins of 3.02–3.07
 pig/egg paradigm 3.32–3.36
 risk 1.42–1.43, 1.46,
  pooling 3.49
 risk transfer 3.47–3.49
  as the foundation for lending banking 3.48
  money as the vehicle for 3.47
 study of 3.10–3.13
 usefulness of payment to the creditor 3.41–3.45
 usefulness of payment to the debtor 3.37–3.40
currency
 area 4.21
 crypto- 9.56
 cyber- 1.11
 historical units of account 1.02
 in hyperinflating economies 0.06
 legal character of money 7.28–7.45
 negotiability and 7.36–7.39
 school 5.17
 theory 7.32
 tokens 8.04
 virtual currency as 7.40–7.45
 *see also* virtual currency

damages 1.53, 9.108
Davies, Glyn 5.05
debasement 2.41–2.44
 *see also* multiple currencies
debt 0.07, 1.38, 1.53, 2.15
 claims 7.01
 securities 10.14–10.16
  definition of 10.14
 *see also* discharge of debts; financial regulation
Decentralized Autonomous
 Organization (DAO) 10.67
definitions of money 0.06, 0.11
 legal 7.02–7.25
 as a unit of account 1.03
 *see also* characterisation of money
deposit-taking 1.13, 8.33
 business 10.31
 consequences of 6.30–6.33
 creation of PPIs by deposit-takers 6.29
 ownership of deposited money 6.37–6.44

*Index* 219

private money and 6.27–6.44
virtual currency 10.60–10.61
*see also* Private Payment Instruments
**deposits**
  accepting 10.61
  banks 5.12, 5.15
  definition 10.30–10.31
**development of money** 1.08
**devolution of power** 2.45
**digital currencies**
  payment instruments vs 8.10–8.11
  *see also* virtual currency
**discharge of credit obligations** 3.30–3.49
**discharge of debts** 1.44–1.48, 2.31, 3.14
  legal tender 7.65–7.66
  set-off and 9.41–9.42
  unilateral:
    by the creditor 7.68
    by the debtor 7.67
  *see also* debt
**distributed ledger technology** 1.33, 7.42–7.44, 8.02, 9.08–9.11
**dividend payments** 10.44
**double coincidence of wants** 3.31
**Dutch currency** 9.90

**e-money** 6.15, 10.33–10.39, 10.62
  definition 10.35
  institutions 10.37–10.38
  regulation of 10.39
  *see also* virtual currency
**earmark theory** 7.51
**economy-wide access** 8.14
**Edward II, King of England** 7.58
**Einzig, Paul** 2.07–2.08, 2.10
**electronic communication** 9.47
  exclusion 10.44
**electronic payment instruments** 10.63
**electronic presentation of instruments** 9.48
**electronic transfer** 7.92
  private payment and 6.49
**endogenous money** 6.57
**English coinage** 5.10
  currency crisis (1695–1698) 5.15
  farthing 2.40
  guinea 2.38
  pound coins 1.17, 1.34–1.36
  shilling 0.06, 1.02, 2.33, 3.42, 4.35, 5.10, 7.43
**equity** 9.44–9.45
**estoppel** 6.41
**ether (ETH) virtual currency** 10.68
**etherium**
  blockchain 10.68
  tokens 8.04
**euro** 7.09, 8.08
  area 2.02, 2.45
**Euroclear** 9.77
**European Central Bank (ECB)** 8.08, 9.56

**European Community Trademark** 9.80
**European Economic Area (EEA)** 9.81
**existence of money** 1.16–1.33; *see also* bank money; intangible money; payment instruments; traditional money

**Faster Payments system** 6.56
**Fedcoin** 8.08
**fiat money** 6.06, 9.45, 10.50
**Filecoin** 8.04
**Financial Conduct Authority (FCA)** 6.64
**financial institutions**
  access to CBDCs 8.13
  intermediated access 8.15
**financial regulation** 0.11, 10.01–10.71
  CFTC-futures and derivatives regulation 10.65–10.66
  collective investment scheme regulation 10.21–10.28
  financial regulatory structures 10.02–10.09
  investments 10.10–10.28
    debt securities 10.14–10.16
    public offering 10.17–10.18
    receipts and units with underlyings 10.19–10.20
  payment systems 10.29–10.50
    e-money 10.33–10.39
    lending and credit 10.50
    payment services 10.40–10.49
  regulatory frameworks 10.01
  SEC securities regulation 10.67–10.71
  US experience 10.64–10.71
  virtual currency 10.13, 10.51–10.63
    deposit-taking 10.60–10.61
    e-money 10.62
    investment business 10.51–10.59
    payment services 10.63
    regulatory structures 10.02–10.09
    securities regulation 10.13
**Fisher, Irving** 8.07
**Florentine gold florin** 2.38
**food as money** *see* staple commodities
**foreign currencies**
  as PPIs 5.10
  recognition of non-UK currency as money 9.92–9.96
  virtual currency 9.88–9.89
**Fox, David** 7.58
**free banking era (US)** 4.37
**free coinage** 2.28
**freedom of the courts** 7.12–7.14
**French currency**
  ecus 9.88
  francs 7.07
**full-bodied coins** 2.37, 4.29
**function of money** 1.03, 2.15–2.19
  alternatives to state money 2.17–2.19
  scorekeeping function 2.16
**futures** 10.19

# Index

game theory 1.08, 3.49
General Purchasing Power 1.03
German monetary law 9.23
   Reichsmark 1.49, 7.64
   Rentenbankscheine 7.64
   Rentenmark 7.63
Ghanaian cedis 9.101–9.102
girobank(s)
   as substitutes for money 3.23–3.24
gold 1.40, 4.05, 4.27, 5.17, 6.58
   standard era 1.02, 4.09, 4.28, 6.59
goldsmith's notes 5.13, 5.15
Goodhart, Charles 2.02, 8.22, 8.24
goodwill 1.14
Gosbank 8.26–8.32
governmentalist school 4.11
Graeco-Roman world 3.11, 4.24–4.25
   *see also* Roman law
Great Depression 8.07
Greek debt crisis 2.45
Gresham's law 2.39, 3.05, 4.16–4.18, 8.39
   *see also* metallism
gross domestic product (GDP) 3.01

Henry VIII, King of England 7.58
Hesiod 6.27
historical units of account 1.02
history of money 2.46
Holy Roman Empire 4.21
Homeric period 4.05
Hong Kong dollar 7.11
Hume, David 1.06
hyperinflating economies 0.06, 7.63

ICO offerings 10.01
'idea' of money 1.10
immobilisation structure 8.04
inflation 2.41–2.44
   *see also* multiple currencies
information sensitivity 4.47–4.52
   *see also* market risk
Innes, Mitchell 3.03, 3.37, 7.54
institutional theory of money 6.10
institutions *see* sociology of money
instrument
   definition of 10.15
   of payment 10.18
intangibles
   intangible money as a 'thing' 1.23–1.26
   legal obligations 9.01
   as things 1.19
intellectual property 9.80
international trade 4.24–4.25
   *see also* metallism
investment
   business 10.51–10.59
   contract, definition of 10.69
IOUs 2.23–2.24, 2.27, 2.45, 4.36
   transferable 5.04

Irish currency 2.33
   pound 7.58
irregular deposits 6.54
Italian lire 9.103
*ius commune* 7.57

Jackson, Andrew, President of the US 5.09

Keynes, J. M. 1.03, 2.31, 4.04, 4.29, 4.42–4.43, 5.17, 6.05, 6.21,
Kings Lynn
   medieval era 3.03–3.04
Knapp, G. F. 7.08, 7.64

labour bank 6.14
language and linguistics 1.06–1.07
leases and licencing 7.23
legal certainty 7.25
legal character of money 7.01–7.97
   abstraction 7.46–7.48
   attributes of money 7.26–7.28
   breach of an obligation to pay money 7.01
   currency 7.29–7.45
   debt claims 7.01
   legal definitions of money 7.02–7.25
   tender 7.53–7.97
   untraceability through mixtures 7.49–7.52
   virtual currency 7.01
   *see also* tender
legal classification
   hard and soft boundaries 7.23–7.25
legal definitions of money 7.02–7.25
   *see also* definitions of money
legal doctrine of money 0.09
legal tender *see* tender
legislative policy 1.54
'lemons' problem 2.39, 4.54
lending
   banking 3.48
   credit and 10.50
Lewis, David 1.07
*lex mercatoria* 7.14
*lex monetae* doctrine 9.22–9.23
*Lex Paulus* 2.38
limited network exclusion 10.44
*littera* payment 6.25
Locke, John 4.51

Mann, F. A. 7.08, 7.10
market risk 4.42–4.58
   information sensitivity 4.47–4.52
   near-money 4.55
   unit of value as risk free 4.53–4.54
   virtual currency 4.56–4.58
Marxism 3.38
McLeod, H. D. 3.12
medieval societies 3.37

# Index

medium of exchange
  status of money as a  1.03, 7.64
**Mengerian theory**  1.03, 2.02, 2.04, 2.06
mercantile agency
  merchants  0.08
  as a substitute for money  3.25
**mere right to transfer**
  ownerships vs  9.12–9.16
**metallism**  2.02, 2.25–2.26, 4.11, 4.13–4.29
  Gresham's law  4.16–4.18
  international trade  4.24–4.25
  metal content:
    of coins  4.26–4.27
    as a constraint on money creation  4.28–4.29
  metallic coin  4.19–4.23
  *see also* value of money
**misappropriation of money**  1.13
**monetary base**  6.07, 6.13
**monetary neutrality doctrine**  2.41
**monetary sovereign**  2.45
**money-backed tokens**  8.04
  non-bank  8.04
**moneylenders**  3.47
**moneyness**  0.06–0.07, 0.11, 1.01, 1.04
**mortgage, definition of**  9.50
**Muldrew, Craig**  3.03, 3.35
**multiple currencies**  2.38–2.44
  debasement  2.41–2.44
  inflation  2.41–2.44
  rationale for  2.40
  valuing coins  2.39

**Napoleonic wars**  4.28
**National Equitable Labour Exchange**  7.11
**near-money**
  riskiness of  4.55
**negotiability**
  currency and  7.36–7.39
**negotiable instruments**  0.05
*nemo dat quod non habet*  7.30–7.31, 7.82, 7.94
**Newton, Isaac**  4.51
**nominalism**  7.61
  virtual currency and  9.21–9.29
**non-bank financial institutions (NBFIs)**  8.13–8.15, 8.35–8.38
**non-money**  7.49
**Northern Irish banks**  4.37
**Northian institutions**  1.08–1.10
**'not-money'**  1.14, 1.47, 1.50–1.51
  money vs  0.02, 0.12
**notes**  5.07–5.09

**Offa, King of England (757–96)**  2.13, 2.36–2.37
**options**  10.19
**Ovid**  6.25
**Owen, Robert**  6.14, 7.11
**ownership**
  interest  9.16
  mere right to transfer vs  9.12–9.16
  transfer of  9.17–9.20

*pari passu*  6.51
**paymasters**  6.03–6.04, 6.26
**payment**  0.11
  definition of  7.84
  mechanism for  7.72–7.73
  moment of  2.17
  services  10.40–10.49, 10.62
    definition  10.41, 10.44
  transaction, definition of  10.46, 10.62
**payment by delivery of money'**  7.85
**payment instruments**
  definition of  10.49
  digital currencies vs  8.10–8.11
  money and  1.20–1.22
  *see also* Private Payment Instruments
  personal restitution  9.67–9.69
  physical tokens  5.05–5.06
  pig/egg paradigm  3.32–3.36
  Polo, Marco , 7.63
  prestige articles  4.05
  price, determination of  7.89
  primitive money  2.07
  prisoners-of-war  7.21
  private banking system  2.18
**private credit money**
  rationale for  6.21–6.26
**private intention**
  as determinative of money status  7.12–7.14
**private law**  1.52
**private money**  1.28–1.29, 5.01
  commercial bank credit money as  6.54–6.64
  credit money, rationale for  6.21–6.26
  deposit-taking and  6.27–6.43
  *see also* Private Payment Instruments
**private payment**
  bills and notes  5.07–5.09
  book credit  5.02–5.09
  electronic transfer and  6.55
  instruments  6.14–6.16
  physical tokens  5.05–5.06
  private monies  5.01
  private payment instruments  5.04
  transfers  6.49–6.50
  in virtual currency  6.51–6.53
**Private Payment Instruments (PPIs)**  5.01–5.20
  book credit  5.02–5.09
    bills and notes  5.07–5.09
    physical tokens  5.05–5.06
    private monies  5.01
    private payment instruments  5.04
    shortcomings of  5.03
  commercial bank money and  6.01–6.64
  deposit-taking  6.27–6.43
  electronic transfer  6.55
  foreign currencies as  5.10
  negotiability of PPIs  6.45–6.53

# Index

Private Payment Instruments (PPIs) (*cont.*):
  payment in a modern economy 6.02–6.21
    central bank money, role of 6.10–6.11
    commodity money, role of 6.08
    credit money, role of 6.09
    exogenous and endogenous credit money 6.13
    private payment instruments 6.14–6.15
    sovereign-issued money 6.01
    virtual money 6.17–6.21
  private banknotes and bank cheques 5.11–5.19
    banknotes vs cheques 5.18–5.19
    banknotes as PPIs 5.13–5.14
    limitation of the power to create 5.15–5.17
  private credit money 6.20–6.25
  private money 6.27–6.43
  private payment 6.49
    transfers 6.49–6.50
    in virtual currency 6.51–6.53
    transfer of 6.45–6.53
  virtual currency issued by banks 5.20
  *see also* commercial bank money; deposit-taking
Proctor, Charles 7.10
promissory notes 9.46–9.47
  non-negotiable 9.74
property
  bank money as imaginary 1.30–1.33
  entry in a distributed ledger 9.08–9.11
  intangible 1.20
  rights 1.19
  transfer of 1.19, 1.31
  virtual currency as 9.04–9.20
    legal factors 9.02–9.03
proprietary restitution 9.63–9.66
public law 1.52
public offering 10.17–10.18
public policy 1.12

real bills doctrine 8.28
Real Time Gross Settlement System (RTGS) 8.10, 8.13
receipts 10.19–10.20
recovery, doctrines of 1.29
redelivery obligation 9.57
regulated activity 10.55
  definition of 10.10
restitutionary claim 9.63
right of publicity 9.06
rights *ad rem/in rem* 9.10
risk
  market 4.42–4.58
  pooling 3.49
  transfer 3.49
  *see also* market risk
Roman law 2.36, 6.54, 6.62
  *coactores argentarii* 3.25

contract *fenus nauticum* 3.49
*datio in solutum necessaria* 7.54
deposit-takers (*argentarii*) 6.28
royal proclamation 7.58

'sale', definition of 7.86–7.87
Sale of Goods legislation 7.94
*sceat* (*sceattas*) 2.12
Schumpeter, Joseph 3.11–3.12
Scottish Banks 1.25, 4.37
search-friction approach 3.08–3.09
Securities and Exchange Commission (SEC)
  regulation 8.08, 10.67–10.71
selling, definition of 10.56
set-off 6.35
  rules of 9.35–9.38
  solvent 9.35
  solvent non-contractual 9.36
  Statutes of 9.37
  statutory 9.38
  virtual currency and 9.30–9.45
share sales 10.44
slavery 3.38–3.39
Smith, Adam 4.54, 7.54
social perception
  of bank money 1.27–1.29
sociology of money 1.05–1.17
  formation of new institutions 1.12–1.17
  origins of the money institution 1.09–1.11
  social behaviour 0.06
  social institution of money 0.07, 0.11, 1.08
  social practice 0.08, 0.10
South African gold mines 5.17
sovereign authority 2.02–2.37
  origins of money 2.07–2.14
sovereign money
  commodity of money 1.36–1.39
  sovereign currency as 'money' 7.06–7.11
  sovereign-issued money 6.01
sovereign values 2.33–2.37
  real values vs 2.33–2.37
Soviet Union
  economic architecture 8.26–8.32
specified activities, definition of 10.10
specified instruments 10.10–10.11
  definition of 10.10
staple commodities 7.54
State money
  alternatives to 2.17–2.19
State sovereignty 2.20–2.37
  banknotes 2.32
  coins 2.23–2.28
  sovereign values vs real values 2.33–2.37
  weight vs tale 2.29–2.31
state theory of money 7.64
status of money
  as a medium of exchange 1.03

private intention as determinative
of 7.12–7.14
stock exchange 10.70
stolen goods 7.33, 9.62, 9.64
store of value 4.42–4.43
commercial bank money as a 4.09–4.10
concept of 1.04
substitute for money
clearing houses as a 3.20–3.22
girobank(s) as 3.23–3.24
mercantile agency as a 3.25
suing for damages instead of a price 7.95
supply of services 7.97
Swiss Vollgeld 8.08

tale *see* coins
taxation 2.15, 2.20
technical service providers 10.44
tender 0.07, 1.49, 7.28–7.29, 7.53–7.97
*Case de Mixt Moneys* 7.58–7.60
compulsory 7.54–7.56
contractual provisions regarding
payment 7.69–7.71
determination of the value of the
thing tendered 7.59–7.57
discharge of debts and 7.65–7.66
unilateral discharge of debt by
the creditor 7.68
unilateral discharge of debt by
the debtor 7.67
divergence of common and civil law 7.61
legal 7.53, 7.54–7.55
legislation, practical significance
of 7.62–7.64
of money and goods 7.76–7.77
payment 7.84–7.85
methods of 7.91–7.92
two elements of 7.88–7.90
in virtual currency 7.93–7.97
relevance of tender 7.74–7.75
'sale', definition of 7.86–7.87
through payment mechanism
provisions 7.72–7.73
of virtual currency 7.78–7.83
Tether and Ripple 10.01
theft *see* stolen goods
'thing-ness' *see* intangibles
thing value 4.02–4.03
*see also* value of money
Thirty Years War (1618–1648) 2.31
time-of-breach rules 9.91–9.92
tokens
asset-backed 8.04
bank money-backed 8.04
currency 8.04
investment 8.04
money-backed 8.04
non-bank money-backed 8.04
utility 8.04

warrant 8.04
tort 9.90
for conversion or trespass 9.64–9.65
traditional money 1.17–1.18
transfer of money 1.31
Tucker, George 5.12

UK Civil Procedure Rules (CPR) 7.77, 7.83
unilateral discharge of debt *see* discharge
of debt
United States monetary system
banking system 3.14
central bank 5.09
dollars 5.09, 7.94
federal currency 5.15
Federal Reserve 8.08
financial regulation 10.64–10.71
trade dollars 7.54
*see also* financial regulation; Securities and
Exchange Commission (SEC)
units
of account 1.02–1.04
defining money as a 1.03
historical 1.02
virtual currency as 9.87–9.112
immediate delivery of 10.58
redemptions 10.44
transactions in units 10.27
with underlyings 10.19–10.20
of value as 'risk free' 4.53–4.54
unjust enrichment 1.54, 9.63
untraceability
through mixtures 7.28, 7.49–7.52
USC model 8.04
usefulness of payment
to the creditor 3.41–3.45
to the debtor 3.37–3.40
utility tokens 8.04

value added tax (VAT) 7.97
value of money 1.40–1.54, 4.01–4.58
characterisation as money 1.53–1.54
coins 2.39
commercial bank money 4.09–4.10
Court decisions 1.51–1.52
government 4.30
central bank money 4.41
central banknotes 4.38–4.40
government bonds 4.31–4.33
money as a credit claim 4.34–4.35
private banknotes 4.36–4.37
intertemporal reallocation of value
4.04–4.08
law and monetary value 1.49
market risk and money 4.42–4.58
metallism 4.13–4.29
real value 2.33–2.37
reasons for 1.42–1.48
society's role in the 1.50

**value of money** (*cont.*):
  sovereign value  2.33–2.37
  theories of  4.11–4.12
  thing value and money value  4.02–4.03
  *see also* market risk; metallism
**vindication approach to recovery
  of money**  9.62–9.63
**virtual currency**  0.01, 0.08, 0.11, 2.01,
  4.01, 8.01–8.39, 9.01–9.112
  central bank virtual currencies  8.05–8.39
    CBDC  8.17–8.25
    centralised banking model  8.26–8.32
    commercial bank money  8.17–8.25
    designs for  8.12–8.16
    economic consequences of  8.33–8.37
    payment instruments  8.10–8.11
  classes of  8.01
  as commercial bank money  6.62–6.63
  as currency  7.40–7.45
  date of breach  7.81
  financial regulatory structures and  10.02–10.09
  foreign money and  9.88–9.89, 9.92–9.96
  function of  2.19
  issued by banks  5.20
  and the law  9.01–9.45
    intangible legal obligations  9.01
    property  9.02–9.03
  legal character of money  7.01
  legal tender  7.78–7.83
    virtual payment  7.93–7.97
  nominalism and  9.21–9.29
  obligations  9.109–9.112
  private  8.02–8.04, 8.38–8.39
    payment in  6.51–6.53
  as property  9.04–9.20
  'pure'  10.16, 10.51
  recovery of misappropriated  9.62–9.69
    personal restitution  9.67–9.69
    proprietary restitution  9.63–9.66
  regulation of  10.51–10.63
  repo of  9.57–9.61
  riskiness of  4.56–4.58
  securities regulation  10.13
  set-off and  9.30–9.45
    common law  9.39–9.43
    equity  9.44–9.45
    rules  9.35–9.38
  situs of  9.70–9.83
  taking security over  9.49–9.61
  taxonomy of private  8.04
  third party beneficiaries  1.15
  transfer of ownership of  9.17–9.20
  transferability and negotiability  9.46–9.48
  as a unit of account  9.87–9.112
    commodities  9.90–9.91
    contracts  9.97–9.108
    unit balances maintained with
      a bank  9.53–9.56
    units, loan of  9.84–9.86
  value of  4.06
  virtual money in the monetary
    system  6.17–6.21
  *see also* e-money
**vouchers**  6.15, 7.97

**Walker, F. A.**  7.07
**Walrasian models**  3.08
**warrant tokens**  8.04
**web of credit problem**  3.35
**Wergild**  2.09
**weight of coins** *see* coins

**Yap** ('Island of stone money')  0.06, 6.25
**Young, H. P.**  1.09

**Zambian currency**  9.105
**zero-sum games** *see* game theory
**Zimbabwean Dollar**  1.49